Human Trafficking

Exploring the
International Nature,
Concerns, and Complexities

Human Trafficking

Exploring the International Nature, Concerns, and Complexities

Edited by
John Winterdyk
Benjamin Perrin
Philip Reichel

CRC Press
Taylor & Francis Group
Boca Raton London New York

CRC Press is an imprint of the
Taylor & Francis Group, an **informa** business

CRC Press
Taylor & Francis Group
6000 Broken Sound Parkway NW, Suite 300
Boca Raton, FL 33487-2742

First issued in paperback 2022

© 2012 by Taylor & Francis Group, LLC
CRC Press is an imprint of Taylor & Francis Group, an Informa business

No claim to original U.S. Government works

Version Date: 20111020

ISBN 13: 978-1-03-247759-6 (pbk)
ISBN 13: 978-1-4398-2036-0 (hbk)

DOI: 10.1201/b11555

Visit the Taylor & Francis Web site at
http://www.taylorandfrancis.com

and the CRC Press Web site at
http://www.crcpress.com

Contents

Acknowledgments

I am honored to acknowledge both Ben and Phil as coeditors for this thematic volume. To collaborate with two such fine scholars has been a genuine pleasure. I, and the book, have only benefited from their involvement. I would also like to express particular appreciation to Carolyn Spence, the acquisition editor for CRC Press who was kind enough to embrace this project and remained encouraging and supportive throughout the preparation of the book. I am also very pleased to acknowledge all the contributors who participated in this project because without their contributions this book would not have come to fruition. Finally—last but not least of all, to my endearing wife Rose, who somehow finds the strength to support and tolerate my passion for such ventures. I can only hope that the readers of this book value and appreciate the fruits of our collective effort to make this undertaking worthwhile.

John Winterdyk

I would like to acknowledge and thank John Winterdyk for his friendship and support over the years. John has provided me with professional opportunities and social interactions that have expanded my areas of interest, professional contacts, and world view. I am also remarkably fortunate to have Eva Jewell as my wonderful wife and best friend. Despite spending too many nights and weekends in more solitary endeavors than she might otherwise have liked, she remains my strongest supporter.

Philip Reichel

I am grateful to John and Phil for their invitation to work together on this edited volume. Both were models of efficiency and experts in their own rights, making the project both enjoyable and intellectually stimulating. I am pleased to recognize graduate student Bethany Hastie for her research assistance and her own continuing work in the field of forced labor trafficking and exploitation. Ongoing institutional support from the University of British Columbia Faculty of Law, Liu Institute for Global of Issues, and Maytree Foundation have been instrumental in furthering my research agenda related to trafficking in persons. Finally, I want to thank my wife for her steadfast support and encouragement during this project, especially in the midst of pregnancy and the birth of our first child.

Benjamin Perrin

Editors

John Winterdyk is the director of the Centre for Criminology and Justice Research (CCJR) at Mount Royal University. He is also an adjunct professor at St. Thomas University (Fredericton, New Brunswick, Canada) and the Polytechnic in Namibia (Windhoek, Namibia). He has published extensively in the areas of youth justice, human trafficking, international criminal justice, and criminological theory. To-date he has authored/(co)edited some 20 textbooks and is currently working on a new young offenders book, and coedited a textbook on fear of crime and punishment as well as a new textbook on Canadian corrections. In addition to his numerous peer-reviewed articles, John was the recent (2009) guest editor for a special issue of the journal *International Criminal Justice Review* on genocide. Current areas of research interest include identity theft, corrections, death in custody, prison gangs, teen courts, and crime prevention.

Benjamin Perrin is an assistant professor at the University of British Columbia Faculty of Law and a member of the Law Society of British Columbia. He is the author of several academic articles on human trafficking and *Invisible Chains: Canada's Underground World of Human Trafficking* (2010). Professor Perrin has advised the Government of Canada on the human trafficking issue as a senior policy advisor and as a witness before several parliamentary committees. He has also worked overseas with victims and assisted in the prosecution of child sex offenders as executive director of The Future Group, a nongovernmental organization that he founded in 2000 to combat human trafficking. In 2009, Professor Perrin was named a Hero Acting to End Modern-Day Slavery by Secretary Hillary Clinton and the U.S. State Department; he is the first Canadian to receive this honor.

Philip Reichel is a tenured full professor in the Department of Criminal Justice at the University of Northern Colorado and adjunct professor in the Department of Justice Studies at Mount Royal University in Calgary, Alberta, Canada. He is the author of *Comparative Criminal Justice Systems: A Topical Approach*; coauthor of *Corrections: A Contemporary Introduction*; editor of *Handbook of Transnational Crime and Justice*; and has authored or coauthored more than 30 articles, book chapters, and encyclopedia entries. He has lectured at universities in Austria, Germany, and Poland, participated in a panel for the United Nations University, presented papers at side events during the United Nations Congress on Crime Prevention and Criminal Justice (Brazil) and the United Nations Commission on Crime Prevention and Criminal Justice (Vienna), and was an invited speaker at Zhejiang Police College in Hangzhou, China.

Contributors

Karin Bruckmüller
Department for Criminal Law and Criminology
University of Vienna
Vienna, Austria

Sanja Ćopić
Institute for Criminological and Sociological
    Research
Belgrade, Serbia

Yvon Dandurand
Research and Graduate Studies
University of the Fraser Valley
Abbotsford, British Columbia, Canada

Claude d'Estrée
Josef Korbel School of International Studies
University of Denver
Denver, Colorado

Amy Farrell
School of Criminology and Criminal Justice
Northeastern University
Boston, Massachusetts

Jo Goodey
Department of Freedoms and Justice
European Union Agency for Fundamental Rights
Vienna, Austria

Annette Herz
Federal Criminal Police Office
Wiesbaden, Germany

Kristiina Kangaspunta
United Nations Interregional Crime and Justice
    Research Institute
Turin, Italy

Julie Kaye
Department of Sociology
University of Saskatchewan
Saskatoon, Saskatchewan, Canada

Sanja Milivojevic
Department of Criminology
University of West Sydney
Sydney, Australia

Benjamin Perrin
Faculty of Law
University of British Columbia
Vancouver, British Columbia, Canada

Philip Reichel
Criminal Justice
University of Northern Colorado
Greeley, Colorado

Stefan Schumann
Department of Criminal Law, Criminal Procedure
    Law and Criminology
University of Graz
Graz, Austria

Marie Segrave
Department of Criminology
Monash University
Melbourne, Australia

Biljana Simeunović-Patić
Institute for Criminological and Sociological
    Research and Victimology Society of Serbia
Belgrade, Serbia

Cindy J. Smith (retired)
Formerly with the Department of Criminal Justice
University of Baltimore
Pasadena, Maryland

Marianne Wade
Birmingham Law School
University of Birmingham
Edgbaston, United Kingdom

John Winterdyk
Centre for Criminology and Justice Studies
Mount Royal University
Calgary, Alberta, Canada

Introduction

1

JOHN WINTERDYK
BENJAMIN PERRIN
PHILIP REICHEL

Contents

It has only been a little more than a decade since the international community committed to confront what Kevin Bales (2007), and Kara (2009), among others, have referred to as modern-day slavery (the "oldest oppression"), with the landmark adoption of the United Nations' *Protocol to Prevent, Suppress and Punish Trafficking in Persons* on November 15, 2000. In response to this milestone international treaty, a growing number of countries have enacted, or amended, their laws and policies to prosecute human traffickers, provide assistance and protection to trafficked persons, and to prevent this criminal activity that undermines fundamental human rights and a broader sense of global order. Meanwhile, 2010 marked the 10th anniversary of the *Trafficking in Persons (TIP) Report* compiled by the U.S. Department of State, a key document in the fight against modern day slavery.

Alongside this international community response, numerous countries have taken important steps to make important contributions to intervene on behalf of trafficked persons and advocate for enhanced measures to provide its victims with various types of support (e.g., rehabilitation and reintegration services) (see Chapter 12). At the same time, academic researchers and scholars have sought to enhance the understanding of both the nature and extent of trafficking in persons involved in sexual exploitation and forced labor at a national, regional, and global levels as well as providing evidence-based research to support more effective public policy responses. While both pure research and action-based research continue to be of ongoing importance, interest has grown, in recent years, in how to improve our assessment of the laws, policies and programs, as well as the pedagogical perspectives of human trafficking that have been implemented to combat/ understand trafficking in persons. This evaluative goal is an important one, both to ensure that responses are indeed achieving their objectives as well as for the identification of promising practices.

This handbook represents another contribution to a recently burgeoning body of (academic) literature on the complex problem of human trafficking.

In addition to the growing list of scholarly publications on the subject (e.g., Bales 2007; Lee 2007, 2011; Perrin 2010a; Scarpa 2008; Segrave et al. 2009; Zhang 2007), there has also been a proliferation of journal articles and even Special Issues produced by some peer reviewed criminology/criminal justice journals with a focus on human trafficking. Most notable was the *International Journal of Comparative and Applied Criminal Justice* [2007, 31(2)], edited by Shoham* and Knepper, and the *European Journal of Criminology* [2010, 7(1)], edited by Winterdyk and Reichel. Shoham and Knepper's Special Issue included six articles which covered such themes as the exploitation of women and children within a European context, to "interest groups and the development of the U.S. Congress's response to human trafficking," to systematic aspects and tendencies of the criminal sex trade. In their Introduction, the editors point out that "the discussion focuses on policies taken to combat human trafficking" (p. 119). Meanwhile, Winterdyk and Reichel also assembled six peer-reviewed articles that focused largely on trafficking in persons in Europe. Among the countries included are Finland, Scotland, Serbia, as well as a contribution from Brazil, which focuses on the impact and effect of government corruption in relation to trafficking in persons.

In addition to academic researchers, governmental and international organizations have made important global contributions to assess both the extent of trafficking in persons (TIP) and evaluate the response of various governments around the world. The U.S. State Department's annual *Trafficking in Persons Report* has, despite some criticism (see, e.g., Friedrich et al. 2006), evolved from a cursory discussion to more comprehensive narratives with statistical data for many of the countries of the world in its effort to monitor and evaluate global strategies to combat TIP since 2001. The United Nations Office on Drugs and Crime's *Global Report on Trafficking in Persons* (UNODC 2009) has also provided a further perspective on national responses by highlighting gaps in the prosecution of TIP at the national level as well as challenged views about who are the traffickers in many cases. Finally, the International Organization for Migration (IOM 2008) has built upon the foundation of the obligations in the *Palermo Protocol* to identify a detailed set of measurable counter-trafficking performance indicators to facilitate both comparative analyses across jurisdictions as well as trends over time within a given jurisdiction.

Although our synopsis is not exhaustive (see Laczko and Gozdziak 2005 for a slightly dated, yet comprehensive listing of work on TIP up to 2004), it appears evident that the issue of human trafficking is garnering the attention of academics as well as researchers in governmental, NGOs, and international organizations.

To-date most of these efforts have tended, despite their rich content, to have either a comparatively narrow focus or, as in the case of the special journal issues (see above), be limited in depth and scope (due to practical constraints). Given the complex transnational nature of TIP, there is a need for a collected work to provide a comprehensive overview of the topic covering the diverse scope and impact of TIP, while recognizing the diversity of views about the characterization of this phenomenon and approaches to addressing it. This book represents the one of the first attempts to provide a cross-sectional and internationally representative examination of various broad themes and issues as they relate to a contemporary understanding of TIP. More specifically, this book will cover, within a comparative and/or international context, key topics ranging from a detailed review of the

---

* Shoham is also a contributor in the aforementioned book.

meaning and various explanations of human trafficking (Chapter 4), to articulating some of the different types of human trafficking (Chapter 5), to how the criminal justice system tries to respond to (i.e., prosecute and prevent—see Chapters 6 through 9), the challenges of assessing the merits of programs and policies designed to protect victims of human trafficking (Chapter 12), as well as the difficulties for national and international capacity building (Chapter 10).

Fitchelberg (2008) points out that the crime of human trafficking has been classified by the United Nations as the third most profitable crime in the world and one for which there are no easy solutions.* Furthermore, as a fairly recent UNICEF report noted: "(t)here is a clear need for effective laws and plans of action, for the investigation and efficient prosecution of all cases, as well as for successful return and reintegration of victims" (Innocenti insight . . . 2005). Hence, this compilation is the result of efforts by a wide range of international contributors and experts who agreed to prepare a specific chapter that allows the book as a whole to address most of the key themes necessary for understanding and developing better responses to human trafficking.

The genesis for this handbook evolved out of a major project completed in 2007. The project was led by Philip Reichel in which he, and an international team, examined the Canadian and American practices of combating TIP. In addition, the project explored a range of initiatives used in Europe and proposed by the United Nations.[†] Subsequent networking with others, engaged in the study of human trafficking, particularly at the 2008 meeting of the European Society of Criminology (ESC) and the 2009 meeting of the American Criminal Justice Academy (ACJS), led Winterdyk and Reichel to the idea of trying to prepare a special issue for a criminological journal. The efforts of this work can be found in the *European Journal of Criminology* [2010, 7(1)]. In addition, follow up with some related work and collaboration has been done with Benjamin Perrin, whose own work in the area has garnered both national and international attention. We welcomed his wealth of expertise and strong legal background to broaden our collective perspectives on the subject. In addition to publishing numerous academic articles on the subject of trafficking persons, his recent book, *Invisible Chains: Canada's Underground World of Human Trafficking* (2010b), explores Canada's connection to this global problem based on empirical research and evidence-based policy analysis.

To-date there has been no single body of work that has attempted to examine the nature, extent, and complexity of the main issues confronting TIP from an international/global perspective. More specifically, since human trafficking is a transnational crime—a crime that transcends borders—it is deemed valuable to explore varying perspectives which either directly or indirectly address the practices or issues for responding to concerns in those regions which are recognized as exporters of trafficking victims versus those regions which are recognized as destination countries (see, e.g., Chapters 11 and 12). However, while most research on trafficking tends to focus on international trafficking, there is also a need to examine the plight of internal trafficking and trafficking for forced labor (see Goodey 2008), which is frequently a more common occurrence in many countries but lacks the same attention as foreign trafficking responses. The general lack of research on domestic trafficking and trafficking for forced labor may in-part be due to the

---

* The first and second most profitable crimes are drugs and arms trafficking.
† See http://www.ncjrs.gov/pdffiles1/nij/grants/223286.pdf for a copy for the final report.

fact that, according to Laczko and Gozdziak (2005), scholarly work on human trafficking, in general, did not really begin to emerge until the late 1990s.

In their research, Laczko and Gozdiak found but one TIP reference dating back to 1993. The majority of the 260 titles they identified were published between the mid-1990s and 2003 followed by a precipitous drop-off in 2004. So, while there now exists a diverse body of literature on TIP given that a number of international agreements have been established (e.g., Palermo Protocol), it is timely to offer a consolidated look at some of the key presenting issues from a national, regional, and international perspective.

In addition to a general lack of scholarly work on internal trafficking, there is a need to examine the techniques used to protect/support victims of trafficking as well as the need to examine which strategies might work best to prosecute those found guilty of trafficking. This thematic volume attempts to explore some of these issues and move the discourse beyond simply reiterating that there is a problem and mapping the routes and relationships between countries, such as countries from which people are trafficked out of (i.e., source countries), countries to where trafficked persons end-up (i.e., a country of *destination*), or a country of *transit*. Transit involves countries through which trafficked persons are moved en-route to their final destination.[*] Rather, we aim to provide a richer comparative-based understanding of the issues so as to forge evidence-based knowledge to better guide policy-makers.

While most of the key themes surrounding TIP will be addressed throughout this book, we thought it instructive to provide a synopsis of some of the fundamental issues involved in TIP. Our thinking is that a discussion of these more general, descriptive, theoretical, and practical issues, though brief, would provide readers' unfamiliar with issues of TIP a common base from which to understand—and critically reflect upon—this handbook's content. To begin, we first offer an overview on the controversial debate regarding the difference between human trafficking and migrant smuggling.

Trafficking versus Migrant Smuggling: What's the Difference?

Given the heated debates and lobbying around the legal definition of trafficking, it is prudent to briefly discuss the difference between *migrant smuggling* and *human trafficking* as uncertainty over the relationship between these two concepts has confounded how the international community responds to TIP. In particular, trafficking and smuggling are often seen as synonymous (see Ogrodnik 2010; Lee 2011) and "borders between smuggling and trafficking are sometimes blurred" (Aronowitz and Perfuffo 2003: 395). While there are some important overlaps, the two concepts should be treated as distinct (David 2010). Yet, the media, researchers, and even some government agencies use the terms interchangeably (Zhang 2007). While in principle they appear to represent the same thing, academics, policy-makers, and vested agencies/organization have begun to provide clearer definitions of these terms. Although the difference will be discussed in more detail in Chapter 2, we will provide a brief overview of the two concepts.

Although there are a number of definitions that can be found in the literature, for the purpose of introducing the difference between human trafficking and migrant smuggling,

---

[*] See http://www.pbs.org/wnet/wideangle/episodes/dying-to-leave/business-of-human-trafficking/trafficking-routes/1428/ (accessed May 10, 2010). This PBS site provides a description as well as maps showing the movement of human beings throughout the world.

we will refer to the international definition as forwarded in the 2000 UN **Palermo protocol** or more formally known as the *Protocol to Prevent, Suppress and Punish Trafficking in Persons, especially Women and Children* (also referred to as the **Trafficking protocol**).[*] The Palermo Protocol states:

> Trafficking in persons shall mean the recruitment, transportation, transfer, harboring or receipt of persons, by means of the threat or use of force or other forms of coercion, of abduction, of fraud, of the abuse of power or of a position of vulnerability or of the giving or receiving of payments or benefits to achieve the consent of a person having control over another person, for the purpose of exploitation.

Meanwhile, the protocol for migrant smuggling, which entered into force in 2004, states[†] that the smuggling of migrants shall mean the procurement, in order to obtain, directly or indirectly, a financial or other material benefit, of the illegal entry of a person into a State Party of which the person is not a national or a permanent resident. Once smuggled persons arrive in the country of destination, they are free to make their own way and generally have no further debt or servitude to the smuggler. Or as Zhang (2007) points out: "human smuggling is the act of assisting or facilitating, often for a fee, the unauthorized entry of a foreign national into another country" (p. 1). However, Zhang further notes: "there are those who claim to be doing their relatives or friends a favor and charge only enough to cover actual costs" (p. 1) when they help smuggle them into another country. For example, Ogordnik (2010: 10) points out that "smuggled migrants consent to the illegal transaction ..." This could involve, for example, illegal Mexicans as well as other ethnic/cultural groups in Canada and the United States who send for their family members or relatives to join them (also, see David 2010). However, as reflected below, such incidents might turn into trafficking. Hence, the line between migrant smuggling and human trafficking are sometimes blurred by the underlying intent or motive (i.e., *mens rea*) (see Lee 2011 for further discussion as well). This perhaps also partially explains why most books on human trafficking include some discussion on migrant smuggling.

Although sometimes used synonymously, efforts to confront human trafficking and migrant smuggling have very different underlying purposes. As Perrin (2010b) points out human trafficking is primarily about the exploitation of the individual to reap ongoing illicit profits, whereas the purpose of migrant smuggling is to "obtain a financial or other material benefit from procuring the illegal entry itself." Although trafficking is generally accompanied by cross border movement, it is not a requirement, whereas it is a required element of human smuggling (ibid). Consequently, victims of human trafficking can be of any nationality, whereas smuggled migrants are always foreign nationals. At its core, human trafficking is a violation of individual human rights whereas migrant smuggling is a violation of state sovereignty.

Part of the confusion may lie in the fact that both terms are relatively contemporary and were introduced in response to varying social and criminal activities that have

---

[*] By 2009, 117 countries had signed the Protocol. The other major Palermo Protocol signed in 2000 was the Protocol against the Smuggling of Migrants by Land, Sea and Air. The first UN convention to deal with trafficking was the 1949 Convention on the Suppression of Trafficking Women and the Exploitation of Prostitution of Others (Goodey 2008).

[†] By 2009, 112 countries had signed the Protocol (Goodey 2008).

accompanied expanding migration trends. As Zhang (2007) clearly states, since the 1980s, "global population migration has reached unprecedented levels ..." (p. 3). Several of these issues are explored further in Chapter 2.

Yet, regardless of their operational differences, smuggling and TIP can both result in the mistreatment of persons. However, from a legal and investigative perspective, trafficking centers on *exploitation* while migrant smuggling centers on cross-border *transportation*. So, while this book offers some discussion about migrant smuggling, the primary focus is on the problem of human trafficking.

A Checkered Past

As prominent as our concern about human trafficking has become today, we should not be remiss in remembering that human trafficking has a long and checkered past. In fact, TIP is commonly referred to as "modern day slavery" (see, e.g., Bales 2007). Moreover, the practice of trafficking and slavery was not always viewed with a degree of disdain. As far back as antiquity the Romans and Greeks used trafficked slaves to build their economies and expand the Roman Empire. It is estimated that at one point as much as 25% of the Roman population were slaves who were brought to Italy against their will to serve the Roman's varied needs (Lee 2011).

The more recent history of trafficking and slavery can be traced back to 1562 when the British imported slaves from the coast of Guinea to work in the West Indies. First initiated by the English navigator Admiral John Hawkins (1532–1595) the practice quickly spread and was embraced shortly after by the Spaniards as they colonized the "New World."

Upon learning of the practice, the British monarchy initially expressed disdain towards slavery, but Hawkins' and others convinced the monarchy that, in addition to it being a very lucrative enterprise, they would be saving the "heathens" by introducing them to Christianity and civilization (*History of Slavery* 2009).

Slavery in the United States did not emerge until 1619 when a Dutch trader sold 20 slaves in Jamestown, Virginia. The practice grew and spread rapidly after that. In fact, as described in *History of Slavery* (2009), in "1663 the Maryland legislature enacted a law that 'all negroes and other slaves within the province, and all negroes and other slaves to be thereafter imported into the province, should serve during life; and all children born of any negro should be slaves, as their fathers were, for the term of their lives.'" The practice flourished until 1865 when then President of the United States, Abraham Lincoln, by the Thirteenth Amendment of the United States Constitution freed the slaves in Richmond, Virginia (*History of Slavery* 2009). Even though 2007 marked the 200th anniversary of the abolition of the slave trade in Britain's colonies, the general practice still continues in most parts of the world.

Albeit a brief overview on the historical legacy of human trafficking, it is apparent that our past is not only rich with examples of human exploitation, but also perhaps reflective of a greater social malaise that seems to have befallen human kind for as long as there has been recorded history. It is only recently that on an international scale we have recognized that human trafficking represents: (1) a gross human rights challenge, (2) a possible migration problem, (3) a (transnational) organized crime, and (4) a grave social malaise of humanity (see Chrucky 2004 for a more detailed accounting of the history of slavery). Unfortunately, as we will see below, and as discussed in further detail in Chapter 3, the plight is still very much present today.

Overview of TIP: A Form of "Modern Day Slavery"

It is generally acknowledged that TIP, or modern day slavery, is a heinous crime and a gross abuse of fundamental human rights (see Fitchelberg 2008; Lee 2011). However, as Zhang (2007) observed: "human trafficking has found supporters throughout the world who hold fundamentally differing views towards the rights and welfare of human beings" (p. 105). While the term "supporters" may be somewhat contextually misplaced, Zhang points out that both developed and developing countries have this problem to some extent. This is reflected in the quote above and discussed in various capacities in Malarek's journalistic account of the sex trade in Eastern Europe. In addition, one can readily find in the media stories relating to such tragic incidents of cases of trafficked victims drowning in unsafe vessels (Eight dead … 2009); or, trafficked victims suffocating to death in overcrowded truck compartments (Siddique 2009); and cargo ships (Harrold and Scott 2010), or, Kenyans seeking to escape poverty and social unrest are being targeted by traffickers in a country that is also void of adequate laws and resources to combat the problem (Clifford 2010); or, young victims being trafficked within such prosperous countries as Canada and the United States (i.e., domestic human trafficking) for the purpose of forcing the victim into the sex trade (Bales 2009; Perrin 2010a; Sher 2011). Trafficking victims represent a diverse group, from those wanting to improve their lives to those desperate to escape civil unrest or situations that appear futile (Zhang 2007). Furthermore, Lee (2011) begins her book on human trafficking by pointing out that the "trafficking of human beings has attracted considerable public and political concern in recent years" (p. 1) but that there is little consensus among countries about what constitutes the rights and welfare of people (also, see Lee 2011: Chapter 1). While international human rights law does establish universal norms governing the rights of individuals, the implementation of these rights at the national level may reflect a different reality in practice. There can be no real argument, however, that the exploitation manifested in the form of trafficking in persons is an affront to individual liberty and dignity. In addition, research on the topic is hampered by the fact that victims/survivors of trafficking have been referred to as part of a "hidden population," where it is "almost impossible to establish a sampling frame and draw a representative sample of the population" (Laczko and Gozdiak 2005: 1) in a manner that is both safe and ethical. These and related issues will be discussed in Chapters 7 and 12.

One of the issues that contributes to the difficulty in combating human trafficking is how best to define it and how to measure it. For example, while scholars such as Bales (2007), Goodey (2008) and Lee (2011), among others, have referred to trafficking in persons as a form of "modern day slavery," the League of Nations in 1926 introduced legal measures to combat slavery and then in 1956 the United Nations expanded international legislative protocols with the Supplementary Convention on the Abolition of Slavery, the Slave Trade, and Institutions and Practices Similar to Slavery (Goodey 2008). But, as noted above the specific protocol defining and establishing guidelines to combat human trafficking are found in the Palermo Protocol. As Goodey (2008: 422) points out "the association of slavery with prostitution … came to a fore at the beginning of the 20th century. Since this time, the specific crime of trafficking has been linked with prostitution … children … and … exploitation in the labour market." The Palermo Protocol also marked a shift from viewing human trafficking simply as a form of slavery to situating trafficking within a transnational crime context (see Chapter 4).

Although many countries have adopted the definition developed by the United Nations (UN), it is not universal (see Chapter 2). While Smith, in Chapter 2, points out that the definition is not devoid of its challenges and nuances, Kleimenov and Shamkov (2005), in their discussion of defining human trafficking in Russia, offer a similar definition to the one developed by the UN but add: "… or can result in human rights violations" (p. 30). By contrast, in preparing a paper for the Canadian Centre for Justice Statistics, Ogrodnik (2010: 12) surveyed 90 different Canadian agencies and among the questions asked was what their definition of TIP was based on. While most used the human trafficking offences in the *Criminal Code* or in conjunction with the *Immigration and Refugee Protection Act*, almost a quarter used their own definition! Only 20 percent were even familiar with the guidelines contained in the UN Protocol.

As will be described and discussed in Chapters 3 and 12, human traffickers tend to victimize the most vulnerable of the global community—young women, children and young adolescents as well as boys and men from impoverished countries. They are typically exploited in the sex-trade industry (see Segrave et al. 2009) or illegal labor markets such as sweatshops. Other sites of human trafficking can include farm work (see Justicia for migrant workers 2009) and domestic servitude (see Bales 1999; Chin 1997, 1998). Trafficked persons can also include child soldiers (see *Child Soldiers: Global Report* 2008). In Chapter 5, Claude provides a rich overview of the various examples of trafficking through the use of "stories."

While there is considerable variation as to how we should or might define human trafficking, the crime can be characterized as involving three basic elements. TIP involves a *process* (e.g., harboring, receiving, recruitment, transferring, and/or transportation), a *method* (e.g., abuse, abduction, coercion, deceit, deception, fraud, and/or threats), and a *goal* (e.g., debt bondage, forced labor, involuntary servitude, pornography, prostitution, and/or sexual exploitation). It is generally recognized that if one component from each of the three elements is present then the result is human trafficking (Finding freedom 2010).

In 2001, Interpol estimated that human trafficking was a $19+ billion enterprise and still growing (Gemmell 2009). Meanwhile, recent estimates from the United Nations peg the total global market value for TIP at around $32 billion annually. Although the exact financial impact is not precise, the financial scope is staggering. Why? With globalization, increasingly competitive economic markets and the population boom, the environment is unfortunately ripe for human exploitation whether it consists of slave-trade, child pornography, sex tourism, organ trafficking, or labor slaves. However, Goodey discusses in Chapter 3 some of the challenges in trying to obtain an accurate account of the extent of human trafficking in a European context and the consequences that such challenges pose for developing the necessary policies to combat the problem. Any reliability of the financial cost or extent of the problem is further compounded by the inconsistencies that exist around a universal definition of human trafficking. In Chapter 2, Smith and Kangaspunta discuss these issues and conclude by recommending that "the only way to be successful is through one basic principle: high quality, unbiased, contextualized research."

Admittedly, we cannot address all the possible factors that might impact our efforts to obtain accurate counts of the problem. For example, other explanations reflect social and cultural aspects unique to individual countries. For example, Stoecker and Shelley (2005a) suggest that in Russia, human trafficking is a composite of: "an organized crime problem, a labor problem, and consequence of regional conflict with the country's borders" (p. 5).

Furthermore, with the growing global phenomenon of people migration, more-so than at any other time in contemporary history, it is not as readily possible at this time to detect and interrupt incidents of migrant smuggling or human trafficking. Nonetheless, as previously discussed, it is important to try to operationally and legally understand how the two concepts are intertwined and yet distinct. In addition, according to the United Nations International Migration Population Division, in 2006, over 190 million persons, or 3.1% of the worlds' population, currently reside in a country other than their country of birth (International Migration 2009). According to International Migration (2009), the United States has by far the largest number (over 38,000 in 2006) of illegal immigrants followed by Germany (over 10,000) and then Canada (over 6000). The challenges associated with mass migration, particularly the exploitation of would-be migrants, are but some of the issues that confront us and should serve to reinforce the need for continued discourse, ongoing research, and refined efforts to address this grievous blight on humanity.

An Enduring Presence

In addition to having a resilient history it is, therefore, perhaps no surprise to read that, according to a United Nations report, no country is immune from the scourge of human trafficking even though citizens in western countries, such as Canada and the United States, the United Kingdom, and New Zealand have difficulty imagining human trafficking occurring in their own country (UNODC 2009). One of the primary reasons why virtually every country is implicated in the network of human trafficking is because a country can serve as a country of *origin*, a country of *destination*, and a country of *transit* (see definitions above). Transit involves countries through which trafficked persons are moved en-route to their final destination.* In fact, according to the UN Office on Drugs and Crime (UNODC), which has compiled the first such study from open sources, there are 127 countries of origin, mainly developing countries, and 137 destination countries, mainly in the industrialized world. The report also highlights 98 transit countries (Penketh 2006). However, it should also be noted that many countries, such as Canada, while being largely a destination country are also transit countries for victims who are trafficked for the purposes of sexual exploitation (Perrin 2010a). The implications and significance of these designations will be explored to varying degrees throughout this anthology. In particular, Herz (Chapter 7) discusses the role and challenges of police investigations within different social and cultural contexts, Wade (Chapter 8) explores some of the issues around jurisdiction and prosecution of human trafficking cases, while Dandurand (Chapter 10) examines the issue of international cooperation—and the lack thereof—in combating human trafficking.

Finally, while there has been an explosion of media coverage (i.e., secondary source data) on human trafficking (see Table 1.1), Brennan (2005) cautions that researchers must be vigilant to not be swept up by the nature and tone of current media attention. Rather, researchers of human trafficking need to remain objective and engage in research that provides the various stakeholders with necessary information. To this end, the chapters of this handbook examine how we can/do contextualize human trafficking (see Chapter 2); explain and describe some of the dimensions of trafficking (see Chapters 3 through 5); analyze how

---

* See http://www.pbs.org/wnet/wideangle/episodes/dying-to-leave/business-of-human-trafficking/trafficking-routes/1428/ (accessed May 10, 2009). This PBS site provides a description as well as maps showing the movement of human beings throughout the world.

Table 1.1   Number of Media TIP Articles: 2000–2010[a]

2000: 236 documents found for: (human trafficking)
2001: 192 documents found for: (human trafficking)
2002: 104 documents found for: (human trafficking)
2003: 136 documents found for: (human trafficking)
2004: 332 documents found for: (human trafficking)
2005: 387 documents found for: (human trafficking)
2007: 611 documents found for: (human trafficking)
2008: 509 documents found for: (human trafficking)
2009: 685 documents found for: (human trafficking)
2010: 742 documents found for: (human trafficking)

[a] Canadian Newstand (a collection of the full text of articles, columns, editorials and features from most major Canadian daily newspapers (e.g., *Globe and Mail, National Post, Toronto Star, Calgary Herald*) and many local dailies and weeklies.

we react to human trafficking incidents (see Chapters 6 through 10); question what types of prevention initiatives are currently in place and what we might expect to see in the future (see Chapter 11); and study what we know about human trafficking and what we are doing for its victims and witnesses (see Chapter 12). As a result, this handbook represents an effort to move beyond simply providing accounts of human trafficking incidents and describing the woes of what human trafficking means by engaging in a diverse, yet thorough, examination of the complexity of systemic responses to trafficking and its victims.

Extent of Human Trafficking

Some readers might assume that TIP is something that happens only in impoverished countries where civil and human rights may be less valued or less honored. However, as reflected in Chapters 5 and 12, human trafficking victims do not only come from impoverished countries, nor are they always sent to industrialized countries, such as Canada, Western Europe, or the United States. For example, a recent incident in the United States involving two American judges charged with being involved in "human trafficking,"* illustrates that this is not the case. The two Pennsylvania (USA) judges accepted over $2.6 million in kickbacks to send young children to two privately run detention centers PA judges accused ... 2009). And while it could be argued that they were not directly exploiting the children being sent, they did profit from their actions. As a recent U.S. government report has observed, victims are routinely "tricked" with false promises of employment, educational opportunities, marriage, and a better life (U.S. Department of State 2008).

Due in large part to its' underground nature, human trafficking is a difficult crime to detect and gather reliable statistics on (see, generally, Chapters 2 and 3 in this book; Lehti and Aromaa 2007; Ogrtodnik 2010). In fact, according to some, it is not clear what methods have been used to generate the documented counts of human trafficking we do have (see van Dijk 2008; Viuhko 2010). Nevertheless, bearing in mind the needed degree of caution about available statistics, the figures are alarming. Again, while related statistics may

* See http://www.thepeoplesvoice.org/TPV3/Voices.php/2009/02/21/us-judges-involved-in-human-trafficking (accessed April 27, 2009) for an accounting of the event.

be underreported due to the hidden nature of human trafficking, estimates for trafficked victims range from 600,000 to 800,000 in the United States (U.S. State Department 2005). Based on his research, Kevin Bales (1999), one of the few who has done extensive research in the area, estimated that worldwide the number of people involved in human trafficking or "slavery" is around 27 million. By contrast, however, a 2005 report by the International Labour Organization estimated that the number of victims of human trafficking is around 2.4 million and another 12.3 million victims are forced into labor. If we are going to be able to effectively combat the practice of trafficking, we need to obtain a clearer understanding of its nature and characteristics. Several years ago, *Innocenti Insight ...* (2005) attempted to create just such a picture in the human trafficking blighted continent of Africa. While the efforts of the UNICEF sponsored project drew attention to the gravity of the problem in Africa, the authors of the report concluded with the observation that there was "ground for guarded optimism regarding the capacity and resolve to tackle the problem" (Innocenti Insight, 2005, p. 37). In Chapter 2, Smith and Kangaspunta examines most of these issues.

Formal Efforts to Combat Human Trafficking

The "4Ps" paradigm: Prevention, protection, prosecution, and partnership.

Many countries have their own legislation regarding human trafficking.* As noted earlier, the first international attempt to standardize the definition of the crime came in 2000 with the *UN Convention Against Transnational Organized Crime and the Protocols*. The UN *Convention Against Transnational Organized Crime* obligates States that have ratified the instrument to commit themselves to take a series of measures against transnational organized crime, including the creation of domestic criminal offences (addressing participation in an organized criminal group, money laundering, corruption and obstruction of justice) (see Chapter 10).

More specific protocols did not come into effect until a few years later. First of these was the *UN Protocol to Prevent, Suppress and Punish Trafficking in Persons*. This protocol was directed specifically against the trafficking of women and children and adopted by General Assembly Resolution 55/25. It entered into force on December 25, 2003. It is the first international protocol that served not only to recognize the gravity of the crime, but also to establish an international standard by which to define trafficking (Art. 3.a of the Protocol). And, while the practice of contemporary slavery has existed for several centuries (see Jordon and Walsh 2007), the 2003 Protocol also represented the first international attempt to develop a uniform definition on trafficking in persons. As reflected in the protocol, the overarching intention behind providing the definition is to facilitate convergence in national approaches by which to create domestic criminal offences that would support efficient international cooperation in investigating and prosecuting trafficking in persons' cases (see Chapters 7 and 8 for further discussion). An additional objective of the Protocol is to protect and assist the victims of trafficking by ensuring that their human rights are fully respected and honored (see Simeunovic-Patic and Copic 2010).

---

* For example, Australia holds illegal migrants arriving by sea and sometimes keeps them on remote islands before sending them to other countries to have a refugee hearing (Jason Kenney... 2010). By contrast, Canada also detains illegal migrants, but provides them with a hearing on Canadian soil before possible deportation. In Canada, they can be held for up to 18- months, but as a recent report by Auditor General Sheila Fraser suggests, Canada's system is highly inefficient (Canada has lost track... 2008).

In order to effectively combat trafficking at a national and international level it is necessary to form a single definition of trafficking that can be used to create effective policy.* However, as will be discussed in Chapters 2 and 3, there are a number of critical challenges in trying to define and measure trafficking. Drawing on a UNICEF report, some of the key challenges include:

1. Avoiding the tendency to approach the issue one-dimensionally as being a crime, or as being only a human rights issue. Both dimensions are linked and are essential to prevent and combat trafficking (see Chapter 4).
2. As victims are a key element of the Palermo Protocol, any definition needs to be able to clearly define when exploitation begins (see Chapter 12).
3. Under the Palermo Protocol exploitation occurs after trafficking has taken place. However, the Protocol does not allow for the determination or consideration of identifying the "pushes" that precede the process (see Chapter 6).
4. The Palermo Protocol, while addressing cross-border movement, does not provide for the more complex movement of people through several transition phases (see Chapters 7 and 8).
5. As there is greater movement of people today than ever before, some legal migrants may become exploited and drawn into the trafficking network and then have no access to legal advice or protection (Innocenti Insight . . . 2005) (see Chapter 12).

Finally, Segrave et al. (2009, p. 28), in their discussion of sex trafficking argue that: "trafficking discourse has been increasingly simplified and packed into narrowly defined and simple polarized dichotomies, leaving the definition of trafficking vague and prone to manipulation by various political agendas." In Chapters 2 and 4 the authors, while not disagreeing with the assertion, question and explore this observation.

As is evidenced above, the international community has begun to mobilize itself in an effort to combat human trafficking, whether offending states are those of destination, origin, or transit points for this criminal activity. And, while not all cases of human trafficking involve trans-border migration, the majority are transnational in scope. However, domestic trafficking remains a substantial problem. As noted on the humantrafficking.org website, in China, it is estimated that between 10,000 and 20,000 victims of trafficking are internal cases (China 2009). Many other countries are also identified as having similar domestic trafficking problems on the Washington, D.C. based website. Again, as already stated, no country appears to be immune to trafficking—regardless of its unique social, political, or economic conditions. As with any initiatives to combat a crime that typically transcends borders, there are numerous practical issues that need to be addressed first at a local and national level and then within the larger context of a global community. Fundamentally, the issue of trafficking is inextricably linked to the existence of porous borders, a decline of police control and organized crime—an area examined in Chapters 7 and 9. Other contributing factors can involve the limitation of support networks and programs/services for homeless youth and adults (see Stoecker and Shelley 2005b).

---

* Comparatively speaking, Europe has been fairly progressive in combating human trafficking. For example, the "Brussels Declaration" on Preventing and Combating Trafficking in Human Being, in 2002, was instrumental in establishing an expert group on trafficking of persons. Similar strong initiatives have arisen through the Office for Security and Cooperation in Europe as well as Europol (see Goodey 2008).

Although researchers have experienced numerous challenges in trying to define the construct of HT, prosecute transgressors of HT, and obtain reliable estimates of the extent, breadth, and trends of human trafficking, fortunately these (and other) challenges covered in this handbook have not prevented the ability of counter-trafficking responses to gain traction. In 2003, for example, the U.S. Government supported some 190 antitrafficking programs in 92 countries (Laczko and Gozdiak 2005). Also, in Chapter 12, Copic and Simeunovic-Patic, citing Goodey (2008, p. 434) point out that there has been an increasing emphasis and application of resources placed on victim assistance. However, there is a risk that any effort to control trafficking or assist its' victims without first establishing a richer understanding of its socio-cultural and political meaning may do little to abate the problem (see, e.g., Lee 2011). Chapter 4 explores some of the alternate explanations of trafficking and concludes with the recommendation that the issue should perhaps be understood and studied from a social malaise perspective.

As will be presented in various chapters throughout this book (e.g., Chapters 6 through 9, 12), there exists a wide range of programs and strategies specifically designed to prevent and/or facilitate countries and organizations in identifying risk factors associated with trafficking. In short, the responses to human trafficking can, as described by Herz (Chapter 7), and Smith and Kangaspunta (Chapter 2), be classified into three major approaches—the three "Ps":

1. Prevention of trafficking;
2. Protection and support of victims; and
3. Prosecution of traffickers.

In Chapter 5, Bruckmuller and Schumann introduce a fourth "P" that refers to "paradigm," which they argue is entrenched in the Palermo Protocol as well as the EU *Council Framework Decision on Combating Trafficking in Human Beings.*

Yet, in-spite of the increased attention to combat trafficking in persons and growing international antitrafficking industry, the plight of trafficking continues to expand (Bales 2007; Goodey 2008, Malarek 2003, Lee 2011).* In light of such dismal accounts, it can be argued how little we really do know or understand about deterring and preventing human trafficking, or supporting victims of trafficking. Similarly, as reflected above, there is a transparent need for a careful analysis in how to formulate effective legislation and plans of action that result in productive investigation and efficient and effective prosecution of all cases. Such an analysis not only needs to take place at a local and national level but also needs to be scrutinized with the larger global context in which trafficking expresses itself. However, a clearer understanding of the nature, extent, and circumstances of human trafficking in the context of the region, country, or continent in question is necessary to develop the capacity and legislation to effectively address trafficking.

---

* While examining the legal response to human trafficking in Japan, Yokoyama (2010) attempts to argue that even though Japan has a Tier 2 ranking that their recent legal responses to combat trafficking in persons has been effective in reducing the incident rates. Japan has restricted the issuance of entertainer visas, especially to Filipina workers, required finger printing and photographing of foreign workers, as well as engaged in an aggressive education campaign involving videos, posters, brochures, etc. However, Yokoyama concludes with a less then ensuring comment when he states: "(w)hat is problematic is that people do not think that human trafficking is a serious social problem...Japan will need to implement education programs" (p.37).

Furthermore, it is necessary to examine and critically evaluate how best to support victims of trafficking. For example, as noted in the 2005 Innocenti Insight report, there is a need to better understand "the clandestine nature of child trafficking ... and how often the risks of trafficking are ill-perceived by families and communities" (*Innocenti Insight ...* p. vii). However, any such initiatives must not only focus on victims of foreign trafficking, but also those who are victims of domestic trafficking.

Again, as evidenced by the growing body of literature and the establishment of formal and informal agencies and organization to address the problem of trafficking, there is, or should be, elevated expectations of not only considerable attention being directed towards combating trafficking but genuine expectations of indisputable progress (generally, see Galleger and Holmes 2010). The time has perhaps never been more urgent to move forward with our efforts to not only understand the issues related to TIP, but develop informed concrete plans of action that will allow us to have a positive impact on all levels of this complex phenomenon.

Overview of the Book

As reflected in the title and illustrated in the Table of Contents, this book represents the bringing together of a diverse range of international experts who are immersed, in varying capacities, with the topic/theme they prepared for this book. The Editors intentionally invited an internationally diverse group of experts to not only reflect that trafficking is being addressed globally, but to also demonstrate and allow for various perspectives to be presented.

We have attempted to provide a cogent structure to the book and, other than obvious pragmatic issues (such as chapter length, number of contributions, etc.), we have attempted to not restrict the authors in the preparation of their chapter.

We are deeply appreciative of such a fine collection of individuals coming together to help us better enunciate and examine the phenomena of trafficking within a truly international context.

In summary, we consider the following to be the most distinctive features of this book:

1. First book on human trafficking that, in addition to having international representation, offers perspectives, to varying degrees, within a regional context. Yet, through the use of discussion questions, can explore and examine the themes within the readers (or other) regional, political, and/or cultural contexts.
2. A comprehensive overview of all major elements/issues related to HT. The topics range from a discussion of how best to move towards a uniform definition HT, to different forms of trafficking, to different ways of explaining HT, to models of control and issues relating to police investigation, as well as the plight of victims.
3. All the chapters include Review and Discussion Questions, as well as (where possible) additional Useful Resources for further reading. In other words, we have included several pedagogical features that are intended to extend the content beyond a mere narrative discussion of the issues.
4. Also considered unique is the fact that the contributions bridge a variety of disciplinary perspectives, which is reflective of the complexity of HT and representative of how the issue is being addressed.

Conclusion

Overall, this thematic handbook serves to demonstrate that while we are gaining a richer grasp of human trafficking across a number of critical areas, as clearly reflected in the recent report by Ogrodnik (2010), much research is still left to be done on the topic. Among other issues, the various forms of human trafficking point to the need to consolidate measures to better support and assist countries identified as transit, destination, or origin, particularly by establishing a common, universally concise definition. As reflected in the chapters contained in this book, there remain, unfortunately, many more aspects of human trafficking that still command exploration.

With the rapid growth of globalization there have been a number of global forces that have contributed to the expansion and growth of human trafficking on an international scale. Among such global forces are the growth of tourism, migration, and commoditization and the illegal movement of millions of people across international borders. While many do it willingly (e.g., people looking for employment and opportunity), others are coerced and/or lured under false promise and pretense—a segment of whom are exploited by the sex trade and/or illegal labor market industry. At the same time, a localization of exploitation is also observable in certain countries, where traffickers have found a pool of vulnerable individuals much closer to home to recruit and target—demonstrating that even the long-standing globalization discourse on human trafficking is not without exception.

Human trafficking is recognized by the UN as the third most profitable crime next to drug smuggling and the smuggling of illegal weapons. For example, the United Nations estimates that the total global market value for TIP is $32 billion annually. However, the human toll is one that reaches beyond the victim and the social, political and economic impact of TIP are far reaching. It is the gravity of the human rights violation that is human trafficking above all else that has likely compelled action by governments, nongovernmental organizations, activists and law enforcement even as the contours of the nature and extent of this problem remain ambiguous and uncertain at times.

We trust that with this thematic book we have been able to not only add to the base knowledge of the phenomenon but, more importantly, we hope to further stimulate research and critical dialogue, which remains relatively limited compared to the social, cultural, economic impact of TIP. And while eradicating trafficking may seem like an unobtainable goal, or at least ominously daunting, as the old Chinese proverb says, "a journey of a thousand miles must begin with a single step" and with this book we hope that we have taken at least a step, if not several, in the right direction.

References

Aronowitz, A.A. and Perfuffo, M. 2003. Trafficking in human beings and related crimes in West and Central Africa. In C. Summer (Ed.), *The Blackwell Companion to Criminology*. Malden, MA: Blackwell Pub.

Bales, K. 1999. New slavery. The transformation of an ancient curse. *Global Dialogue*, 1(Summer): 102–113.

Bales, K. 2007. *Ending Slavery: How We Free Today's Slaves*. Berkley, CA: University of California Press.

Bales, K. 2009. *The Slave Next Door: Human Trafficking and Slavery in America Today*. Berkley, CA: University of California Press.

Brennan, D. 2005. Methodological challenges in research on human trafficking: Tales from the field. *International Migration* 43(1/2):35–54.

Canada has lost track of 41,000 illegals: Fraser. May 6, 2008. http://www.ctv.ca/CTVNews/ TopStories/20080506/ag_report_080506/ (accessed October 2, 2010).

Child Soldiers: Global Report. 2008. http://www.child-soldiers.org/library/global-reports (accessed November 28, 2009).

Chin, C.B.N. 1997. Walls of silence and late twentieth century representations of the foreign female domestic... *International Migration Review*, 31(2): 0353–0385.

Chin, C.B.N. 1998. *In Service and Servitude: Foreign Female Domestic Workers and the Malaysian Project.* New York, NY: Columbia University Press.

China: China National Plan of Action on Combating Trafficking in Women and Children (2008–2012). 2009. http://www.humantrafficking.org/countries/china (accessed June 1, 2010).

Chrucky, A. 2004. Slavery. Retrieved November 29, 2009 from: http://www.ditext.com/moral/ slavery.html.

Clifford, C. January 9, 2010. Human trafficking news ... Retrieved May 22, 2010 from: http://children.foreignpolicyblogs.com/2010/01/09/human-trafficking-news/.

David, F. 2010. Migrant smuggling and human rights: Notes from the field. *RCMP Gazette*, 72(3): 16–17.

Eight dead after vessel capsizes in Aegean Sea. October 27, 2009. Retrieved November 29, 2009 from: http://www.monstersandcritics.com/news/europe/news/article_1509544.php/ Eight-dead-after-vessel-capsizes-in-eastern-Aegean-Roundup.

Fitchelberg, A. 2008. *Crime without borders: An introduction to international criminal justice.* Upper Saddle River, NJ: Pearson.

Finding freedom. 2010. ACT brochure. Edmonton, AB.

Friedrich, A.G., Meyer, A.N., and Perman, D.G. 2006. Trafficking in persons report: Strengthening a diplomatic tool. *UCLA School of Public Affairs.* Retrieved December 22, 2010 from http://www. spa.ucla.edu/ps/research/J-Traffic06.pdf.

Galleger, A.Y. and Holmes, P. 2010. Human trafficking: Challenges and opportunities for police. *RCMP Gazzette*, 72(3): 18–19.

Gemmell, N.A. 2009. *Human trafficking: The effects of modern-day slavery on the global economy.* http://cndls.georgetown.edu/applications/posterTool/index.cfm?fuseaction=poster. display&posterID=1752. (accessed September 8, 2010).

Goodey, J. 2008. Human trafficking: Sketchy data and policy responses. *Criminology and Criminal Justice*, 8(4): 421–442.

Harrold, M. and Scott, M. October 8, 2010. Nine foreigners found in container at Montreal port. *Calgary Herald*, A12.

History of slavery. 2009. http://www.sonofthesouth.net/slavery/history-slavery.htm (accessed November 28, 2009).

Innocenti insight: Trafficking in human beings, especially women and children, in Africa. 2005. Florence, Italy: Unicef Innocenti Research Centre.

International Migration. 2009. United Nations. Retrieved from http://www.un.org/esa/population/ migration/ (accessed December 04, 2009).

International Organization for Migration. 2008. *Handbook on Performance Indicators for Counter-Trafficking Projects.* Geneva: IOM.

Jason Kenney, Australian officials discuss how to deal with human smuggling (September 20, 2010). Theglobeandmail.com/news/politics/Jason-kenney-australian-officials-discuss-how-to-deal-with-human-smuggling/article1713616 (accessed October 02, 2010).

Jordan, D. and Walsh, M. 2007 *White cargo: The forgotten history of Britain's white slaves in America.* New York: New York University Press.

Justicia for migrant workers. 2009. http://www.justicia4migrantworkers.org/ (accessed November 28, 2009).

Kara, S. 2009. *Sex Trafficking: Inside the Business of Modern Slavery*. New York: Columbia University Press.

Kleimenov, M. and Shamkov, S. 2005. Criminal transportation of persons: Trends and recommendations. In S. Stoecker and L. Shelley (Eds.), *Human Trafficking and Transnational Crime*. New York: NY: Rowman & Littlefield (Chapter 2).

Laczko, F. and Gozdiak, E. (Eds.). 2005. *Data and Research on Human Trafficking*. Geneva, Switzerland: IOM International Organization for Migration, *International Migration*, 43(1/2).

Lee, M. (Ed.). 2007. *Human Trafficking*. Cullompton, Devon, UK: Willan Pub.

Lee, M. 2011. *Trafficking and Global Crime Control*. London: SAGE.

Lehti, M. and Aromaa, K. 2007. Trafficking in humans for sexual exploitation in Europe. *International Journal of Comparative and Applied Criminal Justice* 31: 123–45.

Malarek, V. 2003. *The Natashas: The New Global Sex Trade*. Toronto: Penguin Books.

Ogrodnik, L. 2010. *Towards the Development of a National Data Collection Framework to Measure Trafficking in Persons*. Ottawa: Statistics Canada (cat. No. 88-561-M, no. 21).

PA judges accused of jailing kids for cash. 2009, February 11. Retrieved December 18, 2010. http://www.msnbc.msn.com/id/29142654/ns/us_news-crime_and_courts/.

Penketh, A. 2006. *Human Trafficking is "Slavery That Shames World."* Retrieved November 30, 2009 from: http://www.commondreams.org/headlines06/0424-05.htm.

Perrin, B. 2010a. *Invisible Chains: Canada's Underground World of Human Trafficking*. Toronto: Viking Press.

Perrin, B. 2010b. Just passing through? International legal obligations and policies of transit countries in combating trafficking in persons. *European Journal of Criminology* 7(1): 11–27.

Scarpa, S. 2008. *Trafficking in Human Beings: Modern Slavery*. New York, NY: Oxford University Press.

Segrave, M., Milivojevic, S, and Pickering, S. 2009. *Sex Trafficking: International Context and Response*. Portland, OR: Willan Pub.

Sher, J. 2011. *Somebody's Daughter: The Hidden Story of America's Prostituted Children and the Battle to Save Them*. Chicago: Chicago Review Press.

Siddique, A. April 11, 2009. *Afghan Container Deaths Reflect Wider Human-Trafficking Problem*. Retrieved November 29, 2009 from: http://www.rferl.org/content/Afghan_Container_Deaths_Reflect_Wider_Human_Trafficking_Problem/1606823.html.

Simeunovic-Patic, B. and Copic, S. 2010. Protection and assistance to victims of human trafficking in Serbia: Recent developments. *European Journal of Criminology* 7(1): 45–60.

Stoecker, S. 2005. Human trafficking: A new challenge for Russia and the United States. In S. Stoecker and L. Shelley (Eds.), *Human Trafficking and Transnational Crime*. New York, NY: Rowman & Littlefield (Chapter 1).

Stoecker, S. and Shelley, L. (Eds.). 2005a. *Human Trafficking and Transnational Crime*. New York, NY: Rowman & Littlefield. (Chapter 1).

Stoecker, S. and Shelley, L. (Eds.). 2005b. *Introduction. Human Trafficking and Transnational Crime*. NY: Rowman & Littlefield.

United Nations Office on Drugs and Crime. 2009 (February). *Global Report on Trafficking in Persons*.

U.S. Department of State 2008. *Trafficking in Persons Report*. Washington, DC: US Department of State.

Viuhko, M. 2010. Human trafficking for sexual exploitation and organized procuring in Finland. *European Journal of Criminology* 7(1): 61–76.

Van Dijk, J. 2008. *The World of Crime*. Los Angeles, CA: SAGE.

Yokoyama, M. 2010. A legal response: Measures against human trafficking in Japan. *Women and Criminal Justice*, 20: 27–39.

Zhang, S.X. 2007. *Smuggling and Trafficking in Human Beings: All Roads Lead to America*. New York: Praeger Pub.

Defining Human Trafficking and Its Nuances in a Cultural Context

2

CINDY J. SMITH
KRISTIINA KANGASPUNTA

Contents

Introduction

During 2010, there were numerous cases of human trafficking. For example, in Switzerland, four defendants were accused of trafficking women from Hungary and Romania for sexual exploitation (Gigon 2010). In Mozambique, the police accused seven suspects of selling women into South Africa for $670 each (*NY Times* 2010a). Two dozen Cambodian women were sold into marriage to Korean men (*NY Times* 2010b). All 50 states within the United States have reported trafficking (USED 2009) with nearly 500 cases prosecuted over the last decade (USDOJ 2010). In the largest case to date, South Korean businessman KilSoo Lee trafficked about 300 Chinese and Vietnamese victims into American Samoa for labor, resulting in a 40-year sentence and $1.8 million in restitution (Wong 2005). All over the world, those in poverty are being exploited in labor or commercial sex markets (see Box 2.1).

This chapter provides an introduction to the topic of human trafficking (also referred to as trafficking in persons, slavery, modern-day slavery, debt bondage, and labor trafficking). It is an ancient global problem (see the Introduction to this book), and the United Nations and its Members have a long history of leading policy development against trafficking in persons. This history leads to the discussion of the theoretical contextual framework to explain how, after all this time, trafficking in persons has emerged into the social conscience of society. Next, the chapter will define human trafficking,

**BOX 2.1   ONE EXAMPLE OF TRAFFICKING
FOR SEXUAL EXPLOITATION**

Of the 5 million people living in Moldova, approximately 1 million have left the country to pursue employment (Jandi 2003). Considering the dire poverty of the country, most have returned "successful" (as measured by sending home money to help the family), but returning "unsuccessful" results in tremendous shame (personal interview with NGO 2007). This pressure for success enables traffickers to take advantage of women, encouraging them to leave home through false promises and ensuring that they will do what is necessary to be "successful." Local nongovernmental organizations report that a typical scenario for trafficking for sexual exploitation is as follows: Emma was trafficked by her boyfriend who deceived her into thinking he was in love with her. She moved to his country where he forced her to perform sexual acts with other men. He convinced her that she could stop if she replaced herself. Thus, she was a victim who became a trafficker. Emma returns to her neighborhood in rural Moldova dressed in designer clothes and adorned with jewels. She convinces (*recruitment*) her long-time friend, Ana, to join her in her new country. Emma assures Ana that she will be equally successful in a modeling career (*deception*). On their arrival in the new country, Emma's live-in boyfriend forces Ana to perform several sexual acts (*exploitation*) every week with various men.

and discuss what is and what is not human trafficking using the three-pronged approach found in the *Protocol to Prevent, Suppress and Punish Trafficking in Persons, Especially Women and Children of the United Nations Convention against Transnational Organized Crime* (hereafter referred to as the Protocol). The Protocol was adopted by the General Assembly Resolution 55/25 of November 15, 2000 (United Nations 2000). In addition to the definition, the chapter provides examples of the various ways in which trafficking is manifested (e.g., sexual exploitation, labor exploitation, debt bondage, trafficking for the removal of organs, illegal adoptions). After the terms are defined, the typologies of human trafficking are identified and discussed, followed by an overview of the main trends of each region of the world. Contextualizing trafficking in persons' activities is paramount to understanding the complexity and nuances of trafficking. The chapter provides a discussion to emphasize the importance of context. There has been a plethora of publications, but a relative lack of high-quality studies and data (Gozdziak and Bump 2008). The few databases that have emerged are discussed later in this chapter, which concludes with a discussion of the future pathway and themes of particular interest that should be examined.

History of Slavery

Slavery has a long history throughout the world (see Figure 2.1). Its occurrence is recorded as early as 539 BC and was not completely illegalized until the late 1900s. With over 200 countries in the world and the various countries and empires that have developed and disappeared throughout history, it is impossible to list every country and its activities

Year	Event
539 BC	Cyrus the Great (Persian Emperor) abolishes slavery
1102 AD	Slave trade illegal in London
1315	King Louis X, France frees all slaves
1335	Sweden and Finland make slavery illegal
1588	Polish-Lithuanian Commonwealth abolish slavery
1683	Spain abolishes slavery in Chile
1723	Russia abolishes slavery
1787	Society for the Abolition of the Slave Trade is founded in Britain
1802	First Consul Napoleon re-introduces slavery on French colonies
1804	Haiti abolishes slavery
1807	British Empire abolishes slave trading
1810	Mexico abolishes slavery
1818	Britain, Spain, Portugal, France abolish slavery via treaties
1834	Canada abolishes slavery
1842	Uruguay abolishes slavery
1863–65	United States abolishes slavery
1910	China abolishes slavery
1923	Afghanistan abolishes slavery
1924	Iraq abolishes slavery
1924	League of Nations (beginning of the United Nations) is formed, with one of its primary goals being the resolution of the slavery issue
1926	Convention to Suppress the Slave Trade and Slavery
1928	Iran abolishes slavery
1948	Article 4 of the UN Declaration of Human Rights bans slavery globally
1962	Saudi Arabia, Yemen abolish slavery
1981	Slavery is illegal everywhere
1994	Inter-American Convention on International Trafficking in Minors
2000	United Nations Convention against Transnational Organized Crime; Protocol to Prevent, Suppress and Punish Trafficking in Persons, Especially Women and Children

Figure 2.1 Timeline of selected events of trafficking.

related to slavery. The timeline depicts randomly selected countries, documenting their legal movement toward eradication, though one entry in 1802 represents the counter-movement. The early United Nations was formed as a result of human rights against slavery. Thus, it is fitting that the United Nations takes the lead in continuing to eradicate modern-day slavery, and so their activities have been documented in the timeline. For a full discussion on United Nations activities, the reader should refer to the United Nations website (www.unodc.org). Even though slaves have always been subject to different forms of abuse and exploitation, the discussion on human trafficking from the exploitation point of view has a much shorter history (see Kangaspunta 2008).

The most recent effort of the United Nations is the Protocol supplementing the United Nations Convention against Transnational Organized Crime (UNTOC). Now, let us turn our attention to the activities leading up to the Protocol within a theoretical contextual framework.

Theoretical Contextual Framework

Although trafficking has been around since early recorded history and continues today, why did it not emerge into the social conscience of society as a major issue until the Protocol in 2000? How does a social problem—one of many—become *the* issue? This question is best answered by putting trafficking in a contextual framework (see Box 2.2). According to sociologist Herbert Blumer's (1971) model, issues move through a five-step process as they travel from obscurity to an implemented plan of action. An issue may stall or drop out of the collective consciousness (i.e., society's focus) at any point in the process. Because of the risk of losing attention, more successful social movements often have advocates who work to keep society's focus on the issue. In trafficking, nongovernmental organizations, the United Nations (i.e., UNODC Antihuman Trafficking Unit implemented the work as the hands of the Member States), together with other international organizations and the United States State Department (and its international counterparts) have all advocated to keep the issue of trafficking in persons moving through the following five-step process:

1. **Emergence**: Society recognizes a problem. Sometimes problems worsen, but at other times nongovernmental organizations advocate for attention. Unfortunately, the pathway to recognition is a little known phenomenon (Blumer 1971).
2. **Legitimation**: The issue acquires respectability and social endorsement. There is little known about what catches the attention of media and stimulates discussions (Blumer 1971). However, one event surely caught the attention of the research and policy-making community of the United Nations when the UNODC Antihuman Trafficking Unit completed a research project (UNODC 2006a), which generated considerable discussion, particularly about the research methods used. Regardless of why it was discussed, the fact that it was discussed in detail at many meetings among many scholars and policy makers was enough to generate the momentum needed to mobilize discussions and activities.
3. **Mobilization**: Truths and falsehoods frame the discussion. During this phase, advocates from all perspectives make claims about the problem. Although generally the claims are well intended, some turn out to be false, while others are true. It is in this phase that estimates of the size of the problem are useful to garner support and attention. In the case of human trafficking, there have been numerous estimates. At the time of mobilization, none of the estimates were reliable. They were mere guesses using unknown methods.

BOX 2.2   TRUTHS OR FALSEHOODS?

Estimates are useful to help policy makers determine the amount of support and funding necessary to remedy a specific problem (Steinfatt 2003). Of course, the larger the problem, the more attention and funding are needed. For those trying to gain this support and funding, high estimates are helpful. Thus, when two estimates are provided, it is likely that the higher one will be repeated. The estimates of trafficking have varied widely. One estimate, which originated with the CIA in 1999, suggested that there were approximately 700,000 victims of trafficking worldwide between 2000 and 2004. This estimate has also been attributed to the FBI or the U.S. State Department in many publications. Meanwhile, the United Nations' original estimate of 4 million victims was lowered to 1 million in 2000, while the International Organization on Migration estimated there were 400,000 victims in 2001. There are very few studies that have data collection sufficient to provide a reliable estimate (see, e.g., Steinfatt

2003). The truth or falsehood of these "guesstimates" are yet to be determined. Challenges to developing transparent and reliable estimates are numerous, including lack of basic systematic data collection systems at a national level in most countries, hidden/unreported nature of the crime, and nuances found in the interpretation of the definition that make it difficult to identify trafficking.

As we move into the mobilization phase of the model, estimates are helpful in understanding the size of the problem in different countries. However, trafficking in persons is largely a hidden crime, meaning that it is usually not reported to the authorities (Goodey 2008). It is believed, but unknown, that only a small number of trafficking cases come to the attention of any officials and therefore only a minor portion is represented in crime statistics. For this reason, the severity of human trafficking is difficult to measure using official criminal justice statistics. The culmination of the mobilization phase was the agreement to develop the Protocol.

4. **Formation of the official plan of action:** Compromises are made as a plan is developed. The plan, the Protocol, and the United Nations Global Plan of Action against Trafficking in Persons adopted in July 2010 by the General Assembly were developed at the United Nations. There is no formal assessment plan for the Protocol, but parts of it are assessed in the annual United States Trafficking in Persons (http://www.state.gov/g/tip/rls/tiprpt/index.htm) "report card," albeit limited in its ranking decision (Government Accountability Office 2006). Nonetheless, it has increased awareness and encouraged governments to act on the issue. It is in this step that large estimates of trafficking in persons become counterproductive as countries search for an unreported, unrecognized, and hidden crime. They find only a small percentage of the estimated cases, pitting advocates against government officials instead of developing cooperative working relationships. As much of the world has moved beyond this step, the reader will notice that most estimates are absent from this chapter, so as not to add fuel to the conversation of why we cannot find an estimate that is a mere guess. The estimates that do appear are recent and are reliable due to a transparent and supportable method.

5. **Implementation of the official plan:** The planned action is implemented in each Member State, with adjustments for cultural needs. First, countries became signatories and, eventually, parties to the UNTOC. Next, model legislation was developed and technical assistance was offered by the United Nations to help Member States modify and implement legislation, investigation, prosecution, and protection of victims. For example, a country assessment was completed in Lebanon to determine what needed to be done to comply with the legal and social commitments in the Protocol (Smith et al. 2008). The process of assessing the state of being, recommending changes to legislation, building consensus, educating the public, and modifying and developing appropriate treatment programs, takes considerable time.

Having worked through the first three steps, the problem of trafficking in persons has achieved sufficient status such that large estimates originally intended to garner support are no longer necessary, and, in fact, may cause some loss of credibility for those who use them. At the very least, espousing huge estimates by advocates and the reality of the relatively few victims found (GAO 2006) cause considerable discussion and finger pointing between the two parties, instead of cooperation toward the common goal of finding victims (Smith 2006). According to Blumer's (1971) model in the fourth step, instead of perpetuating unsubstantiated estimates, it would be better to publish statistics of known cases with the caveat that this is a hidden crime and the numbers do not reflect the magnitude or "dark figures" of the problem. Official crime statistics can provide very valuable information on how the police, prosecutors, and courts are responding to trafficking cases. Moreover, many other methods to measure severity are not suitable for assessing trafficking because of the nature of this crime (Kangaspunta 2007).

Even though it is difficult to find information on trafficking cases, for policy formulation it would be useful to seek a better understanding of traffickers and victims. Issues related to gender, age, form of trafficking, and victim background can give valuable insight into designing policies focusing on the right victim targets. Equally, it would be useful for law enforcement to have a profile that effectively identifies traffickers. However, one profile will not be able to capture the diversity found in the characteristics of traffickers and trafficking victims. For example, according to a recent UNODC report (2009), between 2003 and 2006, 86% of the traffickers convicted in Azerbaijan and Georgia were women. During the same period, 53% of convicted traffickers in Latvia were women. In Western Europe, between 10% and 35% of convicted traffickers were women. In France, 32% of convicted traffickers were women. Women are also involved in trafficking cases in Asian and African countries. Among convicted traffickers in the United Arab Emirates, 29% were women in both 2004 and 2005. In Nigeria, half of the convicted traffickers were women. Thus, a one-size-fits-all profile would reveal that between 10% and 86% of the traffickers were women, a range which is not as useful as looking at the specific statistics for individual countries or regions.

On the other hand, gender is more equally distributed among victims. While in many countries identified victims tend to be women, there are some exceptions (see, e.g., IOM 2008). In Belgium, the gender distribution among identified victims was more balanced: in 2006, 46% were male and 54% were female (UNODC 2009). It should be noted that in Belgium, the victim protection programs have been open to both men and women for several years. Similarly, in 2007, of 1780 victims identified by the police in Romania, 54% were women and 46% men. At the same time, the main form of trafficking was forced labor (UNODC 2009) (see Chapter 14 for further discussion about human trafficking victims).

Based on these statistics, analyzing trafficking according to location is the only way to develop accurate information on gender. However, because trafficking is a hidden crime, data collected on the crimes are limited in terms of explanatory usefulness. That is to say, a description of gender (e.g., 46% male, 54% female) only describes the relatively few cases believed to occur. The descriptors do not include the dark figure of crime, which is believed to be substantial in number. Moreover, using official statistics can be misleading. For example, recent statistics in the United States show that out of reported alleged human trafficking incidents, 12% of victims were trafficked for forced labor and 83% for sexual exploitation. Of all cases, 32% involved children trafficked for sexual exploitation (Kyckelhahn et al. 2009). Because of the dark figure of crime, it is difficult to know whether labor trafficking or sexual exploitation constitutes a larger percentage.

A serious effort to identify the number of trafficking victims was carried out in Cambodia from 2002 to 2003 (Steinfatt 2003). Based on carefully planned interviews in urban and rural communities around the country, a total of 1074 trafficking victims were found, approximately 20% of all individuals in the sex industry in Cambodia. All of the victims were identified in cities or towns and 18% were under 18 years of age (Steinfatt 2003). Steinfatt and his data collection team used a stratified sampling strategy that included all sizes of urban areas, as well as rural areas by visiting the 24 provinces in Cambodia to collect data from over 200 locations. In each data collection site, he asked three to five taxi drivers to identify locations active in the sex industry (e.g., brothels, massage parlors). By the third driver, no new locations were identified. Next, he visited the locations. Using triangulation, he asked various individuals, including the managers, the number, race, age, and status (i.e., ability to leave) of the women in the establishment. He further verified these counts by a personal visual count when the establishment was open. The data collection team focused on counting the younger women. This example shows that a combination of qualitative and quantitative methods seems to be useful in identifying the human trafficking severity at the country level. Additionally, it demonstrates that accurate data collection of this hidden population is time and labor intensive, involves a significant amount of traveling, and is thus expensive.

Definition

What is Trafficking?

The definition of trafficking in persons has met with some confusion, but generally people, including those in law enforcement (Farrell et al. 2008), do not know how to define trafficking. Part of this confusion may be due to legal and cultural differences. For example, in Lebanon, law enforcement officials give the documentation (e.g., passport) of domestic workers to the employers because, by law, the employers must produce the documentation periodically for inspection by officials. During interviews, one project determined that usually the passports were kept with other family members' passports. This, by itself, does not constitute trafficking. Additionally, as each Member State struggles to implement the Protocol within their own legal structure, differences do occur. A second confusion may be due to the liberal interpretation of the trafficking elements by service providers, who have the victim's best interest at heart. This is opposed to the very strict legal, provable elements of trafficking in persons by prosecutors. However, there is a generally clear definition in the Protocol.

The definition in the United Nations Trafficking in Persons Protocol has a three-pronged approach. One element of each of the three components must be present to constitute trafficking for adults (see Figure 2.2):

> "Trafficking in persons" shall mean the recruitment, transportation, transfer, harboring or receipt of persons, by means of the threat or use of force or other forms of coercion, of abduction, of fraud, of deception, of the abuse of power or of a position of vulnerability or of the giving or receiving of payments or benefits to achieve the consent of a person having control over another person, for the purpose of exploitation. Exploitation shall include, at a minimum, the exploitation of the prostitution of others or other forms of sexual exploitation, forced labor or services, slavery or practices similar to slavery, servitude, or the removal of organs. [Article 3(a) Protocol] (United Nations 2000)

Process/The Act	Way/Means	Goal/Purpose
What is done?	How is it done?	Why it is done
Recruitment	Threat	Sexual exploitation
or	or	or
Transportation	Coercion	Forced labor
or	or	or
Transferring	Abduction	Involuntary servitude
or	or	or
Harboring	Fraud	Slavery/similar practices
or	or	or
Receiving	Deceit	Removal of organs
	or	
	Deception	
	or	
	Abuse of power	

Figure 2.2   Components of trafficking in human beings.

This chart, extrapolated and simplified from the Protocol (United Nations 2000) definition, is a useful tool for analyzing individual cases to determine whether or not they constitute trafficking. For a situation to be considered trafficking, it must have at least one of the elements within each of the three criteria of process, means, and goal.

What is Not Trafficking?

Although there are minor differences in definitions among the various legislations around the world (see, e.g., the Introduction to this textbook), there are two common activities that are not human trafficking*). Smuggling and labor or wage disputes are not human trafficking. Let us look at these activities in more detail.

The *Protocol against the Smuggling of Migrants by Land, Sea and Air*, supplementing the United Nations Convention against Transnational Organized Crime, describes migrant smuggling as follows:

> Smuggling of migrants shall mean the procurement, in order to obtain, directly or indirectly, a financial or other material benefit, of the illegal entry of a person into a State Party of which the person is not a national or a permanent resident. [Article 3(a), United Nations 2000].

The smuggler and the migrant are involved in a commercial transaction that often ends after the border crossing. In other words, the migrant willingly pays a smuggler to assist him or her in gaining illegal entry into a country. Smuggling does not have all three of the components required to meet the definition of trafficking as it is devoid of the element of exploitation and the profit is generated from the fees to move people (i.e., the act, the means, or the purpose as in Figure 2.2). In addition, smuggling of migrants is always transnational and involves illegal entry to the destination country while persons can be trafficked within a country and they can enter the destination country legally as well (see UNODC 2008).

---

* Compare, for example, Turkey Penal Code 80 (MFA n.d.), United States Trafficking Victims Protection Act of 2000 (TVPA 2000), and the United Nations 2000 Protocol Article 3(a).

Many individuals have difficulty identifying victims of human trafficking when the *victim* is or was involved in illegal activity (Farrell et al. 2008). For example, identification of a human trafficking victim is difficult when a smuggled person becomes a trafficked person (Smith 2009; Zhang 2007). An individual who illegally gains entrance into a State is a criminal, but when he or she is forced to work in a field or is forced to perform sexual acts, another illegal activity in many countries, he or she becomes a *victim* of trafficking.

Wage disputes are not human trafficking, but rather focus on the amount of money promised for the amount of work done. These disputes do not meet the three-pronged test of human trafficking. It could be argued that the recruitment process was deceptive, but is devoid of the element of control and exploitation. In other words, the individual is free to leave, although it is sometimes a very difficult decision to leave a job not knowing from where one's next meal will come.

Types of Trafficking

The Protocol (United Nations 2000) identifies several forms of trafficking including sexual exploitation, forced labor or services, slavery or practices similar to slavery, servitude or the removal of organs. Sexual exploitation may take different forms of forced sexual acts in the sex industry. Labor exploitation may include domestic workers, field laborers, and other forms of physical labor that are often referred to as the 3-D jobs: dangerous, dirty, and degrading. Some victims find themselves in situations where they owe more to their trafficker than can ever be repaid. This might occur when the trafficker pays for housing and other basic needs, overcharging to the point where the individual is unable to leave, known as debt bondage. Trafficking for the removal of organs involves persons who are trafficked to remove their organ and then sell them to patients who need an organ transplant. One example is when an individual is recruited to remove and sell one of his or her kidneys, although the process could be more deadly. Another form of trafficking takes the form of illegal adoptions, including the selling of children who are given willingly or kidnapped. In some parts of Africa, it is a practice to give one's child to a community elder, who provides an "advance" of money that the child will earn after he or she is educated in a foreign country. However, sometimes the elder traffics the child into adoption, labor, or the sex industry. More details about the forms of trafficking are found in the Toolkit (UNODC 2008), as well as Chapter 5 of this text.

Typologies of Trafficking

Trafficking can be categorized in many ways. For example, it can be categorized by each stage of the trafficking process: recruitment, transportation, and exploitation. They can all be carried out in a variety of ways, depending on the geographical location, the identity of victims and traffickers, and the method of exploitation. Trafficking could be examined based on these three groupings to develop prevention programs at each stage of the process.

Similarly, trafficking is categorized in terms of process, such as place of origin, transit, or destination (see Kangaspunta 2004). While this provides a meaningful process description for prevention and intervention, it is less useful when developing legislation or techniques for identifying victims.

Alternatively, trafficking may be categorized as international, when victims are exploited after being transported across country borders, or it can be domestic, when the victims are recruited and exploited in the same country. Movement is not one of the criteria in the definition of trafficking in persons. However, the United Nations focuses more on international trafficking because its mandate is transnational crime. Domestic trafficking falls under each Member State's sovereignty.

The dynamics of human trafficking have often been explained or categorized by push and pull factors. Push factors are those which have an impact on the desire to leave the origin country, while pull factors are those which make a destination country inviting. The same phenomenon also can be explained in terms of supply and demand, with the supply side representing the group of people ready to leave their origin country and the demand side being the need for labor or services in different markets in a destination country. Trafficking also could be explained through factors related to the motivation and opportunity to commit a crime (Van Dijk and Kangaspunta 2000).

As presented in the introduction to this book, the three Ps of trafficking include prosecution, protection, and prevention. Prosecution includes activities related to legislation, investigation, prosecution, conviction, and punishment of offenders. Protection is related to the support and protection of victims, while prevention seeks to reduce vulnerabilities and other factors contributing to people's victimization, as well as raising awareness on the issue. In addition, national and international cooperation as a response to trafficking should be addressed. All responses should focus on the victims' rights as the starting point of the action (Goodey 2008).

Thus, it is necessary to examine the context of trafficking from various perspectives. This includes the location, the individuals involved and their motivations and opportunities, as well as the factors that may push or pull them into or out of the situation. Once trafficking is placed in context, examining the trends within these contexts will further inform developing effective strategies in the three "Ps."

Trends

The type of trafficking varies by the country and region (also see Chapter 5 in this collection). The type of exploitation and the profile of trafficking victims might also change in different parts of the world. In Western and Central Africa, the main trafficking trends include children trafficked within the region for forced labor, women and girls trafficked both inside and outside of the region for sexual exploitation, and large volumes of internal trafficking within national borders (UNICEF 2005). Both international trafficking to and from the region, as well as internal trafficking are also present in East Africa. Women and girls are trafficked for domestic labor, forced prostitution and forced marriage, while men and boys are trafficked for agricultural labor, fishing, construction work and criminal activities. Boys and girls are also exploited by armed rebel forces as child soldiers (GTZ 2003; UN GIFT 2007).

Trafficking in persons occurs in practically all countries in Western and Central Europe. While in previous decades women were mainly trafficked from Asia and South America to Western Europe, by the beginning of 2000 the most voluminous flows took place within Europe where victims, mainly women, were trafficked to Western Europe from Southeast and East Europe, including Russia and Ukraine. Currently, there is a clear decrease in the number of victims coming from these regions, but new nationalities are present among the trafficked victims in many Western European countries, particularly from East and Central Asia and Latin America (Sarrica 2009). Women remain the biggest group of trafficked persons followed by children. In many countries, trafficked men are being increasingly noted. There have been reports of trafficking of Cambodian and Thai men to work in numerous labor industries (Olivie 2008), while male victims of trafficking in Belarus and Ukraine have been documented by IOM (2008). Trafficking victims are often circulated between countries, and so there is no clear distinction between countries of origin and destination. Persons are trafficked both across and within borders for sexual exploitation, forced labor, begging, criminal activities, and other forms of exploitation (UNODC 2009; Kelly 2005; UNICEF 2007).

The Commonwealth of Independent States (CIS)* includes countries of origin, transit, and destinations for trafficked victims. People are trafficked both internally within a region, as well as to other regions of the world, particularly to Europe and Middle East (UNODC 2009). While it is generally women who are trafficked for sexual exploitation, both women and men are trafficked for forced labor. Those most vulnerable to trafficking for forced labor are usually young or middle-aged men and women with low education levels, who are already working illegally in the shadow economy as unskilled labor in CIS countries. They are exploited in sectors such as construction and renovation, transportation, trade, lumbering, or in seasonal farming, but also in the criminal economy, such as the production of counterfeit goods. Child trafficking, mainly for sexual exploitation and forced labor, is a widespread phenomenon both within CIS and across their national borders. Children are also trafficked for begging: they are either used as "little beggars" or are "rented out" for the purpose of begging (Tiurukanova 2006).

North America is generally considered a destination for men, women, and children trafficked largely from Latin America and East Asia, as well as from countries in South Asia, Africa and Europe. Internal trafficking is a problem and trafficking routes also go through the North American region. People are trafficked for sexual and labor exploitation as well as for debt bondage and illegal adoptions (U.S. State Department 2009; UNODC 2009). In Canada, human trafficking seems to disproportionately affect indigenous women (Ratansi 2007).

In Latin America, trafficking in persons occurs both within countries and across borders. Children and adults are trafficked for sexual exploitation, forced labor, and domestic work when traffickers take advantage of poor people in countries with political instability, high unemployment, and serious problems of corruption. Trafficking in women for sexual exploitation is a major business both at interregional and intraregional levels. Additionally, the number of sexually exploited children is increasing in the region, while the average age of these children is decreasing. Children are also trafficked for illegal adoptions, to be used as soldiers in armed conflict, to be used as domestic servants, or to be used as agricultural and mining laborers. There is a growing number of victims trafficked for forced labor both within the region and internationally (Ribando 2005).

---

* Azerbaijan, Armenia, Belarus, Georgia, Kazakhstan, Kyrgyzstan, Moldova, Russia, Tajikistan, Turkmenistan, Uzbekistan, and Ukraine.

From South and East Asia, victims are sent to other countries within the region and to other parts of the world. Trafficking in women and girls for sexual exploitation is the main purpose for this form of trafficking, although the exploitation of Asian domestic workers in the Middle East and in other parts of the world is also well documented. Trafficking for other types of forced labor is reported as another major problem within the region (UNODC 2008). Men and boys deceived onto fishing boats sailing the waters of the South China Sea are among the worst exploited in the region (Olivie 2008).

Many Middle Eastern countries are reported to be destinations for trafficking victims. Women are trafficked from Eastern Europe, Central Asia, and Southeast Asia mainly for sexual exploitation. One of the most common problems related to trafficking in the region is the abuse of domestic workers and other guest workers engaged in unskilled work (UNODC 2006a, 2009). A significant number of children are trafficked every year from Southeast Asia and Sudan to the Gulf States to be used as jockeys in the popular camel races; however, the international attention to the problem has resulted in considerable efforts to abolish the practice. Another form of trafficking specific to the Middle East is that of customary marriages involving young women and girls from poorer Islamic countries in the region and other parts of Asia or North Africa being trafficked for false marriage. Once they are married, these brides can find themselves quickly divorced, forced into unpaid jobs, or married to someone else (Calandruccio 2005; UNODC 2006b).

In the past, the main focus of studies concerning trafficking routes has been on international trafficking. And in the past, traffickers have been reported to be in wealthier countries, while the victims were transported from poorer countries. However, the recent information shows that domestic trafficking is a major problem in all parts of the world. This challenges the concept of trafficking across borders between wealthier and poorer countries. However, the underlying concept remains the same. Trafficking occurs most frequently with the victims coming from poverty and the purchasers coming from more affluent society. Crossing borders is not the primary issue.

Based on the discussion so far in the chapter, it is apparent that there is no one-size-fits-all solution. Thus, one approach to identifying and preventing trafficking in persons will not work. To this end, every incident must be contextualized. How is that accomplished?

Contextualizing Trafficking in Persons

Contextualizing is the process of attending to details in such a way that the researcher places these details in a broader picture without letting the broader picture cloud, cover-up, and dismiss the details (Smith 2009). This occurs within the scientific rigor within the research design (e.g., language translation and back translation) and often includes qualitative data. This attention to detail accounts for the cultural variables and enables analyses of subgroups (Smith 2009). These factors improve research methods, something that is urgently needed in trafficking in persons research (Gozdziak and Bump 2008). In examining the context of trafficking, it is useful to first explore the causes that make people vulnerable to trafficking and those that have an impact on market demands.

There are several causes that make potential victims vulnerable to trafficking. The same causes also may have an impact on the criminal career of offenders. Root causes and their connection to vulnerability is a complex issue, and there is no single causal relationship between vulnerability and human trafficking, thus further supporting the need to contextualize the data.

Vulnerability in origin countries could relate to age, gender, and economic situation. Children are vulnerable to the demands and expectations of those in authority, such as their parents, extended family, and teachers. For example, in some cultures, children are sent by their parents to work outside home or sometimes commit crime to pay off debts of the family (Romea 2007). Women are vulnerable to trafficking because they might be excluded from employment, higher education, as well as legal and political parity. Many forms of gender-based violations, such as rape, domestic violence, and harmful traditional practices, are linked to social and cultural situations that contribute to women's vulnerability to being trafficked.

Repatriation from a destination country should ensure the safe and dignified return of each victim. It should involve a risk assessment of the country to which the victim is being returned, coordination between the authorities and service providers of origin and destination countries, supported travel, reception, and referral on arrival and transportation within the home country. Sadly, many return processes are not carried out in an ideal way and may themselves pose risks to victims, making them vulnerable to retrafficking (Surtees 2005).

There is a growing understanding that trafficking in persons is not an isolated crime, but occurs in a web of crime. It may occur within the web of crime that exists in organized crime (Felson 2006), or it may occur outside organized crime, while coexisting with the web of crime (NeuhausSchaan 2009). In other words, the trafficking of persons might occur on the same routes as smuggling of small arms or drugs, whether or not they are a part of organized crime. Or, offenders can be involved in trafficking through forgery of documents, corruption, money laundering, or other criminal activities. As human trafficking is a predominantly hidden crime and very little research has been carried out on offenders, the main source of information concerning offenders other than recruiters are official records, including cases recorded by the police as well as cases of prosecuted and convicted perpetrators. Understanding traffickers and their relationships will assist the criminal justice system in investigating and prosecuting traffickers.

Plethora of Publications

As indicated in the Introduction of this book, trafficking in persons is a developing field in academic criminology, despite the existence of trafficking in persons throughout history. Although there have been many publications over the last few years, few have included scientific rigor. To systematically document this weakness, the National Institute of Justice funded the development of a comprehensive literature review (Gozdziak and Bump 2008). This study found a rich number of published studies in government and nongovernmental literature ($n = 2388$), but only 741 publications met a basic level of scientific rigor and most of them used minimal methods (i.e., convenience samples) (see Table 2.1), while even fewer were peer reviewed. There have been several other collections of the literature (see, e.g., Laczko and Gozdziak 2005, or for a list of bibliographies see http://andromeda.rutgers. edu/~wcjlen/WCJ/mainpages/bibliogs_body.html). Despite the growth of the field (i.e., finding victims, successful prosecution, increased research opportunities), there has not been an equal improvement in the rigor of the methods of research (see, e.g., Laczko and Gozdziak 2005).

Table 2.1   Publications Identified by Gozdziak and Bump (2008)

	Reports	Journal Articles	Books
Total reviewed	1249	736	403
Research-based publications	429	218	94

Source: Adapted from Gozdziak, E.M. and Bump, M. 2008. *Data Research on Human Trafficking: Bibliography of Research-Based Literature.* Institute for the Study of International Migration. NIJ Grant-2007-VT-BX-K002.

With the most pressing complaint about trafficking in persons' literature being the lack of unbiased, data-driven, (policy and practitioner) result-oriented publications, the most important next step for building knowledge in trafficking is data collection. The ASEAN report (IOM n.d.) develops principles for collecting and using data as a tool to combat trafficking in persons. The report indicates that knowledge is built from information, which is developed from data. Data must be policy relevant and focused on practitioners' needs to achieve the three Ps at both national and local levels. The report calls for the data collected to be regular and reliable, to be held to the highest level of security, to be focused on what works, and to include the whole picture—quantitative and qualitative data to place trafficking in context—and be turned into usable information. The sources of data are endless and deciding what to collect is problematic. Erring on the side of collecting too much is preferred to ensure that cases from the dark figure of crime are included. The ASEAN report (IOM n.d.) recognizes that the effort has begun with, for example, the International Organization of Migration's Counter Trafficking Module.

It is agreed that some data does exist. However, each dataset has its limitations. For example, the International Organization of Migration's Counter-Trafficking Module database, which in 2009 contained approximately 13,500 cases, collects data directly from the victims. The Government Accountability Office (2006) suggests that the data are limited to countries with the presence of the International Organization of Migration, thus not generalizable to all victims. This, again, points out the need for contextualization of all reports based on any data collected for trafficking in persons. The Government Accountability Office (2006) report identifies three other data collection efforts (e.g., United States Government, International Labor Organization, United Nations Office on Drugs and Crime), each with limitations. The United States government data include both reported and estimates of unreported international victims. However, these data may not be replicable and are thus unreliable. The International Labor Organization has created data similar to the United States data from information published in 11 languages, but it faces the same limitations. The United Nations Office on Drugs and Crime counted the number of times each country was reported by various institutions (UNODC 2006a). These data are at the macrolevel, providing no information at the individual level (see Kangaspunta 2010).

Finally, the Government Accountability Office (2006) report outlines data collected by eight United States government entities. In combination, the data provide pieces of the whole picture of trafficking that comes to the attention of the government. It includes variables, such as type of trafficking, descriptive information on victims and traffickers, points of entry, logistics including illegal documents, and information on child labor in 144 countries. Many countries collect similar types of data to varying degrees. Some of the data collection focuses on victims and to a lesser degree on offenders. None of it is adequate because the whole picture is needed.

One of the basic principles of quality research is replication. Thus, it is incumbent on the researcher to adequately describe the methods used and to make the data available to outside scrutiny to ensure replication and verification of results. Unfortunately, many of the databases currently being collected are not available to independent verification and results replication. Thus, although knowledge is being built, it is not yet the highest quality. As mentioned previously, the tightest security of the data is necessary to protect the victims. However, deidentification techniques and application processes for data access exist. Those holding data—especially data collected with government funds—need to be open to independent use to ensure that maximum knowledge can be built.

Future Pathways

There is much to be done in moving toward total abolition of slavery, so much so that it is difficult to select a pathway forward. Additionally, research for the purpose of policy and practitioner improvement is circular (see Figure 2.3). Exploratory research feeds into descriptive research, which provides the context for explanatory research, which identifies the unknown. Exploratory research is used to answer the unknown and the cycle begins again. As outlined in the ASEAN (IOM n.d.) report, a full understanding of what is needed to assist policy makers at the macrolevel and practitioners at the individual level is the primary goal. In thousands of publications, some of which were categorized in Gozdziak and Bump (2008), the field has identified some of the information needed. Using the knowledge base, the following four steps outline the way forward

1. Determine what policy makers need, what has been effective for prevention, prosecution, and protection?
2. Using the list of needs developed by the policy makers, develop the knowledge base whenever possible. For example, if the policy makers need a predictor of trafficking, the knowledge base is lacking. The United Nations Office on Drugs and Crime has identified indicators of trafficking in persons, but warns that the existence or absence of any indicator(s) is not a definite sign of trafficking. The research field needs to clarify risk and protective factors in context, develop validated risk assessments in context (i.e., these may need to be skip pattern instruments), develop validated indicator instruments that identify which combination of indicators best predicts trafficking (Smith et al. 2008), and focus on community-level indicators (i.e., trafficking in persons often occurs in a web of crime and other public health

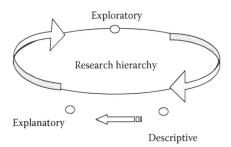

Figure 2.3 The hierarchy of research design.

issues). Some of these data are available (e.g., IOM databases), but other data must be collected. Funds for this research may come from a variety of sources (e.g., U.S. Department of State G/TIP Office or other Member State funds, NGO funding).

3. General public awareness is key to hidden crimes. Continued media and public awareness forums are needed.

4. Repeat steps 1–3.

However, there is one caution. The only way to be successful is through one basic principle: high-quality, unbiased, contextualized research. Adequate funding of those who are committed to this basic principle will provide quicker, albeit research by definition takes time, and more accurate results, although research by definition takes time.

Conclusion

Human trafficking is a global problem. This chapter provides an introduction to the issue, opening with a series of recent successful arrests and prosecutions of traffickers around the world. A series of historical events are provided to place modern-day slavery activities in a historical context. If human trafficking has existed for so many years, why has it not become a major global social issue until 2000? To explain this process, Herbert Blumer's (1971) model is used. This five-step model outlines the political support that is necessary for any issue to sustain momentum to arrive at the implementation phase of the official plan of action. One of the key explanations provided by the model is the usefulness of estimates of the size of the problem in the beginning of the process and how these same estimates can create a problem with credibility later in the process. Trafficking is defined in a way that separates it from migration and labor or wage disputes. This clarification of the definition is followed by a discussion on the various types of trafficking, such as groupings by process (e.g., recruitment, transportation, and exploitation) or by jurisdiction (e.g., international and domestic). A series of trends are provided to help the reader envision which type of trafficking or victim one might expect to see in the various regions around the world, keeping in mind that these trends are based on what is known, that is to say, what is reported. Due to the diversity of victims, situations, and activities that coincide with human trafficking, contextualization is the only way to ensure accurate, useful data for future studies. There has been a plethora of publications over the last 10 years, but very few of them include high-quality research findings. In fact, of the 2388 publications reviewed by Gozdziak and Bump (2008), only 741 met a basic level of scientific rigor and most of these used minimal methods. This has resulted in a large body of knowledge built on weak or nonexistent foundations. The biggest problem is the lack of available good data and the high cost of collecting it. The future must include more effective ways of identifying victims and assisting prosecutors and policy makers to prevent future victimizations.

Discussion Questions

1. If Gilberto assists Juan across the Mexican border into the United States and then tells him he must work on the Southwest Farm until Juan pays Gilberto his fee, is it trafficking? Why or why not? What additional information do you need?

2. Why is it so difficult to identify trafficked victims?

3. Have you seen something that could have been trafficking in persons? What were the characteristics?
4. What circumstances could you imagine that would make you a victim of trafficking? How could it happen?
5. What is contextualization? Provide an example that demonstrates the difference between findings that include contextualization and findings that do not.
6. What is the key difference between advocacy research and the highest-quality research?

References

Blumer, H. 1971. Social problems as collective behavior. *Social Problems*, 18(3): 298–306.

Calandruccio, G. 2005. A review of recent research on human trafficking in the Middle East. In Laczko, F. and Gozdziak, E. (Eds.), *Data and Research on Human Trafficking: A Global Survey*, Offprint of the *Special Issue of International Migration*, Vol. 43(1/2), Geneva: IOM.

Farrell, A., McDevitt, J., and Fahy, S. 2008. *Understanding and Improving Law Enforcement Responses to Human Trafficking: Final Report*. Grant #2005-IJ-CX-0045. Washington, DC: U.S. Department of Justice. (Available at http://www.ncjrs.gov/pdffiles1/nij/grants/222752.pdf). Federal Bureau of Investigation (2001).

Felson, M. 2006. *The Ecosystem for Organized Crime*. HEUNI Paper #26, Helsinki, Finland.

Gigon, A. 2010. Zurich takes aim at human trafficking. *Swissinfo.ch August 26, 2010*. Siwssinfo.ch http://www.swissinfo.ch/eng/swiss_news/Zurich_takes_aim_at_human_trafficking.html?cid=27040094&rss=true (Accessed August 27, 2010).

Goodey, J. 2008. Human trafficking: Sketchy data and policy responses. *Criminology and Criminal Justice*, 8(4): 421–442.

Government Accountability Office. 2006. *Human Trafficking: Better Data, Strategy, and Reporting Needed to Enhance U.S. Antitrafficking Efforts Abroad*. Washington, DC: GAO. (Available at: http://www.gao.gov/highlights/d06825high.pdf).

Gozdziak, E.M. and Bump, M. 2008. *Data Research on Human Trafficking: Bibliography of Research-Based Literature*. Institute for the Study of International Migration. NIJ Grant-2007-VT-BX-K002.

GTZ. 2003. *Study on Trafficking in Women in East Africa*. Deutsche Gesellschaft für Technische Zusammenarbeit (GTZ) GmbH, Sector Project against Trafficking in Women, Bundesministerium für wirtschaftliche Zusammenarbeit und Entwicklung/ Federal Ministry for Economic Cooperation and Development.

International Organization for Migration (IOM). (n.d.). *ASEAN and Trafficking in Persons: Using Data as a Tool to Combat Trafficking in Persons*. Geneva: International Organization of Migration.

International Organization for Migration (IOM). 2008. *MRS N°36- Trafficking of Men—A Trend Less Considered: The Case of Belarus and Ukraine*. Geneva: International Organization of Migration.

Jandi, M. 2003. *Moldova Seeks Stability Amid Mass Emigration*. Vienna, Austria: International Centre for Migration Policy Development. http://www.migrationinformation.org/feature/display.cfm?ID=184.

Kangaspunta, K. 2004. Mapping the inhuman trade: Preliminary findings of the database on trafficking in human beings. *Forum on Crime and Society*, 3(1–2): 81–103. New York: United Nations.

Kangaspunta, K. 2007. Collecting data on human trafficking: Availability, reliability and comparability of trafficking data. In Savona, E.U. and Stefanizzi, S. (Eds.), *Measuring Human Trafficking. Complexities and Pitfalls*. New York: Springer.

Kangaspunta, K. 2008. A short history of trafficking in persons. *Freedom from Fear*, October 2008, pp. 38–41.

Kangaspunta, K. 2010. Measuring the immeasurable. Can the severity of human trafficking be ranked? *Criminology and Public Policy*, 9(2): 257–265.

Kelly, L. 2005. "You can find anything you want": A critical reflection on research on trafficking in persons within and into Europe. In Laczko, F. and Gozdziak, E. (Eds.), *Data and Research on Human Trafficking: A Global Survey*, Offprint of the *Special Issue of International Migration*, Vol. 43(1/2), Geneva: IOM.

Kyckelhahn, T., Beck, A.J., and Cohen, T.H. 2009. *Characteristics of Suspected Human Trafficking Incidents, 2007–08*. Bureau of Justice Statistics, Special Report. U.S. Department of Justice, Office of Justice Programs, http://www.ojp.usdoj.gov/bjs/pub/pdf/cshti08.pdf.

Laczko, F. and Gozdziak, E. (Eds.), 2005. *Data and Research on Human Trafficking: A Global Survey*, Offprint of the *Special Issue of International Migration* Vol. 43 (1/2), Geneva: IOM.

Ministry of Foreign Affairs (MFA). (n.d.). *Turkey on Trafficking in Human Beings*. Republic of Turkey (Penal Code 80). http://www.mfa.gov.tr/turkey-on-trafficking-inhuman-beings.en.mfa (Accessed September 1, 2010).

NeuhausSchaan, J. 2009. *Developing the U.S.—Mexico Border Region for a Prosperous and Secure Relationship: Security in the U.S.—Mexico Borderlands: The Crisis, the Forces at Work and the Need for Honest Assessment and Action*. Houston, TX: James A. Baker III Institute for Public Policy of Rice University.

New York Times. 2010a. Mozambique: Police accuse 7 suspects of trafficking women into South Africa. http://www.nytimes.com/2010/03/27/world/africa/27briefs-Mozambique.html (Accessed August 28, 2010).

New York Times. 2010b. Cambodia: Ban on Marriages to South Korean Men. http://www.nytimes.com/2010/03/20/world/asia/20briefs-Cambrf.html (Accessed August 28, 2010).

Olivie, A. 2008. *Identifying Victims of Human Trafficking Among Deportees from Thailand*. Bangkok: United Nations Inter-Agency Project on Human Trafficking (UNIAP).

Ratansi, Y. 2007. *Turning Outrage into Action to Address Trafficking for the Purpose of Sexual Exploitation in Canada*. Ottawa: Report of the Standing Committee on the Status of Women.

Ribando, C. 2005. *Trafficking in Persons in Latin America and the Caribbean*. Washington, DC: CRS Report for Congress (RL33200).

Romea. 2007. MP warns of Roma children trafficked into crime. Romea.cz http://www.romea.cz/english/index.php?id=detail&detail=2007_744 (Accessed August 28, 2010).

Sarrica, F. 2009. *Global Report in Trafficking in Persons 2009, the Data Collection, the Methodology and the Results*. Paper presented at the IX. Conference of the European Society of Criminology, Ljubljana, Slovenia, September 9–12, 2009.

Smith, C.J. 2006. *Trafficking in Human Beings in Turkey: Overview and Findings About Traffickers*. Ankara, Turkey: U.S. Embassy in Turkey.

Smith, C.J. 2009. Comparative methods: Going beyond incorporating international research methods with traditional methods. *International Journal of Comparative and Applied Criminal Justice*, 33(2): 211–228.

Smith, C.J., Nakib, W. Hanna, C., and Statistics Lebanon. 2008. *Measures to Prevent and Combat Trafficking in Human Beings: Lebanon Country Assessment*. Republic of Lebanon, Ministry of Justice & UNDC with UNICEF. (Available at: http://www.unodc.org/documents/human-trafficking/Lebanon-HTreport-Oct08.pdf Accessed August 29, 2010.)

Steinfatt, T.M. 2003. *Measuring the Number of Trafficked Women and Children in Cambodia: A Direct Observation Field Study*. Part—III of Series.

Surtees, R. 2005. *Second Annual Report on Victims of Trafficking in South-Eastern Europe 2005*. Geneva: IOM.

Tiurukanova, E.V. 2006. *Human Trafficking in the Russian Federation, Inventory and Analysis of the Current Situation and Responses*. Report conducted by E.V. Tiurukanova and the Institute for Urban Economics for the UN/IOM Working Group on Trafficking in Human Beings, Moscow.

Trafficking Victims Protection Act. (TVPA) 2000. *Victims of Trafficking and Violence Protection Act of 2000*. United States. (Available at: www.state.gov/documents/organization/10492.pdf).

UN GIFT. 2007. *Vulnerabilities of Conflict and Postconflict Countries*. Report of the UN.GIFT Regional event for Eastern Africa, Uganda, June 19–22, 2007. Vienna: UNODC.

UNICEF. 2005. *Trafficking in Human Beings, Especially Women and Children in Africa*. Innocenti Research Centre, Innocenti Insight, Second Edition. New York, NY: United Nations Children's Fund (UNICEF).

UNICEF. 2007. *Child Trafficking in Europe: A Broad Vision to Put Children First*. Innocenti Research Centre, Innocenti Insight. New York, NY: United Nations Children's Fund (UNICEF).

United Nations. 2000. United Nations Convention against Transnational Organized Crime its Protocols. (Protocol against the Smuggling of Migrants by Land, Sea and Air, supplementing the United Nations Convention against Transnational Organized Crime Online) (Protocol to Prevent, Suppress and Punish Trafficking in Persons, Especially Women and Children, supplementing the United Nations Convention against Transnational Organized Crime). Available at: http://www.unodc.org/unodc/en/treaties/CTOC/index.html#Fulltext.

UNODC. 2006a. *Trafficking in Persons, Global Patterns*. Vienna: UNODC.

UNODC. 2006b. Trafficking in Persons and Smuggling of Migrants in the Middle East and North Africa. Unpublished material.

UNODC. 2008. *Toolkit to Trafficking in Persons: Global Programme Against Trafficking in Human Beings*. New York, NY: UNODC. (Available at: http://www.unodc.org/unodc/en/human-trafficking/electronic-toolkit-to-combat-trafficking-in-persons—index.html.)

UNODC. 2009.*Global Report on Trafficking in Persons*. Vienna: UNODC.

U.S. Department of Education (USED). 2009. *Human Trafficking of Children in the United States: A Fact Sheet for Schools*. Washington, DC. http://www2.ed.gov/about/offices/list/osdfs/factsheet.html (Accessed August 28, 2010).

U.S. Department of Justice (USDOJ). 2010. *Attorney General's Annual Report to Congress and Assessment of U.S. Government Activities to Combat Trafficking in Persons. Fiscal Year 2009.* Washington, DC: USDOJ.

Van Dijk, J. and Kangaspunta, K. 2000. Piecing together the cross-national crime puzzle. *NIJ Journal*, January 2000. Washington, DC: National Institute of Justice.

Wong, B. 2005. Largest U.S. human trafficking case leads to 40-year sentence. *Seattle Post—Intelligence Reporter*. Seattle, WA. http://www.seattlepi.com/business/230480_trafficker29.html (Accessed August 27, 2010).

Zhang, S. 2007. *Smuggling and Trafficking in Human Beings: All Roads Lead to America*. Westport, CT: Praeger/Greenwood (ISBN-13:978-0-275-98951-4).

Data on Human Trafficking
Challenges and Policy Context

3

JO GOODEY[*]

Contents

Introduction

Other chapters (i.e., Chapters 1 and 2) in this book variously address legal definitions and the diverse manifestations of human trafficking—ranging as it does from sex trafficking through labor exploitation and trafficking in human organs. The focus of this chapter is on what we do, and do not, know about human trafficking with respect to data collection challenges, and it looks specifically at the European Union (EU) policy context in which data collection takes place.

Throughout much of the developed world, and in some parts of the developing world, the need for data collection is becoming increasingly important in governmental and nongovernmental circles.[†] Evidence-based advice is promoted as the bedrock of policy responses to the social and economic concerns of the day. Reliable data and information are now regarded as essential tools in the development of policies and action that address

---

[*] The opinions of the author expressed in this chapter do not represent those of the European Union Agency for Fundamental Rights.

[†] In the European Union (EU) a European Statistical System (ESS) exists, which is a partnership between the Community's statistical authority—namely, Eurostat (the Directorate General of the Commission with responsibility for the harmonisation of data collection on different policy issues across the EU's 27 Member States)—and national statistical institutes and other national authorities with responsibility for the development, production and dissemination of EU statistics. These data are seen as an essential tool for the development of informed policy at EU and national level; see: http://epp.eurostat.ec.europa.eu/portal/page/portal/about_eurostat/corporate/introduction (accessed December 30, 2010).

anything from child poverty through inequalities in the labor market—including the field of human trafficking. In the absence of robust data, there is a real risk that policy responses are developed which do not reflect realities on the ground, which in turn can mean that initiatives are misdirected and their positive impact is limited. The human and financial costs of misdirected policies is also something that has to be carefully considered—and particularly during economic downturns when resources are stretched and competed for. It is apparent, as presented in this chapter, that we are far from having robust and comprehensive data on human trafficking that can serve to inform policy responses.

The evidence presented here draws on developments in Europe, and more specifically within the EU. In this chapter, the reader will not find an overview of the situation concerning data collection on trafficking in other regions in the world; however, the points made here with respect to the EU should resonate with other regions. In summary, the first part of the chapter explores a selection of key challenges for data collection on trafficking, while the second part examines the policy context against which data are collected. The chapter concludes with an indication of possible ways forward with respect to data collection in the field of human trafficking.

Challenges for Data Collection

Judging the Scale and Nature of Human Trafficking

Since the early 1990s, various estimates have been forwarded by different organizations concerning the extent of trafficking on a global and regional scale—focusing mainly on sex trafficking. At the end of the 1990s and during the first decade of the twenty-first century, the figure of 500,000 women and children being trafficked annually for prostitution into the "old" (pre-2004) 15 Member States of the EU was regularly referred to by non-governmental organisations (NGOs); yet this figure's source, although likely to have been the International Organisation for Migration (IOM), and how it was calculated, remains uncertain (Aromaa and Lehti 2007). In comparison with this "guesstimate" figure, perhaps the most concerted attempts to capture the extent of trafficking have been developed by the UN's International Labour Organisation (ILO), which has explored various methodologies that aim at capturing the global extent of trafficking for both labor and sexual exploitation. ILO's 2007 report on "Methodologies for global and national estimation of human trafficking victims" (Kutnick et al. 2007) compares findings between ILO's own analysis and that of the U.S. government—with the former estimating that between 275,068 and 508,931 people are in the process of being trafficked both within and between countries at any given time, while the latter estimates that between 600,000 and 800,000 people are trafficked across international borders each year. What is apparent from these large but very divergent figures, and when comparing data between and within countries, is that different sources and different definitions of trafficking are being drawn on when attempting to calculate the scale of the problem.

Both NGOs and intergovernmental organizations, such as the UN, regularly make reference to the large scale of human trafficking. It is understandable that these large figures serve a purpose in that they highlight the extent of human suffering from trafficking. In this regard, the accuracy of the figures—give or take a few 100,000s—is perhaps less important than the image created of the scale of the potential problem, which is typically related alongside harrowing personal histories of trafficking victims. However, inaccurate "guesstimates" can serve to undermine the credibility of efforts to address trafficking, a situation that is encapsulated neatly by an example from the 2006 World Football Cup, which was held in Germany.

In March 2006, a European Parliament resolution addressed forced prostitution in the context of world sports events, which was followed a month later by the Presidency of the Council of the European Union emphasizing—"the fact that major international events, including sports events, have shown to pose the risk to contribute to a temporary increase in trafficking in human beings."[*] In contrast with, or perhaps because of, these dire warnings, only five cases concerning sex trafficking were investigated in connection with the 2006 World Football Cup in Germany. At the same time, over 300 online German articles were published that made reference to sex trafficking in connection with this sporting event (Hennig et al. 2007). As the International Organisation for Migration (IOM) noted, in its March 2008 bulletin on trafficking, the actual extent of sex trafficking for the World Cup "was unrealistic and unfounded hype."

It can be argued that the concerted efforts of the World Cup organizers, together with the German police and NGOs, served to warn potential traffickers away from the 2006 World Cup. At the same time it can also be argued that, against all these efforts to combat trafficking, cases of trafficking still went unreported and undetected. A more plausible explanation rests with the conclusion reached by the IOM—that the dangers of sex trafficking surrounding the World Cup were exaggerated.

A similar critique of exaggeration has been leveled at police operations in the United Kingdom that have set out to combat trafficking—often in the full glare of the media. Writing in *The Guardian* newspaper about the UK police's "Operation Pentameter," O'Connell Davidson (2007) referred to the "hyperbole and emotive rhetoric about sex slaves" in the United Kingdom, which she critiqued as lacking a focus on the actual circumstances and needs of prostitutes (O'Connell Davidson and Anderson 2006). In 2006, Operation Pentameter identified 84 trafficking victims, and a year later, Operation Pentameter II identified 164. While this shows a twofold increase in the operation's identification of victims, the numbers still appear low and reflect figures collected in 1998 by Kelly and Regan in their research that was based on questionnaire replies from 36 of the 43 police forces in England and Wales—which concluded that of the 71 victims identified in 18 trafficking cases in 1998, the "real" number of victims could be anywhere in the range from 2–20 times greater (Kelly and Regan 2000).

The above numbers would seem to indicate that relatively slow progress is being made by the police in their efforts to identify victims in trafficking cases. Yet, it has to be acknowledged that official police data on known trafficking cases can only hope to scrape the proverbial "tip of the iceberg" when it comes to the true extent of this type of crime. Given, as we know from victim surveys, that so much of conventional or common crime never comes to the attention of the police, it is hardly surprising that serious and organized criminal activities remain elusive. At the same time there are elements of police work that cannot be made known to the public for fear of jeopardizing investigations. Concerted police efforts to identify and bring to justice cases of human trafficking should not be conflated with the media's desire to focus on a story that serves to both inform and titillate the public about sex trafficking.[†] Here, it is

---

[*] Council of the European Union 2725th Justice and Home Affairs Council Meeting, Luxembourg April 27–28, 2006, Council Conclusions on Trafficking in Human Beings, paragraph 9.

[†] For an example of some of the more sensationalist reporting on trafficking; see: Daily Mail newspaper, UK (December 8, 2009) "Human Traffickers Sell Sex Slave on Britain's Busiest Street"; www.dailymail.co.uk/news/article-1233780

important to consider the context in which data on trafficking are generated to understand what is and what is not possible to know, at present, about this crime.

Within the EU, the quality of data collection on human trafficking differs extensively. A diverse range of source material exists, of varying quality—from criminal justice and government-produced data, through to local and international NGO databases. One of the best examples of data collection comes from the Dutch National Rapporteur[*] on trafficking in human beings, which was established in 2000 as an independent mechanism for data collection that reports to the government. The Rapporteur uses a wide range of sources, including criminal justice sources, in its annual reporting on the situation in the Netherlands, the results of which are used to formulate policy recommendations to address trafficking. Data collection and reporting are also undertaken on a regular basis by specialized police units in some countries—such as the German Federal Police (Bundeskriminalamt [BKA])[†] and the National Criminal Police of Sweden.[‡] This kind of reporting typically provides a breakdown of information concerning the background typology of victims and offenders according to their countries of origin, and, in the case of victims, their gender and age.

Police and criminal justice data, where available in the public domain, can provide a good introduction to the nature of trafficking cases; yet, the mainstay of detailed police and prosecutorial knowledge in this field must, necessarily, remain hidden (see Box 3.1 referring to the work of Europol and Eurojust). Other useful sources that offer an insight into the nature of trafficking incidents are provided by the Office for Democratic Institutions and Human Rights (ODIHR, of the Office for Security and Cooperation in Europe [OSCE]; see Aronowitz et al. 2010) and the European Commission,[§] which variously provide data on selected trafficking cases that serves to inform about the nature of the exploitative process; including traffickers' personal histories and the makeup of trafficking networks.

In comparison, the majority of material on the nature of trafficking is typically focused on victims as it originates from NGOs, such as La Strada (which, in September 2010, celebrated its fifteenth anniversary as an NGO focusing on trafficking in women[¶]) and the Coalition against Trafficking in Women (founded in 1988[**]), and intergovernmental organizations, such as IOM and the UN, which are primarily working with victims in the fields of trafficking and migration. What we know less about in the trafficking equation is the traffickers themselves (see Goodey 2008; Surtees 2008; Troshynski and Blank 2008). This situation reflects the fact that it is difficult and potentially dangerous to undertake research or some form of data collection with criminals—that is, human traffickers. In comparison, researching victims is, relatively speaking, easier (see Chapter 12 for further discussion on victims of human trafficking). However, data collection does pose potential problems for victims who may fear reprisals for having spoken with anyone about their experiences—be it NGOs, the police, or researchers.

---

[*] Dutch National Rapporteur on Trafficking in Human Beings—English website: http://english.bnrm.nl

[†] http://www.bka.de/lageberichte/mh/2009/bundeslagebild_mh_2009.pdf

[‡] http://www.polisen.se; in English—"Trafficking in human beings for sexual and other purposes" Situation Report 11.

[§] European Commission "Fight Against Trafficking in Human Beings" website; http://ec.europa.eu/anti-trafficking—contains examples of case law.

[¶] http://lastradainternational.org—European network against trafficking in human beings.

[**] http://www.catwinternational.org

BOX 3.1   EUROPOL AND EUROJUST[*]

Europol and Eurojust are two operational European Union (EU) agencies that are engaged in work that directly addresses trafficking cases of a trans-border or trans-European nature—the former in relation to police cooperation in investigations, and the latter in relation to judicial cooperation.

Europol can be understood as the EU's equivalent of Interpol. The mandate of Europol is to "improve the effectiveness and cooperation in preventing and combating various forms of serious international forms of organized crime, including human trafficking." Europol does share some limited information on trafficking in its regular situation reports, but it only shares detailed information with authorized users in the EU's 27 Member States, which are subject to data protection control under the Europol Convention.

Eurojust is the EU's agency for judicial cooperation, which includes a number of cases dealing with human trafficking. Eurojust releases general figures about the number and nature of cases it has successfully prosecuted that specifically relate to trafficking (83 cases in 2008, 74 cases in 2009, and 70 cases up to the end of September 2010; data presented by Michele Coninsx, Vice-President of Eurojust at the fourth European Anti-Trafficking Day conference, which took place in Brussels on October 18 and 19, 2010), but maintains strict data protection in relation to the details of ongoing prosecutions.

Europol and Eurojust engage in Joint Investigation Team operations (JITs) with respect to certain cross-border cases of serious and organized crime in the EU; including trafficking cases. Occasional "success stories" from JIT operations are made public (presentation by Bernie Gravett, London Metropolitan Police at the fourth European Anti-Trafficking Day conference).

Different Data Collection Sources[*]

Apart from the police and other branches of the criminal justice system, and the work of antitrafficking NGOs, there are many alternative sources that can produce data on the scale and nature of human trafficking. As illustrated by the ILO's work, trafficking encompasses diverse forms of labor exploitation besides sex trafficking, and therefore can be detected and documented through different avenues that include, for example, labor and health inspectorates (ILO 2009). As an illustration—a 2010 report by the NGO "Environmental Justice Foundation," which investigates potential cases of illegal and exploitative fishing practices, revealed not only environmental concerns but also the extreme exploitation of workers under "modern-day slavery" conditions onboard ships sailing off the west coast of Africa (Environmental Justice Foundation 2010). In other words, trafficking cases can be unearthed in diverse settings and as a by-product of other investigations.

A range of different sources for data collection on potential trafficking cases is to be welcomed. However, a number of challenges arise when trying to work with these diverse sources. Chief among these is the existence of different legal definitions and hence different criminal justice responses to trafficking across the various jurisdictions of the

---

[*] Europol—http://www.europol.europa.eu; Eurojust—http://www.eurojust.europa.eu

EU.[*] In turn, this impacts on if and how data are collected on trafficking as a specific offence or offences, or whether trafficking is subsumed under other offences. Given that different agencies—both criminal justice and noncriminal justice based—collect data differently, there is the ever-present problem of data comparability both within and between countries. For example, this lack of comparability and consistency can mean that the same case, as well as the same victim or offender, may be recorded more than once and identified differently in each database. The current absence of harmonized and transferable data between sources can seriously hamper the investigation and prosecution of trafficking cases, as well as the identification of vulnerable victims for the purpose of assistance and protection.

In response to this situation, the European Commission's 2006–2010 Action Plan for the development of a comprehensive and coherent EU strategy on measuring crime and criminal justice, which is soon to be followed by a second Action Plan from 2011, is the clearest illustration of the desire by the "users" of such data—those who initiate and develop policy responses—to have comprehensive, reliable, and comparable data on key areas of crime where the EU has legal competence. To this end, an expert group on the policy needs for data on crime and criminal justice was set up by the Commission in 2006, and was followed by the creation of different expert subgroups to address key areas of crime,[†] including one on "trafficking in human beings." The objective of the trafficking subgroup was to "develop harmonized definitions and associated indicators that will facilitate greater comparability of data across EU member states on the crime area under consideration."

A direct outcome of this subgroup's work was a joint ILO and Commission working group, which applied the Delphi method of "consensus building" among different experts in the trafficking field, for the identification and prioritization of indicators on human trafficking. The subgroup's work resulted in the development of four operational indicator sets concerning different victims: (1) adult victims of labor exploitation; (2) adult victims of sexual exploitation; (3) child victims of labor exploitation; and (4) child victims of sexual exploitation. The indicators are like a "checklist" for those working in the field who might encounter potential victims—such as labor inspectorates. The outcome of this exercise was tested in Moldova (a small country located in the Balkan region of SE Europe) in 2008 in a special module on labor migration that was introduced into the country's Labor Force Survey, and which was able to capture sufficient numbers of returnee migrants on whom the module could be tested. There are also plans (as reported in the 2009 joint ILO—European Commission publication) to test the survey on other administrative data collection instruments in "western" Europe (International Labour Organisation and European Commission 2009).

The European Commission has also supported other efforts at harmonized data collection in the field of trafficking. Notable among these are the so-called SIAMSECT

[*] For an understanding of some of the challenges of trying to collect and compare diverse European criminal justice data sources on different types of crime, see: European Sourcebook of Crime and Criminal Justice Statistics, 4th edition published in 2010, www.europeansourcebook.org; see also United Nations surveys on Crime Trends and the Operations of Criminal Justice Systems, of which the 10th survey included data on trafficking in human beings, www.unodc.org.

[†] European Commission Decision of August 7, 2006 setting up a group of experts on the policy needs for data on crime and criminal justice; 2006/581/EC; Official Journal L 234, 29/08/2006, p. 0029–0032—of which the author is a member.

files that were funded by the Commission's DAPHNE II[*] program and developed by the Institute for International Research on Criminal Policy (IRCP) at the University of Ghent, together with the Joint Research Centre on Transnational Crime (Transcrime) at the University of Trento (Vermeulen et al. 2006). This research developed a series of standardized templates for the collection of EU-wide indicators on missing and sexually exploited children and trafficking in human beings. In the project description, the authors indicate that the templates are designed for law enforcement authorities, judicial authorities, NGOs and governmental organizations, as well as social and labor inspectorates. The results of this project were tested in practice, in Belgium and Italy, using an IT tool developed by the same research teams as part of the "MONTRASEC" project; cofinanced by the Commission's "Prevention of and fight against organized crime" program (Vermeulen and Paterson 2010).

Alongside the above, a number of parallel initiatives exist in the EU and with countries external to the EU that variously address the need for improved and comparable data collection on trafficking. Some examples, among many, include

> An initiative by the IOM and the Austrian Ministry of the Interior resulted in the publication of recommendations concerning data collection for core indicators in the field of human trafficking at the level of Member States and the EU. Another international actor in the field, this time the International Centre for Migration Policy Development (ICMPD), has been developing a system for data collection and information management in southeastern Europe that relates to two distinct databases—one for information relating to victims, and the other for information regarding traffickers and the criminal justice system.[†] And in September 2010, another project was launched at a high-level ministerial roundtable in Vienna—hosted by the Austrian government, under the project leadership of Helga Konrad (the former OSCE special rapporteur on trafficking in women), and in cooperation with IOM—to put in place "concrete partnership initiatives" between Austria and its neighboring countries to improve coordination and cooperation initiatives against trafficking. Part of this initiative makes reference to a joint mechanism for data coordination and sharing—a trafficking "index"—in line with the Action Oriented Paper on strengthening the EU external dimension on action against trafficking, which emerged under the 2009 Swedish Presidency of the EU.

In summary, numerous data collection initiatives on trafficking have been launched in the last few years across the EU. At best, these initiatives set out to improve and harmonize data gathering in the region; at worst, they run the risk of duplicating efforts towards improved data collection.

Looking beyond the regional EU level, the goal of developing indicators in the field of human rights—including trafficking in human beings—has been taken up by the UN Office of the High Commissioner on Human Rights. A series of expert consultations have taken place, and a draft practical guide has been developed that explores working methodologies for indicator development. Under the project template that deals with violence

---

[*] The European Union has initiated a number of programmes since the mid-1990s that have supported anti-trafficking initiatives; including the DAPHNE programme, which specifically addresses violence against women and children, as well as programmes that have focused on police and judicial cooperation such as STOP and AGIS.

[†] International Centre for Migration Policy Development (2010) Handbook on Anti-Trafficking Data Collection in South-Eastern Europe: Developing Regional Criteria.

against women, a basic list of indicators has been developed for the grouped categories of "violence at work, forced labor, and trafficking," which are put under the framework of structural, process, and outcome indicators. This work serves to remind us about the different levels of indicators, or different types of data collection, which can be utilized in the field of human rights abuses. These range from structural indicators that include the transposition of legislation; through to process indicators that can measure the proportion and frequency of businesses inspected for conformity with labor standards through outcome indicators that seek to record reported cases of trafficking.

As a reflection of the fact that data on serious and organized crime—and hence data on trafficking—are difficult to collect, we are still a long way from having harmonized data collection on outcome indicators that can present robust information on the number and nature of trafficking incidents. This is currently the case for data collection on trafficking at both the national and international levels. In other words, there still remains a lack of consistency in how data are collected, managed, and reported. Therefore, it is important to utilize a range of indicators—such as structural or process indicators—that can be used to monitor developments with respect to human trafficking. Herein, reference to multiagency responses to trafficking—or "partnerships"—has entered the policy discourse on trafficking in the last 2 years. This reference to "partnership," or what has been termed the fourth "P" response to trafficking (the other three being prevention, protection, and prosecution), reflects the need for joined-up work, including data collection and intelligence gathering on a range of indicators, between different actors in the field; ranging from NGOs through the police and judiciary.

Sharing Data and Security Concerns

As already previously suggested, it is likely that much information about the extent and nature of trafficking is not put in the public domain by the police and other criminal justice agencies, beacuse to do so could compromise efforts at investigation and prosecution. At the same time, the need to protect victims from further abuse is also a factor to consider with respect to how much detail can enter the public domain. These concerns are particularly shared by NGOs that work directly with trafficking victims; concerns that may also impinge on these organizations' ability and willingness to enhance data compatibility and exchange of data between different organizations.

Whereas police and judicial authorities necessarily have to limit who they exchange detailed case information with, it is arguable that the same restrictions should not be imposed on sharing aggregate data on trafficking that reports on general numbers and trends (as this poses very little risk for the parties concerned). In other words, databases that do not allow for the identification of individuals or small groups can be used by a range of actors in the development of policy responses and action on the ground to address trafficking. This kind of information exchange—particularly if it is coordinated across agencies and countries—is invaluable as a means for exploring current and emergent trends in trafficking, and ideally can operate as an early warning system for police and NGOs alike.

It has to be remembered that set against the repeated calls for improved and comparable data collection across the EU on trafficking, there is much that will remain below the surface and in the hands of those who are responsible for criminal investigations and prosecution. Yet at the same time we have to acknowledge that the police and the judiciary

BOX 3.2   ECPAT: END CHILD PROSTITUTION, CHILD PORNOGRAPHY, AND THE TRAFFICKING OF CHILDREN FOR SEXUAL PURPOSES

ECPAT is a nongovernmental organization that was founded in Thailand in the early 1990s. It began by highlighting the problem of child prostitution in many Asian countries, and steadily extended its work to cover other regions of the world. ECPAT consists of a network of groups in over 70 countries that work to eliminate child prostitution, pornography, and trafficking for sexual purposes. In the field of trafficking ECPAT serves to underline the particular problem of *child* trafficking, and provides vital information about the extent and nature of this crime in many parts of the world.

For further details about the history and current mandate of ECPAT, see: http://www.ecpat.net

are also heavily reliant on the willingness of victims to report their victimization and to testify against their offenders. Here, the work of NGOs in identifying and working with victims—and referring them to the authorities where appropriate—is essential. In essence, what we know about the extent and nature of trafficking owes a great deal to NGOs working on the ground (see Box 3.2).

The latest policy vogue in the field of trafficking—the "partnership" response—is an indication of the increased acknowledgment that is being given to the essential role played between different actors in combating trafficking. These "partnerships" are important in the development of a more coherent and joined-up response to trafficking, which in turn can enhance efforts at improved data collection between different actors.

With respect to the need for improved data collection and exchange, partnerships between NGOs, on the one hand, and the police and judicial authorities, on the other, can only work when NGOs trust the police to protect vulnerable victims. *ICMPD's Handbook on Antitrafficking Data Collection*, as referred to earlier, sets out considerations in this area with regard to the victim's right to privacy and confidentiality, the issue of consent, the duty of data providers to ensure adequate safeguards for data storage, and maintenance and transmission of data. With the increased need to collect and process data electronically, it is clear that harmonized guidelines and systems for data collection are the way forward to achieve this goal. The need for data encryption to ensure privacy and data protection is also a key factor for the future development of any trafficking databases; however, who is best placed to do this and how it will be resourced are questions that are particularly poignant in times of economic austerity (writing in 2010).

Policy Developments in Response to Trafficking

From a Crime Control Model toward a Victim-Centered One?

The so-called three "Ps'" response to human trafficking—prevention, protection, and prosecution (see Chapter 8)—has been characterized as a polarized response between different organizations working to address trafficking. In summary, prevention and protection have been characterized as victim centered (Goodey 2003a,b, 2004a,b), whereas prosecution has been labeled as offender centered. Responses to trafficking have also been characterized as follows (Lindstrom 2007): migration based (exemplified by the work of the IOM); human rights based (as exemplified by NGOs working to assist victims, and by the work of the Council of Europe); economics based (i.e., focusing on economic push and pull factors, and characteristic of some of ILO's work); and law enforcement based (typified by the work of Europol in the EU [see Box 3.1 in this chapter]); and to an extent by the U.S. government's Trafficking in Persons (TIP) reports that rank different countries' (primarily) criminal justice responses to trafficking*—but which have a limited impact within the EU). To an extent, the reference in EU policy circles to a "partnership" response, as the fourth "P" in addition to the above, has sought to alleviate what was, and in some quarters still remains, a polarized response to trafficking—be it characterized under the three Ps heading or on the basis of other response models.

The responses of different agencies to trafficking can be understood with respect to the different mandates of these various actors in the area of trafficking. In turn, what we know about the extent and nature of trafficking largely reflects the origins of responses to trafficking, and hence which organizations are collecting data. For example, if the identification of trafficked people for labor exploitation had first emerged through the work of health and safety inspectorates, it might well be the case that data collection would have been dominated by work in this field; hence, a "health and safety" response to trafficking could have evolved. Likewise, if the medical establishment had identified the problem of trafficked women as part of a broader exercise collecting data on sexually transmitted diseases, then a "medical" model of responding to trafficked women could have developed. As it is, since the 1990s data collection on trafficking has been dominated by a "crime" model—and more specifically as an *international* crime model rather than a *domestic* one—as a reflection of the fact that the police and criminal justice system took the lead in responding to trafficking under the broader framework of work addressing transnational organized crime; a model that can be characterized as prosecution and law enforcement focused, and one which only recently recognized that trafficking did not necessitate the crossing of borders.

The "crime" model is embedded in the 2000 United Nations Convention against Transnational Organised Crime, which is the legal blueprint from which responses to trafficking have developed in recent years. The Convention is supplemented by two protocols; one to "Prevent, Suppress and Punish Trafficking in Human Beings, Especially Women and Children," and the other concerning the "Smuggling of Migrants by Land, Sea and Air." The Vienna-based United Nations Office on Drugs and Crime (UNODC)—previously the UN Centre for International Crime Prevention (CICP) at the time the Convention was being negotiated—took the lead with respect to the Convention's development, and was supported in this through the work of its Global Programme against Trafficking (GPAT), which subsequently developed a citation index of text-based references to countries of origin, transit, and destination, that offered a limited interpretation of trafficking routes as a reflection of the methodology employed by the study.

Although the Convention and its protocols are wide-ranging in scope—encompassing labor exploitation and trafficking in human organs—the mainstay of UNODC's focus throughout the 2000s has been on trafficking for sexual exploitation. This approach

* http://www.state.gov/g/tip/rls/tiprpt/2009/index.htm.

needs to be seen in the light of the UN's first Convention to explicitly address trafficking, which was the 1949 Convention on the "Suppression of Trafficking in Women and the Exploitation of Prostitution of Others." Hence, UNODC's response to trafficking and data collection has been dominated by a crime control model that has focused on the particular problem of trafficking in women, and laterally children, for sexual exploitation—and more specifically, prostitution.

Legal developments to address trafficking in the EU have taken the UN Convention and its Protocols as the basis for developing legislation; for example, the EU's 2002 Framework Decision on combating trafficking in human beings. This has meant that legal responses to trafficking in the EU have also developed under what can be described as a predominantly crime control model. This is exemplified to a degree by the EU's 2004 Directive on residence permits issued to third-country nationals who are victims of trafficking, or who have been the subject of an action to facilitate illegal immigration, as it stipulates *cooperation with the authorities* (in the investigation of cases) as a factor in granting residence permits. The 2004 directive can be characterized as offering "protection" to victims within the main goal of securing "prosecution" of traffickers.

More recently, in 2010, the European Commission tabled a proposal for a Directive on "Preventing and combating trafficking in human beings, and protecting victims," which will repeal the earlier Framework Decision from 2002 [Trafficking Directive COM (2010) 95 final; repealing Framework Decision 2002/629/JHA]. The inclusion of "protecting victims" in the new legislation, as well as the insertion of new articles directly dealing with child victims, reveals a more victim-centered response to trafficking; yet the provisions for victim protection are laid out in the proposal within the context of criminal proceedings (see Box 3.3). By embedding victim protection within criminal proceedings, a victim-centered response to trafficking is delimited by a response that appears to be grounded in the goal of a criminal trial—which, as a stressful and potentially dangerous undertaking, might not be in the best interests of the victim.

Outside the EU's legislative developments, the Council of Europe offers a more holistic response to trafficking with respect to victims' rights. The 2005 Convention on Action against Trafficking in Human Beings is described on the Council of Europe's website as the "most important human rights treaty of the last decade."[*] Arguably, however, the Council of Europe's human rights-focused response to trafficking is one that countries feel they can

---

BOX 3.3   THE EUROPEAN UNION'S RESPONSE TO TRAFFICKING[†]

The European Union is taking an increasingly active role in responding to trafficking in human beings. On December 21, 2010 the Commission launched its antitrafficking policy website, which summarizes work at EU and Member State level that is variously addressing trafficking. For example, the website refers to: legislation and case law; the work of the EU Group of Experts on Trafficking; EU-funded projects in the field of antitrafficking; EU national rapporteurs on trafficking; and the work of the EU Anti-Trafficking Coordinator.

---

[*] www.coe.int/t/dghl/monitoring/trafficking/Docs/News/AUT-web-article-en.asp; see also GRETA—the Council of Europe's (CoE's) Group of Experts on Action against Trafficking in Human Beings.
[†] http://ec.europa.eu/anti-trafficking/index.htm

afford to sign up to; in comparison, EU legislation carries the weight of sanctions for non-adherence. What the Council of Europe (like the UN's Treaty monitoring bodies) is keen to prioritize, but unable to enforce, is data collection on trafficking. In comparison, the EU is better placed to promote harmonized data collection on trafficking, and has begun to do this through existing channels such as Eurostat—which is beginning to work in the field of data collection relating to crime and criminal justice.

To date in the EU, in line with the dominant crime control response to trafficking, data collection has largely developed within the scope of efforts to harmonize EU figures in the field of crime and criminal justice—as described earlier with respect to the European Commission's 2006–2010 Action Plan for an EU strategy on measuring crime and criminal justice, which includes data on trafficking. The focus in the Action Plan on data collection concerning crimes with a cross-border element needs to be understood with respect to where the EU has legal competence to address crime without infringing on national sovereignty—that is, with respect to crime with a cross-border dimension (including trafficking and other forms of organized crime, such as money laundering).

Looking outside the narrow confines of the existing legal responses directed *specifically* at trafficking, the EU has progressively been developing legislation that addresses the needs of crime victims—such as the 2001 Framework Decision on the Standing of Victims in Criminal Proceedings and the 2004 Directive relating to Compensation of Crime Victims,* and is in the process of developing a new Victims Directive to replace these two. In parallel, specific initiatives, such as the Daphne program, which was launched in 1997, have financed work on the ground by NGOs, local authorities, and research institutions to address all forms of violence against women, young people, and children—which includes trafficking.[†] In this regard, the European Commission's responses to trafficking and to victims, more generally, cannot be so readily characterized as a single-model approach that is law enforcement or crime control based. A range of actors from labor inspectors through environmental health inspectors can potentially provide alternative sources of information and also data on trafficking; sources of information that are outside the strict confines of what can be considered as a law enforcement or crime control approach, hence the recent "partnership" approach.

The Stockholm Programme and the Lisbon Treaty

Where the 2004 Hague Programme has left off in 2009, the Stockholm Programme, for the period 2010–2014, seeks to further strengthen the EU as an area of freedom, security, and justice (see Box 3.4).[‡] Trafficking in human beings is addressed in the Stockholm Programme under the heading of "Protecting against serious and organized crime." This would appear to locate trafficking within a crime control and law enforcement response; which would also appear to be the case with respect to aspects of the proposed Directive on trafficking (as described earlier). The clear connection made in the Stockholm Programme

---

* Council Framework Decision of March 15, 2001 on the standing of victims in criminal proceedings (2001/220/JHA); Council Directive of April 29, 2004 relating to compensation of crime victims (2004/80/EC)—http://eur-lex.europa.eu.
† http://ec.europa.eu/justice/funding/daphne3/funding-daphne3_en.htm.
‡ European Council 2010/C 115/01 "The Stockholm Programme—An open and secure Europe serving and protecting citizens"; http://eur-lex.europa.eu.

BOX 3.4   THE STOCKHOLM PROGRAMME*

The Stockholm Programme forms the basis of the European Union (EU) policy and action in the fields of "freedom, security, and justice" for the years 2010–2014. It builds and develops on its predecessors the Tampere and Hague Programmes. The core elements of the Programme are addressed under seven headings: (1) Towards a citizens' Europe in the area of freedom, security, and justice; (2) Promoting citizens' rights: A Europe of rights; (3) Making people's lives easier: A Europe of law and justice; (4) A Europe that protects; (5) Access to Europe in a globalized world; (6) A Europe of responsibility, solidarity, and partnership in migration and asylum matters; (7) Europe in a globalized world—the external dimension of freedom, security, and justice.

"Trafficking in human beings" is addressed under its own heading (4.4.2), which is under the general framework of "Protecting against serious and organised crime" (4.4). Other parts of the Programme directly address specific aspects of trafficking (such as child trafficking victims under 2.3.2 on the "Rights of the child"), or indirectly encompass elements of trafficking through reference to "Vulnerable groups" (2.3.3) or "Victims of crime" (2.3.4)—such as women who are victims of gender-based violence, or persons who are harmed in a Member State of which they are not nationals or residents.

between the "migration-crime-security" nexus (see Goodey 2005), in response to an intertwined approach to the social and criminal issues of the day, means that a crime control response to trafficking remains dominant. Having said this, it is also apparent that major changes are taking place in relation to responses to crime, as reference to fundamental rights is inserted in the Programme.

The EU's response to trafficking has also to be understood within the broader framework of major changes that have recently taken place at the political, legislative, and policy level in the Union. Namely, with the entry into force of the Treaty of Lisbon in 2009, the Charter of Fundamental Rights of the European Union becomes legally binding, and the Union will accede to the European Convention on Human Rights. The Charter entrenches fundamental economic, political, and social rights for the EU citizens into EU law.[†] More specifically, these developments are significant with respect to the importance they bestow on fundamental rights as a core component of security and crime concerns; including the specific area of trafficking in human beings. Importantly, the Charter of Fundamental Rights makes explicit reference to prohibition of trafficking under article five "Prohibition of slavery and forced labour." The appointment of a Commissioner with a portfolio to address "justice, fundamental rights, and citizenship" is also an important development that raises the position of fundamental rights in the European Commission's work.

The enhanced role of fundamental rights within the fields of crime and security can be seen in the language of the Stockholm Programme—which refers to a "Europe built on fundamental rights." What this concretely means beyond the language of the Programme,

---

* http://eur-lex.europa.eu/LexUriServ/LexUriServ.do?uri=OJ:C:2010:115:0001:0038:EN:PDF
† Charter of Fundamental Rights of the European Union (2000/C 364/01); www.europarl.europa.eu/charter/pdf/text_en.pdf.

and the specific reference to trafficking in the Charter, is yet to be determined. The importance of inserting this fundamental rights language in the Programme and accompanying documents that address trafficking, such as the Action Oriented Paper on trafficking in human beings which was adopted by the Council on November 30, 2009, should not, however, be underestimated.

What the implications of this could be for data collection is difficult to say. However, the Stockholm Programme does refer to statistics as a "necessary prerequisite inter alia for evidence-based decisions on the need for action, on the implementation of decisions and on the effectiveness of action";* but does so while referring only to existing and future Action Plans to measure more effectively crime and criminal justice. Whether other EU Action Plans that are noncrime related will also address the need for data collection on trafficking is to be seen. Where the Stockholm Programme deals specifically with trafficking, it encouragingly refers to the need to be guided by an improved understanding of and research on trafficking and smuggling; and herein, Europol is called upon to step up its ongoing work with respect to information gathering and strategic analysis in cooperation with countries of origin and transit. A comprehensive and fundamental rights response to trafficking would demand that alternative data sources are drawn on, where they exist, outside the traditional arena of policing and criminal justice. This means looking at areas such as economic and social rights and gender equality, and hence the push and pull factors that influence patterns of trafficking. Here, Eurostat could have a stronger role to play with respect to data collection in areas that can be explored as indicators of vulnerability to exploitation from trafficking.

Alongside the limited reference to statistical data, the Stockholm Programme invites the Council to consider establishing an EU antitrafficking coordinator—in the same mould as the European antiterrorism coordinator. As of December 2010, the Commission selected a European antitrafficking coordinator—Myria Vassiliadou—who is mandated to provide a coordinated and consolidated EU response to trafficking. But the role of such a coordinator vis-a-vis divergent developments at the Member State level to install or enhance the role of existing rapporteurs, or offices for the collection of data and information on trafficking, is, as yet, unclear.

New Arenas for Data Collection

The most significant development in recent years in the field of trafficking has been the shift from focusing mainly on trafficking for sexual exploitation—which primarily looked at trafficking in women. In the EU, a broader response to trafficking has emerged that encompasses forms other than sexual exploitation, and which looks at a wider spectrum of groups that are vulnerable to trafficking.

Children have received a renewed focus as a specific group that are vulnerable to trafficking for sexual and labor exploitation (Beddoe 2007; CEOP 2007; Dottridge 2007). Although the UN's Trafficking Protocol specifically refers to "women and children" in its title, it is apparent that the mainstay of work in the trafficking field has focused on trafficking in women for sexual exploitation. To some extent, this situation reflects the

---

* European Council 2010/C 115/01 "The Stockholm Programme—An open and secure Europe serving and protecting citizens"; http://eur-lex.europa.eu—paragraph 4.3.3.

fact that work on vulnerable children tends to be separated from work with adults—hence the existence of UNICEF, Save the Children, and specialist NGOs working with sexually exploited children such as ECPAT (End Child Prostitution, Child Pornography and the Trafficking of Children for Sexual Exploitation; ECPAT 2007—see Box 3.2 in this chapter referring to ECPAT; Sillen and Beddoe 2007). On the other hand, it can be argued that the volume of trafficking cases that have come to light involving children has been less than for adult women, and hence the focus has been on women.

In response to what was seen as a gap in existing EU-wide research to map responses to and data collection on child trafficking, the European Union Agency for Fundamental Rights (FRA) decided to publish a report on Child Trafficking in the EU (2009). This report emerged on the back of the Agency's ongoing work on the rights of the child, which has looked at indicator development in selected areas concerning children—one of which is trafficking. In addition to a specific focus on trafficking, the FRA has undertaken research on separated asylum seeking children—the results of which can be read in consideration of children who are vulnerable to being trafficked when in the care of different State agencies in the EU.

The Roma have also emerged as a specific focus in the EU with respect to concerns about trafficking in Roma children, by Roma, for purposes of begging and petty crime.* The expulsions of Roma EU citizens from the territory of France in September 2010, and the subsequent political fallout from the European Commission, has served to refocus attention on the Roma "problem" in the EU. In the same period, developments in France could be seen alongside news media items about a joint police operation between the United Kingdom and Romania, which involved Europol and Eurojust operatives and saw the arrest of a number of members of a Roma gang who had trafficked children into the United Kingdom for the purpose of exploitation.† It can be envisaged that these developments on the ground, which in themselves are not perhaps new but which reflect shifting political and policing priorities, might encourage the collection of more comprehensive data that is able to disaggregate and share information on the basis of ethnicity, age, and the relationship between victim and offender. Yet in some Member States, such as Hungary and France, it remains the case that open data collection on personal characteristics such as ethnicity remains a problematic area in which to launch renewed calls for improvements in data collection on trafficking.

Linked to the theme of begging are broader concerns about trafficking for labor exploitation. The ILO currently leads the way with respect to global research and data collection initiatives in this area, while in Europe the OSCE (with its mandate covering 47 countries) has also addressed the theme of labor exploitation (OSCE 2006, 2008). In the Member States of the EU a great deal of work is yet to be done before attention is *equally* focused on trafficking for sexual and labor exploitation. Interesting developments can be seen in this regard in areas that focus on illegal immigration and control of the EU's external borders, as this field also encompasses victims of trafficking alongside victims of human smuggling. To this end, it can be noted that the 2005 EU border agency Frontex is looking at border guard training, in consultation with the FRA, to see how human rights can be incorporated as a key element. If such initiatives are rolled out in practice, the potential for enhanced recognition of trafficking victims within the framework of border control and management is significant. Any developments in this regard would likely necessitate

---

* "EU warns France of action over Roma" (September 29, 2010); www.bbc.co.uk/news/world-europe-11437361.
† Presentation by Bernie Gravett, police superintendent, London Metropolitan police—4th EU Anti-Trafficking Day Conference, October 18–19, 2010, Brussels.

improvements in data collection to be able to identify and separate victims of trafficking from others who are trying to enter the EU.

Concluding Comments

The current status of knowledge about the extent and nature of trafficking in the EU reflects a number of factors—not least of which is the fact that the Commission, as the entity that could enhance data collection across the EU, is relatively new to the area of data collection in the field of crime and criminal justice statistics. Having said this, in the aftermath of the 9/11 terrorist attacks in the United States and the subsequent terrorist attacks in Spain and London, the EU upped its efforts to provide a coordinated and coherent response to terrorism in the form of the EU's antiterrorism coordinator. In comparison, it is notable that it has taken a lot longer for the EU to consider the establishment of an equivalent office to coordinate efforts to address trafficking in the EU—including data collection.

Legislation on trafficking is yet to make data collection by policing and judicial authorities a compulsory part of any antitrafficking response. However, there are developments with respect to the mainstreaming of data collection in other areas that can be looked at when considering how to improve the current situation regarding trafficking. Notable among these is the United Nations Convention on the Rights of Persons with Disabilities, which in Article 31 explicitly refers to State Parties undertaking to collect appropriate information, including statistical and research data, to enable them to formulate and implement policies to give effect to the Convention. Importantly, the article refers to data protection and privacy, the disaggregation of collected data, and the dissemination of statistics so that they are accessible to persons with disabilities and others.

Data collection on human trafficking can also be improved when more emphasis is laid on a concerted dialog between the users and producers of data to determine what is possible to collect, and what is useful to collect. At present, policy makers and politicians typically call for improved data collection, but often do so with limited information about what this might mean with respect to the need to reform and harmonize the way different jurisdictions and agencies currently operate. For example, it is good to be reminded that data collection in the area of conventional crime—such as burglaries or assault—is currently not standardized or "high tech" across much of the EU; the lesson being that data collection on trafficking needs to reflect on the current set-up in Member States concerning other areas of crime data collection before ambitious or impractical initiatives are introduced (see Alvazzi del Frate [2010] with respect to the some of the challenges concerning the collection of data on "complex crimes").

Finally, it is clear that the EU and its Member States are at a point where talk about improved data collection on trafficking is being transferred into different "pilot actions" to test various methodological approaches for data collection in specific Member States, and often concentrating on specific areas of trafficking. The real test will be whether the Commission is able to select and support initiatives for data collection that it has supported through different actions—such as the SIAMSECT and MONTRASEC project, as well as the Commission-ILO initiative. The year 2010 saw the 10th Anniversary of the Palermo Convention on Transnational Organised Crime, and its accompanying protocols on human trafficking and smuggling, which means that a great deal of reflection is taking place at the international level in consideration of the successes and shortcomings in addressing trafficking. The absence of comprehensive, robust, and comparable data on trafficking remains one of the key areas where improvements are still much needed.

Critical Review and Discussion Questions

1. Why is data collection an essential element for effectively addressing trafficking in human beings?
2. Can different "models" be identified in response to trafficking, and what might their influence be on current data collection practices?
3. In Europe—what are the ongoing challenges facing data collection on trafficking in human beings?
4. How can the European Union's policy response to trafficking in human beings be characterized? What developments have recently taken place that can be expected to have a major impact on how trafficking is responded to and, potentially, on how trafficking data are recorded?
5. What are the emerging arenas for data collection on trafficking?
6. How do the European Union's responses to data collection in the field of trafficking compare with those in other parts of the world?

References

Alvazzi del Frate, A. 2010. Complex crimes. In S. Harrendorf, M. Heiskanen, and S. Malby (Eds.), *International Statistics on Crime and Justice* (pp. 65–86). Helsinki, Finland: HEUNI, UNODC.

Aromaa, K. and Lehti, M. 2007. Trafficking in human beings: Policy problems and recommendations. In P.C. van Duyne, A. Maljevic, M. van Dijck, K. van Lampe, and J. Harvey (Eds.), *Crime Business and Crime Money in Europe: The Dirty Linen of Illicit Enterprise* (pp. 97–109). Nijmegen: Wolf Legal Publishers.

Aronowitz, A., Theuermann, G., and Tyurykanova, E. 2010. *Analysing the Business Model of Trafficking in Human Beings to Better Prevent the Crime.* Office of the Special Representative and Coordinator for Combating Trafficking in Human Beings, Office for Security and Cooperation in Europe (OSCE).

Beddoe, C. 2007. *Missing Out: A Study of Child Trafficking in the Northwest, Northeast and West Midlands.* UK: ECPAT UK.

CEOP 2007. *A Scoping Project on Child Trafficking in the UK.* London: CEOP.

Dottridge, M. 2007. *A Handbook on Planning Projects to Prevent Child Trafficking.* Lausanne: Terre des Hommes Foundation.

ECPAT 2007. *Missing Out: A Study of Child Trafficking in the Northwest, Northeast and West Midlands.* UK: ECPAT.

Environmental Justice Foundation. 2010. All at Sea: the abuse of human rights aboard illegal fishing vessels—www.ejfoundation.org (accessed September 30, 2010).

European Union Agency for Fundamental Rights (FRA) 2009. *Child Trafficking in the European Union.* Vienna: FRA.

Goodey, J. 2003a. Migration, crime and victimhood: Responses to sex trafficking in the EU. *Journal of Punishment and Society, 5(4),* 415–431.

Goodey, J. 2003b. Recognising organised crime's victims: the case of sex trafficking in the EU. In A. Edwards and P. Gill (Eds.), *Transnational Organised Crime: Perspectives on Global Security* (pp. 157–173). London: Routledge.

Goodey, J. 2004a. Promoting good practice in sex trafficking cases. *International Review of Victimology Special Issue on Trafficking, 11(1),* 89–110.

Goodey, J. 2004b. Sex trafficking in women from Central and East European countries: Promoting a "victim-centred" and "woman-centred" approach to criminal justice intervention. *Feminist Review Special Issue on 'Post-Communisim: Women's Lives in Transition'*, 76, 26–45.

Goodey, J. 2005. Sex trafficking in the European Union. In J. Sheptycki and A. Wardak (Eds.), *Transnational and Comparative Criminology* (pp. 269–285). London: Cavendish.

Goodey, J. 2008. Racist Crime in the European Union: Historical Legacies, Knowledge Gaps, and Policy Development In J. Goodey and K. Aromaa (Eds.), Hate Crime (pp.16–28). Helsinki: HEUNI (European Institute for Crime Prevention and Control, affiliated with the United Nations).

Hennig, J., Craggs, S., Laczko, F., and Larsson, F. 2007. *Trafficking in Human Beings and the 2006 World Cup in Germany*. Geneva: International Organisation for Migration (IOM).

Kelly, L. and Regan, L. 2000. *Stopping Traffic: Exploring the Extent of, and Responses to, Trafficking in Women for Sexual Exploitation in the UK*. London: Home Office, Police Research Series Paper 125.

Kutnick, B., Belser, P., and Danailova-Trainoer, G. 2007. *Methodologies for Global and National Estimation of Human Trafficking Victims; Current and Future Approaches*. Geneva: ILO.

ILO 2009. *The Cost of Coercion: Global Report under the follow-up to the ILO Declaration on Fundamental Principles and Rights at Work*. Geneva: ILO.

International Labour Organisation and European Commission (March 2009, revised September 2009). *Operational Indicators on Trafficking in Human Beings*.

Lindstrom, N. 2007. Transnational responses to human trafficking: The politics of anti-trafficking in the Balkans. In H. R. Friman and S. Reich (Eds.), *Human Trafficking, Human Security and the Balkans*. Pittsburgh: University of Pittsburgh Press—accessed on-line at: www.maxwell.syr.edu/moynihan/programs/ces/pcconfpdfs/lindstrom.pdf.

O'Connell Davidson, J. 2007. Sex slaves and the reality of prostitution. *The Guardian*, December 28.

O'Connell Davidson, J. and Anderson, B. 2006. The trouble with trafficking. In C.L. van den Anker and J. Doomernik (Eds.), *Trafficking and Women's Rights* (pp. 11–26). Basingstoke: Palgrave.

OSCE 2006. *A Summary of Challenges Facing Legal Responses to Human Trafficking for Labour Exploitation in the OSCE Region*. Warsaw: OSCE/ODIHR.

OSCE 2008. *Human Trafficking for Labour Exploitation, Forced and Bonded Labour: Identification, Prevention and Prosecution; Human Trafficking for Labour Exploitation, Forced and Bonded Labour: Prosecution of Offenders, Justice for Victims*. Vienna: OSCE.

Sillen, J. and Beddoe, C. 2007. *Rights Here, Rights Now: Recommendations for Protecting Trafficked Children*.UK: UNICEF and ECPAT.

Surtees, R. 2008. Traffickers and trafficking in Southern and Eastern Europe: Considering the other side of human trafficking. *European Journal of Criminology*, 5(1), 39–68.

Troshynski, E.I. and Blank, J.K. 2008. Sex trafficking: An explanatory study interviewing traffickers. *Trends in Organised Crime*, 11(1), 30–41.

Vermeulen, G., Balcaen, A., Di Nicola, A., and Cauduro, A. 2006. *The Siamsect Files*. Antwerp: Maklu.

Vermeulen, G. and Paterson, N. 2010. *The Montrasex Demo*. Antwerp: Maklu.

Useful Resources

1. European Commission "Fight Against Trafficking in Human Beings" website: http://ec.europa.eu/anti-trafficking
2. United Nations surveys on Crime Trends and the Operations of Criminal Justice Systems, of which the 10th survey included data on trafficking in human beings: www.unodc.org.
3. Dutch National Rapporteur on Trafficking in Human Beings—English website: http://english.bnrm.nl
4. European Council 2010/C 115/01 "The Stockholm Programme—An open and secure Europe serving and protecting citizens": http://eur-lex.europa.eu

Explaining Human Trafficking

4

JULIE KAYE
JOHN WINTERDYK

Contents

Introduction

Trafficking in persons gained considerable attention in the early twenty-first century when it was cast alongside terrorism and drug trafficking "as one of the three 'evils' that haunts the globe" (Kempadoo 2005, p. vii). Global and regional perceptions and responses to human trafficking (HT) have elevated HT from a "women's issue," driven by nongovernment organizations (NGOs), in the 1980s to "the global agenda of high politics" of the European Union and the United Nations (Lee 2007, pp. 1–2). While HT remains the subject of much research, debate, and advocacy in diverse disciplines and fields, such as criminology, politics, law, sociology, human rights, migration studies, gender, and public health (Lee 2011), explanations of HT are varied and, at times, contradictory. Moreover, studies of HT are frequently polarized by moralistic debates that cluster around a number of contentious issues, evoking strong sentiments of morality, justice, citizenship, and sexuality. From these perspectives, HT has variously been understood as, and often conflated with, prostitution and sex slavery, irregular migration, labor exploitation, transnational organized crime, and a threat to national sovereignty and security (Sanghera 2005). While HT occurs within each of these sites, a broad understanding of HT is necessary to address the multiple ways in which individuals are trafficked and the unique experiences of each trafficked person.

    With this in mind, this chapter reviews various explanations of human trafficking and the limitations of these explanations. In particular, we discuss HT from the perspective of gender inequality, transnational crime, globalization, development, and human rights. Each of these explanations has been key in informing dominant understandings of HT and has influenced the formation of existing antitrafficking approaches. Although each of these perspectives offers a functional platform upon which to objectively explain and understand HT, as with all theoretical models, they also have their limitations. In particular, we find that these explanations have been unable to overcome dichotomous interpretations and politicized discourses of HT. Therefore, we will conclude with an argument for, and discussion about, understanding human trafficking as a complex social phenomenon, which has the ability to depoliticize understandings of HT by taking into account the diversity of experiences faced by trafficked persons.

The chapter has three overarching objectives:

1. To examine key theoretical explanations of human trafficking
2. To discuss the strengths and limitations of existing explanations
3. To highlight the benefits of understanding HT as a complex social phenomenon

We begin with an explanation of human trafficking from a gender inequality and feminist perspective.

Human Trafficking, Gender Inequality, and Feminist Explanations

Until recently, HT was perceived as predominantly a woman's issue and explanations of trafficking centered on discussions of gender-based forms of discrimination and the feminization of trafficking (Popli 2008; Lee 2007; Williams and Masika 2002). While important for understanding the issue of HT, especially the overrepresentation of women and girls among victims of trafficking, gender-based explanations have been plagued by polarized debates over the "victim" or "agent" status of trafficked persons. In this section, we discuss gender-based explanations of human trafficking, such as *gender inequality* (i.e., the overt and covert disparity between men and women) and patriarchy as well as global economic disparities and the feminization of poverty. We further examine how these explanations have been limited by ongoing cycles of definitional casuistry over the "victim" or "agent" status of trafficked women.

Although reliable estimates of human trafficking remain scarce, Williams and Masika (2002) assess that women and girls comprise approximately 80% of individuals trafficked across international borders. As is discussed in Chapter 5, while men and boys are also trafficked, with the trade of young boys dominating in some regions and sectors (e.g., boys are disproportionally trafficked into agricultural work in Côte d'Ivoire, Nigeria, and Benin [Adepoju 2005]), women and girls remain the primary targets for HT (see, generally, Di Nicola et al. 2009; Territo and Kirkham 2010). In light of this, gendered explanations of HT focus on the inequalities perpetuated by patriarchal values. In regions where the sociocultural values of patriarchy prevail, the position of women and girls in the household, family, and community are devalued (Williams and Masika 2002). In such settings, girls are often withdrawn from school to work in domestic service (Adepoju 2005; Dottridge 2002). Alongside domestic servitude, their lack of access to education and economic resources makes them especially vulnerable to the tactics employed by human traffickers.

In addition to patriarchal values, current global economic configurations have also disproportionately affected women, particularly women of the global South, leading researchers and advocates to explain HT in terms of the socio-economic disadvantage faced by women. Global economic restructuring policies—including structural adjustment programs, international trade agreements, the relocation of foreign firms to developing countries, the growing importance of export-oriented industries, and diminutive social welfare and service programs—disproportionately affect women of the Global South (Kempadoo 1998; Sassen 2002). This is because women comprise the primary source of labor for the exporting industries of textile, garment, toy, and shoe production, as well as electronic factories and agribusinesses (Kempadoo 1998; Territo and Kirhham 2010). Immigrant and migrant women also form a new "serving class" because the pressures of managerial and professional work in global cities entail increasing dependence on domestic assistance (Sassen 2002, p. 94). Heightened demand for low-wage labor, alongside diminishing workforces in the Global North, encourages women from the Global South to migrate. Yet, as will be discussed, in the name of antitrafficking, a number of Western countries have adopted polices that dissuade legal migratory routes. In the absence of viable migratory options, women may rely on the services of a human smuggler and, potentially, fall victim to the exploitative practices of a trafficker (see Chapter 12 in this volume for further discussion).

While many agree that sociocultural and socioeconomic factors contribute to the disadvantages faced by women and girls and their disproportionate representation among victims of HT, feminist discussions (i.e., *feminist theory*) of HT have been polarized by debates over the "victim" or "agent" status of trafficked women (see, e.g., Leidholdt 2003; Raymond 2005; Doezema 2002; Kempadoo 2005; Thorbek and Pattanaik 2002).[*] On the victim side of the debate, feminist scholars and activists argue that trafficked persons are coerced and thereby victimized by their experiences and that human trafficking can be equated to a modern-day form of slavery (see, e.g., Leidholdt 2003; Raymond 2005). Advocates of this perspective generally seek to equate HT with prostitution, claiming that all prostitution exploits the rights of women and should appear under the umbrella of HT (see Di Nicola et al. 2009).

On the flip side of the debate, the agent side, are feminist scholars and activists who believe there is a distinction between human trafficking and prostitution. They argue for a broad understanding of trafficking that includes the trafficking of men, women, and children into a number of positions, including forced prostitution (which they believe is distinct from voluntary sex work), forced marriages, domestic services, agricultural labor, and factory work (see, e.g., Agustín 2007; Doezema 1998; Kempadoo 1998). Advocates from this perspective further argue that women must be distinguished from children in antitrafficking legislation (Sanghera 2005). According to Sanghera (2005), grouping women and children under the same documentation, "infantilizes women and denies them both their right to autonomy and to make decisions" (p. 13). From this perspective, women have the right to move from region to region in search of a better life and employment without being subjected to the abuses of traffickers or the authorities responding to trafficking (such as police or immigration officers). They argue that counter-trafficking initiatives should focus on addressing the abuse, coercion, and human rights violations that occur in multiple labor sites, rather than seeking to eradicate one particular form of labor (e.g., sex work) or limiting the ability of women to migrate in search of a better life (see, e.g., Jana et al. 2002).

---

[*] Dichotomous discussions over the status of women as "victims" or "agents" have dominated a number of areas of interest to feminists, particularly those associated with violence against women (for general discussions see Schneider 1993; Chancer 1998).

Plagued by these moralizing ideologies, feminist discourses of trafficking polarized around categories of victim versus agent and coercion versus consent (Kempadoo 2005). As a result, polarized coalitions of non-government organizations, such as the Human Rights Caucus (HRC) and the Coalition Against Trafficking in Women (CATW),* became especially influential in framing recent international definitions of human trafficking, specifically the 2000 United Nations Trafficking Protocol Supplementing the UN Convention Against Transnational Organized Crime (hereafter, Trafficking Protocol). HRC adopted an "agency" perspective, arguing that HT definitions distinguish between trafficking and prostitution. By arguing that prostitution is a form of labor, whereas HT requires some form of coercion or deception, the HRC aimed to develop a framework to protect the labor rights of women in the sex industry (Nagle 1997; Kempadoo 1998; Doezema 1998).

CATW, on the other hand, adopted a "victim" standpoint by arguing that trafficking and prostitution are synonymous. From their perspective, women are unable to offer consent because they are exploited and thereby victimized through the very act of engaging in prostitution. With this in mind, Janice Raymond (2005), co-executive director of CATW, suggests that views equating prostitution with labor are "out of touch with the majority of women in prostitution who want not 'better working conditions' but a better life" (p. 45). In this way, CATW aimed to protect the rights of women by protecting prostitutes from the inherent violence of prostitution (see Perrin 2011). Claiming to draw on the experiences of trafficked women and to represent the "true" feminist standpoint, both coalitions argued that their research and ideology protect the rights of women in the sex trade and thereby the rights of trafficked women. Yet, their polarized positions limited the advancement of antitrafficking measures that provide resources and protective services to trafficked persons.

The debates culminated in the signing of the 2000 UN Trafficking Protocol. Despite inherent differences, feminist advocates on both the "victim" and "agency" side of the discussion claim to have "won" the lobbying debate to shape the Trafficking Protocol toward their respective standpoints. This reflects the compromises established in the Protocol as well as the ambiguous nature of the document and ongoing struggles to shape trafficking discourses and antitrafficking agendas. In the end, from a feminist perspective (see Box 4.1), debates about the status of trafficked women as "victims" or "agents" and "prostitutes" or "sex workers" dominated Protocol discussions, which meant there was little time taken to consider protective measures, such as appropriate housing, counseling, access to legal information, medical and material assistance, as well as employment, training opportunities, and education. Although the Protocol urges signatories to protect victims of trafficking, there is little elaboration on how their rights can be protected and there is no obligation for signatories of the protocol to provide such protective services. Thus, the final Protocol is predominantly a law enforcement instrument that has redefined HT in terms of a transnational crime.

---

* Members of the HRC include: International Human Rights Law Group, Foundation Against Trafficking in Women, Global Alliance Against Traffic in Women, Asian Women's Human Rights Council, La Strada, Ban-Ying, Fundacion Esperanza, Foundation for Women, KOK-NGO Network Against Trafficking in Women, Women's Consortium of Nigeria, Women, Law and Development in Africa (Nigeria) (Jordan 2002). The Network of Sex Work Projects (NSWP) also supported the position of the HRC. CATW, on the other hand, worked with a coalition of NGOs called the International Human Rights Network (IHRN) (CATW n.d.).

BOX 4.1   FEMINIST THEORY AND PERSPECTIVE

There are numerous different theoretical perspectives in criminology that can be used to explain, describe, predict, and understand behavior. They range from microlevel-oriented explanations grounded in the biological and psychological perspectives to more macrolevel explanations such as strain theory, left realism, critical criminology, and the feminist perspective (see, e.g., Williams and McShane 2008). Drawing on some key themes from critical criminology, feministic criminology is centrally concerned with issues of power, the unequal distribution of wealth and social resources, as well as the differential position of specific groups in society. Although there are different forms of the feminist perspective (e.g., liberal, Marxist, radical, and cultural feminism), it is the sexist nature of the criminal justice system and its agents that underpins feminist criminology. Feminist theorists argue that social and political reform is necessary to bring about gender equality or parity in the system (White et al. 2009). Feminist perspectives are limited by their tendency to focus on questions pertaining to social class, ethnicity, and race. Moreover, findings from this perspective are similar to the kinds of evidence supported by more conventional theories. In addition, some critics argue that feminist criminology should extend its focus to a more gender relation's orientation (Naffine 1997). Not withstanding these critiques, feminist criminology has also been credited for transcending the typical masculine approach to theories of crime and what Vold et al. (1998, p. 283) refer to as "appreciative relativism"—that is, for criminologists to embrace a feminine approach to crime.

In summary, explanations of HT that focus on gender inequality are important for understanding the overrepresentation of women and girls among trafficked persons. The sociocultural values of patriarchy, as well as socioeconomic factors associated with global economic relations, reinforce the devaluation of women and girls, restricting their access to education and viable employment. In turn, traffickers rely on such forms of deprivation to specifically target women and girls into exploitative situations of forced labor or debt bondage. Despite the importance of gendered explanations of HT, feminist contributions to effective strategies to address HT have been limited by the impasse over the victim or agent status of trafficked women.

Human Trafficking as a Transnational Crime

Since the adoption of the 2000 Trafficking Protocol (see Chapter 10), antitrafficking approaches equate human trafficking with *transnational crime* (i.e., crimes that are cross-border or potentially cross-border and, which while being intra-State, also violate the fundamental values of the international community—Box 4.2), employing restrictive border controls and immigration policies to combat HT and illegal forms of migration, such as human smuggling. Thus, criminologists and other researchers and advocates that explain HT trafficking in terms of transnational crime, focus on the relationship between HT and human smuggling, the use of surveillance mechanisms and restrictive immigration controls to combat HT, and the nature and activities of transnational organized crime

BOX 4.2   TRANSNATIONAL CRIME BY ANY OTHER NAME

The lexicon in criminology is ever adapting to the changes in crime trends and patterns. With the end of the Cold War and rapid growth of globalization in the early 1990s, the terms "global crime," "international crime" and "transnational crime" began to appear more regularly in the literature. Reichel (2005) points out that "global crime" is more reflective of a crime's distribution and that, while not necessarily a unanimous agreement, "international crime" are acts that: "threaten world order and security (e.g., crimes against humanity, . . .), whereas 'transnational crimes' affect the interest of more than one state" (p. xiv). Within such a context, human trafficking, smuggling, money laundering, and terrorism are prime examples of transnational crime. Further to this point, transnational crimes also speak to the need for a different approach to law enforcement, prosecution, obtaining reliable statistics, international cooperation for exchange of information, and dealing with the victims of such crimes. Most of these issues are discussed at some point throughout this thematic volume.

syndicates. In this section, we review each of these approaches to understanding HT and the limitations of existing transnational crime perspectives.

While there are clear legal distinctions between HT and human smuggling, as outlined in the United Nations Convention against Transnational Organized Crime (2000), discussions of HT are frequently conflated with irregular migration and smuggling discourses. Human smuggling, which can include human rights abuses and dangerous travel routes, is contractual and for the purpose of facilitating the illegal movement of persons across borders for financial or other material gain (UN 2000; Salt 2000; also see Chapter 2, this volume), whereas HT is for the purpose of exploitation, involving the use of fraud, coercion, or abuse. Additionally, trafficking does not require the movement of individuals across borders, as in cases of domestic trafficking, or movement at all (Perrin 2011). However, in international trafficking cases, the line where a contractual relationship ends and exploitation begins is often unclear, making it difficult for frontline workers to distinguish between HT and human smuggling while in the field (Bruckert and Parent 2002). This is particularly the case when migrants willingly employ the services of smugglers; yet find themselves in a situation of debt bondage on their arrival in the destination country. In these cases, the distinction between a smuggled individual and victim of trafficking "can only be determined after the individual has arrived in the destination country" and is either free to make their own way or exploited by the smuggler, turned trafficker (Aronowitz 2001, p. 167). Moreover, since traffickers often withhold proper documentation from trafficked persons, they are perceived as illegal migrants and vulnerable to criminalization.

In light of this, Lee (2007) suggests that "trafficking as transnational organized crime" approach rests on the relationship between the state and the problem of HT. Since organized crime networks pose a threat to national security and state sovereignty, restrictive immigration controls and heighted surveillance mechanisms are employed to address the threat posed to the state by human traffickers. However, restrictive border controls, alongside the problematic distinction between HT and human smuggling, has led to trafficked persons being criminalized as illegal migrants violating immigration or criminal laws (Oxman-Martinez et al. 2005a).

Restrictive border controls and immigration policies to combat illegal forms of migration limit legal migratory avenues, particularly for marginalized populations, without reducing demand for cheap, exploitable labor (Kapur 2003). In the absence of legal migratory routes, individuals may depend on illicit options and potentially fall into the hands of traffickers (Jana et al. 2002). Meanwhile, heightened surveillance mechanisms targeting illegal forms of migration risk criminalizing victims of HT. This corresponds with the increased border security implemented by numerous nations in the aftermath of 9/11 (see Winterdyk and Sundberg 2010). Consequently, trafficked persons, alongside undocumented migrants, are deported and potentially prosecuted for violating immigration standards, creating a reluctance of trafficked persons to rely on authorities for fear of incarceration or deportation. Traffickers, in turn, rely on the illegitimate status of trafficked persons to restrain their victims in oppressive positions of forced labor. By threatening deportation, public exposure, and harm to the victim or their families, traffickers draw on the limitations of antitrafficking and antismuggling approaches to prevent women from escaping their control. Such immigration-centered approaches also neglect the experiences of trafficked persons that are trafficked within national boundaries (see, e.g., Oxman-Martinez et al. 2005a).

In light of restrictive immigration policies, the demand for illegal migration services has increased (Nikola 2000), creating space for organized criminal networks to participate in HT. According to Nikola (2000), organized criminals "exploit legislative loopholes and regulatory asymmetries in countries to maximize their profits and reduce their risks" (p. 182). In light of this, analyses of the relationship between HT and transnational crime emphasize the role played by transnational organized crime syndicates in facilitating the movement of trafficked persons. According to the UN Convention Against Transnational Organized Crime, an organized criminal group refers to:

A structured group of three or more persons, existing for a period of time and acting in concert with the aim of committing one or more serious crimes or offences established in accordance with this Convention, in order to obtain, directly or indirectly, a financial or other material benefit (Article 2, UN 2000).

For the purposes of HT, transnational cooperation among criminal groups occurs in a number of ways. For instance, organized criminal groups cooperate across borders, work in multiple countries at one time, network with other criminal groups to facilitate the movement of trafficked persons, and often maintain ethnic or family ties in cross-border settings (UNODC 2008). The latter creates specific problems for antitrafficking approaches aiming to offer culturally specific services to trafficked persons.

Motivated by economic and political gain, organized criminal groups have modified their activities to include the profit-making opportunities associated with HT and, in some cases, exert significant political influence in the regions where they operate (UNODC 2008; Shelley 2010). In this way, Shelley (2010) emphasizes the movement of organized crime syndicates in and out of the realms of legitimacy and illegitimacy: "they obtain false documents for their victims from criminal specialists, thugs from outside their networks to intimidate women and traffic laborers, and move their proceeds through established money-laundering channels" (p. 83). At the same time, trafficking networks obtain visas from public officials, transport their victims using public transportation, and advertise the services of their victims in legitimate job banks, and more recently, Internet sites (Shelley 2010). While some organized criminal groups are highly sophisticated, exerting substantial influence over regional politics, others are smaller in nature, such as family-run operations or other groups that may capitalize on profit-making by moving back and forth between or overlap criminal activities, such as human and drug trafficking (UNODC 2008). Regardless of their degree of sophistication, Lee (2007) indicates that transnational organized crime syndicates drive the highly profitable smuggling and trafficking trades.

Despite the proclaimed importance of transnational crime and HT, much of the research in the area remains speculative, at best. This stems from a lack of reliable data (see Chapter 2, this volume) on the subject and the lack of coherence in definitional understandings of HT and migrant smuggling (Bruckert and Parent 2002). Not only do individual countries lack a unified approach to collecting data, there is little systematic exchange of information between countries on the issue of HT (see, Chapter 10, this volume). Moreover, according to the UNODC, some countries fail altogether to collect data on HT (e.g., China, Iran, Saudi Arabia, Yemen, Libya, Tunisia, Madagascar, while others only began to record data in recent years (see, generally, UNODC report on human trafficking exposes modern form of slavery, 2010)). Others only recently began to collect HT statistics. The federal government of Canada, for instance, only started recording cases of human trafficking in 2006 and the statistics that do exist only represent international forms of human trafficking (University of British Columbia 2008). In countries where statistics are collected, they are often compiled by a number of different agencies with varying definitions and objectives. As an alternative, the Geneva-based International Organization for Migration (IOM), has been working to develop a standardized methodology for collecting data on victims of human trafficking and then housing all the data in their IOM Global (Victim-Centered) Human trafficking database. The IOM currently houses the largest database of its type in the world (IOM Global Human Trafficking Database 2010).

In summary, explaining HT in terms of transnational crime has dominated trafficking discussions since the adoption of the UN Protocol. Proponents of this approach argue that a crime and security lens was necessary to advance the issue of human trafficking in the public sphere, particularly in the context of post-9/11 antagonism toward migrants. However, critics argue that such approaches conflate HT with human smuggling, which has resulted in restrictive border controls and the criminalization of trafficked persons.

Development, Economic Globalization, and Human Trafficking

To account for the broad socioeconomic context that underlies HT, developmental theorists explain HT in the context of socioeconomic inequality stemming from the modernizing agendas underlying colonization, development, and economic globalization (see, generally, Brysk and Shafir 2004) (see Box 4.3).

From this perspective, HT and antitrafficking initiatives occur in the context of colonial legacies such as poverty, inequality, and lack of social support networks (Oxman-Martinez et al. 2005b; Kempadoo 2007). A history of colonial exploitation, including the intentional break-up of families, communities, and nations through imposed borders and residential schools has placed many Indigenous people, especially women, in positions of marginalization and economic dependency. Although many indigenous women traditionally enjoyed more "respect, power, and autonomy" than their European counterparts, contemporary Indigenous women are specifically targeted for acts of violence and sexual exploitation based

BOX 4.3 MODERNITY AND THE MODERNIZING AGENDA

There are numerous discussions about the conceptualization and consequences of modernity (see, e.g., Giddens 1990; Beck 1994; Habermas 1996). Modernity includes a number of variables, such as capitalist production, industrial technology, rationalist knowledge, and bureaucratic state institutions to name a few. Yet, underlying modernity, what we refer to as the modernizing agenda, are Enlightenment ideas of progress wherein modern (i.e., European) social institutions create "vastly greater opportunities for human beings to enjoy and secure a rewarding existence than any type of pre-modern system" (Giddens 1990, p. 7). This assumption that "modern" is superior to "traditional" paved the way for European civilizing missions during the period of colonial expansion (Mann 2004). Later, similar assumptions of progress-oriented development (specifically economic development) justified postwar theories of economic modernization. Economists, such as Walter Rostow (1960), depicted development as a process of modernization or industrialization within the capitalist system, arguing that Western-initiated and state-led development in the First World could be replicated in the Third World (Parpart and Veltmeyer 2004). Under recent trends of neoliberal economic globalization, modernization-oriented theories have resurged to occupy an increasingly "hegemonic position" within the development literature (Unwin 2007, p. 1). Thus, while we are aware of the broader dimensions of modernity, in the context of HT we use the term to refer primarily to the assumption of progress underlying colonial expansion, economic modernization, and neoliberal economic globalization.

on their race, class, and gender within "settler society" (Green 2007, p. 22). Although there is much speculation about the prevalence of the trafficking of Indigenous women, there is little detailed knowledge about the scope or experiences of trafficked Indigenous women (for Canadian examples, see Amnesty International 2004; Native Women's Association of Canada 2010; Sikka 2009).

Meanwhile, postcolonial and postdevelopment theorists question representations of "Third World subjects" and the failure of development to achieve its goals. Despite a persistent focus on development as modernization or progress, postdevelopment thinkers indicate that very little has shifted in global hierarchical relations[*] since contemporary development agendas were set in the 1940s[†] and instead, internal disparities have only

---

[*] The rise of the so-called "Asian Tigers" or Newly Industrializing Countries (NICs) are frequently cited as an exception and, although these countries reveal that the global economic system is anything but static, proponents of post-development thought argue they have not substantially altered global economic inequalities. Rather, they suggest the expansion of NICs undermined Third World resistance to the liberalization of international financial markets and structural adjustment programs (McMichael 2007). Therefore, the debt crisis concentrated the power of international financial institutions (i.e., the World Bank and International Monetary Fund) to disproportionately influence development strategies in the Global South. The NICs were also affected by the debt crisis in 1997, a decade later than most of the Global South. Post-development theorists also note, the rise of NICs was not primarily driven by a neo-liberal capitalist strategy; rather, NICs adopted a mixed economy that included forms of state management.

[†] Kothari (2005) problematizes conventional discussions of development history that identify 1945 as the "start date" of development. Rather, she traces the relationship between colonialism and contemporary development studies.

increased. With respect to human trafficking, Sassen (2002) describes the systemic connection between the rise of alternate global circuits, such as trafficking in women, and "conditions in developing countries that are associated with so-called 'development,' particularly through economic globalization" (p. 89). For Sassen (2002), these conditions include the rise of unemployment, shrinking employment opportunities for men, debt, and falling government revenues.

In addition to these arguments, feminist postcolonial thinkers like Spivak (1988) and Mohanty (1991), underscore the problematic representations of women in development discourses. Spivak's (1988) discussion of the representation of the subaltern subject caused sustained reflection on how Western development discourses portray Third World women. In this vein, Mohanty (1991) criticizes the portrayal of women from the Global South as "ignorant, poor, uneducated, tradition-bound, domestic, family-oriented, victimized, etc." (p. 56). As discussed above, trafficking discourses parallel development literature in pursuing ideologically driven information about trafficked women and drawing on women's narratives to justify preconceived ideas about the "victim" or "agent" status of trafficked women. In turn, this information largely reproduces existing structures, enabling "dominant cultures to continue their domination, rather than shedding light on how social domination is reproduced" (Elabor-Idemudia 2002, p. 231). By asserting a break with conventional ideas of progress-oriented development, where "developing" countries are in the process of "catching up," advocates argue for subsistence-based approaches that emphasize on local control and autonomy over resources (see, for instance, Mies and Shiva 1993).

Economic globalization, under the current direction of neoliberal market ideologies, extends the developmentalist logic of early colonization and postwar modernization theorists. Based on the ideals of capitalist economic accumulation, the concept, "economic globalization," like its predecessor, "development," attempts to convey an inclusive movement where all regions are "marching together towards some future Promised Land" (George 2003, p. 16). However, critics argue that both development and economic globalization have been realized through market forces that inevitably exclude and, in some cases, impose undesirable consequences (such as environmental degradation or usurping subsistence-based relations) on some members of society, thereby increasing inequality both within and between nations (Mies 1998). As a result, "alternative circuits" or "counter-geographies" that derive profit "on the backs of the truly disadvantaged" emerge and flourish to supplement global labor supplies (Sassen 2002, p. 89). In this way, the exportation of human beings in global labor markets occurs in the context of rising inequality between industrialized countries of the global North and developing countries of the South and unequal distribution of resources within these counties (Elabor-Idemudia 2003).

In the context of rising inequality, the trafficking of human beings is influenced by a number of "push" and "pull" factors (Lee 2011; Di Nicola 2000). People are pushed to leave their home communities and countries to avoid conflict, natural disasters, political instability, discrimination, impoverishment, a general lack of opportunities, and so on. At the same time, they are pulled to countries of the global North or more prosperous regions of their home countries in search of economic opportunities, education, healthcare, and other perceived benefits of the location of destination.

In general, developmental theorists have attempted to account for the broad socioeconomic factors underlying HT by explaining trafficking in terms of the socioeconomic deprivation created by legacies of colonization and development, which have been further perpetuated by economic globalization. While key for understanding HT, such critical theories have offered little in terms of strategies for addressing trafficking in persons and alleviating global economic disparities. Moreover, as will be discussed, by focusing solely on the "dark" side of globalization, such approaches neglect the ways in which existing boundaries of social organization (namely, nation-states) are being challenged to address the rights of trafficked persons.

Globalization and Human Trafficking

While discussions of HT frequently focus on economic factors associated with globalization (see above), debates about the definition, extent, chronology, and value of globalization reveal the contested and often elusive nature of the concept. Although it is beyond the scope of this chapter to expound on each of these debates,[*] it is important to note that the relationship between human trafficking and globalization cannot be understood in solely economic or sociopolitical terms. Globalization is a complex set of processes that are "political, technological and cultural, as well as economic" in nature (Giddens 2000). With respect to the nation-state, scholars have debated whether globalization is depriving the state of sovereignty, leading to the decline of the nation-state (e.g., Sassen 1996; Schmidt 1995; Strange 1997) or whether the state will continue to play a key role in the twenty-first century (e.g., Hirst and Thompson 1996). While the flow of people, capital, goods, services, information, and culture certainly challenge existing state-centric boundaries, heightened national security in response to perceived external threats reinforce the role of the state. Clearly, globalization is contributing to the reconstruction of the state, which is "neither given nor fixed, and it is certainly not a fully formed political agent" (Nyers 2006, p. xii).[†] Meanwhile, the experiences of trafficked persons both challenge existing boundaries of the state and are subject to the criminalizing effect of heighted border security.

Given the recent emphasis on the relationship between trafficking and transnational crime, the experiences of trafficked persons are increasingly intertwined with the territorial boundaries of the state, political boundaries of citizenship, and symbolic boundaries of national identity. A "citizenship gap" has emerged as a growing number of people "whose lives are subject to global markets and mobility without secure membership in a national community" lack access to social services, employment, and voice in political matters (Brysk and Shafir 2004, p. 6). At the same time, globalization, while intensifying the disparities within and between states, also "creates new opportunities and multiple venues in which to claim rights in other states and global institutions" (Brysk and Shafir 2004, p. 8). In this way, trafficked persons, alongside refugees and irregular migrants, pose a challenge to neatly bounded national identities and existing conceptions of citizenship (Lamont and Molnár 2002).

Existing national boundaries are held together by the concept of citizenship. Citizenship is a conceptual space where the state defines its relationship to the "other" (Brubaker 1992). By defining membership in a polity, citizenship, by nature, "involves a dialectical process between inclusion and exclusion" (Kivisto and Faist 2007, p. 1). Again, a conflict emerges between humanitarian principles (i.e., human rights, such as the rights of irregular migrants

---

[*] For further discussion see, for example, Scholte (2000, 1997); Waters (1995); and Giddens (2000).
[†] Also see Anderson (2006) on the socially constructed or "imagined" nature of nations.

and trafficked persons)—which have the perceived ability to challenge sovereign modes of inclusion and exclusion—and the sovereignty of the nation-state to insist on the role of citizen as the primary political entity (Nyers 2006). In antitrafficking debates, arguments have ranged from a call for unrestricted movement across international borders and global citizenship[*] (Kapur 2003; Sharma 2003) to heightened border security to apprehend traffickers and illegal migrants.[†]

In summary, globalization is a complex set of processes that cannot be solely understood in socioeconomic or sociopolitical terms. In explaining HT, a broad understanding of globalization reveals that trafficked persons, alongside irregular migrants, are challenging existing conceptions of citizenship and boundaries of the nation-state. At the same time, heightened national security in response to perceived external threats criminalizes trafficked persons and limits their ability to access basic services and viable employment.

Rights-Based Approaches

> Man was born free, and he is everywhere in chains. One man thinks himself the master of others, but remains more of a slave than they.
>
> **—Jean-Jacques Rousseau**
> *1762, The Social Contract*

As described in his recent book on crime and human rights, Savelsberg (2010, p. 1) points out the "emergence of human rights law and the criminalization of atrocities is one of the most important developments in recent criminology and penal law." Yet, other than being politically, legally, and socially recognized as representing a gross violation of *human rights*, the concept of HT has not benefitted from criminological insight (*ibid*). Perhaps the closest criminological analogy can be associated with the principle of the "social contract," first introduced by Jean-Jacques Rousseau (1712–1778). Rousseau claimed that without law and order and a declaration of human rights (although he did not use this terminology directly), we would remain primitive in nature. It can arguably be said that by using human rights as a guiding compass, criminal justice policy, welfare policy, and political policies can help create strategies that better address and serve the rights and needs of trafficked persons. Yet, as we will point out, attempting to formulate a universally accepted understanding of these rights remains problematic, particularly in a context where there is little consensus on the definition of HT and debates are driven by polarized agendas and ideologically driven discourses.

Nonetheless, rights-based approaches have been effectively used to explain HT. In particular, rights-based approaches center on the needs and experiences of HT victims. For example, victims can suffer from mental and physical abuse, as well as lack of resources and social stigmatization (see Chapter 12 in this volume) and thereby require a multi-faceted response that addresses the complexity of their experiences. In addition, the phenomena of HT is a complex concept in that it also involves, to varying degrees, the issue of organized crime, matters pertaining to migration, aspects of discrimination (e.g., the Roma in the

---

[*] Also see debates about cosmopolitan citizenship, global civil society, and "post-sovereign" or "post-Westphalian" world order (e.g., Linklater 1996, 1998; Keane 2003; and MacCormick 1996).

[†] Winterdyk and Sunberg (2010) include several chapters that address the issue of the removal of borders within the European Union and the implications thereof.

Balkan region—see Chapter 12), as well the efforts (or lack thereof) of the criminal justice system (see, generally, Chapter 8). However, while there is general consensus that HT is a violation of human rights, not all countries have rights-based legislation concerning HT (e.g., Turkey, Ireland, Thailand, etc.).* Moreover, rights-based approaches frequently represent polarized standpoints about HT.

Claiming to protect the rights of trafficked persons, a number of conflicting perspectives draw on rights-based discourses in their explanations of HT. Dominating this discourse are human rights NGOs and advocates that explain HT trafficking in terms of modern-day slavery (see, e.g., Bales 1999) and feminist abolitionist groups that focus on female sexual exploitation and prostitution as a particular form of slavery (see Leidholdt 2003; Raymond 2005). Others emphasize on a human rights perspective by distinguishing their understanding from approaches that explain HT in terms of organized crime, migration, and prostitution (Jordan 2002). From this perspective, scholars and activists argue that a rights-based approach is necessary to challenge existing perceptions of HT and question whether anti-trafficking measures adequately protect the rights of trafficked persons (see, e.g., Dottridge 2007; Sanghera 2005). Or, more specifically, do the various protocols, State legislations, and the mandate of respective criminal justice systems clearly reflect and express the rights of victims over addressing the vested interests of the State?

In this section, we review these approaches and argue that rights-based discourses have failed to overcome dichotomous understandings of HT (also see Chapter 6 for a similar discussion in terms of seeing HT intervention as either being a "crime control" or "social work" response). In turn, this has limited their ability to effectively advance the rights of trafficked persons.

Arguing that HT constitutes a modern-day form of slavery, rights advocates reference the 1807 *Act for the Abolition of the Slave Trade* in the British Empire (Perrin 2011) and the 1948 *Universal Declaration of Human Rights*, which includes the right to be free from slavery or servitude (Lee 2007). Proponents of this approach further emphasize the widespread nature of HT and the profits it derives for a criminal underworld. Quoting the frequently recited statistic that: "2.5 million people are in forced labor (including forced sexual exploitation) at any given time as a result of trafficking" (ILO 2007), abolitionists highlight the magnitude of the problem. Alongside this statistic are other widely cited figures; in particular, that HT constitutes the third worst form of organized crime in the world (next to drug and arms trafficking) and generates annual profits of 32 billion dollars (Besler 2005). Bales (1999) further estimates that proportionately more people are held in bondage today than any other period of history. The reliability of such statistics notwithstanding, abolitionists highlight the magnitude of the problem in order to stir moral sentiments (if not "moral panic") in response to this new form of slavery. In doing so, abolitionists frequently reference themselves alongside historical figures, such as the former British politician William Wilberforce (1795–1833), who led a sustained campaign to abolish the Atlantic slave trade in the early nineteenth century (see Pollock 1977).

By drawing on historically rooted sentiments of outrage and guilt, connections between the Atlantic slave trade and modern-day slavery effectively generate a moral response to the issue of HT. Yet, in doing so, such approaches overemphasize extreme cases of HT and romanticize collective action against "evil" perpetrators (e.g., organized crime syndicates,

---

* For a review of countries and their legislation on human trafficking see: http://www.legislationline.org/ topics/subtopic/46/topic/14/country/4 (accessed January 14, 2011).

Johns, and corrupt officials in developing countries, to name a few). In critique of such "unmitigated victimization," Sanghera (2005) indicates, "in this dominant frame, men prey upon women, the rich countries gouge out resources, including women, of the poorer ones, poor women are not human beings but merely commodities, and on and on" (p. 13). In turn, such oversimplification can lead to widespread misunderstanding and disillusionment given the complex set of realities encompassed under the umbrella of HT.

Bales (1999), in particular, identifies HT as a form of modern-day slavery by outlining the factors that distinguish "Old Slavery" from "New Slavery." First, while new slave owners collect substantial profits from their slaves, they avoid legal ownership. Second, new slaves receive minimal care from their slave masters because the period of exploitation is relatively short; thus, new slaves are seen as "completely disposable tools for making money" (Bales 1999, p. 4). Last, ethnic differences are not necessarily relevant in the New Slavery. Despite these distinctions, abolitionists argue, "the catastrophic impact on the lives of the victims has changed little" (Perrin 2011, p. 7). In the end, Bales (1999) contends that New Slavery involves "the total control of one person by another for the purpose of economic exploitation" (p. 6). Yet, as O'Connell (2006) highlights, this definition creates a dichotomous relationship between "total control" and "choice," neglecting the questions of "how much choice, and choices between what?" (O'Connell 2006, p. 7). In doing so, such approaches claim to protect the rights of trafficked persons, but eliminate important discussions from occurring under the umbrella of trafficking discourse, such as debates over voluntary and consensual versus involuntary and nonconsensual forms of migration.

Another position, recently put forth by Malarek (2009) in his book *The Johns: Sex for Sale and the Men Who Buy It*, argues that as serious as human trafficking is that it is as much a problem about men as it is about human rights (for an alternate perspective see Atchison 2010). On the one hand, such perspectives conflate human trafficking with prostitution and rely on the aforementioned worldview where "men prey upon women" (Sanghera 2005, p. 13). This not only neglects the complexity of motives and experiences (which can include the exploitation of women) underpinning sex industries, but also does little to resolve such gender-based conflict. On the other hand, as an explanatory model, Malarek's standpoint suggests that human rights may not be encompassing enough to fully address the causes of HT, particularly in a context where cultural relativities, economic disparities, and power imbalances fuel the demand for trafficked persons.

In line with Malarek's view, feminist abolitionist groups further rely on discourses of modern-day slavery to emphasize their belief that prostitution constitutes a particular form of modern-day slavery (see, e.g., Leidholdt 2003; Raymond 2005). As previously discussed in this chapter, such approaches claim to protect the rights of women who are subject to the abuse of what they perceive as the inherently exploitative act of prostitution. In other words, they claim that all prostitution is sexual slavery, a standpoint in direct opposition to those arguing for labour rights for sex workers (see Kempadoo and Doezema 1998; Kempadoo 1998; Nagle 1997). Yet, as previously discussed, both sides of the debate limit appropriate dialog about effective ways of protecting the rights of trafficking persons as well as the rights of "sex workers" or "sex slaves." The assumption that all prostitutes are sex slaves prevents dialog about effective ways of responding to the rights of other forms of exploitation faced by women in sex industries, regardless of the woman's desire or ability to exit the trade. Further, by conflating HT with sex slavery, such approaches also neglect other forms of exploitation that fall under the definition of HT as well as avoid examining those who abuse trafficked women and children, such as traffickers or some law enforcement agents.

Rights-based approaches have also contrasted their perspective with other explanations outlined in this chapter (i.e., approaches that explain HT in terms of organized crime, migration, and prostitution). Scholars from this standpoint challenge existing conceptions of HT, particularly the limitations of the UN Protocol to disassociate HT from prostitution (see Miller 1999), to protect the rights of trafficked persons (Jordan 2002), and to limit the widespread acceptance of stringent immigration policies that restrict legal migratory routes and further endanger trafficked persons. As Gallagher (2001) indicates, the UN Protocol is not a human rights treaty and does not grant new rights to trafficked persons. The absence of mandatory protections for trafficked persons likely reflects a compromise with the "organized crime objectives" of the Protocol discussions (Gallagher 2001, p. 1004). Yet, by focusing on crime control and security concerns, such approaches neglect the "full range of rights needed by trafficked persons," such as safe migration and movement or equitable economic conditions in home or destination counties (Miller 2004, p. 32).

Drawing on critiques of the UN Protocol, other human rights advocates question whether antitrafficking measures adequately protect the rights of trafficked persons, let alone adequately target the traffickers. For instance, Sanghera (2005) argues that antitrafficking strategies in "the arenas of policy and legislation, rescue and repatriation, and interception of 'seemingly potential victims' at border points during the process of transportation or migration" (p. 21) have adopted restrictive measures that have little consideration for the rights of trafficked persons. Sanghera further argues, "in some instances prevention initiatives at source have been tantamount to restricting women and girls' right to freedom of movement" (p. 21). Similarly, Kempadoo (2005) argues that human rights violations continue to escalate despite the antitrafficking policies derived from the Trafficking Protocol. In a report prepared for GAATW, Dottridge (2007) indicates that existing antitrafficking measures are "counter-productive" in their attempt to help trafficked persons (p. 2). Although a number of women have refused to participate in such programs, their voices remain peripheral in the construction of anti-trafficking measures.

While such critiques offer important challenges to existing antitrafficking approaches, they often derive from an antistate perspective that does little to encourage existing state actors to better respond to the rights of trafficked persons. For many, national security is an important policy concern and, thus, must be taken into consideration when assessing the rights of migrants, including irregular migrants and trafficked persons. However, it is our assertion that the notion of security does not support the classical principle of building a sense of connectedness or community, but one that establishes a sense of detachment. To borrow a term from Liz Elliott, a Simon Fraser University (Vancouver, Canada) criminologist, national security is more reflective of "macho politics" than it is of community building, or capacity building (Elliott 2007). To this end, the human rights agenda can be used to at least bring into question the rights violations that may exist within the criminal justice system, border-protection policies, and a plethora of other social and political dynamics that impact our approach to HT.

A final cautionary comment about a rights-based explanatory approach is the challenge of trying to reconcile the issue of *cultural relativism* with universal human rights (see Reichert 2007). For example, the jury is still out on whether human rights are able to promote economic and social development or simply empower the economically and politically rich and stable societies to exploit less developed or less stable communities.

In light of this, any attempt to understand and define HT from a rights-based perspective, should not omit an examination of the power relations underpinning discourses of human rights. For instance, who is defining the rights? Who has the right to define oppression on behalf of another? Are the voices of the oppressed heard in the process of defining and responding to their rights? Within such a context, the rights agenda is as complex a concept as HT is a complex phenomenon and therefore its explanatory capacity should be positioned within a broader global, national, and regional level of analysis.

In this section we focused on HR as an explanatory model for HT. While it is undeniable that HT represents a gross violation of human dignity and human rights and that it represents a promising perspective by which to justify a formal response to such acts, the HR agenda cannot, or at least should not, be viewed in isolation of the broader social complexity that underlies HT. To be used in isolation of such consideration is seen to be both naïve and ultimately limiting in understanding, explaining, and effectively responding to the issue of HT. In the final section we will both summarize the main themes of this chapter as well as offer a sociologically based paradigm that may better serve to explain and respond to HT.

Conclusion

Trafficking as a Complex Social Phenomenon

Criminologists, political scientists, lawyers, journalists, sociologists, human rights advocates, and scholars in the fields of migration studies, gender, and public health have all examined the issue of HT, leading to a diverse set of explanations and interpretations. In particular, trafficking has been explained in terms of gender inequality, transnational crime, globalization, development, and human rights. While each of these explanations is important in their own right, they have also been limited in their ability to overcome dichotomous understandings and politicized discourses. Moreover, in an attempt to examine the individual parts of the phenomenon, scholars and activists have conflated the individual parts of HT with the whole. In turn, we suggest, this has prevented the advancement of constructive dialog, the development of effective strategies, and the improvement of the rights of trafficked persons. To overcome such politicized discourses and dichotomous understandings, we suggest that HT should be understood as a complex social phenomenon and thereby reflect the diversity of experiences encompassed by the single concept.

As we have demonstrated, trafficking discourses have been simplified into loosely defined polarized dichotomies, such as rights versus restrictions; state versus nongovernment actors; victims versus agents; and coercion versus consent. Such dichotomous understandings reflect the vague nature of international definitions of HT. In turn, lack of a clear understanding about the concept of HT has left discussions about HT vulnerable to the manipulation of a variety of political agendas (see Segrave et al. 2009).

On the one hand, this reflects the importance of considering whether the multitude of experiences covered by the single concept of HT requires more definitional precision. As Ahmed (2005) argues, "many of the elements and definitions for this social phenomenon are often limited in their scope and do not adequately reflect the totality of the problem"

(p. 199). While the UN Protocol offers an important starting point in providing a universal definition of HT, it provides little direction for responding to the complexity of experiences encompassed by the concept. Recognizing HT as a complex social phenomenon requires more precise definitions of the various types of HT. In turn, such definitional precision would help develop standardized instruments for assessing the different types of HT and more effective responses to the unique experiences of trafficked persons.

On the other hand, the vulnerability of trafficking discourses to the manipulation of political agendas reveals the importance of bipartisan dialog and interdisciplinary analysis on the topic. In this way, the more nuanced understanding of human trafficking as a complex social phenomenon is necessary in order to depoliticize trafficking discussions. For example, discussions polarized around the issues of national security versus human rights, have led to the adoption of restrictive border controls, on the one hand, and calls to unrestricted movement across borders, on the other. While such dichotomous standpoints are not easily overcome, it is important to create dialog that considers and respects both issues of national security and the rights of migrants, including irregular migrants and trafficked persons. In doing so, antitrafficking advocates, who have so far made limited progress in advancing the rights of trafficked persons, can develop realistic approaches for responding to the issue of HT within the constraints of contemporary state-centric models of governance. At the same time, critical assessments of the role of the state in HT are necessary and advocates to this effect can, and should, continue to question the structures that they perceive reinforce HT and other forms of exploitation. As a complex social phenomenon, discussions of HT cannot (or at least should not) be isolated from broader dialog about, for example, economic inequality, globalization, national boundaries, and flows of people across borders.

Further, HT trafficking analysis requires an interdisciplinary lens because, by definition, HT encompasses the study of migration, prostitution, labour flows, the users of trafficked victims, and so on that necessarily interact with other areas of analysis, such as development, postcolonial studies, globalization, race and ethnicity. Rather than presenting HT as a single event (e.g., prostitution or irregular movement across borders), trafficking should be presented as "a series of interrelated events along an extended continuum that spans a given period of time" (Ahmed 2005, p. 208). An examination of the interrelated events that make up an instance of HT requires a cross-disciplinary analysis that does not isolate HT from its associate parts (i.e., discussion of globalization, migration, human rights, gender inequality, and so on).

Thus, while existing explanations of HT would appear to have served many of us well, we align ourselves with Lee's (2011) recent approach in arguing that the current explanatory models presented in this chapter fail to adequately reflect the complexity of this social phenomenon. For example, as reflected (directly and indirectly) throughout this thematic handbook, HT is unquestionably linked to the imbalances between differential migration and immigration policies and practices, political ideologies, globalization, gender-role perceptions, interpretation of human rights, border-control/protection policies, and so on. Again, as Lee (2011) encourages, if we are to gain a better understanding of HT we need to reassess "the language of human trafficking and the dominant enforcement of trafficking control" (p. 13). However, in addition to simply calling for a sociological approach that focuses on the mere criminalizing of HT, or viewing HT purely as a social issue of gender inequality, or bringing into question the "macho politics" of the criminal justice system, we also suggest extending the lens of understanding and explanation to include an examination and explanation of the role that various types of consumers[*] play in the dynamic relationship that allows HT to exist and often flourish as well as positioning the human rights framework to challenge "the criminalization of non-citizens and to test states' obligations under international human rights law to protect the rights of trafficked victims" (Lee 2011, p. 154).

We set out to provide an overview of some of the dominant explanatory models of HT. To this end, we provided an overview of key existing explanations of HT (i.e., gender inequality, transnational crime, globalization, development, and human rights) and showed that, while instructive, none offered an explanatory framework that clearly accounts for the complex nature of HT. Thus, we conclude with an alternative model that embraces a sociological approach that understands HT within a richer social context and reflects the intrinsically complex interplay between the many networks of relationships and politics that underlie HT. We also suggest that this explanatory model be critical in its approach to expose the overt and not-so-overt interplay of human rights, feminization, globalization, and the social milieu that comprise contemporary societies and increasingly intertwined networks of global relations.

Review and Critical Discussion Questions

1. Which of the three theoretical models of explanation resonates the best for you? Explain why.
2. Use one or more of the explanations and try to apply it to another type of transnational crime. How well does it explain the crime?
3. Identify the strengths and limitations of both the "victim" and "agent" perspectives? Is there a middle ground between these polarized views?
4. What do you consider to be the strengths and weaknesses of the final explanation offered in this chapter? Are there aspects of HT that should receive greater or lesser attention? Explain why.
5. What do you think is missing from existing explanations and responses to HT?

References

Adepoju, A. 2005. Review of research and data on human trafficking in sub-Saharan Africa. In F. Laczko and E. Gozdziak (Eds.), *Data and Research on Human Trafficking: A Global Survey* (pp. 75–98). Geneva, Switzerland: International Organization for Migration.

Agustín, L. 2007. *Sex at the Margins: Migration, Labour Markets and the Rescue Industry*. New York: Zed Books.

Ahmed, A. 2005. Using a dynamic, interactive, and participatory process to develop and redefine the human trafficking paradigm in Bangladesh. In K. Kempadoo (Ed.), Trafficking and Prostitution Reconsidered: New Perspectives on Migration, Sex, Work, and Human Rights. Boulder, CO: Paradigm Pub. (Chapter 11).

Amnesty International. 2004. *Stolen Sisters: A Human Rights Response to Discrimination and Violence against Indigenous Women in Canada*. Retrieved from http://www.amnesty.ca/campaigns/resources/amr2000304.pdf.

Anderson, B. 2006. *Imagined Communities: Reflections on the Origin and Spread of Nationalism* (5th ed.). New York: Verso.

[*] As discussed in Chapter 4 in this book, victims of HT can include being forced into prostitution, domestic servitude, forced labor, child soldier, and so on.

Aronowitz, A.A. 2001. Smuggling and trafficking in human beings: The phenomenon, the markets that drive it and the organizations that promote it. *European Journal on Criminal Policy and Research, 9*, 163–195.

Atchison, C. 2010. Report of the Preliminary Findings for Johns' Voice: A Study of Adult Canadian Sex Buyers. Retrieved from http://www.johnsvoice.ca/

Bales, K. 1999. *Disposable People: New Slavery in the Global Economy*. Berkeley, CA: University of California Press.

Beck, U. 1994. The reinvention of politics: Towards a theory of reflexive modernization. In U. Beck, A. Giddens, and S. Lash (Eds.), *Reflexitve Modernization: Politics, Tradition and Aesthetics in the Modern Social Order* (pp. 1–55). Stanford: University Press.

Besler, P. 2005. *Forced Labour and Human Trafficking: Estimating the Profits*. Geneva: International Labour Organization.

Brubaker, R. 1992. *Citizenship and Nationhood in France and Germany*. Cambridge: Harvard University Press.

Bruckert, C. and Parent, C. 2002. *Trafficking in Human Beings and Organized Crime: A Literature Review. Research and Evaluation Branch: Community, Contract and Aboriginal Policing Services Directorate*. Ottawa: RCMP. Retrieved from http://www.rcmp-grc.gc.ca/pubs/ccaps-spcca/traffick-eng.htm

Brysk, A. and Shafir, G. 2004. *People out of Place: Globalization, Human Rights, and the Citizenship Gap*. New York: Routledge.

Coalition Against Trafficking in Women. (n.d.). *An Introduction to CATW*. Retrieved from http://www.catwinternational.org/

Chancer, L.S. 1998. *Reconcilable Differences: Confronting Beauty, Pornography, and the Future of Feminism*. Berkeley: University of California Press.

Di Nicola, A. 2000. Trafficking in human beings and smuggling of migrants. In P. Reichel (Ed.), *Handbook of Transnational Crime and Justice*. pp. 181–203. Thousand Oaks, CA: Sage.

Di Nicola, A., Cauduro, A., Lombardi, M. and Ruspini P. (Eds.). 2009. *Prostitution and Human Trafficking: Focus on Clients*. New York: Springer.

Doezema, J. 1998. Forced to choose: Beyond the voluntary v. forced prostitution dichotomy. In K. Kempadoo and J. Doezema (Eds.), *Global Sex Workers: Rights, Resistance, and Redefinition* (pp. 34–50). New York: Routledge.

Doezema, J. 2002. Who gets to choose? Coercion, consent, and the UN trafficking protocol. *Gender and Development, 10*(1), 20–27.

Dottridge, M. 2002. Introduction. In M. Dottridge (Ed.), *Collateral Damage: The Impact of Anti-Trafficking Measures on the Human Rights Around the World*. pp. 1–27. Bangkok: GAATW. Retrieved from http://www.gaatw.org/Collateral%20Damage_Final/singlefile_CollateralDamage final.pdf

Dottridge, M. 2007. *Collateral Damage: The Impact of Anti-Trafficking Measures on the Human Rights around the World*. Bangkok: GAATW.

Elabor-Idemudia, P. 2002. Participatory research: A tool in the production of knowledge in development discourse. In K. Saunders (Ed.), *Feminist Post-Development Thought: Re-Thinking Modernity, Post-Colonialism, and Representation* (pp. 227–254). London, Zed Books.

Elabor-Idemudia, P. 2003. Race and gender analyses. *Canadian Women Studies, 22*, 116–123.

Elliott, L. 2007. Macho Politics—Liz Elliott PhD SFU criminology. Retrieved January 4, 2011 from http://www.youtube.com/watch?v=8MJt2vchXvY

Gallagher, A. 2001. Human rights and the new UN protocols on trafficking and migrant smuggling: A preliminary analysis. *Human Rights Quarterly*, (4):975–1004.

George, S. 2003. Globalizing rights? In M. Gibney (Ed.), *Globalizing Rights* (pp. 15–33). New York: Oxford University Press.

Giddens, A. 1990. *The Consequences of Modernity*. Cambridge: Polity Press.

Giddens, A. 2000. *Runaway World: How Globalization is Reshaping Our Lives*. New York: Routledge.

Green, J. 2007. Taking account of aboriginal feminism. In J. Green (Ed.), *Making Space for Indigenous Feminism* (pp. 20–32). Black Point, Nova Scotia: Fernwood.

Habermas, J. 1996. Modernity: An unfinished project. In M.P. d'Entreves and S. Benhabib (Eds.), *Habermas and the Unfinished Project of Modernity* (pp. 39–55). Cambridge: Polity Press.

Hirst, P. and Thompson, G. 1996. *Globalization in Question: The International Economy and the Possibility of Governance.* Cambridge: Polity Press.

ILO. 2007. *Forced Labour Statistics Factsheet.* Geneva: International Labour Organization.

IOM Global Human Trafficking Database Counter Trafficking Division. 2010. Retrieved from http://www.iom.int/jahia/webdav/shared/shared/mainsite/activities/ct/iom_ctm_database.pdf

Jana, S., Bandyopadhyay, N., Dutta, M.K., and Saha, A. 2002. A tale of two cities: Shifting the paradigm of anti-trafficking programmes. In R. Masika (Ed.), *Gender, Trafficking, and Slavery* (pp. 69–79). Great Britain: Oxfam.

Jordan, A. 2002. *The Annotated Guide to the Complete UN Trafficking Protocol.* Retrieved from http://www.nswp.org/

Kapur, R. 2003. The 'other' side of globalization: The legal regulation of cross-border movements. *Canadian Women Studies, 22,* 6–15.

Keane, J. 2003. *Global Civil Society?* Cambridge: Cambridge University Press.

Kempadoo, K. 1998. Introduction: Globalizing sex workers' rights. In K. Kempadoo and J. Doezema (Eds.), *Global Sex Workers: Rights, Resistance, and Redefinition* (pp. 69–79). New York: Routledge.

Kempadoo, K. 2005. Introduction: From moral panic to global justice: Changing perspectives on trafficking. In K. Kempadoo, J. Sanghera, and B. Pattanai (Eds.), *Trafficking and Prostitution Reconsidered: New Perspectives on Migration, Sex Work, and Human Rights* (pp. vii–xxxiv). Bolder, CO: Paradigm Publishers.

Kempadoo, K. 2007. The war on human trafficking in the Caribbean. *Race & Class, 49*(2), 79–85.

Kivisto, P. and Thomas F. 2007. *Citizenship: Discourse, Theory, and Transnational Prospects.* Oxford: Blackwell Publishing.

Kothari, U. 2005. From colonial administration to development studies: A post-colonial critique of the history of development studies. In U. Kothari (Ed.), *A Radical History of Development Studies: Individuals, Institutions and Ideologies* (pp. 47–66). London: Zed Books.

Lamont, M. and Molnár, V. 2002. The study of boundaries in the social sciences. *Annual Review of Sociology, 28,* 167–195.

Lee, M. 2005. Human trade and the criminalization of irregular migration. *International Journal of the Sociology of Law, 33,* 1–15.

Lee, M. 2007. Introduction: Understanding human trafficking. In M. Lee (Ed.), *Human Trafficking* (pp. 1–25). Devon: Willan.

Lee, M. 2011. *Trafficking and Global Crime Control.* Thousand Oaks, CA: Sage Pub.

Leidholdt, D. 2003. Prostitution and trafficking in women: An intimate relationship. *Journal of Trauma Practice, 2,* 167–183.

Linklater, A. 1996. Citizenship and sovereignty in the post-westphalian state. *European Journal of International Relations, 2*(1): 77–103.

Linklater, A. 1998. Cosmopolitan citizenship. *Citizenship Studies, 2*(1), 23–41.

MacCormick, N. 1996. Liberalism, nationalism and the post-sovereign state. *Political Studies, 44*(3), 553–567.

Malarek, V. 2009. *The Johns: Sex for Sale and Men Who Buy it.* Toronto: Porter.

Mann, M. 2004. "Torchbearers upon the path of progress": Britain's ideology of a "moral and material progress" in India. In H. Fischer-Tiné and M. Mann (Eds.), *Colonialism as Civilizing Mission* (pp. 1–29). London: Anthem Press.

McMichael, P. 2007. *Development and Social Change: A Global Perspective.* (3rd ed.). Thousand Oaks, London: Pine Forge Press.

Mies, M. 1998. *Patriarchy and Accumulation on a World Scale: Women in the International Division of Labour* (6th ed.). New York: Zed Books.

Mies, M. and Shiva, V. 1993. *Ecofeminism*. Halifax, Nova Scotia: Fernwood.

Miller, A. 1999. Human rights and sexuality: First steps towards articulating a rights framework for claims to sexual rights and freedom. *American Soceity of International Law, 1999 proceedings*, 288–303.

Miller, A. 2004. Sexuality, violence against women, and human rights: Women make demands and ladies get protection. *Health and Human Rights*, 7(2): 16–47.

Mohanty, C. 1991. Under western eyes: Feminist scholarship and colonial discourses. In C. Mohanty, A. Russo, and L. Torres (Eds.), *Third World Women and the Politics of Feminism* (pp. 51–80). Bloomington: Indiana University Press.

Nagle, J. (Ed.). 1997. *Whores and Other Feminists*. New York: Routledge.

Naffine, N. 1997. *Feminism and Criminology*. Sydney, Australia: Allen and Unwin.

Native Women's Association of Canada. 2010. *What Their Stories Tell Us: Research Findings from the Sisters in Spirit Initiative*. Retrieved from http://www.nwac.ca/sites/default/files/reports/2010_NWAC_SIS_Report_EN.pdf.

Nyers, P. 2006. *Rethinking Refugees: Beyond States of Emergency*. New York: Routledge.

O'Connell, J. 2006. Will the real sex slave please stand up? *Feminist Review, 83*, 4–22.

Oxman-Martinez, J, Hanley, J., and Gomez., F. 2005a. Canadian policy on human trafficking: A four-year analysis. *International Migration, 43*(4), 7–26.

Oxman-Martinez, J., Lacroix, M., and Hanley, J. 2005b. *Victims of Trafficking in Persons: Perspectives from the Canadian Community Sector*. Retrieved from http://www.justice.gc.ca/eng/pi/rs/rep-rap/2006/rr06_3/rr06_3.pdf.

Parpart, J. L. and Veltmeyer, H. 2004. The development project in theory and Practice: Of its shifting dynamics. *Canadian Journal of Development Studies*, (1): 39–59.

Perrin, B. 2011. *Invisible Chains: Canada's Underground World of Human Trafficking*. Toronto, Ontario: Penguin Group.

Pollock, J. 1977. *Wilberforce*. New York: St. Martin's Press.

Popli, U. K. 2008. Contemporary gender issue: Feminisation of trafficking. *Rajagiri Journal of Social Development, 4*(1), 15–32.

Raymond, J. 2005. Sex trafficking is not "Sex Work." *Conscience, 26*, 45.

Reichel, P. (Ed.). 2005. *Handbook of Transnational Crime & Justice*. Thousand Oaks, CA: SAGE.

Reichert, E. 2007. *Challenges of Human Rights*. New York: Columbia University Press.

Rostow, W.W. 1960. *The Stages of Economic Growth: A Non-Communist Manifesto*. Cambridge: Cambridge University Press.

Salt, J. 2000. Trafficking and human smuggling: A European perspective. *International Migration, 38*(3), 31–56.

Sanghera, J. 2005. Unpacking trafficking discourse. In K. Kempadoo, J. Sanghera, and B. Pattanaik (Eds.), *Trafficking and Prostitution Reconsidered: New Perspectives on Migration, Sex Work, and Human Rights* (pp. 3–24). Bolder, CO: Paradigm Publishers.

Sassen, S. 1996. *Losing Control?: Sovereignty in an Age of Globalization*. New York: Columbia University Press.

Sassen, S. 2002. Women's burden: Counter-geographies of globalization and the feminization of survival. In K. Saunders (Ed.), *Feminist Post-Development Thought: Re-Thinking Modernity, Post-Colonialism, and Representation* (pp. 89–104). London: Zed Books.

Savelsberg, J.J. 2010. *Crime and Human Rights*. Thousand Oaks, CA: Sage Pub.

Schmidt, V.A. 1995. The new world order, incorporated: The rise of business and the delcine of the nation-state. *Daedalus, 24*(2), 75–106.

Schneider, E.M. 1993. Feminism and the false dichotomy of victimization and agency. *New York Law School Review, 38*, 387–401.

Scholte, J.A. 2000. *Globalization: A Critical Introduction*. New York: Palgrave.

Scholte, J.A. 1997. Global capitalism and the state. *International Affairs, 73*(3), 427–452.

Segrave, M., Milivojevic, S., and Pickering, S. 2009. *Sex Trafficking: International Context and Response*. Portland, OR: Willan Publishing.

Sharma, N. 2003. Travel agency: A critique of anti-trafficking campaigns. *Refuge, 21*(3), 53–65.

Shelley, L. 2010. *Human Trafficking: A Global Perspective*. Cambridge: University Press.

Sikka, A. 2009. *Trafficking of Aboriginal Women and Girls in Canada*. Retrieved from http://www.iog.ca/publications/2009_trafficking_of_aboriginal_women.pdf.

Spivak, G. 1988. Can the subaltern speak? In C. Nelson and L. Grossberg (Eds.), *Marxism and the Interpretation of Culture* (pp. 271–313). Urbana: University of Illinois Press.

Strange, S. 1997. *The Retreat of the State: The Diffusion of Power in the World Economy*. Cambridge: Cambridge University Press.

Territo, L. and Kirkham, G. (Eds.). 2010. *International Sex Trafficking of Women and Children: Understanding the Global Epidemic*. Flushing, NY: Looseleaf.

Thorbek, S. and Pattanaik B. (Eds.). 2002. *Transnational Prostitution: Changing Patterns in a Global Context*. New York: Zed Books.

United Nations. 2000. *Protocol to Prevent, Suppress and Punish Trafficking in Persons, Especially Women and Children*. Retrieved from http://www.unodc.org/.

United Nations Office on Drug and Crime (UNODC). 2008. *The Vienna Forum Report: A Way Forward to Combat Human Trafficking*. Retrieved from http://www.un.org/ga/president/62/ThematicDebates/humantrafficking/ebook.pdf.

United Nations Office on Drug and Crime (UNODC). 2010. *UNODC Report on Human Trafficking Exposes Modern Form of Slavery*. Retrieved from http://www.unodc.org/unodc/en/human-trafficking/global-report-on-trafficking-in-persons.html.

University of British Columbia. 2008. *UBC Legal Expert Releases Canada's First Stats on Foreign Human Trafficking Victims*. Retrieved from http://www.publicaffairs.ubc.ca/media/releases/2008/mr-08-143.html.

Unwin, T. 2007. No end to poverty. *Journal of Development Studies, 43*(5), 929–953.

Vold, G., Bernard, T., and Snipes, J. 1998. *Theoretical Criminology* (4th ed.). New York: Oxford University Press.

Waters, M. 2001. *Globalization* (2nd ed.). London: Routledge.

White, R., Haines, F., and Eisler, L. 2009. *Crime and Criminology: An Introduction*. Toronto: Oxford University Press.

Williams, S. and Masika, R. 2002. Editorial. *Gender and Development, 10*, 2–9.

Williams III, F.P. and McShane, M.D. 2008. *Criminological Theory*. (5th ed.). Upper Saddle River, NJ: Prentice Hall.

Winterdyk, J.K. and Sundberg, K. (Eds.). 2010. *Border Security in the Al-Qaeda Era*. Boca Raton, FL: CRC Press.

Useful Websites

Feminist theory: http://www.cddc.vt.edu/feminism/enin.html

Agency Perspective on HT: http://www.gaatw.org/

Victim Perspective on HT: http://www.catwinternational.org/

Human Right Watch: http://www.hrw.org

Global Rights http://globalrights.org

Globalization http://www.cddc.vt.edu/feminism/enin.html

International Organization for Migration (IOM): http://iom.org

Office of the High Commissioner for Human Rights: http://ohchr.org

United Nations Office on Drugs and Crime: http://www.unodc.org/unodc/en/human-trafficking/

Voices from Victims and Survivors of Human Trafficking

5

CLAUDE D'ESTRÉE

Contents

Human Trafficking Introduced

The primary focus of this textbook is on human trafficking. In fact, most books on trafficking tend to focus on the trafficking of women and children. This is understandable because, as reflected in various UN reports (see UNODC/UN.GIFT Global Report on Trafficking in Persons, 2009), trafficking of women and children is the third most profitable crime. However, as we will see in this chapter, there are a host of other forms and variations of human trafficking which are worthy of attention. This chapter adopts an approach using the "victims' voice" to illustrate the variation and complexity of human trafficking and as a means to show other examples of human trafficking.

In the emerging field of forced labor and human trafficking we tend to break down the occurrences into types, such as sex trafficking, agricultural slavery, forced marriage, forced begging, forced organ removal, or by regions of the world, thematically or geographically. At the Human Trafficking Clinic (HTC) at the Josef Korbel School of International Studies we discuss the "**3 Cs**," the causes, conditions, and cures of human trafficking to parallel the "**3 Ps**," of punishment, protection, and prevention that is oft quoted by the U.S. Department of State's Office to Monitor and Combat Trafficking in Persons. The U.N. *Palermo Protocol* and the U.S. *TVPA* (Trafficking Victims Protection Act of 2000) tout themselves to be "victim centered." While the effectiveness of the victim-centered policy of either the *Palermo Protocol* (see Chapters 1 and 2 for further discussion) or the *TVPA* might be called into question, there is at least a recognition that the wrong committed is directed at an individual human being and that it should be the center of concern. This immediately raises a conflict with the traditional jurisprudence of criminal law and its relationship between the individual and the community as expressed by municipal law. Criminal statues, and the *Palermo Protocol* and the *TVPA* are both criminal statues at their core, are expressions of community mores in their relationship to criminal behavior. A crime committed against an individual becomes a crime committed against the community. Once a crime has reached the level of prosecution by the state, the victim has little to no say in the proceedings and merely acts as a potential witness of the crime committed against the community. We know this because even if an individual victim of criminal activity were to forgive the perpetrator of the act against his/her, the state would continue to move against the perpetrator (also, see Chapter 12 in this volume). Should the victim, as part of his/her act of forgiveness, refuse to testify against the person who had criminally violated their rights and liberties, the state could bring criminal sanctions against her for refusing to testify! Once the state is involved in criminal proceedings their victim plays only a small part. While there has been a movement toward victim-centered crimes and procedures, again as seen in international and national statues like the *Palermo Protocol* and the *TVPA* and at international criminal proceedings like the International Criminal Tribunal for the Former Yugoslavia (ICTY), and the International Criminal Tribunal for Rwanda (ICTR), the place of the victims in criminal proceedings is still in question.

Perhaps one of the driving forces behind a victim-centered focus on crime is the emergence of the validity of stories, or narratives. In the 1970s and 1980s a movement developed in the study of anthropology that began to look at stories of individuals about themselves as having as much value as a more objective, scientific approach to observing individuals and their communities. An example among historians was the discovery of slave narratives in the United States (see, e.g., Rawick, 1996). It is not as if the slaves' narratives were not available to historians, but rather, guided in part by their colleagues in anthropology, historians began to put value to these first-person accounts of slavery. The 2004 U.S. Public Broadcasting System (PBS) series, *Slavery and the Making of America* (produced by Thirteen/WNET New York), offered an understanding of slavery in the United States with an amalgamation of first-person slave narratives and historic research and analysis through the medium of a docudrama. It has become important to hear the voices of the victims and survivors. On the other hand, while these stories have gained a place in our understanding of modern slavery and human trafficking, it can be said that we only really give them lip service. A more radical idea has begun to emerge, which suggests that victims and survivors actually participate in the decision-making process that would possibly help alleviate not only their suffering, but the suffering of others facing a similar plight. The question is raised as to what weight these stories should have in formulating policy and the crafting of law. For example, when the U.S. Congress calls as a witness a victim of human trafficking to testify before one of its committees are they really listening to the story, or is it more a publicity, or public relations process? Should the U.S. Congress, or any other international jurisdiction, even be crafting law based on the testimony of one or two witnesses? The author of this chapter very much doubts that when a particular legislative committee of the U.S. Congress gathers to debate and craft a law that impacts on forced labor and human trafficking that they have brought in, as equal partners to the process, the views and opinions of the victims of human trafficking to help them craft that law.

Although this chapter will focus on American-based stories, the message and lessons transcend international borders because of the transnational nature of most human trafficking incidents. Stories are used to sell the idea of outrage at forced labor and human trafficking. Human rights organizations use the stories of human trafficking to raise awareness and funds. Sometimes a non-government organization (NGO) actually travels on a speaking tour with victims in tow so that the audience can hear their stories directly. On the one hand this is a powerful tool, on the other hand it has an uncomfortable feeling of exploitation, especially as most of these victims tend be young women who are survivors of sex trafficking. Stories can also be used in books (see, e.g. Perrin, 2010; Malarek, 2004), articles, stage plays (e.g., "She has a name"—www.burnttickettheatre.com), and documentaries (e.g., see resource guide at end of chapter), as a way of illustrating the human dimension to what might otherwise be an objective, and therefore distancing, analysis of human trafficking. Unfortunately, these stories are sometimes used to mask poor methodology and questionable data, so that the reader is caught up emotionally with the story and is not applying a critical eye to the data or the analysis.

Nonetheless, the story of individuals who are victims and survivors is at the heart of the matter. It is their story that connects us, as human beings, to them. We identify with their suffering. We imagine ourselves or our children in the same situation and reel back in horror. It is the story of the victim that is told to law enforcement officers and prosecutors that initiates criminal inquiry. It is the story of the survivor heard by the legislature that leads to the formulating of law, policy, and financial allocations. The same story may be heard in very different ways. The police officer hears the story through a different set of ears than does the human rights advocate. Law enforcement and NGOs represent very distinctive cultures, each with its own set of priorities and bound by a different set of missions and rules. Therefore, it is not surprising then that the response to the same story can be very different, often causing tension between law enforcement and NGOs (see the HTC website listed at the end of the chapter). Law enforcement is guided by a much narrower definition of what legally constitutes human trafficking and NGOs are guided by their focus on victim's services and therefore broaden their definition. While both groups, both institutions, are ostensibly there to serve victims of human trafficking, see, for example, how they hear the story of the victims can lead to very different, even opposing, outcomes. There is one more important point that, at least for the author, has become apparent. Victims of human trafficking are often thought of as guilty, until proven innocent. This turns the legal norms and legal mores, the jurisprudence, on its head. Since the stories we hear most are about prostitution and illegal immigrants, the victims and survivors do not receive the benefit of "innocent, until proven guilty." In addition to the already immense suffering they have already gone through the victims now have to seemingly "prove" their innocence. Truly hearing their story becomes critical not only for their own psychological well-being, but so that they are also afforded full protection of the law.

Using victim-based stories, this chapter reviews the many types of modern human trafficking. Well-known forms include sex trafficking, child labor, and agricultural slavery.

In addition to these well-known forms of human trafficking, newer and less well-known forms of trafficking are also included such as organ trafficking, football. and the dancing boys of Afghanistan.

The stories in this chapter are a mix of amalgamated stories and stories taken from U.S. cases as a means of showing patterns of behavior and issues of both the victim of human trafficking and the trafficker. Amalgamated stories are created from a variety of sources to bring together multiple elements to best explain, in this case, the complexity of human trafficking.

The old scourge of "slavery" has clearly returned. Of course, if we were to follow the story of Douglas A. Blackmon's (2008) book, *Slavery by Another Name: The Re-Enslavement of Black People in America from the Civil War to World War II*, we might note that slavery, at least in the United States, never went away, it only morphed into a new terminology called "human trafficking." Terms of art, however, are not unimportant.

For this chapter, I will be using definitions developed by the HTC at the Josef Korbel School of International Studies. It became apparent that there were a host of different definitions and assumptions about those definitions, when it came to understanding forced labor, human trafficking, and modern slavery. Most of the definitions have been borrowed from legal documents, such as the U.N. *Palermo Protocol (The 2000 Protocol to Prevent, Suppress and Punish Trafficking in Persons especially Women and Children)*, and the U.S. TVPA (*Victims of Trafficking and Violence Protection Act of 2000*), as well as the various International Labour Organization's (ILO) various conventions on forms of forced labor. These documents, while important, constitute legal definitions that are ultimately used to define who are the transgressors and who are the victims and survivors for the purpose of criminal and civil litigation. The HTC felt that while these definitions had their place, they were not particularly useful for purposes of research, especially research in the social sciences. Furthermore, the HTC has sought, through its "**Taxonomy Project**" to craft a set of terms that were integrative, interlocking, and supportive of each other.

The HTC defines Human Trafficking as a subcategory of slavery or forced labor. *Slavery* is the condition of being under the control of another person, in which violence or the threat of violence, whether physical or mental, prevents a person from exercising her/his freedom of movement and/or free will. *Forced Labor* is all work or service, legitimate or otherwise, which is exacted from any person under violence or the threat of violence, whether physical or mental, which prevents a person from exercising his/her freedom of movement and/or free will. The subcategory, *Human Trafficking* is the recruitment and/or movement of someone within or across borders, through the abuse of power/ position with the intention of forced labor exploitation, commercial, or otherwise.

Some Dominant Forms of Human Trafficking

Sex Trafficking

Sex trafficking is the recruitment and/or movement of someone within or across borders, through the abuse of power/ position with the intention of forced sexual exploitation, commercial, or otherwise.

A **prostituted person** is a person under the control of another who has limited agency and/or choice and is coerced to perform sexual acts in exchange for monetary and/or nonmonetary compensation.

A **sex worker** is a person who claims agency and/or choice to perform sexual acts in exchange for monetary and/or nonmonetary compensation.

The rationale for defining "prostituted person" and "sex worker" is that they constitute very different, and often opposing, camps in the sex trafficking debate.

There are a number of controversies with the human trafficking community. The chief of these concerns the issue of sex trafficking and the scope of its potential victims. This essay does not delve into that particular controversy other than to note that terms of art again play an important role, such as the use of the term "prostituted women" or "women who are prostituted" in one camp and the term "sex worker" in another camp. One camp would insist that no women would ever willingly engage in prostitution whatever her age, making force, coercion, and fraud unnecessary elements of the crime of trafficking and making all "pimps" and "johns" traffickers. The other camp insists that while prostitution may not be an ideal first choice, women over the age of 18 have agency and have the right to use their bodies as they wish. This disagreement often brings out the knives when discussing sex trafficking. These arguments almost always ignore the phenomena of men as potential victims of human trafficking, as illustrated below, when talking about "romance tourism."

Anastasia was a young, university-educated woman in her early twenties. Born and raised in Eastern Europe, she possessed the legendary porcelain beauty of many Ukrainian women. She lived with four other women in a cold-water flat on the seventh floor of a large apartment building built during the heyday of the Soviet Union. Anastasia lived in a country that, following the breach in the Berlin Wall, had slipped from being a first world nation to a third world nation. None of the young women could find full-time jobs, but they were resourceful and pooled their money for rent and food.

But she was very ambitious and intelligent. She wanted more—much more. She dreamed of a well-paying job, a spacious home, a loving husband and, one day, children. While out at a club she had overheard that there were well-established men in Europe and America who were looking for wives. When Anastasia mentioned this to her manager at work, she was surprised when her manager said that her brother owned a company that connected men to women all over Eastern Europe. She discussed it with her housemates, and they joked that it did not sound like a bad arrangement. The worst that could happen was that she would have to marry some middle-aged professor. Then after a couple of years when she was a legal resident, she could divorce him. Then she could then get a good job while she looked for the husband of her dreams. Maybe she could even get her master's degree in computer programming.

When Anastasia's manager's brother took her to lunch during her break, he was charming, witty, and full of smiles. He told her that he could post her profile on his website for just a small fee. In fact, since she worked for his sister, he would feature her profile all of the next month for no extra charge. Then, when she was selected, all the visa fees, travel costs, and finder's fees to his company would be paid for by her future husband. She would be under no pressure to pick someone and could take as much time as she liked. After all, this could be the most important decision of her life. In fact, he told her that since groups of American and European men sometimes stopped in her city to meet the women they might marry, she would likely have the chance to meet her future husband face-to-face before making a final decision.

Several weeks later, Anastasia was invited to a party for Western European men to meet with selected women featured on the website. Her manager's brother told her that he had someone very special who seemed to be interested in her. When she met "Max" at the party the following week, she was surprised at his complete command of Russian even though he was from Germany. "Max" said that he was the CEO of a small but prosperous computer software company, and a partner in a Russian club in Berlin. He owned a large home outside Berlin, but kept an apartment in the city for business. "Max" explained that he was looking for a companion to play hostess to his customers and various business partners. And as though reading her mind, he told her that she was free to go her own way after 2–3 years as his "wife and companion."

After the deal with her manager's brother was concluded and her visa put in order, Anastasia flew to Berlin to join her new fiancé. She was surprised when she was met, not by "Max," but by his driver. The driver told her he was taking her to "Max's" apartment in Berlin and asked her for her papers and her passport for safekeeping. "Max," he reported, was in England on business and would join her the next day.

When they arrived at the apartment, four men in business suits were sitting in the living room having drinks. These people, the driver told her, were important customers and so she should be on her best behavior, as "Max" had requested that she entertain them. In the bedroom she would find a white satin negligee to change into.

When the full impact of what was going on descended upon her, she began to cry and yell at the driver. He shoved her across the room, snapping that she knew exactly what she was getting into, and not to play innocent.

The four men proceeded to rape her repeatedly. The days and nights that followed were a blur of violent sex and forced drugs mixed with large quantities of alcohol. Weeks turned into months, and when her health and porcelain beauty began to crack, her "husband" "Max," who she now knew to be a member of the Russian Mafia, sold her to the Japanese Yakuza and she was flown to Tokyo.

Her eventual contracting of HIV Aids and disappearance is another story.

There are variations on the aforementioned amalgamated story. The other classic variation is the young girl from a small village in southern Nepal. She, too, is valued for her exotic beauty. In this story it is either an older woman, exquisitely dressed from the same village, or a man from a large Indian city, who comes to the village with promises of jobs. Education and a monthly stipend for the family entices the young girl or her family to follow. The girl is entranced with the idea of nice clothes and the night life of a big city. The parents, who may have many more children than they can feed, are seduced by the earning power of a girl child, who would normally be considered a burden to the family, both socially and economically. The young girl soon finds herself in Chawri or GB Road in New Delhi or Sonagachi in Kolkata. The story does not end well for her either. Like Anastasia she contracts HIV/Aids and is cast out of the brothel to fend for herself. She manages to make it back to her village where she is a pariah, even to her family, because of her status as a former prostitute and their ignorant fear about HIV/AIDS.

The stories of sex trafficking, whether obtained through research, gathered from court records, and/or told to victim advocates, have a number of common themes. As we will see in other stories, they begin in a country that is economically distressed. There is little opportunity for individuals or families to make enough money to sustain themselves, let alone acquire any consumer goods that would give them comfort. They are approached by someone who offers them either financial security or a vision of a better future. Though not a requirement within the legal definition of human trafficking, the victims travel across an international border to another country where they lose the protection of their own state. Should they have any personal or travel documentation, like passports, driver's license, or birth certificate, they are taken from them by the trafficker. In the case of sex trafficking the girls and women in these stories are beaten, raped, and drugged to break their will, their desire to escape, and make them compliant. The end is always the same—disappearance, death, or shunning by her community.

There are complicating variations of these stories that are told less often. The first is the woman (in the majority of cases it is women) who manages to work off the debt, yet remains in the commercial sex trade. The second is the woman who has been the victim of sex trafficking who then, as a means of self-preservation, becomes the Madame of the brothel, who, in turn, enslaves other women. Is she a victim or a criminal? Finally, there is hardly a mention of men, or even boys, in these stories. Granted, the number of men and boys who are victims of sex trafficking are minor in relationship to the number of women and girls, but the lack of male-oriented stories is significant. One aspect of the male sex trade can be found under the expression, "**romance tourism**."

"Sex tourism" and "romance tourism" are both terms associated with the commercial sex trade and sex trafficking. Sex tourism refers to men engaging/exploiting women and girls, and sometimes boys, while romance tourism is a euphemistic term referring to women who engage men for short-term sexual encounters. Romance tourism is the phenomenon by which tens of thousands of women (Rent a Rasta 2006), mostly from Canada, United States, and Europe, purportedly descend on the Caribbean each year "in search of the big bamboo," black men with legendary sexual prowess. The stories are strikingly similar to those in Thailand, the difference being a gender reversal with more than a tinge of racism. Prof. Jacqueline Sanchez Taylor (2006) correctly notes the problem in the title of her insightful article, *Female Sex Tourism: A Contradiction in Terms?*

While romance tourism would likely not meet the HTC's definition of sex trafficking, it should, by all logic, meet the definition espoused by those who use the term prostituted women. If one stated view is that no woman willingly engages in prostitution and thus all such women are victims of sex trafficking, and all men who sexually exploit these women, the john/punter/hobbyist/pimp, are traffickers, then by extension, men are equally victims of sex trafficking when involved in romance tourism. The question raised by romance tourism is the contradiction of agency between men and women in the commercial sex trade and sex trafficking and the almost completely ignored issue of men and boys, heterosexual and homosexual, who are also victims of sexual exploitation and sex trafficking. Strikingly, while there are numerous domestic and international laws dealing with sex tourism there are no such laws when it comes to romance tourism.

U.S. Legal Cases Dealing with Sex Trafficking

For convenience and practical reasons throughout this chapter, I will focus on offering American-based legal cases to exemplify the various topics to be covered. In this section, we present two legal cases that typify sex trafficking in the United States. The first, *The People v. Rodney Lyndell Tillis* [(2010) Cal.App. Unpub. LEXIS 958] is set in San Diego, California. The defendant, Rodney Tillis, is a professional pimp who encounters a young, inexperienced woman, Breanna B., prostituting herself in an area called the "Blade," a popular area for sexual services. This might have been a normal story of pimping and pandering, except for several factors that become important. Breanna, while not a minor, is only 21 years old and is prostituting herself for the first time because she has no job and no income. Seemingly within moments of Breanna arriving in the Blade she is picked up by Tillis who spots her as a neophyte. In a very short span of time, Tillis sexually abuses Breanna, tells her that she must earn $1000 per night and turn over all her earnings to him. Tillis physically intimidates and threatens Breanna and puts her under the charge of a more experienced prostitute, then takes her to a motel room to rest where she can be watched at all times to make sure she does not escape. After taking Breanna back to the Blade, Breanna approaches a stranger and tells him that she has been kidnapped and gets a ride home. Breanna reports her encounter to the police the next day and they arrest Tillis. The response by the police, I believe, is based on the belief in Breanna as an "innocent," that is to say, a young woman who had never prostituted herself before, set upon by a vicious pimp. Breanna's sexual assault in Tillis' car would, unfortunately, not have elicited much sympathy from the police had she been an experienced, professional prostitute, nor would her kidnapping or being forced to work for no compensation. However, because of her innocence, these actions by Tillis constituted the elements of sex trafficking. The fact that California law does not require proof of an actual sex act to define human trafficking and that pandering does not require a completed act of prostitution [*Wooten v. Superior Court* (2001) 93 Cal.App.4th 422, 437] is helpful for making the trafficking case.

The second case, *State of Iowa v. Leonard Ray Russell* [(2010) Iowa App. LEXIS 145] is seemingly simple and straightforward. Two girls, aged 15 and 16, run away from a juvenile home and are picked up by two adults on their way to Washington, D.C. The girls are told that they can help pay their way across the country by performing in strip clubs and engaging in prostitution. Both girls willingly do so and there is no indication in the story that the girls were forced to give up all their earnings nor were they sexually assaulted by Russell or his girlfriend, Jazzie. The story makes clear that one of the girls decides to go on to Washington, D.C. to better learn the prostitution trade, while the other decides to stay in the Iowa area to work in commercial sex trade, including strip clubs and prostitution. The two girls' services were also featured on an internet website.

While the outcome for the defendant Russell is the same as for Tillis, the stories of the victims are very different. Breanna was an adult and the two girls are minors, under the age of eighteen. We are not even given their first names so as to supposedly protect their innocence. The two girls, however, seem to very willingly engage in prostitution and the commercial sex trade, and unlike Breanna, are not physically harmed or threatened by Russell or his companion, Jazzie. However, the critical element of this story is the age of the two girls. Their willingness to engage in prostitution and dance at strip clubs is completely immaterial since an adult moving a minor is by definition an abuse of power since the minor lacks the ability to give consent explained hereafter. They lack agency. The *TVPA* is quite clear that anyone under the age of 18 cannot give their consent to engage in the commercial sex trade and it does not matter that Russell is unaware of this provision in the law. Like California, Iowa requires no proof of a sex act, and the internet advertising of the two girls' sexual services is enough to convict him of pandering and human trafficking.

Debt Bondage and Bonded Labor

Perhaps the most common form of human trafficking deals with debt bondage and bonded labor and it is regularly found in agricultural slavery or slavery at the very lowest end of the production line [see, e.g., Owed Justice: Thai Women Trafficked into Debt Bondage in Japan (2000)].

Debt bondage is a creditor–debtor arrangement by which a person is forced to work off a debt, legitimate or otherwise, in which his/her movement and/or free will is controlled. When external factors, such as custom or force, eliminate the possibility of repayment by the victim and/or succeeding generations the condition becomes **bonded labor**.

In a typical debt-bond slavery case the individual borrows money from a local land owner. As collateral against the debt, the individual works for the land owner. The worker may be paid a small sum—just enough to feed themselves and no more. But whenever a need arises—money for medicine, a wedding, or funeral—the worker borrows more from the land owner. Since the debt can actually never be paid off by the worker, the debt may be passed on to future generations of the family. This debt-bond may be for as little as $50 or $100. The only hope is for some outside source, a well-to-do relative, to step in and pay off the debt. But even if the debt is paid what is the worker and his family to do? If their skill sets only include the making of bricks, or breaking rocks, or the tilling of someone else's fields there is no one to turn to but the very same person to whom they were originally bound. The threat or use of violence is a common factor in debt-bond slavery.

Angel had been out of work for months, only finding the odd repair job. His family lived in a Mexican village a few kilometers from a mid-sized town some distance south of the U.S. border. The rain had been very scarce for several years and the promise of NAFTA (North American Free Trade Agreement) had yet to reach them. This was not a place that tourists found beautiful, culturally interesting, or even quaint. His wife seemed to produce miracles everyday providing meals for their family of eight. This purgatory may have gone on indefinitely had his second youngest child not become ill. The doctor told him that his son needed to go to a hospital and would need expensive medicine for an extended therapeutic regime. There was no money to even begin treatment.

Angel had heard of a man offering jobs—good jobs—across the border. He could make more money in a week than he could in a month at home. He had never even been tempted before—the thought of leaving his family made the lure of even serious amounts of money unthinkable, not to mention that the price for a "coyote" to smuggle an adult across the border was astronomical—$500! Even though the jobs across the border picking produce all day, seven days a week, were almost demeaning for a skilled carpenter and electrician like himself, the men from his village who had gone to the United States were sending money to their families. Children in those families got proper food, went to school in decent clothes, and could go to the doctor and get medicine.

When Angel approached the "coyote," he was told that if he could come up with $200, he could pay the rest from his earnings once he got to his job in the United States. So he gathered up the family's meager savings, borrowed the rest from relatives, and paid the coyote $200.

The journey across the Arizona–Sonora Desert was long; the 120 degree heat, searing. Two members of his party disappeared before they reached a safe house in southwest Arizona. At the safe house the coyote told him and his companions that they were going to be taken by van to their jobs. The driver asked for all their identification papers for safe-keeping.

What Angel did not know was that the coyote had just sold each of them to the van driver.

For the next 3 days he traveled with 16 other companions. The only breaks were brief stops at gas stations. Each time they stopped they were allowed to use the restroom, but only accompanied by the driver of the van. They were given water, but no food. Sleep was virtually impossible. When they finally reached Florida, they were all exhausted, hungry, weak, and disoriented. He did not even know where he was in the United States.

Before being shown to the room he would share with five other men he was informed of the terms of his employment, all written up in English in a very official-looking contract. One of the men working for the labor contractor translated it into Spanish for him: If he met his orange-picking quota, he would earn $200 per week, minus any days he was sick and could not work. The labor contractor would also deduct his rent and meals. In addition to the $300 he stilled owed the coyote, he also owed $3500 to the labor contractor. He could pay back this "loan" over time, with interest. However, until the debt was paid off he would have to work exclusively for the labor contractor. He was required to sign the contract before being fed and allowed to sleep.

The next morning Angel was then taken to orange groves. There had been a damaging frost recently, so each tree only had a few oranges. To make his quota that day he worked 14 h. He ate his lunch of tortillas, beans, rice, and coffee while working.

After working a full 7 days, Angel was told that the deductions of what he owed the labor contractor and his rent and food came to $225. The $25 difference would be added to what he already owed. No money would be going home that week. This went on day after day, week after week, month after month. The dozen or so guards, extended family members of the labor contractor, would remind any grumblers that anyone caught trying to escape before paying off their debt would be severely beaten or disappear into the crocodile-infested pond.

His eventual escape is another story.

This story combines many of the tales that could be found in the case files from the Coalition of Immokalee Workers in Florida. Others follow similar outlines that are well told in Binka le Breton's *Trapped: Modern-Day Slavery in the Brazilian Amazon.* These are men, and occasionally women, trapped by a system of **enganche** (hooking), which is a widespread system of recruitment whereby workers receive wage advances from intermediaries (Andrees and Belser, 2009). The workers usually use the small advancement on drink and prostitutes and then are required to pay back the advancement by working for months on deforestation projects in the remaining Amazon forests. As in other forms of debt bondage the men never pay off the debt and are simply released when the project is completed. The cycle repeats itself *ad nauseum.*

Again, for convenience and practicality, we will focus on two U.S. cases that will serve to tell international stories that wind up in U.S. Courts via the Alien Tort Statute (28

U.S.C. § 1350) and the Racketeering Influenced and Corrupt Organizations Act (RICO) (18 U.S.C. § 1962). The Alien Tort Statute has been used extensively to bring human rights violations that take place outside the United States into U.S. Courts. RICO is an effective tool in bringing multiple defendants together as coconspirators. *Alberto Justo Rodriguez Licea, et al., v. Curacao Drydock Company, Inc.* (2008) 584 F.Supp.2d 1355, is played out in the Southern District Court of Florida and tells a story of government complicity in human trafficking and modern slavery. The Cuban government, in its a desire to generate U.S. currency and foil the Embargo, send Cuban workers to Curacao to work 16-h days for up to 45 days straight. Their passports are taken and they are held in captivity while living in slave-like barracks. The work is very dangerous and there is no safety measures taken or medical care provided. Should they try to escape they are told that their families will be prosecuted. Some manage to escape but are then hunted like criminals until they make it to the United States. The Cuban authorities make good on their word and continue to punish their families back home. The ships they work on belong to the international community, including oil ships and cruise liners, and the defendant, Curacao Drydock Company make huge profits by forcing the labor of 50–100 workers over a period of 15 years.

The second case, while set in a foreign country, strikes a bit closer to home. *Ramachandra Adhikari et al., v. Daoud and Partners et al.* (2009) 697 F.Supp.2d 674. The case was told in Houston, Texas, where one of the codefendants KBR (which for 44 years, until 2007, had been the engineering, contracting, and construction arm of Halliburton) has its headquarters. The laborers were recruited by an agency in Nepal and were charged substantial brokerage fees that would have to be paid before receiving any compensation to be sent home to their families. Most of the men were told that they would be working in a luxury hotel in Amman, Jordan. A few others were told they would be working in an American camp, though none of them were told where and they were led to believe that they would be sent to the United States. None were told that they would be sent to an extremely dangerous place.

After having their passports confiscated, they were flown Al Asad Air Base, north of Ramadi, Iraq, where they were under constant mortar fire. KBR was aware of the primitive and unsafe conditions that they were being kept in, but insisted that they could not leave until they had fulfilled their 15-month contract. Daoud and Partners had previously been involved with a case where they had kept 18 Indian nationals in forced labor in Fallujah, Iraq, for months after they had quit their jobs. In the process of trying to fulfill their labor contract, more than 10 of the laborers were executed by insurgents.

The common threads to their stories are somewhat obvious. Many are double victims. They have left their own country out of economic desperation and a desire to feed, clothe, educate, and provide medical care to their families. Once they have taken the very great risk to leave hearth and home, they are victimized again by the trafficker. Their passports and means of identification are taken from them and they are transported to a strange country (often not even knowing where they are), where they do not speak the language and have no access to those who might represent their interests (Consulates and Embassies). They are forced to work long hours in either exhausting or dangerous conditions where they are provided little or no medical care. They are told that they owe large sums of money to the labor contractor, often after the fact, which will be deducted from their earnings. There are a series of monetary fines and physical punishment for failing to meet quotas or even being sick. Food, clothing, and housing expenses are also deducted from their earnings. The classic story results in a worker owing the contractor more each week than they are, in fact, able to earn. They cannot leave their place of work, and it is a common practice that their families back home are threatened if they should try to escape. A curious part of these stories is that large, organized crime is not involved. Most of this form of forced labor is perpetrated by small "mom and pop" outfits. On the other hand, it is also telling that two of the stories implicate nation-states, Cuba and the United States, operating under the cover and veil of contractors and a series of subcontractors.

Child Labor

The use of children in labor poses a number of potential problems. The ILO's *Worst Forms of Child Labour* (C183, 1999) states that a child is defined as someone under the age of 18. The arbitrary age distinction between being a child, with no agency, and an adult, with full agency, is reflected in a number of other modern conventions that deal with children, such as child soldiers. Yet the ILO's *Minimum Age Convention* (C138, 1973), states that the minimum age that a child should be able to work is 15, or the end of compulsory education, unless there is economic need in a developing county, in which case the minimum age is fourteen. This leaves a 4-year gap between the ages of 14 and 18 where children are allowed to work, but are considered not to have agency. This has prompted some in the antitrafficking movement, as it relates to **child labor**, to take the same stance as those who use the term prostituted women. They argue that since children lack agency, no one under the age of 18 should be working. Any child who is working, therefore, is a victim of human trafficking and those who insist that a child works, including the child's parents, are traffickers. Most would critique this stance as flying in the face of cultural norms and economic necessity (see, e.g., Hudson, 2007). Children have been part of the workforce for as long as adults have worked. Even in the United States, the labor laws make special provisions for children to work on family farms and ranches and to work in family businesses, as long as it does not interfere with education. The conundrum exists between anyone under the age of 18 engaging in the commercial sex trade being presumed to be trafficked for lacking agency, and someone under the age of 18 working in the labor market who are presumed to be legitimate workers despite not having agency. Indeed the ILO's *Worst Forms of Child Labour* (C183, 1999) is explicit in its title. We are concerned only with the worst forms of child labor, not child labor in itself.

C182 Worst Forms of Child Labour Convention, 1999

Article 3 For the purposes of this Convention, the term *the worst forms of child labor* comprises:

1. all forms of slavery or practices similar to slavery, such as the sale and trafficking of children, debt bondage and serfdom, and forced or compulsory labor, including forced or compulsory recruitment of children for use in armed conflict;
2. the use, procuring, or offering of a child for prostitution, for the production of pornography, or for pornographic performances;
3. the use, procuring, or offering of a child for illicit activities, in particular for the production and trafficking of drugs as defined in the relevant international treaties; and
4. work which, by its nature or the circumstances in which it is carried out, is likely to harm the health, safety, or morals of children.

While the actions against the worst forms of child labor are commendable the ILO states that there are in excess of 215 million children in the workforce. The latest ILO report, *Accelerating Action Against Child Labour*, while noting a decrease of 15% among young girls, stated an increase of 7% among young boys and a substantial increase of 20% among children ages 15–17. Additionally, around 70% of child labor is in agriculture, where children are exposed daily to dangerous tools and machinery as well as pesticides and poisons now used commonly around the world to increase yield (Global View: Farm Work is not Child's Play, 2006).

They were a middle-class family originally from Central America. Ernesto had emigrated to the U.S. 18 years earlier with his wife from the same small town. In those years he had worked at several jobs before settling into the custom auto parts business. The business he started provided a good life for him, his wife, and four children. Now, at this critical juncture in the growth of his company he needed his wife to help in the office on a regular basis.

Their three eldest children were in elementary school and middle-school, and so they checked with an au pair service about child care for their youngest. The yearly fee of $20,000 that they were quoted was outrageous. Next they checked with members of his Central American community to see they could find someone who could help them out at home, but all they could find was an older woman who could come to their house for only a few hours each day and they needed someone from early morning until after the children went to bed. They finally contacted relatives back in their home town, asking if there was a young woman who could do child care and some light house-keeping in exchange for clothes, medical care, going to school in the United States, and accompanying them on periodic family vacations. To his cousin's family, this offer sounded like paradise; a once-in-a-lifetime opportunity for their 14-year-old daughter.

When Janice arrived a few months later she was shown a tiny bedroom in their unfinished basement, furnished with a bed and a cast-off dresser. Her day started at 5 a.m. and rarely ended before midnight. She cared for the children, prepared all the family's meals, and cleaned the house. The slightest infraction earned her a beating. Janice's food was only what was left over from family meals. She never did go to school. In fact, she never left the house. She was told that if she tried to leave, they would call the police who would hurt her and then deport her.

Neighbors on a couple of occasions noted that the family's "fifth" child did not attend school with the other children. Their concerns were satisfied when told that Janice was being home-schooled because of a mental impairment. Being good neighbors also meant not being too inquisitive, too nosey.

Three years later, neighbors called the police after repeatedly hearing screaming between the husband and wife. The responding police officer noticed that the oldest of the couple's five children seemed very shy and frail, and did not move from her chair in the corner of the room. The officer's instincts said that something about the situation was not right, but she could not identify an obvious problem. Even though the officer had received training about human trafficking, the truth of the situation still eluded her. It took five further visits—visits undertaken in direct disobedience to her superior officer's orders—before she found herself in Janice's room and realized what exactly was going on in the family.

The prosecution of Ernesto and his wife is another story.

The aforementioned amalgamated story also has other versions. The most common ones come from India where children work alongside their parents packing mud forms to make bricks or crushing rock and carrying gravel to make roads. It is not unusual in these stories to find children at the age of 8 or 10 expected to work long hours and very hard labor. In many cases the stories are set in villages where the entire population has been enslaved by another caste or by the local Brahmin farmer. The families may have been victims of bonded labor for multiple generations over a debt of less than $100. The children are required to carry on the debt load until it is paid in full, which almost by definition cannot be done.

Outside of India probably the best-known stories of human trafficking involving children are the **restavèks** of Haiti—the forgotten children of Haiti. In her article, *Haiti's Restavèk Children: The Child Servitude Crisis* (*The Huffington Post*, March 29, 2010), Marian Wright Edelman, President, Children's Defense Fund states that half of Haiti's population is under the age of 18 and quoting the 2010 Annual Report of the U.S.-based NGO Beyond Borders, 300,000 (data unverifiable) of Haitian children are caught up in the *restavèk* system. Fueled by chronic poverty, lack of resources, and often misguided governments, the history of *restavèks* in Haiti is a long one. The story is fairly straightforward. A family in one of the larger cities like Port-au-Prince, or Cap-Haïtien, is in need of some domestic help. They seek out a child in one of the many small mountain villages whose family is large and unable to properly feed them. They make the offer to take one of the children, aged 10–14 usually, back to Port-au-Prince where they will be asked to do light housework in exchange of food, a place to live, and education. The family from Port-au-Prince is most often not well-to-do, but they are considerably more financially solvent in comparison with the families in the mountain villages. Once the child gets to the city, the story is similar to many other places on the globe. The hours are long and hard. The children are mistreated and the girls are often sexually abused. They receive neither any education nor compensation for their work. When they get too old or unruly they are simply thrown out into the street and replaced by another child. It is interesting to note that the *restavèk* system may have had benign origins. Families in cities would try and be helpful to their poorer country cousins by providing an opportunity to benefit from the vastly improved conditions in the city. It has, however, become one of the most abusive and exploitive child labor systems in the world, amounting to human trafficking, only 1 h and 50 min by air from Miami, Florida!

The stories of child labor have several themes in common and they collectively serve to help the reader identify the stories as being examples of human trafficking. The children come from areas of extreme poverty, often in situations where there is not enough calorie intake to sustain life (everyday 24,000 people die of malnutrition, usually a child under the age of 5—UNICEF at www.unicef.org/mdg/poverty.html). Through abuse of power/position, they are moved away from parental supervision and oversight and placed under the control of abusive adults. Cultural mores, caste, race, and law enforcement inaction result in little action to alleviate the exploitive labor conditions and provide basic education and health needs as required by international human rights law.

Some Less Dominant/Less Visible/Less Known Forms of Human Trafficking

There are stories that depart from more classic forms of human trafficking that despite being fairly common are not well known, or publicized. This may be because they are regionalized or there has been some reason to keep the story quiet so as not embarrass a particular group or industry. It may also be that there is no universal acceptance that the story constitutes a form of human trafficking (see Zhang, 2007). There is also a clear prejudice in the reporting of sex trafficking, especially as it relates to girls. News agencies and Congressional testimony seem to gravitate to either the most salacious or emotionally laden stories. The following stories have a significant history and impact, yet receive, in comparison, very little coverage. The following are but a few examples of severely under-reported stories by victims and survivors of forced labour, human trafficking, and modern slavery.

Bacha Bazi

Many first became aware of the phenomena of **bacha bazi** (literally "playing with boys") through the "PBS Frontline" documentary in late 2010 entitled *The Dancing Boys of Afghanistan* and Khaled Hosseini's (2003) best seller novel, *The Kite Runner* (see also Fisher and Shay, 2009). *Bacha bazi* may find its roots as far back as the 9th or 10th century in Baghdad and is found well described in the 1877 writings of Eugene Schuyler in Turkistan and surrounding countries as well as James Silk Buckingham's journal of his travels in Mesopotamia in 1817. *Bacha bazi* is essentially a form of child slavery and child prostitution. Modern *bacha bazi* began to flourish following the fall of the Taliban in Afghanistan in 2001–2002 and is found mostly in Pakistan's Northwest Frontier and the adjoining areas of Afghanistan among the Pashtun. Males are not considered to be men until they are married and are referred to as *bacha bereesh*, a boy without a beard or a beardless youth.

Ghaith Abdul-Ahad wrote in *The Guardian* (September 12, 2009) the following story of one of the dancing boys of Afghanistan.

> Dressed in a flowing shirt and long, red skirt, with sherwal pants beneath and small silver bells fastened to hands and feet, the dancer stepped across the floor, face hidden beneath a red scarf. The bells chimed with the movement, the skirt brushing past the watching men who stretched out their hands to touch it. The sitar player sang loudly, a love song about betrayal. The dancer twisted and sang hoarsely with him, arms thrown high above a lean muscular body, moving faster and faster until finally the scarf dropped, revealing a handsome young man's face with traces of a moustache and beard. One of the men quickly grabbed up the scarf and started sniffing it.

It is then common practice to bid on these *bacha bereesh* who are then taken home by their owner for the sexual pleasure of the master. The cultural and religious norms governing this behavior are complex and certainly confusing to the outsider. Pashtun society is governed by a cultural code called *pashtunwali*, whose supreme emphasis is on *nang*, or "honor." But Pashtun society it is also governed by Islamic Shari'a law* and the two often come into conflict. Shari'a, if it does not condemn homosexuality directly, certainly condemns homosexual acts. As found in other cultures, homosexuality and homosexual acts are attributed only to the recipient of the act, whatever the age of the recipient. In Pashtun

---

* For a brief overview of Shari'a law see: http://www.religioustolerance.org/islsharia.htm (retrieved April 3, 2011).

society the lines are even less clear. The *bacha bereesh* (boy without beard) is by definition not a man, but almost a genderless adolescent. Thus, neither the adult male nor the adolescent male would be labeled either as homosexuals or engaging in homosexual acts. This is of critical importance because the *nang* (honor) of the adult male is not diminished by the sexual interaction. Having said that, the life of boys who are part of the *bacha bazi* culture is harsh and unforgiving. They are forced to both dance and participate in homosexual acts. They are bought and sold as though they were chattel. They have no freedom of movement and are subject to harsh physical treatment and punishment at the whim of their owner. Presumably, once these *bacha bereesh* become men, they are free from their life of forced entertainment and sexual encounters. There is very little in the literature that comments on whether or not their *nang* (honor) is completely restored or if they are readily accepted into heterosexual society and can marry. There is certainly no study that shows the possible long-lasting psychological effects of *bacha bazi* on men who spent their entire adolescent years as sexual slaves.

The Body, But Not the Person

A curious aspect of human trafficking is the inclusion of not the whole body but, instead, body parts. In this story, the main part of the human being is left behind, either alive or dead, but one or more of her organs has been removed and transported, to be placed in the body of another person.[*] In fact, the recipient never meets the donor and, presumably, never knows that the organ that is now keeping them alive has been harvested from an unwilling donor, leaving them either without a vital organ, or worse, dead. This is a world that parallels the legitimate buying and selling of organs, or as in the United States, donors placing organs in a bank to be used on either a first-come-first-served basis or by need. *Transplant tourism* is becoming widespread with 109,000 people on waiting lists for transplants, mostly for kidneys, and hundreds die while waiting for a transplant (Bilefsky, 2010). All inclusive package deals can range from $70,000.00 to $100,000.00 (Roberts, 2009). The average annual income in India is $950.00 and a family, or illicit broker, can make $1,000.00 for a kidney. The incentive to harvest is high and the economic disparity between the donor and the recipient is enormous. Like other areas of human trafficking, there are sending countries and receiving countries. On the sending side we find Pakistan, India, China, Philippines, Bolivia, Peru, Israel, Turkey, and Moldova as leading countries. On the receiving side the leading countries are the United States, Japan, Israel, Saudi Arabia, Canada, and Oman (Roberts, 2009). The U.S. strict policy of no sale, or purchase, of organs may prompt those with means to become transplant tourists. Perhaps it is no wonder then, that the United States does not include organ trafficking in its *TVPA* or report on it in its annual blame and shame *Trafficking in Persons Report*, despite it being part of the *Palermo Protocol*. In fact, the United States is the only country not to recognize organ trafficking as a legitimate form of human trafficking (Pugliese, 2007). Stories abound from China where prisoners are executed primarily for their body parts (Woan, 2007) and Africa where children disappear from their villages only to be found eviscerated, their small bodies left on

---

[*] For an official report on the trafficking of human organs and/or body parts see the 2008 UN report available at: http://www.unodc.org/documents/human-trafficking/Marika-Misc/BP011HumanTraffickingfor theRemovalofOrgans.pdf

the side of a dusty trail (see, e.g., Smith, 2009).* The stories are so widespread, that even when proved to be false, can cause deep fear and panic. When the author was in the process of adopting in Ukraine some years ago there was a sudden shutdown of all adoptions by the National Adoption Agency in Kiev. Rumors were flying that Ukrainian orphaned children were being harvested of their organs which were then being sold in Western Europe. The truth turned out to be only slightly better. Ukrainian mothers who had decided to give up their children for adoption at birth were being told that their children had died during childbirth. In reality, the doctors, nurses, and hospitals in some locations were selling those children at a premium price to childless Western European parents seeking to adopt a child. (The buying and selling of children for adoption is yet another widespread human trafficking phenomena only recently being investigated by the United States.)

Unlike other forms of human trafficking, the demand for organs is directly involved in life-and-death situations with the potential recipient facing death without an organ transplant and the donor facing almost certain death from the harvesting of her or his healthy organ. The person whose life has been saved never comes into contact with the person who has been sacrificed. The deep perversity is that the recipient literally keeps alive in their body the mortal remains of what was once a vital, but now discarded, human being.

The World's Sport

Football. Soccer. The world's game. It is difficult to imagine a country on the planet that does not play football with their dreams of 10-year-old players (and the "soccer moms") on lush turf in suburban United States, dusty back lot in Western Africa, or rocky plateau in northern India. All dream of playing for their national team and winning the World Cup. All hope to be the next Pele, Zidane, Marta, Ronaldo, or Hamm, desiring above all desires to have their stories told and retold about the amazing scissor-kick goal, heart-stopping save, or brilliantly timed pass. But the story no one wants to hear in this multibillion dollar industry is about the children who make the balls and the children taken from their homes to foreign lands and abandoned after failing to properly feed the ever voracious maw of world football. In fact, according to the "**FoulBall Champaign**" (see http://www.thirdworldtraveler.com/Reforming_System/FoulBall.html) much of the world's sporting equipment is made with child labor in regions of the world where work standards are virtually nonexistent.

Until 1996, the center of the soccer ball-making world was Sialkot, Pakistan (Hussain-Khaliq, 2004) where thousands of mothers and their children produced balls day in and day out. Children, their families often caught in the cycle of debt-bondage, worked 5–11 h a day sewing balls. In a full day's work they could produce two soccer balls for which they were paid 3–5 rupees per ball (500% less than what the ball retailed for). This was until Schanberg and Dorigny wrote about their plight in the June, 1996 issue of *Life Magazine*. They wrote the story of the conditions of the children, 7000 in Pakistan, 25,000 in India, and their mothers, describing their 6 cents an hour wages and bondage to a naïve and shocked audience. Something good came from the story told in one of the world's most beloved and well-read magazines. There was an immediate outcry and the "FoulBall Campaign" was launched among great fanfare in June 1996 followed shortly by the Atlanta

---

* C. Smith (December 31, 2009). Americans Getting Transplanted Organs from Chinese Inmates. Retrieved March 25, 2011 at http://www.epm.org/resources/2009/Dec/31/americans-getting-transplanted-organs-chinese-inma/

Agreement in 1977 signed by the ILO, UNICEF, and the Sialkot Chamber of Commerce. The agreement called for the prohibition of workers under the age of 15 and for moving the making of soccer balls out of the cottage industry of the home to well-regulated factories. Everyone patted themselves on the back and went home. There was an immediate darker story that emerged from this story of proclaimed success (Khan et al., 2007). Families quickly realized that they had lost a valuable source of income—their children. Mothers had to travel long distances to work at central factories, leaving their children at home uncared-for, and working very long hours under mind-numbing and physically exhausting conditions. Within a short amount of time the soccer ball-making companies moved from the constant watchful eye in Sialkot to the Meerut and Jullander districts in India (van der Schatte Olivier, 2008), where child-labor laws were much more lax and the Atlanta Agreement nonexistent. The roar that greeted the "FoulBall Campaign" became a squeak and eventually faded away altogether.

The next iteration of football and human trafficking then takes place across the planet in Europe. There are estimated to be 20,000 child players brought illegally through Africa into Europe each year. Trafficked players are present in 33 out of 36 UEFA leagues. Africa, which was once exploited for humans during the trans-Atlantic slave trade during the 17th to 19th centuries, then was exploited by the Colonial powers for their rich mineral and forest resources during the 19th to 21st centuries, was once again being exploited. This time neo-colonialism was reaching out to take the resources of talented young football players to lead to the growth of the ever-expanding and vastly rich football economy of Europe. Agents from Europe and within Africa, with little guidance or governance from the African Football Federation, would scour the streets and fields of Africa, promising pure fantasy and wealth, to any child who could do a "round-the-world." They would be taken, perhaps even with joyful parental approval, to unregistered soccer schools (McDougall, 2007, 2008), or, perhaps more correctly, soccer plantations. There they would receive a bit of training, would be fed, given a nice new football uniform, cleaned up, and then smuggled to Europe to try out for teams hungry for new talent. When these starry-eyed young players did not make the cut for the team the agent would unceremoniously dump them on the streets of Europe, with no employment, no money, no passports or travel documents, and no way to get home. It is estimated that in France alone there are 7000 boys and men, 98% of who are illegal immigrants and 70% under the age of 18, who are homeless and on the streets after being cut after tryouts with a football team (see, e.g., Culture Football Solidaire, 2011).

Perhaps the next time Pele's great story of success is told at a World Cup or we buy a new soccer ball when our daughter or son starts their practice season with a promising team, we might do well to remember the story of Adiya in India, or Moussa in Mali. They once shared their dream, their story, with Pele and with us, but their dream turned into a nightmare and their story was lost in the maelstrom of the sports entertainment industry.

Conclusion

Slavery strips away what is so essentially human about each one of us (see Bales, 2007; Bales and Cornell, 2008). Slavery cannot be reduced to a statistic or cold, calculated analysis. We need to connect with the victim and the survivor. This is not to say that we cannot understand many of the issues surrounding the reemergence of slavery under the new rubric called human trafficking by sound methodology, the proper collection of data, and its analysis as reflected in most of the chapters in this collection. This method is important and is, in fact, the basis of the majority of the work of the HTC. We clearly need a sophisticated, multidisciplinary approach (as reflected throughout this book) that combines passion with intellectual rigor. It is precisely because so much of the present work in human trafficking reduces people to statistics that this chapter attempted to both raise issues about dominant forms of forced labor and modern slavery, as well as several lesser known forms through the power of the story of the victims and survivors themselves. The debate will continue as to the efficacy of using the victims' voice.

Some will say that while their stories are helpful at an emotional level that the policy and decision-making to deal with forced labor, human trafficking, and modern slavery should be left to more objective minds. If we do this, then we miss the very important input available to the policy makers, the law makers, from the voices and stories of these victims and survivors. Not only do they indicate a pattern of abuse and techniques used by the traffickers that allows them to effectively create a severe power imbalance, but more importantly the story and voice of human trafficking connects each of us, one-on-one, with those who are suffering and deserve, our sympathy, understanding, compassion, and, most importantly, our action to alleviate their immense suffering.

Review and Critical Discussion Questions

1. Why are the stories of victims and survivors of forced labor, human trafficking, and modern slavery important?
2. What patterns of behavior and circumstance by both the victims and the perpetrators of human trafficking and forced labor can we learn from their stories?
3. What are the definitions from the Taxonomy Project of the Human Trafficking Clinic and how do they differ from the legal definitions as found in documents like the Palermo Protocol and the TVPA?
4. Do you think that there is a difference between "sex tourism" and "romance tourism?"
5. Should the same age criteria apply when discussing sex trafficking and child labor trafficking?
6. Do you think that cultural norms ought to be considered and weighed in understanding forced labor and human trafficking?

References

Abdul-Ahad, G. September 12, 2009. *The Dancing Boys of Afghanistan*. The Guardian. /guardian. co.uk.

Andrees, B. and Belser, P. (Eds.). 2009. *Forced Labor: Coercion and Exploitation in the Private Economy*. NY: Lynne Rienner Pub.

Appiah, K.A. and Bunzl, M. (Eds.). 2007. *Buying Freedom: The Economics of Slave Redemption*. Princeton, NJ: Princeton University Press.

Armstrong, H. C. 2008. *Rebuilding Lives: An Introduction to Promising Practices in the Rehabilitation of Freed Slaves*. Free the Slaves.

Bales, K. 2007. *Ending Slavery: How We Free Today's Slaves*. Berkeley, CA: University of California Press.

Bales, K. and Cornell, B. 2008. *Slavery Today.* Berkeley, CA: House of Anansi Press.

Bilefsky, D. November 15, 2010. Seven charged in Kosovo organ-trafficking ring. *New York Times.*

Blackmon, D.A. 2008. *Slavery by Another Name: The Re-Enslavement of Black People in America from the Civil War to World War II.* New York: Doubleday.

Culture Football Solidaire. 2011. Retrieved April 6, 2011 from: http://www.footsolidaire.org/index/php.

Davidson, J. and O'Connell, J. 2005. *Children in the Global Sex Trade.* Boston, MA: Polity Press.

Edelman, M.W. March 29, 2010. *Haiti's Restavèk Children: The Child Servitude Crisis. The Huffington Post.* Internet newspaper—http://www.huffingtonpost.com/

Farley, M. (Ed.). 2003. *Prostitution, Trafficking, and Traumatic Stress.* Haworth Maltreatment and Trauma Press.

Fisher, J. and Shay, A. (Eds.). 2009 *When Men Dance: Choreographing Masculinity Across Borders.* Oxford, England: Oxford University Press.

Global View: Farm Work is not Child's Play. October 16, 2006. In *Arable Farming.* Retrieved April 18, 2011 from http://business.highbeam.com/411400/article-1G1-152958811/global-view-farm-work-not-child-play

Hochschild, A. 2005. *Bury the Chains: Prophets and Rebels in the Fight to Free an Empire's Slaves.* Chicago, IL: Houghton Mifflin.

Horton, J.O. and Horton, L.E. 2005. *Slavery and the Making of America: Companion to the PBS Series.* Oxford, England: Oxford University Press.

Hosseini, K. 2003. *The Kite Runner.* NY: Riverbend Books.

Hudson, B. 2007. The rights of strangers: Policies, theories, philosophies. In M. Lee (Ed.), *Human Trafficking.* Portland, OR: Willan Pub.

Hussain-Khaliq, S. 2004. Eliminating child labour from the Sialkot soccer ball industry: Two industry-led approaches. *The Journal of Corporate Citizenship* (13) (Spring):101.

ILO. 2010 *Accelerating Action Against Child Labour: Global Report under the Follow-up to the ILO Declaration on Fundamental Principles and Rights at Work.* Geneva http://www.ilo.org/wcmsp5/groups/public/@dgreports/@dcomm/documents/publication/wcms_126752.pdf

ILO, UNICEF, Sialkot Chamber of Commerce. 1997. *Atlanta Agreement: Partner's Agreement to Eliminate Child Labour in the Soccer Ball Industry in Pakistan.* Geneva: International labour Organization.

IOM/BM.I March 2006. *Resource Book for Law Enforcement Officers on Good Practices in Combating Child Trafficking.* Geneva, France: IOM International Organization. Available online at: http://www.ch.iom.int/fileadmin/media/pdf/publikationen/resource_book.pdf

Khan, F. Munir, K., and Willmott, H. 2007. A dark side of institutional entrepreneurship: Soccer balls, child labour, and postcolonial impoverishment. *Organizational Studies,* 28, (7):1055.

Laczko, F. and Gozdziak, E. (Eds.). 2005. *Data and Research on Human Trafficking: A Global Survey.* Geneva, France: IOM International Organization for Migration. (offprint of special issue of *International Migration,* 43 (1/2). Available online at: http://www.iom.int/jahia/webdav/site/myjahiasite/shared/shared/mainsite/published_docs/books/data_res_human.pdf)

Malarek, V. 2004. *The Natashas: The New Global Sex Trade.* Toronto, ON: Penguin.

McDougall, D. June 10, 2007. Inside the football factories that feed the beautiful game. *The Observer.* Retrieved April 12, 2011 from http://www.guardian.co.uk/profile/danmcdougall.

McDougall, D. January 06, 2008. The scandal of Africa's trafficked players. *The Observer.* Retrieved April 12, 2011 from http://www.guardian.co.uk/profile/danmcdougall.

Owed Justice: Thai Women Trafficked into Debt Bondage in Japan. 2000. Human Rights Watch. http://www.humantrafficking.org/publications/64 (retrieved April 6, 2011).

Perrin, B. 2010. *Invisible Chains: Canada's Underground World of Human Trafficking.* Toronto, ON: Viking.

Pugliese, E. 2007. Organ trafficking and the TVPA: Why one word makes a difference in international enforcement efforts. *Journal of Contemporary Health Law and Policy,* 24(1): 181–208.

Rawick, G.P. (Ed.). 1996. *The American Slave: A Composite Autobiography*. Westport, CT: Greenwood Press, 1972–79.

Roberts, E.D. Spring 2009. When the storehouse is empty, unconscionable acts abound: Why transplant tourism should not be ignored. *Howard Law Journal*. 52:749–790.

Sanchez T. J. 2006. Female sex tourism: A contradiction in terms. *Feminist Review*, 83(1), pp. 42–59. www.jstor.org/stable/3874382

Schanberg, S. and Dorigny, M. June 1996. Six cents an hour. *Life Magazine*.

Smith, C. December 31, 2009. Americans Getting Transplanted Organs from Chinese Inmates. Retrieved March 25, 2011 at http://www.epm.org/resources/2009/Dec/31/americans-getting-transplanted-organs-chinese-inma/

UNODC/UN.GIFT. 2009. Global Report on Trafficking in Persons. http://www.ungift.org/doc/knowledgehub/resource-centre/GIFT_Global_Report_on_TIP_2009.pdf)

van der Schatte Oliver, J. and Jetteke, A. October 2008. Child labour in football stitching activity in India: A case study of Meerut District in Uttar Pradesh. *Banchpan Bachao Andolan*.

Woan, S. 2007. Buy me a pound of flesh: China's sale of death row organs on the black market and what Americans can learn from it. *Santa Clara Law Review*, 47(2): 413–444.

Zhang, S. 2007. *Smuggling and Trafficking in Human Beings: All Roads Lead to America*. NY: Praeger Pub.

Zimmerman, Y. C. 2010. From Bush to Obama: Re-thinking sex and religion in the United States' initiative to combat human trafficking. *Journal of Feminist Studies in Religion*, 26(1): 79–99.

Cases Cited

Alberto Justo Rodriguez Licea et al., v. Curacao Drydock Company, Inc 2008 584 F.Supp.2d 1355.

Alien Tort Statute (28 U.S.C.S. § 1350) Racketeering Influenced Corrupt Organizations Act (RICO) (18 U.S.C.S. § 1962).

International Labour Organization (ILO) C138 Minimum Age Convention, 1973.

International Labour Organization(ILO) C182 Worst Forms of Child Labour Convention, 1999.

Ramachandra Adhikari et al., v. Daoud and Partners et al. 2009 697 F.Supp.2d 674.

State of Iowa vs. Leonard Ray Russell (2010 Iowa App. LEXIS 145).

The People v. Rodney Lyndell Tillis (2010 Cal.App. Unpub. LEXIS 958).

Wooten v. Superior Court (2001 93 Cal.App.4th 422, 437).

Helpful Websites

Angel Coalition (MiraMed): http://www.angelcoalition.org/drupal/en

Anti-Slavery International: http://www.antislavery.org/

Coalition of Immokalee Workers (CIW): http://www.ciw-online.org

Coalition to Abolish Slavery and Trafficking (CAST): http://www.castla.org/

Child Sex Tourism Prevention Project—World Vision: http://www.worldvision.org/content.nsf/learn/globalissues-stp

Forced Migration Online: http://www.forcedmigration.org/

Human Trafficking Clinic (Josef Korbel School of International Studies): http://humantrafficking-clinic.org/

HumanTrafficking.org: http://www.humantrafficking.org/

Innocenti Research Centre (UNICEF): http://www.unicef-irc.org/

International Organization for Migration (IOM): http://www.iom.int/jahia/jsp/index.jsp

IOM—Counter-Trafficking: http://www.iom.int/jahia/Jahia/activities/by-theme/regulating-migration/counter-trafficking

IOM at the UN: http://www.un.int/iom/

International Labour Organization (ILO): http://www.ilo.org/global/Themes/Forced_Labour/langen/index.htm
International Rescue Committee: http://www.theirc.org/
Laboratory to Combat Human Trafficking: http://www.combathumantrafficking.org/
Master Human Trafficking Clinic Library:http://www.refworks.com/refshare?site=020081136005200000/RWWEB101388428/HTC%20Master
Migration Policy Institute: http://www.migrationpolicy.org/
National Underground Railroad Freedom Center: http://www.freedomcenter.org/
Organization for Security and Co-operation in Europe (OSCE): http://www.osce.org/cthb/
Polaris Project: http://www.polarisproject.org
UN Interregional Crime and Justice Research Institute (UNICRI): http://www.unicri.it/institute/
UN.GIFT (Global Initiative to Fight Human Trafficking): http://www.ungift.org/
UN Human Rights: http://www.ohchr.org/EN/Pages/WelcomePage.aspx
UN Office on Drugs and Crime (UNODC): http://www.unodc.org/unodc/en/human-trafficking/index.html?ref=menuside
UN Protocol on Trafficking: http://www1.umn.edu/humanrts/instree/trafficking.html
UNICEF: http://www.unicef.org/protection/index.html
U.S. Department of Justice: http://www.justice.gov/crt/about/crm/htpu.php
U.S. Health and Human Services: http://www.acf.hhs.gov/trafficking/
U.S. Law Enforcement—Internet-based Human Trafficking Training: http://www.umcpi.org/index.cfm?option=view&newsitemid=12281&nid=10295&optionid=10295
World Cocoa Foundation: http://www.worldcocoafoundation.org/

Films and Documentaries*

1776 (Columbia TriStar Home Entertainment—2002)
Amazing Grace (Four Boys Films/Walden Media/Bristol Bay Productions—2006)
Anonymously Yours (Berkeley Media LLC/Aerial Productions—2003)
Bling: A Planet Rock (MMVII Image Entertainment/VH1—2007)
Born Into Brothels (Think Film/HBO/Cinemax/Red Light Films—2004)
Call + Response (Fair Trade Pictures—2008)
Child Labor in Brazil (UN/Showtime/RCN Entertainment /Zenger Media—2003)
Child Warriors (Arts & Entertainment Network/History Channel—2008)
Children Underground (Belzberg Films—2003)
China Dolls (Don Barhart Entertainment/Chuklehut Entertainment—2008)
CSA: The Confederate States of America (IFC Films/Spike Lee/Hodcarrier Films—2005)
Dancing Boys of Afghanistan (Frontline/WGBH/More 4—2010)
Dreams Die Hard: Survivors of Slavery in America Tell Their Stories (Free the Slaves/Crisis House—2005)
Dying to Leave (Wide Angle/WNET-New York—2003)
Freedom and Beyond-Bal Vikas Ashram: Freeing Slaves, Fighting Slavery (Free the Slaves—2006)
Global Commute (Invisible Children Inc —2006)
Heading South-Vers le sud (Genius Entertainment—2005)
Human Trafficking (Echo Bridge TV mini-series—2005)
Immokalee: A Story of Slavery and Freedom (Pan Left Productions—2004)
India—The Sex Workers (Frontline—June 2004)
Lilya 4-Ever (Memfis Films/Det Danske Filminstitut—2004)
Lives for Sale (Faith & valies Film/Maryknoll World Publications/Lightfoot Films—2006)
Look Beneath the Surface: Identifying Victims of Human Trafficking in the U.S. (US Department of Health and Human Services—200-?)

---

* Instructors should screen film for age-appropriate content.

Modern Slavery (Free the Slaves—2005)

One Life, No Price—a Bollywood service spot (UN Office on Drugs and Crime—2008)

Rent a Rasta (Yeah But Not Now Productions/International Association of Professional Creators—2006)

Sex Slaves (Columbia Broadcasting System CBS—2006)

Sex Traffic (Granada Television/Big Motion Pictures/Canadian Broadcast Corporation—2004)

Sisters and Daughters Betrayed (Global Fund for Women—1995)

Slavery: A Global Investigation (True Vision Productions/Home Box Office/Free the Slaves/Channel 4—2004)

Slavery and the Making of America (WNET-New York/Ambrose Video Publishing—2005)

Silent Revolution: Sankalp and the Quarry Slaves (Free the Slaves—2005)

Traces of the Trade: A Story of the Deep North (California Newsreel/Ebb Pod Productions—2008)

Trade (Twentieth Century Fox/Lions Gate Films—2007)

Two Marys: Two Views of Slavery (Films for the Humanities and Sciences/BBC Education)—2005

Understanding Trafficking (Ananya Chatterjee-Chakraborty—2009)

Untouchable? (Bullfrog Films/BBC Worldwide Ltd—2000)

Voces Inocentes/Innocent Voices (Warner Home Videos/Muvi Films—2007)

Crime Control versus Social Work Approaches in the Context of the "3P" Paradigm

Prevention, Protection, Prosecution

KARIN BRUCKMÜLLER
STEFAN SCHUMANN

6

Contents

Strategies to Combat and Prevent Trafficking in Human Beings

Surveying international, governmental and nongovernmental reports, scientific articles, and the Internet produces a bewildering variety of approaches to prevent and combat trafficking in human beings (THB). One finds, among others, human rights and victim-centred approaches, criminal justice and law enforcement approaches, free labor approaches, gender-sensitive approaches, and approaches based on women's and children's rights. All these approaches influence the strategies that are at present being employed to combat THB.

Broadly speaking, these approaches can be subsumed under the two categories of *crime control* and *social work/welfare approaches*. Whereas crime control approaches emphasize on the prosecution and the punishment of criminals through criminal proceedings, social work/welfare approaches primarily focus on providing protection and support to victims or other groups of endangered people. Both categories call for a kind of "toolbox" containing measures ("tools") to prevent and combat human trafficking, which will be evaluated, selected, and bundled either from a human right's and victim's point of view or a crime control or criminal justice and law enforcement perspective. While in practice the implementation of social work tools predominantly falls to victim support services, social workers, and nongovernmental agencies, the crime control approach is focused on law enforcement agencies and criminal courts. It is claimed that stakeholders overvaluate their particular approach: Law enforcement officers, and sometimes the legislator itself, are accused to assess victims primarily as witnesses whose statements are needed to detect and prosecute the traffickers. Thereby, victims' needs, which have to be recognized regardless of whether victims are able, or willing, to give their testimony, might be neglected (Women's Commission 2007, p. 1; UNODC 2010a, p. 57). Conversely, police officers sometimes articulate their apprehension that social workers' engagement interferes with the needs of investigation and thereby affects or slows down the detection and prosecution of traffickers. Yet, this chapter will point out that both approaches not only share common roots; but it will be demonstrated that these approaches are not mutually exlusive, rather they must be applied simultanously and coherently.

Whereas the social work approach can easily be associated with strenghtening the victims' human rights, the crime control and law enforcement approach's link to human rights does not seem to be equally obvious. Yet, one must not forget that both perspectives are based on the conviction that trafficking in human beings must be considered a violation of fundamental human rights and human dignity (see Ezeilo 2010; Austin 2007; European Court of Human Rights *Rantsev v. Cyprus and Russia* from 07/10/2010). Both approaches are concerned with the "3Ps"—the prevention of the human trafficking, the protection of victims, and the prosecution of traffickers, as demanded and implemented by various international, regional and national guidelines for combating trafficking in human beings.

Trafficking in Human Beings as a Violation of Human Rights and Human Dignity

The prohibition of trafficking in human beings is an integral part of human rights treaties and other legal instruments, the latter including resolutions of the UN General Assembly as expressions of a globally shared conviction. The prohibition of all forms of slavery, slave-trade, servitude, and, with some restrictions, forced labor, the prohibition of sexual exploitation, the prohibition of organ trade, as well as the children's right to protection and the human right to liberty and security and to respect the dignity inherent to each human being are demanded by human rights instruments such as the *International Covenant on Civil and Political Rights* (1966), the *Universal Declaration of Human Rights*, the *UN Convention on the Rights of the Child* (1989) and its *Optional Protocols*, the ILO's *Worst Forms of Child Labour Convention* (1999)*, as well as the Council of Europe's *European Convention for the Protection of Human Rights and Fundamental Freedoms* (1950) and—as one of the latest transnational human rights treaties—the European Union's *Charter of Fundamental Rights* (2000). The latter explicitly states that "trafficking in human beings is prohibited" (Art. 5 § 3 EU FRC).

In a narrower sense, these human rights treaties demand that law enforcement authorities and other governmental staff must not treat victims in a way that puts them in danger of being victimized a second time. Victims shall be provided with supportive measures (e.g., Declaration of Basic Principles of Justice for Victims of Crime and Abuse of Power 1985). In a broader sense, alongside the United Nations' concept of human security, human rights obligations demand the criminalization of trafficking in human beings and aim to prevent and prosecute those violations of basic human rights and human dignity threatened by other individuals (UNDP 1994, p. 3; UNDP 2009, p. 65). So the human rights treaties and the concept of human security serve more or less as a conceptual basis or a theoretical frame for transnational responses to human trafficking, based on protection, prosecution, and prevention.

Tackling Trafficking in Human Beings: The Extended "3P" Paradigm

In order to fulfill these human rights obligations of protecting victims of human trafficking and of criminalizing human trafficking, there are global as well as regional international agreements that explicitly tackle human trafficking. Demanding measures of prevention, prosecution, and protection, the so-called "**3P**" paradigm serves as the backbone for each of these agreements, while the parallel provisions contained in these agreements differ in details (see Box 6.1). Yet, one should not overlook that these agreements usually form an integral part of international efforts to ensure the criminalization of transnational crime and to improve mutual legal assistance. These agreements might be seen as an explanation for the actual assessment of the "3Ps" in those treaties. We will return to this notion when analyzing the crime control and the social work approach in the sections that follow. Not only do parallel provisions in the various treaties differ in details; in fact, the level of obligation of the provisions within a specific treaty ranges from mandatory measures and measures that State parties must consider applying or endeavor to apply to measures that are optional (UNODC 2004, p. 248).

Since trafficking in human beings is often (though not exclusively) transnational in nature, coordination and cooperation between States is indispensable (see Chapter 10, this volume). Therefore, by attempting to implement the 3Ps, there are various needs for "cooperation" or "partnership" (see UNODC 2009, pp. 12, 45–52); one might speak of the "3P plus C" or the "4P" paradigm (Mattar 2006, p. 15; Clinton 2009).

---

* See also ILO Forced Labour Convention, 1930, and ILO Abolition of Forced Labour Convention, 1957.

BOX 6.1   DIFFERENCES OF OBLIGATIONS IN THE PALERMO PROTOCOL

Article 5. Criminalization

1. *Each State Party shall adopt such legislative and other measures* as may be necessary to establish as criminal offences the conduct set forth in Article 3 of this Protocol, when committed intentionally.

Article 6. Assistance to and protection of victims of trafficking in persons

1. *In appropriate cases and to the extent possible under its domestic law,* each State Party shall protect the privacy and identity of victims of trafficking in persons, including, inter alia, by making legal proceedings relating to such trafficking confidential.

Article 7. Status of victims of trafficking in persons in receiving States

1. In addition to taking measures pursuant to article 6 of this Protocol, each State *Party shall consider adopting legislative or other appropriate measures* that permit victims of trafficking in persons to remain in its territory, temporarily or permanently, in appropriate cases.
2. In implementing the provision contained in paragraph 1 of this article, each State Party *shall give appropriate consideration* to humanitarian and compassionate factors.

This extended paradigm can be found in the UN Protocol to Prevent, Suppress and Punish Trafficking in Persons, especially Women and Children, supplementing the United Nations Convention against Transnational Organized Crime, the so-called Palermo Protocol, from 2000, which is the principal legally binding global instrument to combat THB. Likewise the paradigm was picked up on a regional international level by the EU Council Framework Decision on Combating Trafficking in Human Beings from 2002 and finally by the CoE Convention on Action against Trafficking in Human Beings,[*] signed in Warsaw in 2005. Collectively, these instruments are of binding nature and oblige their State Parties to take the necessary measures at the domestic level.

The various instruments take their direction for measures from each other: Roughly it can be said that regional agreements tend to be more detailed than the global one (e.g., the EU law specify which sanctions shall be applicable while the UN protocol simply demands for sanctions that take into account the gravity of the offence). It has to be assumed that the generally closer framework of police and judicial cooperation in criminal matters within the EU alleviates deeper harmonization than a global treaty-making process allows for (see Chapter 8, this volume; Schumann 2011). Furthermore, posterior treaties tend to go beyond prior ones; unlike the CoE convention from 2005, the posterior EU law from 2002 does not include trade of organs as a means of committing THB. After the CoE Convention

---

[*] See also the CoE Protection of Children against Sexual Exploitation and Sexual Abuse (2007).

came into force, a recent proposal for adapting the EU law includes trade of organs, too (EU Proposal 2010)*, which seems to be consequential since all EU Member States except for the Czech Republic signed the CoE Covention.

Overall, strategies to combat and prevent THB are specified by both transnational and national action plans. Those plans outline the preferred strategies and specify the legislative and practical measures to be taken—measures from the "toolboxes" of the crime control approach and of the social work approach. Transnational action plans such as the *United Nations Global Plan of Action to Combat Trafficking in Persons* (UN 2010), the *African Union's Ouagadougou Action Plan to Combat Trafficking in Human Beings, Especially Women and Children* (African Union, 2006) and the *EU Plan on Best Practices* (EU 2005) are enacted. Furthermore, as of 2009, almost 50% of the countries evaluated by the UNODC have put forward a national action plan against THB (UNODC 2009, p. 9).

The legal and practical implementation of these initiatives is the responsibility of the authorities of the different States and of international organisations (IOs) and nongovernmental organisations (NGOs).

As explained above, the extended "3P" paradigm derives from the need to respond to human trafficking as a violation of human rights and from the need for an effective and transnational criminal justice response to a crime of mostly transnational character. It is the benchmark for effective approaches to combat human trafficking. Therefore, in the following part of this chapter the crime control approach and the social work approach will be analyzed by using the "3Ps."

Crime Control Approach

What's Behind All This?

It has already been said that **crime control approaches** emphasize the penalization of THB and on the prosecution and punishment of the traffickers. Legislators should comprehensively criminalize THB, and police, public prosecutors, and judges should aim to arrest and punish people traffickers. While the focus lies on crime control measures, effective criminalization, prosecution, and punishment are deemed to contribute to victims' protection. Based on a more traditional idea of criminalization they are presumed to have a deterrent effect on prospective offenders and preventing prospective acts of THB (see below: Prevention and Protection). In some legal systems the idea of retribution continues to play a leading role as regards criminalization and prosecution.

Prosecution

The buzzword of "**prosecution**" serves as a generic term which covers both the comprehensive criminalization of acts of THB and the effective detection and investigation of such acts and the prosecution of the offenders (see Chapter 7, this volume).

---

* After this chapter was finalized, the new Directive 2011/36/EU of the European Parliament and of the Council of April 5, 2011 on preventing and combating trafficking in human beings and protecting victims, and replacing Council Framework Decision 2002/629/JHA was agreed, OJ EU 2011 L101/1. It entered into force on April 15, 2011 and will have to be transposed into Members States' domestic laws by April 6, 2013 at latest.

Comprehensive Criminalization

The international agreements, such as the Palermo Protocol, the EU Framework Decision, and the Coe Convention, provide explicitly for each State Party to adopt such legislative and other measures as may be deemed necessary to establish human trafficking as an offence punishable under criminal law. This applies in particular to cases where control of a person is obtained or exercised with a view to their sexual exploitation, their exploitation as forced labor or as organ donors, their enforced marriage, or the adoption of a child. All forms of trafficking shall be made punishable by domestic laws. As offenders shall be regarded not only those who committed an act of trafficking in person, but also those who instigated someone to do so or supported a trafficker. At the same time, rules on the applicability of national criminal laws oblige the states to actually prosecute crimes that fall under their jurisdiction according to spatial or personal criteria.

The UN Palermo Protocol (Art. 5) in conjunction with its "mother" convention (United Nations Convention Against Transnational Organized Crime) demands sanctions that take into account the gravity of the offence, and similarly both the CoE Convention (Art. 23) and the EU Framework Decision (Art. 3) oblige State parties to implement "effective, proportionate and dissuasive criminal penalties"—a phrase shaped by the European Union Court of Justice (ECJ case 68/88 Commission/Greece, ECR 1989, 2965) inspiring treaties, negotiations, and interpretations far beyond Europe's borders. The crime of trafficking in persons is punishable by a prison sentence as a matter of principle. This is expressly stipulated in the mentioned European documents. The EU Framework Decision goes even further. It demands that those who commit an act of THB under specified, aggravating circumstances such as endangering the victim's life or trafficking particularly vulnerable victims are punishable with terms of imprisonment of not less than eight years. The CoE Convention demands in these cases the assumption of aggravating circumstances to be written into national law. For the punishment of legal entities such as travel or recruitment agencies, monetary sanctions and other effective measures are available.

From a conceptual perspective human trafficking is deemed punishable because it violates the rights of the trafficked individual. Nevertheless, there is international consensus that such an act be punishable regardless of whether the victim has consented to being trafficked or exploited or not; it is the trafficker who remains culpable in all cases (UN Palermo Protocol Art. 3b, EU FD Art. 1, CoE Conv. Art. 4). Acts of cross-border trafficking, which is almost the norm, can concurrently constitute an infringement of border security. Yet, this infringement of an elementary state interest is addressed primarily by criminalizing the smuggling of migrants (see Chapter 2 on the difference between THB and smuggling of migrants).

Effective Detection and Prosecution

Even the establishment of a comprehensive criminalization of trafficking in persons by as many states as possible worldwide does not automatically guarantee the desired effect. Any deterrent effect depends on how the pertinent laws are enforced: The most important factors are the probability of detection and of prosecution and the sentencing of the offenders.

In order for the States to effectively enforce the criminal legislation for traffickers, what is needed first of all is for law-enforcement authorities to develop an appropriate awareness. Law-enforcement agencies must become aware both of how widespread trafficking is and what different forms it could include. They must develop to be in a position to recognize cases of trafficking and victims of trafficking. They must be able to distinguish between victims of transnational trafficking in persons from "run-of-the-mill" illegal immigrants so that they can make sure that the victims get the protection they need (see below: social work approach) and that the criminals who are responsible for their plight are caught. This cannot be achieved without adequate training and financial and human resources (UN Palermo Protocol Art. 10; UNODC 2009a,b).

In the light of this complex, three-tier structure of trafficking—the act itself, the exploitation of the victim, and the element of force— it is necessary to also include the training of the skills required to secure the evidence that is necessary to convict the criminals.

The comprehensive training of the members of the pertinent law-enforcement authorities should be complemented by the establishment of special antitrafficking police units, as is demanded, for instance, by the UN Palermo Protocol. Fifty-four percent of 155 States worldwide have already established such special units (UNODC 2009, p. 8), which are designed to improve the chances of the prosecution and conviction of criminals on the one hand, and the identification of victims on the other.

In daily practice, during crackdowns in the red-light milieu, or on illicit employment, priority should be given to identifying individuals who have been trafficked. This will make possible the shift of the detection of both offenders and victims from the gray zone into the open.

Prevention and Protection

The crime control approach is based on the assumption that criminalizing human trafficking as comprehensively as possible will reduce the probability of its incidence and that—following the classical idea of criminalization—prosecution is indeed a factor that contributes to prevention. The preamble of the UN Palermo Protocol underlines "that the protocol shall ensure effective action to punish the traffickers and to protect the victims," otherwise "persons, who are vulnerable to trafficking will not be sufficiently protected" (Preamble §§ 1, 3). Those who are vulnerable to trafficking are potential prospective victims. Resorting to criminalization and punishment with the aim of reducing the danger of actual victimization is considered a measure of protection against victimization. Sentencing criminals to an adequate punishment is intended to have a deterrent effect both on the convicted criminal (special prevention) and on other potential offenders (negative general prevention).

In addition to pursuing the goal of **prevention** and in keeping with the general aims of punishment, the investigation of a specific crime is regarded to contribute directly to preventing additional crimes: As trafficking in human beings, in most cases, is part of organized crime, the arrest and punishment of a criminal attempts to interrupt the smooth functioning of the operative network of a criminal gang. Removing at least one of the actors may render such a network dysfunctional and therefore potentially prevents it from committing further crimes, at least for the time being. However, it is a reasonably well-documented fact that detecting and prosecuting offenders of organized crime is very difficult (see Chapter 7). Detecting and prosecuting offenders might support the identification of their victims, thus allowing for essential support. Hence, the de facto protection of victims might be sort of a side effect within the crime control approach.

Cooperation

To yield satisfactory results, structures must be provided that are required for the collaboration between police authorities, criminal prosecuting authorities and customs and finance authorities, also including victim support organizations. Mechanisms that reflect the seriousness of trafficking are needed for the exchange of information between these authorities. This will contribute not only to the likelihood of a prosecution and conviction in concrete cases, but also to shedding light on the typical structures of relevant criminal acts and groups of criminals and transfer routes (e.g., Europol 2006, pp. 17–18). This kind of information will prove valuable as a basis for crime prevention and crime detection in future.

What has been mentioned above also applies to cross-border cases. These especially entail the necessity of effective cross-border cooperation of criminal prosecuting authorities. Such cooperation needs to take place both at bi- and multilateral levels. Networked forms of centralized and decentralized cooperations are needed and have in part already been established. This applies, for instance, to Interpol. Examples of especially close cooperation can be found within the European Union. Following a "strategy of the shortest routes" (Schumann 2011), contacts between the various agencies involved in transnational cases typically associated with THB are focused on being as direct as possible. The European Police Office Europol in The Hague has been designed to function as a centralized institution capable of handling the collection, evaluation, and exchange of information of THB cases, offenders, suspects, and other relevant facts. The Member States' authorities have a comprehensive duty to pass relevant information on to Europol. Each Member State has a competent national authority in its country and a liaison officer at Europol in The Hague, who is responsible for the exchange of information. These police experts, who are recruited from all Member States, are located in The Hague, and they are familiar with their Member State's legal and law enforcement system and entitled to use their powers. This makes it possible for national police forces to cooperate in concrete cases with a maximum efficiency while using Europol's assistance and resources. The establishment of joint investigation teams are another form of transnational cooperation, which is demanded both by the UN Palermo Protocol and by EU law (UNODC 2010, Chapter 4). Hence, THB is one of the most important areas for the application of this form of investigation.

Does it Work? The Crime Control Approach in Practice: Achievements and Problems

In this section we will analyze which achievements can be made by using a crime control approach to human trafficking. Likewise the inherent problems of a pure or unbalanced crime control approach will be discussed.

Prosecution

Legislation

Even though a consensus has been reached regarding the establishment of THB as a criminal offence, there are differences in the scope of its definition in the above-mentioned international agreements. Not all legislations, for instance, include the trade in organs. As mentioned earlier, the version of the EU Framework Decision that is currently still binding does not consider the trade in human organs as an element of the trafficking in persons; however, an appropriate amendment has already been proposed (EU Proposal 2010).

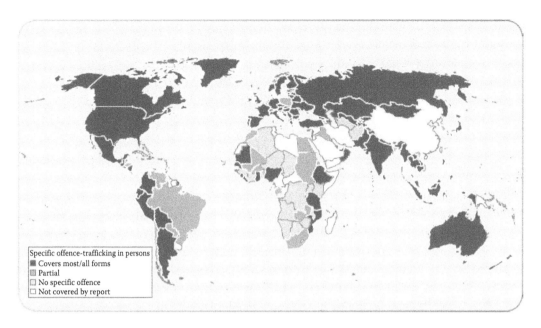

Figure 6.1 Criminalization of trafficking in persons—status of national legislation, by country (November 2008). (From UNODC. 2009. *Global Report on Trafficking in Persons*. http://www. unodc.org/documents/Global_Report_on_TIP.pdf [accessed January 2011]. With permission.)

An interstate comparison of the adoption by individual States of the establishment of trafficking in persons as a criminal offence reveals differences (UNODC 2009, p. 9; FRA 2009, p. 58). The UNODC global report on human trafficking from 2009 criticizes that a number of African countries still do not have legislation that penalizes, or penalizes comprehensively, THB. They might, for example, only criminalize some aspects, such as child trafficking. But this is also true for some of the wealthier countries with more established social and political infrastructures (e.g., Brazil, Estonia, Poland; see Figure 6.1). Criminalization often depends on political will (see Chapter 10 for further disussion).

In addition to these differences in content, we may also note different formal approaches to the transposition of THB into national law: Some legislatures have opted for a specific rubric of "trafficking in persons" or introduced an additional rubric of "trafficking in minors"; others have been content not to make trafficking in persons punishable per se; rather, THB is to be subsumed under a combination of various constellations of elements of crime and is made punishable in this way (UNODC 2009, pp. 8–9; FRA 2009, pp. 57–8).*

For these types of initiatives to be efficacious the worldwide implementaion of these criminal law regulations is regarded to be important, if not necessary. Yet, as of November 2008, only 63% of 155 countries worldwide have provisions against trafficking in persons, punishing the prevalent forms of trafficking such as sexual exploitation and forced labour, with no restrictions as to the victim's age or gender, in their Penal Codes (UNODC 2009, p. 8).

The differences in the definitions of trafficking in persons that we have noted in the international documents are exacerbated by the transposition into national law; they make

---

* This includes intrastate trafficking as a matter of principle.

comparison more difficult both with regard to how the law copes with trafficking in persons and the actual incidence of trafficking on a global and even regional level (to the problem of lack of data: BM.I/IOM 2009; UNODC 2009, p. 18).

As regards aggravating circumstances, again the transposition into national criminal law leads to another set of considerable differences, this time in the threat of punishment (UNODC 2009, pp. 8–9; FRA 2009, pp. 64–7). Usually aggravating circumstances are explicitly assumed, or the crime carries a greater threat of punishment in cases where children or other particularly vulnerable persons are trafficked (UNODC 2008).

In addition to the offenders themselves, the individuals who actually exercise power over the victims, all accessories such as job agencies or dating agencies involved in the case, are likewise guilty of trafficking, even if they have never been in personal contact with the victim.

Trafficking persons often requires the cooperation of travel agencies, job agencies, employers, and other businesses. Consensus prevails in the international agreements that such legal entities may also become culpable and may need to be punished as offenders. The demanded sanctions extend all the way to winding down the businesses in question. In practice, however, the prosecution and punishment of legal entities often runs up against problems, either because no provisions exist, as in some domestic legal orders, there are no rules on criminal liability of legal entities, or because the application of the corresponding laws is still fraught with difficulties.

Suggestions to ensure that those individuals who use the services of a prostitute (even if they know—or must at least seriously consider as a possibility—that they are dealing with a victim of trafficking) should be punished [see also Malarek (2010) for further discussion on this issue] have also been proposed. The debate over whether the clients of prostitutes who are victims of trafficking are also punishable is an ongoing one, especially in countries such as Germany or Sweden (FRA 2009, p. 59).

Prosecution and Conviction Statistics

Drawing on available data, the prosecution and conviction statistics do not support definitive conclusions as to the efficacy of measures to combat THB. The same applies to the crime control approach, as statistics do not reflect the number of cases of THB or how many potential offenders refrained from committing crimes because of the drive for the criminalization of THB. What the figures do reflect, however, is the current level of prosecution. According to a UNODC study from 2009, the global picture is this: "91 countries (57% of the reporting countries) reported at least one human trafficking prosecution, and 73 countries reported at least one conviction per year. A core of 47 countries reported making at least 10 convictions per year, with 15 making at least five times this number" (UNODC, 2009, p. 8) (see Figure 6.2).

According to UNODC, Vietnam has one of the highest conviction rates for traffickers in the world, the reason being that a great deal of effort was put into training law enforcement authorities (also see Chapter 10).* Interestingly, statistics show that, compared to other criminal offences, a disproportionately large number of women play key roles as offenders in traffickers' networks (UNODC 2009, p. 10).

Although in Europe about 1500 criminal proceedings for trafficking were carried out in 2006, and about 3000 victims were assisted in the EU (mostly in Italy, Belgium and

* http://www.unodc.org/unodc/en/human-trafficking/prosecution.html.

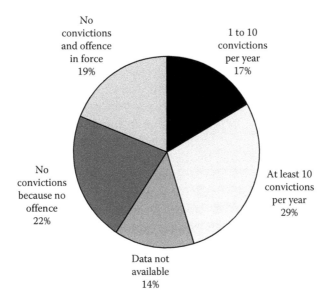

Figure 6.2 Distribution of all countries according to the number of convictions recorded for the specific offence of trafficking in persons during the reporting period. (From UNODC 2009. *Global Report on Trafficking in Persons.* http://www.unodc.org/documents/Global_Report_on_TIP.pdf [accessed January 2011]. With permission.)

Austria),* the prosecution and conviction figures quoted above appear negligible compared to the (estimated) numbers of victims. "Worldwide for every 800 people trafficked, only one person was convicted in 2006."† There are a number of different reasons and problems that account for this state of affairs: There still appears to be a lack of specific and/or adequate legislation on trafficking in persons in the national legislations, which is one of the major obstacles for both an effective intrastate crime control approach and an effective transnational law enforcement cooperation. Moreover, trafficking in persons was not introduced as an offence into most criminal law systems until quite recently. In most countries, THB was included in the Criminal Code after the Palermo Protocol came into force (UNODC 2009, p. 36; UNODC 2006). As a result, criminal prosecutors have not had much time or opportunity to become sufficiently familiar with the offence for it to be actually applied. To solve such problems, so-called "Joint Investigation Teams" were built with the support of Europol and Eurojust in Europe. These teams are networks of national experts, which i.a. share experiences and best practices. They also share decisions of prosecuting human trafficking. Although the legal situation throughout Europe is very familiar due to the EU Framework Decision harmonizing Member States' law and therefore Member States'

---

* http://ec.europa.eu/cyprus/news/speeches_articles/20101029_index_trafficking_en.htm. It is not easy to estimate the extent of victims of human trafficking. The "dark figure" is a very high one, "because criminal activities related to trafficking are hidden behind widespread phenomena such as prostitution or immigration. According to a research of the ILO, there are at least 2.45 million people in forced labour as a result of trafficking in persons worldwide.

† UN.GIFT, Human Trafficking, The Facts: http://www.unglobalcompact.org/docs/issues_doc/labour/Forced_labour/HUMAN_TRAFFICKING_-_THE_FACTS_-_final.pdf

authorities could learn from each other the prosecution of offenders has not increased significantly.

Another problem is that frequently the elements of exploitation and the use of force are not taken into account and the criminal acts are judged solely as instances of "smuggling" or under some other partial aspect. In cases in which victims of trafficking in persons are not recognized as such, offenders are very rarely brought to justice, if at all. What causes additional problems is the fact that in some cases the victim does not know the offender and/or the network of offenders or he/she is unable to identify the offender. This is of course aided and abetted by the very structure of organized crime. Often the evidence is insufficient to secure the offender's conviction for THB. In some countries the drive for criminalization and actual prosecution suffers from the fact that trafficking generates a great deal of money. The annual profit of human trafficking for the purpose of forced labor, including commercial sexual exploitation, is estimated to be $30 billion (ILO 2005, p. 46).

Prevention and Protection

Deterrence Does Not Work

As mentioned above, crime control is seen as well as a form of general and specific **deterrence** and should thereby prevent further victimization. However, practice and the literature show that criminalization and penalization is not a very effective means by which to deter somebody from (re)committing an offence.

Tackling Related Crimes: Criminalizing Victims of THB

An overzealous crime control approach is not without dangers for the victims of THB. Comprehensive criminalization of trafficking in human beings is frequently complemented by separate drives to establish as criminal offences acts that are either included in wider definitions of THB or associated with it, such as illegal border crossings, smuggling human beings, accepting employment illegally, prostitution or making use of the service of prostitutes, child labor and moonlighting. Criminalization in these cases, while it helps to combat THB, is primarily designed to serve other state interests, notably the control of immigration, protecting border regimes and the management of the inland revenue and the welfare state. In practice, however, the effects resulting from these measures may be a mixed blessing. It is quite common for those measures of criminalization to affect victims of THB, and the risk for this to happen is heightened by the tendency of criminal prosecution authorities to single out these forms and collateral materializations of trafficking for investigation (UNICEF 2008).

Legal interests that are protected by the establishment of these criminal offences, such as high immigration thresholds (Chacón 2010) and high thresholds for legal employment (see Pope 2010, pp. 1489–75), may make it even easier for potential migrants or illegal immigrants to become victims of trafficking. Lower migration thresholds and easier access to the labor market would presumably have a preventive effect. Both legal and illegal migration pressure can only be alleviated by supportive measures applied in the typical countries of origin.

The policies of a complete ban on prostitution and of the punishability of the clients of prostitutes are still a source of contention. The supporters of these policies contend that clients of prostitutes are obliged to accept it as a possibility that they are dealing with a victim of trafficking in persons. The policies are supposed to reduce the demand for the services of prostitutes, thereby also reducing the economic incentive for acts of trafficking in the form of sexual exploitation.

Protection for Victim-Offenders

At least in Europe, most victims of THB are not identified straightaway as victims, but as offenders by the police or in criminal proceedings. Subsequent to their trafficking, victims are often made to work as thieves, drug dealers, prostitutes or illicit workers. From a police perspective, they have committed a crime and are therefore predominantly offenders. During the first interrogation at the earliest, police officers realize—sometimes with the help of NGO members—that the offender might also be a victim to human trafficking. In contrast to the classic bipartite scenario, with its clear distinction between the roles of offender and victim, there is in such cases one person, the victim-offender, who simultaneously plays both roles.

For these special cases international guidelines (UNODC 2009b, Art. 10) and the draft EU Directive (EU Proposal 2010) stipulate that victims of trafficking should be exempt from being charged with concomitant crimes (see Box 6.2).

For example, a charge against a victim of human trafficking for using false identity papers to enter a country should be dropped by the police or the prosecutor as soon as possible. This applies especially to those civil law countries where prosecutors are otherwise committed to the principle of compulsory prosecution. They have basically no choice but to bring charges, also against victims of THB. Conversely, in a common law system it is up to prosecutors to decide based on opportunity reasons whether they will pursue charges or not (also see Chapter 8, this volume).

As has been illustrated in this subsection, the topic of victim-offenders is a very complex one. This is partly due to the fact that prosecutors are liable to find themselves at odds with public opinions that might be in favor of a prosecution, especially in cases where a crime committed by a victim-offender results in another victim (e.g., a victim of theft). If charges are pursued against a victim-offender, the possibility must be taken into account that the victim-offender, even though he or she is facing trial as a criminal at that stage, may be a traumatized victim, who must be protected against secondary victimization in the course of his or her testimony.

Therefore, it is worth considering whether it may not be advisable to give such victim-offenders the benefit of certain victim's rights, to which they are entitled to on the basis of their status as victims of THB, already in proceedings conducted against them as offenders. This would mean, for example, that victim-offenders are entitled to psychological and medical assistance, or that the police and the authorities in charge of the criminal proceedings are obliged to do everything in their power to prevent a revictimization of victim-offenders (Bruckmüller 2006).

Based on the demonstrated issues in this section, one has to say that a pure and unbalanced crime control approach does not work sufficiently and effectively. This evaluation is supported by the low rates of prosecution and conviction of THB.

Social Work Approach

What's Behind All This?

The protection of and support for victims of the kind envisaged by the social work and/ or welfare approaches aim to rescue, rehabilitate and reintegrate victims of human trafficking.

In a broader sense, the **social work approach** also includes preventive measures designed to preclude victimization. Appropriate measures include raising awareness both on the part of potential victims and the general public, and all kinds of improvements in

BOX 6.2   NON-PROSECUTION OF VICTIM-OFFENDERS

Council of Europe Convention on Action Against Trafficking in Human Beings
Article 26
Each Party shall, in accordance with the basic principles of its legal system, provide for the possibility of not imposing penalties on victims for their involvement in unlawful activities, to the extent that they have been compelled to do so.

Proposal for a Directive of the European Parliament and of the Council on preventing and combating trafficking in human beings, and protecting victims, repealing Framework Decision
Article 7
Nonprosecution or Nonapplication of Penalties to the Victim
Member States shall, in accordance with the basic principles of its legal system, provide for the possibility of not prosecuting or imposing penalties on victims of trafficking in human beings for their involvement in criminal activities they have been compelled to commit as a direct consequence of being subjected to any of the acts referred to in Article 2.

US Trafficking Victims Protection Act of 2000, 18 U.S.C.
§ 7101—sec. 102(17), (19)
Victims of trafficking should not be "penalized solely for unlawful acts committed as a direct result of being trafficked, such as using false documents, entering the country without documentation, or working without documentation."

UNODC Model Law against Trafficking in Persons
Article 10
1. A victim of trafficking in persons shall not be held criminally or administratively liable (punished) (inappropriately incarcerated, fined or otherwise penalized) for offences (unlawful acts) committed by them, to the extent that such involvement is a direct consequence of their situation as trafficked persons.
2. A victim of trafficking in persons shall not be held criminally or administratively liable for immigration offences established under national law.
3. The provisions of this article shall be without prejudice to general defenses available at law to the victim. .
4. The provisions of this article shall not apply where the crime is of a particularly serious nature as defined under national law.

the living conditions in the countries of origin. Finally, the social work approach does not preclude the prosecution of the traffickers; rather, the prosecution of the offenders can help victims to be identfied and to get access to justice.

The social work approach involves the criminal prosecution authorities to the same extent as does the crime control approach; it is, after all, these authorities who are in charge of the first contact with victims of trafficking. Where the implementation of a social work approach differs from the crime control approach is the involvement of other state agencies, such as the authorities responsible for migration issues, and medical and social services. Significant contributions to the implementation of a social work approach also come from nonstate institutions such as NGOs, self-help groups of former victims of trafficking and charitable organizations, in short, from the so-called civil society.

Protection

The need for and rights to protection of victims of THB have to be followed both by laws and practical measures and need to be center stage of the social work approach. However, victims of THB will receive appropriate protection not until they have been identified as such.

Identification of the Victims

The identification of victims is the precondition for an effective social work approach that offers victims assistance on their road towards rehabilitation and social integration. This can only be achieved if the identification as victims is followed immediately by other aspects of the social work approach coming into play, such as psychological treatment by appropriately trained staff.

However, a word of caution is deemed appropriate here. In practice, as stated earlier, it is often difficult to identify victims of human trafficking (CoE Rec 2008). In most cases, victims are liable to be suffering from the consequences of intimidation and traumatization to such an extent that they are unable to talk candidly about their situation even to the police or in court. Furthermore, in some cases, people might not even be aware that they are in fact victims of trafficking, for example, if exploitation is not subjectively experienced by them as such (see Chapter 12, this volume).

Law-enforcement agencies are called upon to play a key role here (see Chapter 7, this volume). Victims are typically apprehended by the police as offenders in either a criminal activity that has been forced upon them by their handlers or in one of the transgressions that frequently accompany trafficking, such as illegal border crossing or illegal sojourn in the country. This is the reason why the training of members of law-enforcement agencies must be given high priority to (UN Palermo Protocol; CoE Convention; EU Plan 2005). Specifically in cases involving children as potential victims, it is absolutely necessary to call in psychologically trained experts. To help the police identify an offender as a victim, guidelines with telltale indicators should be made available (see UNODC 2009b, Art. 18). In practice, it may prove helpful for the police in their everyday work to involve NGO personnel specially trained in the identification of THB victims.

What is also considered necessary is a raised level of general awareness about THB (see Box 6.3). The sensitization of individual members of the public may very well contribute

---

BOX 6.3   PREPARING MATERIALS FOR RAISING AWARENESS

- Include all relevant information, for example methods of recruitment, focus on successful prosecutions in Member States,
- Be aimed at identified target groups, including children,
- Be based on real case studies,
- Consider approaches needed within and outside the EU, and
- Be aimed at reducing demand.

Campaigns have to be evaluated for effectiveness (EU Plan 2005).

to the identification of victims, especially in certain types of seasonal work (e.g., seasonal farm work), in certain types of employment (e.g., catering and domestic services), in the low-pay manufacturing sector in developing or emerging countries or in the adoption of foreign children in western countries (EU Plan 2005). As an expression of concern and a demonstration of intent, the UN has launched its "Blue Heart Campaign" to draw attention to THB and its victims worldwide.

Protection and Support

The social work approach is particularly focused on the victims' need for protection and support. This includes both establishing certain rights of protection and participation as a law and making sure that pragmatic measures are put into place to guarantee compliance.

In accordance with what has already been said, international agreements require the countries that join them to provide for protection of and support to victims. The obligation resulting from these agreements varies between mandatory requirements, which refer above all to the physical protection and safety of the victims and their access to justice, and optional requirements to those provisions designed to support the victims' physical, psychological, and social rehabilitation once their more immediate needs have been met. The former are designed to make sure that the victims are no longer in harm's way, that they take part in the criminal proceedings against their traffickers and that they become eligible for compensation for the harm that has been done to them. The implementation of the optional measures must be considered, for instance by the State Parties to the UN Palermo Protocol; it is, however, up to the national legislature to decide whether, in what form, and to what extent to implement them. As far as the pragmatic measures are concerned, the States are given a considerable amount of maneuvering space.

As also argued in Chapter 12, victims of THB are entitled to all the same rights that are granted all crime victims. At the most basic level, this includes the right to be treated with respect for one's personal dignity and for one's personal integrity as well as, for example, the right to access to justice. Children have the additional right to have their age and developmental stage taken into account (UNODC 2008, pp. 71–2).

In addition to this, the special needs of victims of THB shall be taken into account. Those needs arise because the victims are mostly in a foreign country and under a very strong domination of an offender. The international documents provide for example, for the right to a residence permit. These special needs should be a matter of concern for the legislative branch of government without losing sight of the implementation of practical measures to provide for the physical, psychological and social recovery of victims (such as secure accommodation). These measures shall be provided for in cooperation with NGOs, where appropriate. Which specific measures are actually offered to victims of THB is a matter to be decided by each particular State (see, e.g., UN Palermo Protocol Art. 6; UNODC 2009b, Art. 18); often such a decision is mainly a question of money.

In the following, those rights and measures for victims of human trafficking, which are recommended by the international guidelines and the UN Model Law against Trafficking in Persons to guarantee an extensive protection, will be analyzed. In doing so, typical victims rights as well as special rights for victims of THB attract interest.

Safety and Privacy

The safety and the private life of the victim have to be protected in a comprehensive manner. High priority has to be given to appropriate and secure accommodation. In cases where these are required, both medical treatment and psychological support (UNODC 2008a, p. 20) must be provided free of charge (see UN Palermo Protocol Art. 6; UNODC 2009b, Chapter VII; CoE Conv Art. 11; EU FD Art. 7*).

If the criminal proceedings result in a trial in which the victim is to give evidence as a witness, the victim and his/her relatives and/or other persons close to him/her need to be offered protection. In particular, data protection is crucial for victims of THB, since misuse of the data may endanger the life and safety of victims and their relatives. In some countries, so-called "restricted notes" have been introduced; a system that allots numbers to the victims' data (UNODC 2009b, Art. 18). Only selected officials know the identity of the person behind the number. If there is reason to assume that data protection in itself will be insufficient, it is incumbent on the authorities to offer also physical protection, such as relocating and permitting residence to the victims.

Access to Justice
The victim has to be granted access to justice (see UN Palermo Protocol Art. 6†), which entails, among other things, the right to be present throughout the trial against their perpetrators. The criminal proceedings and the trial have to be conducted in a manner that precludes the victim's secondary victimization and a further traumatization.

Special methods should enable the victim to give evidence without coming face to face with the offender. CCTV, for example, makes it possible for the court to follow the victim's testimony. Holding the main trial in camera is another measure to protect the victim (UNODC 2009b, Art. 23). Some countries provide legal and psycho-social assistance for victims during the entire trial to facilitate the access to justice for especially vulnerable victims.‡

Restitution and Compensation
The victim has to be awarded restitution or compensation (UN Palermo Protocol Art. 6; CoE Conv Art. 25; UNODC 2009b, Art. 28, 29). The offender is obliged to offer victims, their families or dependants fair compensation for losses suffered. The victim's possessions must be returned or restitution must be made in the form of payment for the harm or losses suffered and for the reimbursement of expenses resulting from victimization. In cases where public officials or other agents acting in an official role are involved in trafficking, it is up to the State to satisfy the victim's claims.

Compensation by the State (or by a fund) should satisfy the claims put forward by all (or at least by certain) groups of victims if the offenders in question are unable to make the requisite payments. Families that have lost one of their members to death as a result of trafficking should also be entitled to claim compensation payments.

Right to Comprehensive Information
For victims to be able to make use of these rights and measures, they have to be comprehensively informed about all the rights they are entitled to and about the assistance and the support that is actually available for them (UN Palermo Protocol Art. 6, 7, CoE Conv Art. 25, UNODC, 2009b, Art. 19§). An interpreter is to be provided for if needed.

---

* In connection with EU Council Framework Decision of March 15, 2001 on the standing of victims in criminal proceedings (2001/220/JHA), Art. 8.
† See also EU Council Framework Decision on the standing of victims in criminal proceedings, Art 3.
‡ EU Council Framework Decision on the standing of victims in criminal proceedings, Art 6.
§ See also EU Council Framework Decision on the standing of victims in criminal proceedings, Art 4.

Recovery and Reflection Period

Each State should create their own legal, or other appropriate, measures which permit victims of trafficking in persons to remain at least temporarily in their territory. Deportation proceedings based on migration law—where they have been set in motion already—should at least be postponed temporarily. The victim should be given the benefit of a recovery and reflection period (UN Palermo Protocol Art. 7, CoE Conv Art. 13, UNODC 2009b, Art. 30).

Such a period shall be sufficient for the person concerned to recover and escape the influence of traffickers and also to take an informed decision on cooperating with the competent authorities. A policy of nonpunishment is necessary to ensure that victims of human trafficking develop a relationship of trust with state authorities to allow the victims to escape their dependence on their traffickers (FRA 2009, p. 154).

The duration of this period is specified in the Convention of the Council of Europe with at least 30 days. The UN Model Law proposes 90 days.

Residence Permit

In practice, the question of whether a victim of human trafficking shall be granted a residence permit is highly controversial. The UN Palermo Protocol demands that each State Party should consider adopting those measures, and in doing so the Party shall give appropriate consideration to humanitarian and compassionate factors. Yet in practice, a victim's cooperation with the law-enforcement agencies in the criminal proceedings against the traffickers is considered a precondition for even a temporary, limited residence permit to be issued. For example, the EU Directive on the Residence Rights of Victims of THB requires Member States after the expiry of the reflection period to assess the benefits presented by a prolonged stay of the victim in the country for investigation or judicial proceedings and to reach a decision on whether the victim has shown a clear intention to cooperate.[*]

In the meantime one has to consider that this respective regulation shall be without prejudice to the protection granted to refugees, to beneficiaries of subsidiary protection and persons seeking protection under international refugee law as well as other human rights instruments. It does not detract from the prerogatives of the Member States as regards the right of residence granted on humanitarian or other grounds (Reasonings 4, 5).

Reintegration

At the end of the day, victims of THB should be reintegrated into society either in the destination country—if they are given a permanent residence permit—or in their country of origin. Coping with the problems caused by repatriation requires cooperation with organizations in their countries of origin.

The UN Protocol demands that the State Party of which a victim of human trafficking is a national or in which the person had a right of permanent residence shall facilitate and accept the return of that person without undue or unreasonable delay (UN Palermo Protocol Art. 8). The state shall also provide the necessary travel documents. While it is paramount that such return shall be with due regard for the safety (privacy, dignity, and health) of that person and for the status of legal proceedings related to the fact that the person is a victim of human trafficking, the consent of the victim is not seen as obligatory.

---

[*] EU Council Directive on the residence permit issued to third-country nationals who are victims of trafficking in human beings or who have been the subject of an action to facilitate illegal immigration, who cooperate with the competent authorities 2004, Art. 8.

The Protocol does state however that such return shall preferably be voluntary (UNODC 2009b, Art. 33, UN Palermo Protocoll Art. 8).*

Prevention of THB in general and the protection of victims of THB in particular are interrelated tasks. The latter must not only exclude secondary victimization during the criminal proceedings, but it should aim at avoiding revictimization, too. In this aspect it is a special way of prevention. Revictimization often lurks if a victim of THB is repatriated without appropriate measures being taken, even if this is done with the victim's consent (U.S. Department of State 2010, p. 18).

Bilateral or regional agreements or arrangements between the countries of origin and the destination countries are to be concluded to make safe repatriation possible. This will pave the way for the reintegration of repatriated victims of trafficking in persons and for the reduction of the risk of revictimization through THB. It is also necessary to harmonize the activities of victims' support groups in the countries of origin and the destination countries. This will make a "soft landing" in their countries of origin easier for victims.

Prevention and Cooperation

In addition to the above-mentioned reintegration as an element of prevention, it is important to strengthen the political dialog between destination countries and countries of origin on the human rights dimensions of antitrafficking policies. Therefore, gender-specific prevention strategies as a key element to combat trafficking in women and girls (e.g., broader measures especially against poverty, insecurity and exclusion, and gender inequalities) should be promoted. This includes implementing gender equality principles and eliminating the demand for all forms of exploitation, including sexual exploitation and domestic labor exploitation (UN Palermo Protocol, Chapter III; CoE Conv Chapter II; EU Plan 2005).

What is also crucial is the early identification of victims to prevent their exploitation and to reduce the demand for trafficked persons in destination countries. Therefore, it is important to study trafficking routes and strengthen operational responses: for example, border agencies should develop common strategies, and cooperate closely to identify victims. Also information seminars should be held (e.g., with the airline industry or immigration services). Human trafficking for labor exploitation requires new types of specialization and cooperation with partners (e.g., agencies responsible for the control of working conditions and financial investigations related to illicit employment). In addition to all this, raising awareness will sensitize people to the solicitations of traffickers and for the task of identifying victims.

In addition to cross-border cooperation, it emerges from what has been said that if the needs of victims of THB are to be met, support is required from many different sides, which can only be achieved through a multiagency approach (UN.GIFT 2008). What is particularly important is the establishment and involvement of IOs, NGOs and especially of victim support organizations capable of leading these efforts and of coordinating and monitoring them. It is indeed the case that in many States, groups specialized in offering support to victims of THB have already formed, which reflects the fact that these types of victims typically require help in ways that are specific to the group.

---

* Any decision to return a victim of trafficking in persons to his or her country shall be considered in the light of the principle of non-refoulement and of the prohibition of inhuman or degrading treatment.

Prosecution

The social work approach does not oppose prosecution. Rather prosecution, even from the perspective of the social work approach, might contribute to the protection of victims and endangered people by arresting, detaining, and punishing the offenders. There is an interaction among social work measures and prosecution conversely to some laws on (restricted) granting of residence permits: the better the vicitims feel protected, the higher the change to get a usable testimony to convict the offender (UNODC 2010a, p. 38).

Does it Work? The Application in Practice: Achievements and Problems

As limited as it is applied in today's practice, the social work approach seems not to be working any more than the crime control approach. The reasons, besides there not being enough money for appropriate and comprehensive support and protection measures, are the focus of the following.

Protection and Prevention

As has already been pointed out, one of the greatest challenges lies in identifying victims as such to give them the benefit of assistance and protection. However, even if someone has been identified as a victim, the basic situation in most countries only allows protection measures that tend to focus on short-term assistance to victims (UNICEF 2008). In most cases, this short term does not exceed the recovery and reflection period and even this is usually tied to the victim's readiness to cooperate with the law-enforcement agencies.

It must however be borne in mind that what victims of THB need in particular is continuous support in the form of mutually adapted measures. Many countries lack the money to pay for such measures, and a rupture occurs in most cases when victims have been repatriated and are not backed up at home in the way that would be required.

Prosecution

An additional problem is the Janus-faced nature of state authorities. The police, for instance, typically find themselves in a double-bind situation. On the one hand, they have identified someone as a victim and want to alleviate their predicament; on the other hand, they need—as a criminal-prosecuting authority—to extract from that person the most detailed evidence possible to incriminate the offender and, with another turn of the screw that makes their situation even more conflicted, they also might need to investigate the offence committed by the THB victim in his or her role as a criminal. Training can certainly relieve some of the tensions here.

In general, the same applies to the authorities responsible for migration. They are faced with the conflicting tasks of, on the one hand, checking the victim's status as a migrant, which may result in his/her deportation, while, on the other hand, they also have to pass verdict on that person's request for a residence permit. Migration law tends to pose an insurmountable barrier or it makes it at least very likely that those who are typically at risk of becoming victims of THB fail to qualify for legal immigration. This means that very restrictive use is made of permanent residence permits for victims of THB.

NGOs frequently complain that they are either not involved at all or at least not sufficiently closely in the evaluation of international agreements and their efficacy and that this means that victims of THB are deprived of an important representative (NGO 2010). The result is a skewering of the evaluation results in favor of the perspective of the law-enforcement agencies and a corresponding neglect of complementary perspectives (GAATW 2010, p. 5). Efficacy is measured primarily in terms of crime control.

Is "Versus" What We Need? Opportunities Created by Melding the Two Approaches

Are the two approaches of crime control and social work compatible or mutually exclusive (see Box 6.4)? As demonstrated, both approaches do not work separately, and hence this is a question that holds a high degree of practical relevance.

There might be a certain apprehension on the part of some law-enforcement agencies that an excessive amount of victim protection and victim rights, which also aim to prevent secondary victimization, might lead to a state of affairs where the victim may no longer be used as a source of evidence and that this might imperil criminal persecution altogether. The extent to which the victim's testimony can be made use of in the trial often clinches the success of the criminal persecution. This is why granting a right of residence to victims is linked in several international agreements to the victim's willingness to testify before law-enforcement agencies.

From the point of view of victim protection, however, the dependence of a (frequently only temporary) right of residence on compliance with law-enforcement agencies might impinge on the victim's human right to protection. An exclusive concentration on the crime control approach in combating human trafficking moreover entails the danger that the victims of human trafficking are not recognized, treated, and offered protection as such. This is particularly relevant in cases where victims are implicated in a criminal offence in their capacity of victim (prostitution; smuggling; accepting paid employment without work permit; crossing borders without valid papers). In all these instances of crimes committed by a victim-offender, a victim becomes a criminal in the eyes of the law and in practice the status of a victim of human trafficking is frequently not discovered or rejected.

BOX 6.4   SUCCESSFULLY COMBATING THB: EXAMPLES OF COMBINING THE CRIME CONTROL AND SOCIAL WORK APPROACH

Presumed victims of THB shall be questioned in joint interviews by a law enfocement officer together with a member of a (human trafficking) victim support. The close cooperation of a police officer and social workers will help to identify victims of THB, while preventing the revictimization during the interrogation. In countries where the interviews are not conducted jointly, nevertheless the police should contact a member of a victim support service, so that he or she can offer the victim comprehensive support.

Police, prosecutors, and judges have to be aware of the victim's/witness's vulnerability during the whole proceeding, especially by questioning and when the victim testifies. An atmosphere of understanding and a questioning without pressure or a hearing in another room with audio/video link can ensure that the witness feels protected, so that he or she is in the condition to testify without psychological difficulties and revictimization. Such an atmosphere brings forward a usable testimony and helps to convict the offender. (UNODC 2010a, p. 38 and 43, UNODC 2008b, pp. 21–2)

It is important for States to recognize that trafficked persons who face immediate deportation or arrest will not be encouraged to come forward, report the crime, or cooperate with the competent authorities. Granting a recovery and reflection period—including corresponding rights, and regardless of whether or not there is a prior readiness to give evidence as a witness—assists States both in the protection of the human rights of trafficked persons and in prosecuting offenders: The protection of basic rights also serves to raise the victim's confidence in the State and its ability to protect his or her interests. A victim with confidence in the State is more likely to make an informed decision and cooperate with the authorities in the prosecution of traffickers. If a victim is put under pressure to press charges immediately, the risk increases that he or she will withdraw the statement at a later stage. A recovery and reflection period is in the interest of both the victim and the authorities to enable proper identification and to start or proceed with investigations.

With respect to child victims of human trafficking it is explicitly demanded that the best interest of the child victim should be a primary consideration for legislation. It has to be recognized that for States important interests are at stake in combating crime and in regulating immigration. However, these policy goals should not be allowed to overshadow the best interests of child victims to trafficking (FRA 2009).

Approaching trafficking from a single perspective often limits the ability to adequately respond to its complexity and to take into account the various needs of victims and society. Obviously, it is imperative to combine crime control and social work approaches: The more victims feel empowered by victim protection, the more prepared they will be to cooperate with law-enforcement agencies and the more adept they will become at doing so.

Questions

1. What is needed to identify traffickers and trafficked persons?
2. Can THB be prevented with these approaches? If so what is needed to do so?
3. Do you believe there is a gain of combining law enforcement and victim-centered approaches to combat THB? If so what is the surplus?
4. Does a balanced crime control and victim-centered approach work out in practice?
5. Should the victim's willingness to cooperate in the investigation be precondition to gain a residence permit? Should the residence permit be limited to the time of the criminal proceedings?

References

Austin, M. 2007. *Human Trafficking a Human Rights Violation and Security Risk.* http://www.america. gov/st/washfile-english/2007/February/20070212140713HMnietsuA0.1229059.html (accessed January 2011).

BM.I/IOM. 2009. *Guidelines for the Collection of Data of Trafficking in Human Beings, Including Comparable Indicators.* Vienna, Austria: BM.I.

Bruckmüller, K. 2006. *The Victim Offender. How to Treat a Young Offender, Who is a Victim Himself.* http://www.oijj.org/plantilla.php?pag=091402 (accessed January 2011).

Chacón, J. F. 2010. Tensions and trade-offs: Protecting trafficking victims in the era of migration enforcement. *University of Pennsylvania Law Review* 158, 1609.

Clinton, H. 2009. *Partnering Against Trafficking.* http://www.state.gov/secretary/rm/2009a/06/125009. htm (accessed January 2011).

Europol. 2006. *Trafficking of Women and Children for Sexual Exploitation in the EU*. Den Haag.

Ezeilo, J. N. 2010. *Promotion and Protection of All Human Rights, Civil, Political, Economic, Social and Cultural, Including the Right of Development*. Report submitted by the Special Rapporteur on trafficking in persons, especially women and children, A/HRC/14/32.

FRA. 2009. *Child Trafficking in the European Union. Challenges, Perspectives and Good Practices*. http://www.fra.europa.eu/fraWebsite/attachments/Pub_Child_Trafficking_09_en.pdf (accessed January 2011).

GAATW. 2010. *Feeling Good About Feeling Bad ... A Global Review of Evaluation in Anti-Trafficking Initiatives*, http://www.gaatw.org/publications/GAATW_Global_Review.FeelingGood.AboutFeelingBad.pdf (accessed January 2011).

ILO. 2005. *A Global Alliance Against Forced Labour*. Global Report under the Follow-up to the ILO Declaration on Fundamental Principles and Rights at Work 2005. http://www.ilo.org/public/english/standards/relm/ilc/ilc93/pdf/rep-i-b.pdf (accessed January 2011).

Malarek, V. 2010. *The Johns: Sex for Sale and the Men Who But it*. Toronto: Key Porter.

Mattar, M. Y. 2006. *Comprehensive Legal Approaches to Combating Trafficking in Persons: An International and Comparative Perspective—The Protection Project*. PP-Chartbook.

NGO. 2010. Joint Statement to be delivered at the close of the UNTOC 5th Conference of Parties (October 18–22, 2010, Vienna, Austria).

Pope, J. G. 2010. A free labor approach to human trafficking. *University of Pennsylvania Law Review* 158, 1849.

Schumann, S. 2011. EU police and judicial cooperation, the Lisbon treaty reform and the Stockholm Programme—Towards a simulation of intra-state conditions? In P. Bárd (Ed.). *Terrorism and the Rule of Law*, forthcoming.

UNDP. 1994. *New Dimensions of Human Security, Human Development Report 1994*. New York, NY. http://hdr.undp.org/en/reports/global/hdr1994/ (accessed January 2011).

UNDP. 2009. *Overcoming Barriers: Human Mobility and Development; Human Development Report 2009*. New York, NY. http://hdr.undp.org/en/reports/global/hdr2009/chapters/ (accessed January 2011).

UN.GIFT. 2008. *Multi-Agency Synopsis of Mandates and Research Activities Related to Combating Human Trafficking*. New York, NY. http://www.ungift.org/docs/ungift/Multy-Agency_Synopsis.pdf (accessed October 2011).

UNICEF—Innocenti Research Centre. 2008. *Child Trafficking in Europe. A Broad Vision to Put Children First*. http://www.unicef-irc.org/publications/pdf/ct_in_europe_full.pdf (accessed January 2011).

UNODC. 2004. *Legislative Guides for the Implementation of the United Nations Convention against Transnational Organized Crime and the Protocols thereto*. New York, NY. http://www.unodc.org/unodc/en/treaties/CTOC/legislative-guide.html#_Full_Version_1 (accessed October 2011).

UNODC. 2006. *Toolkit to Combat Trafficking in Persons. Global Programme against Trafficking in Human Beings*. http://www.unodc.org/pdf/Trafficking_toolkit_Oct06.pdf (accessed January 2011).

UNODC. 2008. *An Introduction to Human Trafficking: Vulnerability, Impact and Action*. Background Paper, New York, NY. http://www.unodc.org/documents/humantrafficking/An_Introduction_to_Human_Trafficking_-_Background_Paper.pdf (accessed October 2011).

UNODC. 2008a. *Human Trafficking. An Overview*. New York, NY. http://www.ungift.org/docs/ungift/pdf/knowledge/ebook.pdf (accessed October 2011).

UNODC. 2008b. *Good Practices for the Protection of Witnesses in Criminal Proceedings Involving Organized Crime*. New York, NY. http://www.unodc.org/documents/organized-crime/Witness-protection-manual-Feb08.pdf (accessed October 2011).

UNODC. 2009. *Global Report on Trafficking in Persons*. http://www.unodc.org/documents/Global_Report_on_TIP.pdf (accessed January 2011).

UNODC. 2009a. *Anti-Human Trafficking Manual for Criminal Justice Practitioners*. http://www.unodc.org/unodc/en/human-trafficking/anti-human-trafficking-manual.html (accessed January 2011).

UNODC. 2009b. *Model Law against Trafficking in Persons*. http://www.unodc.org/documents/human-trafficking/UNODC_Model_Law_on_Trafficking_in_Persons.pdf (accessed January 2011).

UNODC. 2010. *Trafficking in Persons and Smuggling of Migrants*. Guidelines on International Cooperation. UNODC.

UNODC. 2010a. *Human Trafficking in the Baltic Sea Region: State and Civil Society Cooperation on Victims' Assistance and Protection*. New York, NY. http://www.unodc.org/documents/human-trafficking/CBSSUNODC_final_assessment_report.pdf (accessed October 2011).

UNODC. (no year specification). *First Aid Kit for use by Law Enforcement Responders in addressing Human Trafficking*. http://www.unodc.org/unodc/en/human-trafficking/publications.html?ref=menuside (accessed July 2011).

U.S. Department of State. 2010. Trafficking in Persons Report. 10th ed. http://www.state.gov/documents/organization/142979.pdf (accessed July 2011).

Women's Commission for Refugee Women and Children. 2007. *The U.S. Response to Human Trafficking: An Unbalanced Approach*. http://www.humantrafficking.org/uploads/publications/ustraff.pdf (accessed January 2011).

Helpful Web Links

List of publications including materials on law-enforcement training and victim support: http://www.ungift.org/knowledgehub/en/publications.html (accessed January 2011)

About the need of a victim-centered monitoring mechanism to the United Nations Convention against Transnational Organised Crime and its protocols, including the Human Trafficking Protocol: http://www.victimcenteredmechanism.com/ (accessed January 2011)

Interviews with victims of THB to show underlining the importance of a victim centered approach: http://www.unmultimedia.org/radio/english/detail/96624.html (accessed January 2011)

List of reports on law enforcement activities to prevent and combat human trafficking: http://www.europol.europ a.eu/index.asp?page=publications&language= (accessed January 2011)

Legal References

African Union's Ouagadougou Action Plan to Combat Trafficking In Human Beings, Especially Women and Children 2006. http://www.regjeringen.no/upload/kilde/ud/rap/2006/0172/ddd/pdfv/301551-tripolifinal.pdf (accessed January 2011).

CoE Convention on Action against Trafficking in Human Beings 2005. http://www.coe.int/t/dghl/monitoring/trafficking/Docs/Convntn/CETS197_en.asp#TopOfPage (accessed January 2011).

CoE Convention on the Protection of Children against Sexual Exploitation and Sexual Abuse 2007. http://conventions.coe.int/Treaty/Commun/QueVoulezVous.asp?NT=201&CL=ENG (accessed January 2011).

CoE European Convention for the Protection of Human Rights and Fundamental Freedoms 1950. http://conventions.coe.int/treaty/Commun/QueVoulezVous.asp?NT=005&CL=ENG (accessed January 2011).

CoE Recommendations on Identification to Services of Victims of Trafficking in Human Beings 2008. http://www.humantrafficking.org/uploads/publications/council_eur_08_rec_identi_0408.pdf (accessed January 2011).

Declaration of Basic Principles of Justice for Victims of Crime and Abuse of Power 1985. http://www.un.org/documents/ga/res/40/a40r034.htm (accessed January 2011).

ECJ Case 68/88 Commission/Greece, ECR 1989, 2965. http: //eur-lex.europa.eu/smartapi/cgi/sga_doc?smartapi!celexplus!piod!CELEXnumdoc&lg=en&numdoc=61988CJ0068 (accessed July 2011).

EU Charter of Fundamental Rights 2000. http://www.europarl.europa.eu/charter/default_en.htm (accessed January 2011).

EU Council Directive on the residence permit issued to third-country nationals who are victims of trafficking in human beings or who have been the subject of an action to facilitate illegal immigration, who cooperate with the competent authorities 2004. http://eur-lex.europa.eu/LexUriServ/LexUriServ.do?uri=CELEX:32004L0081:EN:HTML (accessed January 2011).

EU Council Framework Decision of March 15, 2001 on the standing of victims in criminal proceedings (2001/220/JHA). http://eur-lex.europa.eu/LexUriServ/LexUriServ.do?uri=OJ:L:2001:082:0001:0004:EN:PDF (accessed January 2011).

EU Council Framework Decision on Combating Trafficking in Human Beings 2002. http://europa.eu/legislation_summaries/employment_and_social_policy/equality_between_men_and_women/l33137_en.htm (accessed January 2011).

EU Plan on best practices, standards and procedures for combating and preventing trafficking in human beings 2005. http://eur-lex.europa.eu/LexUriServ/LexUriServ.do?uri=OJ:C:2005:311:0001:0012:EN:PDF (accessed January 2011).

EU Proposal for a Directive of the European Parliament and of the Council on preventing and combating trafficking in human beings, and protecting victims, repealing Framework Decision 2002/629/JHA 2010. http://eur-lex.europa.eu/LexUriServ/LexUriServ.do?uri=CELEX:52010PC0095:EN:HTML (accessed January 2011).

ILO Abolition of Forced Labour Convention 1957. http://www.ilo.org/ilolex/english/convdisp1.htm (accessed January 2011).

ILO Forced Labour Convention 1930. http://www.ilo.org/ilolex/english/convdisp1.htm (accessed January 2011).

ILO Worst Forms of Child Labour Convention 1999. http://www.ilo.org/ilolex/english/convdisp1.htm (accessed January 2011).

International Covenant on Civil and Political Rights 1966. http://www2.ohchr.org/english/law/ccpr.htm (accessed January 2011).

UN Convention on the Rights of the Child 1989. http://www2.ohchr.org/english/law/crc.htm (accessed January 2011).

UN Global Plan of Action to Combat Trafficking in Persons 2010. http://www.un.org/ga/president/64/issues/ht/input160610.pdf (accessed January 2011).

Universal Declaration of Human Rights 1948. http://www.un.org/en/documents/udhr/index.shtml (accessed January 2011).

UN Protocol to Prevent, Suppress and Punish Trafficking in Persons, especially Women and Children, supplementing the United Nations Convention against Transnational Organized Crime—Palermo Protocol 2000. http://www.unodc.org/unodc/en/treaties/CTOC/index.html#Fulltext (accessed January 2011).

Human Trafficking and Police Investigations

7

ANNETTE HERZ

Contents

Introduction

According to Interpol, estimates have placed human trafficking (HT) and illicit migration as a $28 billion enterprise, steadily catching up with drug and arms trafficking (see www. interpol.int). The total number of victims of cross-border trafficking is now estimated at 600,000–800,000 per year, or 2–4 million if *victims* of internal trafficking are included

(UN/IOM 2010). With regard to a 2010 UNODC report, it is estimated that 140,000 human beings in Europe alone become victims of HT with a view to sexual exploitation every year, thus having yielded a profit of approximately $3 billion. Since the late 1980s and the Fall of the Iron Curtain, trafficking in human beings especially for the purpose of sexual exploitation is increasingly in the focus of the public as well as of politics within Europe. In Europe, Germany and Russia are regarded as the main countries of origin and/or destination for trafficking in women for the purpose of prostitution (see IOM 2000; Oberloher 2003; UN/IOM 2006).

Due to the reports of politicians and representatives of the law enforcement authorities as well as various scientific examinations, it is confirmed that the field of crime "*trafficking in human beings*" (THB) has established itself also in Germany and Russia as part of a worldwide illegal market and that groups of offenders—linked to organized crime and acting at international level—systematically organize the recruitment, (illegal) entry, and exit of the women concerned (Sieber and Boegel 1993; Hofmann 2002; UN/IOM 2006).

As indicated in the Introduction to this volume, trafficking in human beings is one of the most despicable offences because the offenders intentionally use the helplessness of the victims and violate their human dignity, freedom, and physical integrity. The classification of criminal acts into the category trafficking in human beings may vary according to the penal provisions in the respective countries. In principle, the relevant regulations focus on activities in connection with the recruitment and selection of persons for the purpose of sexual or other forms of exploitation. On the basis of the UN Protocol of 2000 (see below), universal trafficking in human beings is defined by three elements: First, the offence comprises the recruitment, transportation, transfer, harboring, and/or reception of persons. Second, in the case of full-aged victims, qualified instruments of crime must be given, such as threat or use of violence or other forms of coercion, exploitation of particular helplessness. Finally, the offender must act with the intention to exploit another person.

An important aspect is the clear distinction between human trafficking (HT) and smuggling of aliens (also see the Introduction to this volume). Although a personal state of distress of a person is frequently exploited in the case of alien smuggling as well, there is a difference between trafficking in human beings and the smuggling of aliens as regards the legally protected interests. Whereas the legal provisions against HT focus on the right of self-determination of the individual, those against alien smuggling concentrate on the integrity of national borders and consequently, not on the interests of the smuggled person because the latter is not regarded as the victim but as the offender in that case.

It is, for example, the police that encounter regularly potential victims of HT when they conduct their occasional checks in the "Red-light" districts commonly found throughout Europe. The police officers in the appropriate departments must be sensitized accordingly to discover and assess indications for trafficking in human beings, to secure evidence and to deal with the special needs of the victims—for example, by establishing contact in a timely manner with a counseling service specialized in rendering assistance to victims of HT; in contrast to other *police investigations*—for example, in the field of drug trafficking where usually a lot of so-called "objective evidence," such as the discovery of drugs or material *witnesses* is available—police depends, in HT cases, on the statement of the victim to prove the guilt of the offender. The key witnesses in trafficking crimes are also the victims, and in most cases have been at least psychologically (if not physically) traumatized. Questioning these victims often requires special techniques and training that takes account of this trauma (see also Chapter 12). From that point of view there are parallels to the investigations in other fields of sexual violence.

Despite the presumed high number of HT victims in Germany and Russia, police statistics do, however, only speak of a comparatively small number of such offences committed every year. The number of cases recorded by police is said to reflect only a part of the actual extent of HT. The assumption of a large number of unreported crimes (i.e., "dark figure" of crime) is based on the following observations:

- Criminal investigation into HT cases is generally complex and time consuming.
- Besides the fact that such cases are often related to the jurisdiction of other countries because of the nature of the crime, it is often difficult to see through the structures of the criminal groups because they are generally very well organized.
- It is, however, not only the central but also a very problematic role of the victimized witnesses that impairs successful investigations (also, see Chapter 12). The victims' ability and willingness to testify as well as the credibility of their testimony are often limited. As will be shown subsequently, this is due to their illegal status, their often basic willingness to migrate, intimidation by the offenders, as well as the fact that many women consent to work as prostitutes, at least temporarily. In order to understand the motivation of the persons concerned it is—on the one hand—necessary to take into account the so-called "push factors" as general socio-economic factors that force the persons concerned to emigrate (e.g., because they are underprivileged, jobless, poor, or have become victims of disasters). On the other hand there are the "pull factors" that make the country of destination attractive under various aspects (e.g., economic prosperity, a better earning potential, demand of prostitution) (see Han 2000; Hofmann 2002).
- HT is often mixed up with or reduced to the smuggling of migrants and triggers conflicting roles of criminal and border police.

These observations raise questions as to how prosecution in HT cases is implemented in practice and how the various authorities deal with these criminal offences (see Chapter 8 for further discussion).

The first section of this chapter provides an overview of the most relevant supranational recommendations and obligations as well as support structures regarding the criminal prosecution of HT [i.e., UN, EU, Organization for Security and Co-operation in Europe (OSCE), Europol and Interpol]. By using Germany and Russia as examples for this chapter, the author will show how two prominent European countries of destination (Germany) as well as origin, transit and destination (Russia) for HT implement these international guidelines on a national basis. The various characteristics of criminal proceedings in HT cases will be discussed. Specifically, the section which reviews how investigations are typically initiated as well as how they develop conducted. The section which describes what types of problems of investigation and evidence arise in practice to the effect that—regardless of numerous initiatives and efforts on the international and national level to successfully combat HT—figures of police statistics on trafficking cases remain low and will likely be on that level in the future. Finally, since sexual exploitation is by far the most commonly identified form of HT (79%), followed by forced labor (18%), this chapter focuses on the former (UNODC 2009).

An essential problem with regard to the prosecution of HT is due to the different suppression approaches of many countries in this field: is HT a punishable offence at all, what criminal activities can be subsumed under the generic term HT, and what sentences are imposed? Therefore, the penal prosecution in HT cases differs from state to state because of the varying degrees of professionalization of the investigative and judicial authorities which depend on the importance that is awarded to that field of crime and/or whether it is prioritized at all. For example, it has been shown over the years that the objectives of the investigative authorities (i.e., the sustainable dismantling of the groups of offenders organizing HT in numerous cases and operating at the international level) can only be achieved by a harmonization of the legal provisions, a close cooperation in the course of investigations and a comparable degree of professionalization of the investigative authorities.

Effective measures to enhance law enforcement cooperation between countries affected by a trafficking case require the need and capacity to establish channels of communication, and enhancing information exchange. For example, in relation to the *organized crime* groups that are involved in HT, it is necessary to establish cooperation around the specific means and methods used by such groups. Information exchange can pertain to the travelling routes and conveyances used; and information pertaining to the use of false identities, altered or forged documents or other means of concealing criminal activities (e.g., providing items or evidence necessary for analytical or investigative purposes or promoting the exchange of law enforcement officers including the posting of liaison officers).

Due to the special and difficult role of the victims in HT proceedings and the high significance of their witness statements to prove the guilt of the offenders, all victim-related regulations are automatically also of central importance for successful investigations in such cases which are, therefore, also described hereafter.

International and Supranational Levels

International regulations regarding the handling of HT victims in the individual states have existed for more than 100 years.[*] Since then, lots of conventions, protocols, guidelines, and recommendations have been adopted. They deal with numerous aspects which are also of central importance for the authorities in charge of the prosecution of HT cases in the States Parties. This can include, among other elements, the kind of criminal acts to be subsumed under the term HT, the close exchange of information about offence and offender structures among the national law enforcement authorities, mutual transnational investigations in the case of internationally operating groups of offenders, the handling of HT victims in view of their possible illegal residence status and protection against the offenders, agreements among the States Parties on the return of the victims to their mother countries, as well as preventive measures (see, e.g., Kreuzer 2001).

Based on the UN Protocol of 2000, an overview of the subsequent activities on international and supranational levels, relevant for the prosecution of HT will be discussed next.

UN Protocol of 2000

The UN 2003 *Protocol to Prevent, Suppress and Punish Trafficking in Human Beings* constitutes the preliminary conclusion of international codifications for the suppression

---

[*] The International Agreement for the Suppression of the "White Slave Traffic" with the purpose to provide effective protection against the criminal traffic in women and girls of 1904—adapted later on by the UN, is the first international convention dealing with the suppression of human trafficking.

of HT. The reason for the necessity of the UN Trafficking Protocol mainly indicated by its authors was the fact that all previous agreements* had failed to cover "all HT aspects" in the framework of a generally valid convention. This failure is intended to be rectified by the objectives outlined in Article 2 (i.e., the prevention and suppression of trafficking in human beings in special consideration of women and children, protection and support of HT victims and furtherance of cooperation between the States Parties) (see Vlassis 1998).

Attention will now shift to a short description of the relevant provisions regarding HT prosecution in the Protocol.

First Universal Definition of HT

Article 3 of the Trafficking Protocol can be regarded as the most important achievement because it contains for the first time a definition of the term "trafficking in human beings"—and it is as such the basis for the adaption of the appropriate penal provisions in the States Parties and makes the *international cooperation* in HT proceedings easier. As already stated above, according to the Protocol trafficking in human beings is made up of three elements. First the recruitment, second any form of coercion and finally, the offender's intention to exploit another person.

The term exploitative relationship in prostitution is extended to the exploitation of manpower in general and the removal of body organs. In accordance with Article 5, all States Parties have the obligation to take all measures necessary to criminalize HT including attempted crime liable to prosecution.

Victim Protection

As stated above, the statement of an HT victim is in most of the cases the primary evidence to prove the guilt of the offender. Due to the difficult situation of many victims, which prevents them from making a statement toward the police (i.e., illegal stays, desire to earn money, and therefore a willingness to cooperate with the offender/s, and intimidation by the offender/s), one provision of the Trafficking Protocol is to avail victims the necessary protection and to ensure the status of the victim during court proceedings (also see Chapter 12). The Protocol herewith tries to account for the special importance of the HT victims' willingness to cooperate during police investigations and in the penal proceedings in order to identify and convict the offender. The Protocol addresses, in detail, the protection of privacy and the identity of the victim. Under Article 6(1), the identity of the victim has to be guaranteed, if necessary, by means of a trial closed to the public. In accordance with Article 6 (3) and (5), the Signatory States have the obligation to guarantee the physical and mental welfare as well as the physical integrity of the victim with explicit emphasis on the importance of a cooperation with NGOs. Finally, in accordance with Article 7 No. 1, the receiving States consider the issue of provisional or permanent residence permits in appropriate cases (see, e.g., Gallagher 2001).

---

* For example, The International Agreement on Fighting the Trafficking of Girls (1904), International Convention for the Suppression of Traffic in girls (1910), International Convention for the Suppression of Trafficking in Women and Children (1921), International Convention for the Suppression of the Traffic in Women of the Full Age (1933) as well as the Convention for the Suppression of the Traffic in Persons and the Exploitation of Prostitution of Others (1950).

Transnational Cooperation

HT investigations often have transnational links because victims and offenders often come from different countries and parts of the offences are committed abroad (e.g., recruitment and smuggling). Therefore, there is a clear need for close cooperation among and between the law enforcement authorities of the countries concerned in any concrete case. Such cooperation is considered decisive for the clarification of any HT case that concerns, for example, the situation of the victim in the originating country, the recruitment methods and smuggling routes applied by the offenders as well as the identification of recruiters and smugglers and finally the connections among the groups of offenders in the countries of origin and destination.

The provisions in Articles 10–13 pertain to the cooperation between the States Parties in the field of prosecution and the protection of national borders. In addition to an intensified exchange of information on possible victims and offenders of HT as well as the respective modus operandi, the Protocol emphasizes the importance of particular training of officers specialized in HT cases. The protection of the borders is to be made possible through an increased frequency and a coordination of the border controls, a stronger observation of commercial carriers potentially supporting HT as well as an increased protection of documents against forgery and a check of identity documents (see www.un.org).

EU Initiatives

As is the situation at most international levels, the plight of HT is also of a crucial importance for the European institutions. In relation to preventative initiatives, several European financing programs were initiated, in particular in countries of "origin." The objective of such initiatives is to improve cooperation between the investigative and law enforcement authorities of the Member States.* Whereas the law enforcement authorities in those countries that are recognized as countries of "destination" for HT within the EU there have been long-standing experiences with HT investigations and, for the most part, they have established specialized antitrafficking units. Unfortunately, however, the issue of HT has frequently been neglected by those of the Member States that have joined the EU only recently (for example, those countries located in Central and Eastern Europe, which are typically acknowledged as countries of "origin" and "transit"). To reach a better level of cooperation among the law enforcement authorities of the Member States as well as to enable countries of origin to combat HT, at the source so-called "twinning-programmes" were set up. These programs were composed of police officers from the "old" EU-Member States to help professionalize police officers from "new" EU-Member States. This includes ensuring the provision of resources and training for developing intelligence-led policing for law enforcement bodies to investigate in trafficking cases including proactive approaches. As many victims are hesitant to lodge a complaint or to trust in the police for the reasons already stated above, HT investigations are often triggered by proactive investigation approaches (i.e., the active collection of information for example by means of systematic police controls in the Red-light districts) (see, e.g., Rijken 2003).

---

* This includes above all the programs STOP I and II (1996–2000, 2001–2002) and see AGIS reports (2002–2007), DAPHNE (1997–1999 initiated by the EU Parliament, subsequently prolonged), ODYSSEUS (i.e., Migration) and FALCONE (i.e., organized crime).

Another important channel for cooperation on the suppression level of HT is the European Police Office Europol (see below). At the normative level, the legislative provisions regarding HT within the EU had to be harmonized (see European Council Tampere 1999, www.europarl.europa.eu).

In 2002, the EU Council adopted a Framework Decision on the suppression of trafficking of human beings (see ABl. EF 2002). The Framework Decision standardized the definition of the criminal offence HT in the Member States. For example, Article 1 of the Framework Decision defines the minimum standards of offences to be criminalized by the Member States as HT, and corresponds with Article 3a of the UN 2000 Protocol. The Framework Decision was adopted by all the existing Member States by 2004.

The Framework Decision represents an extension of the Trafficking Protocol, as the Member States have to criminalize and investigate HT cases irrespectively of the commission of a transnational offence or an organized crime-related one. Thus, it is acknowledged that HT may just as well occur on a domestic level and may also be committed by single perpetrators or smaller networks.

One directive the European Council initiated in 2004 focuses in detail on how to deal with HT victims from Third-world country nationals (countries) during penal proceedings (see Council Directive 2004). For the first time, a legally binding agreement at the European level was made to clarify the residence status of HT victims. Under the decision, the victim must now be granted a reflection period and—where appropriate—will be issued a residence permit so that they are able to assist as witnesses in the penal proceedings (see Articles 6 and 8). If they are willing to cooperate, a residence permit is issued to them for the period of at least 6 months—subject to the fulfillment of further prerequisites—which can be renewed until the end of the penal proceedings at the latest (see Articles 8 and 13). Further provisions deal with the care and support of the victim (see Article 7), working and educational possibilities (see Article 11) as well as reintegration measures (see Article 12). As stated above, these provisions are of fundamental importance to strengthen the victims' role in the investigation process and therefore the likeliness that a victim consents to testify against their perpetrator.

In March 2010, the EU Commission presented proposals for legal provisions which are to place the EU Member States under the obligation to become still more active in matters of HT than in the past, especially in the three fields of prosecution (see Chapter 9), victim protection (see Chapter 12 in the volume) and prevention (Repealing Framework Decision 2002/629/JHA, see www.europa.eu). The proposed directive is to facilitate a harmonization of the national penal law rules. It is requested in the directive to make available investigative tools such as undercover investigation methods for the police and for judicial authorities that are already being used in the efforts to suppress organized crime. The urgency of a comprehensive victim protection initiative to win the prejudiced persons as witnesses for the penal proceedings is once again emphasized (i.e., measures to provide lodging, medical care, witness protection programs and legal advisers free of cost). Furthermore, the proposal of the Commission underlines the importance of information campaigns designed to raise the awareness of potential victims in view of the dangers of HT and to create training programs for law enforcement and judicial officers on how to recognize HT victims and to deal with them. Moreover, tougher sanctions are to be imposed on persons who knowingly employ HT victims or use their services. The proposal of the Commission also includes the establishment of national bodies to monitor the implementation of these measures. At the time of preparing this chapter, it is the intention of the Commission to nominate an EU coordinator who would then be in charge of HT suppression initiatives to make the EU policy more effective, visible, and coherent, as well as to tackle the reasons for HT and to further the cooperation with non-EU countries (see www.europa.eu).

OSCE

With 56 participating States from Europe, Central Asia, and North America, HT is considered one of the most pressing and complex issues in the OSCE (Organisation for Security and Cooperation in Europe) region as every year, thousands of women, children, and men are trafficked to or from OSCE States. HT concerns all Member States of the OSCE—either as countries of origin and transit or as countries of destination. The OSCE forms the largest regional security organization of its type in the world. The Organization deals with three dimensions of security: (1) the politico-military, (2) the economic and environmental, and (3) the human dimension. It therefore addresses a wide range of security-related concerns, including arms control, confidence- and security-building measures, human rights issues, as well as policing strategies. The OSCE is a primary instrument for early warning, conflict prevention, crisis management and postconflict rehabilitation in its area.

The fight against HT has been a top priority for the OSCE in recent years. Actions the OSCE takes include legislative reforms, training of law enforcement authorities and improving the security of travel documents. Currently, the OSCE has 18 missions or field operations in South-Eastern Europe, Eastern Europe, South Caucasus, and Central Asia, some of which are specifically designed to combat HT. These projects are based on key OSCE antitrafficking documents, most importantly the OSCE *Action Plan to Combat Trafficking in Human Beings*, adopted in 2003 and revised in 2005.

By way of example, the OSCE works closely with the Ukrainian authorities to implement projects that address the prevention of HT, strengthening of the prosecution and criminalization of this crime and the facilitation of assistance to victims. This includes providing expertise and technical support in the development of a comprehensive antitrafficking law. The OSCE carries out capacity-building activities for judges, law enforcement officers, lawyers, the media, and NGO representatives. Particularly in view of the Euro 2012 football tournament, which Ukraine will cohost with Poland, capacity-building efforts targeting Ukrainian law enforcement authorities preparing them to prevent and combat trafficking attempts, are needed. Other OSCE projects conducted in Tajikistan, Uzbekistan and Moldova equally focus on enhancing the capacity of law enforcement personnel and institutions to prevent and prosecute HT, including training courses which focus on victim identification procedures, internationally acknowledged models of investigative techniques, the importance of a proactive investigation approach, and good practices for collecting evidence, interviewing techniques as well as the protection of human rights during investigations (see www.osce.org; Kartusch 2002).

Europol

The European Police Office (Europol)[*] set up in 1998 is the European law enforcement agency. Its objective is to support the appropriate authorities of the Member States in the

---

[*] The Europol Convention (OJ C 316, 27.11.1995, p. 2) entered into force on October 1, 1998. On January 1, 2010, Europol became a so-called EU agency.

prevention and suppression of terrorism, unlawful drug trafficking and other serious forms of international crime, including HT. More than 620 staff members at Europol headquarters in The Hague, the Netherlands, closely cooperate with law enforcement agencies in the 27 EU member states and in other nonEU partner states such as Australia, Canada, USA, and Norway. Additionally, the EU member states and nonEU partners have seconded to Europol some 130 Liaison Officers to guarantee fast and effective cooperation based on personal contact and mutual trust (see Voß 2003).

As Europol officers have no direct powers of arrest, they support law enforcement personnel in the Member States by gathering, analyzing and disseminating information and coordinating operations. The partners use the input to prevent, detect and investigate offences, and to track down and prosecute the offenders. Europol experts and analysts also provide operational support and service functions to so-called Joint Investigation Teams (JITs) which help solve criminal cases on the spot in EU countries (see Herz 2006).

To trigger Europol's involvement, at least two Member States must be affected by the forms of crime in such a way as to require a common approach. Europol's core task is to support the police authorities of the Member States in their intelligence work (see, for example, Tolmein 1999; Milke 2003). Accordingly, Europol not only facilitates the exchange of data among the Member States, but also initiates the collection, collation, and analysis of intelligence. The most important working tool available to Europol is a computerized data collection system composed of an information system, work files (AWF), and an index system.* Law enforcement authorities in the EU rely on this intelligence work and the services of Europol's operational coordination center and secure information network, to carry out almost 10,000 cross-border investigations each year.

The relevant data concerning HT have been collected in the AWF Phoenix that was established in July 2007. It contains information on suspects, victims, trafficking networks, trafficking routes and so on. In addition to Germany, another 20 EU Member States as well as Norway, Australia, and Switzerland are associated members who participate in the AWF Phoenix with the purpose of supporting the Member States in their efforts to suppress and counteract the efforts of the traffickers especially from such countries as Romania and Nigeria where trafficking syndicates are seen to be a major problem.

In 2009, three JITs in the field HT under participation of Europol were set up. In the course of "Operation Black Leaves" it was possible to neutralize three organized Nigerian groups who networked together to bring victims to various European countries. As a result of the JIT initiative they were able to make arrest in The Netherlands, France, Italy, Germany, Greece, Spain and in San Marino. As a result of "Operation Longship"; a JIT between Romania and Great Britain, 214 persons were checked, five victims were identified, four children were identified as possible HT victims and were subsequently placed under police protection and important evidence was seized in the course of an extensive investigation for fraudulent failure to provide service as agreed. In November 2009, there was one

---

* The Information System contains data relating to suspects, persons convicted as well as persons who are believed will commit criminal offences for which Europol is competent (Art. 8 Europol Convention). The data may consist of criminal offences, alleged crimes, crime scences, weapons used, departments handling the case, suspected membership of a criminal organization, convictions. Work Files are specifically set up for analysing information to support a criminal investigation and are run by an analysis group. As the files may contain personal data on suspects, possible witnesses, victims, contacts and associates, the access is more restricted (Art. 10 Europol Convention). To regulate the access to the Information System as well as the Work Files, a special Index System was set up (Art. 11 Europol Convention).

further operation involving the participation of France, Greece, Italy, The Netherlands, Great Britain, Europol, Eurojust and Interpol. This operation led to the arrest of 22 persons for suspected facilitating HT worldwide in approximately 2000 cases. In 2010, there have so far been further two JITs having used data of AWF Phoenix. Europol supported these JITs by means of exchange of information and operational analyses.

Europol underlines the necessity to encourage further measures in the future aiming at an identification of victims, the development of transnational investigations as well as the seizure and confiscation of proceeds and assets gained in HT (see www.europol. europa.eu).

Interpol

The International Criminal Police Organisation (ICPO), which is more commonly known as Interpol was founded in 1914 and currently has 188 Member States. Interpol is the oldest and most important global cooperation framework for transnational cooperation on police level (see Stock and Herz 2008). Located in Lyon, France, the main duty of Interpol is to guarantee a quick and secure exchange of police information among the Member States. Further to a resolution adopted on the occasion of the 69th General Assembly, Interpol had constituted a working group on trafficking in women for sexual exploitation in 2000. Since 2000, this working group has been a forum for the exchange of information and strategies among the law enforcement authorities of the Member States and the development of "best practices" to improve international cooperation in this phenomenal domain. The working group decided in 2007 to extend its focus on all forms of HT, among other things on HT for the purpose of forced labor, commercial sexual exploitation of children in connection with tourism and trafficking of body organs. Due to the global significance and the importance of the complex aspects of HT, Interpol has held its first "Global Trafficking in Human Beings Conference" in June 2010.* One of the objectives of the conference was a strengthening of police cooperation in the individual regional areas of Interpol.

Interpol currently makes available to its Member States the following instruments and support programs in the field of HT: Education and training offers assistance during operational measures (e.g., "Operation BIA" in June 2009 under participation of 300 Ivorian officers who could save more than 50 child workers from being forced into child labor as well as resulted in the arrest of eight persons). Similarly, project "Childhood," also developed by Interpol and UNODC, dealt with the issue sex tourism in connection with child trafficking in Thailand, Vietnam, and Cambodia. These measures (including training programs for the officers on-the-spot as well as incident-related and technical assistance during ongoing investigations) were taken to build up partnerships with law enforcement authorities in Asia so that the penal prosecution of offenders can be advanced and the victims be freed from their plight. Interpol also uses so-called "Notices and Diffusions" for search purposes. This system allows for worldwide cooperation and also allows Interpol to search for suspects, to locate missing persons and to gather information. The so-called "green notices" enable any country to warn selectively about the entry of offenders who act

---

* The 1st INTERPOL Global Trafficking in Human Beings Conference took place in Damascus/Syria from 07.–09.06.2010.

at transnational level including those who have come to police notice in the past for trafficking or sexual abuse of children. Since 2005, the Member States have been able to use a so-called "Human Smuggling and Trafficking Message" (HST) via the protected websites of the Interpol General Secretariat to report HT cases in a standardized form to Interpol and enter the relevant data into the Interpol databases. Information on the disclosure of HT cases in an early state (e.g., at the entry into a country), can be collected by means of the so-called MIND-/FIND applications, enabling the law enforcement authorities in the field border protection/entry to make queries on stolen/reported lost travel documents, stolen vehicles, and fugitive offenders. Finally, it is the intention of Interpol to establish a new "Human Smuggling Team" which will serve the Member States as a so-called "one stop shop" in this crime area (see www.interpol.int).

National Level

As already stated above, Germany and Russia are regarded as the main European countries of destination and/or origin for trafficking in women with a view to prostitution. The primary reason for that development is due to the already-mentioned "push and pull factors": especially since the facilitation of the entry possibilities in the late 1980s, young Russian women who are jobless and without a chance try to immigrate to the prosperous Germany for better living conditions. In many cases, however, these women subsequently become dependent on alien smugglers and human traffickers.

The information given below concentrates on the suppression of HT in Germany and Russia focusing on the legal basis for investigation with a view to the various problems arising when applying these in practice. A special focus is on the critical role of the victim witnesses which requires specific knowledge, experience, and qualifications of law enforcement officers as well as close cooperation with NGOs within the specific states of operational, investigatory, and other procedures conducted during criminal prosecution.

Germany

Scope of the HT Problem in Germany
Within Europe, Germany is considered to be the main destination country for trafficked women. Without any reliable empirical basis, the number of female foreign prostitutes in the European Union is estimated at 200,000–500,000. The number of prostitutes who become victims of HT in Germany each year is estimated at 10,000–30,000 (Herz 2005). According to estimations of the government of the Federal Republic of Germany, 85% of the HT victims recorded since 1989 had come from the so-called "Central and Eastern European (CEE) countries"[*] and from Russia. Since 2000, there were repeatedly significant changes as regards the countries of origin. In the 1970s and 1980s, the prejudiced persons mainly came from Southeast Asia, Africa, and Latin America. Since the fall of the Iron Curtain in the late 1980s, above all, women from Central and Eastern Europe

---

[*] Bulgaria, Estonia, Latvia, Lithuania, Poland, Romania, Slovakia, Czech Republic, Hungary, Cyprus, Malta, and Turkey

have come under notice. The CEE countries and Russia are not only exclusively countries of origin and transit but also countries of destination (Herz 2005). However, due to the complexity and clandestine nature of HT, it is difficult to not only obtain reliable data but also to conduct reliable research in this field (see also Chapter 2). In a relevant study in Germany, representatives of police estimated the number of unreported offenders and victims (i.e., "dark figure") at 83% and 91% (i.e., a very high level), respectively. The persons interviewed referred to suspicious circumstances that could not be verified on a regular basis and to the problem to gather valuable information from (potential) persons concerned (Herz 2005).

Legal Situation

In 1973, special legal provisions regarding HT were for the first time adopted in Germany. On February 11, 2005 there was a review of the latest corresponding amendment to the relevant penal provisions—in accordance with the described changes at the UN and EU level—(section 232 Penal Code: HT for the purpose of sexual exploitation; Section 233 Penal Code: HT for the purpose of exploitation of labor; Section 233a *Penal Code:* promotion of trafficking in human beings).[*] Serious aggravated HT cases—if the victim is a child, the offender has severely abused the victim physically when committing the offence or if mortal danger is provoked as well as in the case of a gang-type *modus operandi*—are punished with prison sentences of up to 10 years. Germany joined the UN Convention including the Trafficking Protocol in 2000 (Herz 2005); and the Convention of the Council of Europe has been signed but not yet ratified.[†]

Police Investigation in HT Cases

The German Federal Criminal Police Office (Bundeskriminalamt/BKA) releases an annual report containing updated information on police efforts to investigate HT cases from the various police forces nationwide. According to these situation reports between 2000 and 2009, 303 proceedings involving foreign victims have been conducted each year on average. In addition, 114 proceedings involving German victims are processed each year on average. These cases are registered by the BKA separately. The number of proceedings steadily increased to 534 cases with 710 victims and 777 suspects by 2009 (BKA Annual Reports 2000 to 2009, www.bka.de).

It is interesting to observe that in accordance with the BKA statistics that 50%–60% of the HT proceedings have been initiated in the past due to complaints of victims and third-party persons. Nevertheless, research shows that, especially in the case of foreign HT victims, due to their difficult situation, they are much less willing and able to lodge complaints than other crime victims (the possible reasons are as already stated: illegal stay, dependence, and compulsory structures) (Herz 2005). Trafficking investigations are focused on victims whose human dignity was violated in some way and for whom it is very difficult to resist the offenders and to seek the assistance of third persons. This is primarily observed in cases where the offenders have established dependence between them

---

[*] 37. Strafrechtsänderungsgesetz (Criminal Justice Amendment Act) BGBl. (Federal Law Gazette) 2005 I, page 239). Germany entered into the Convention incl. the Trafficking Protocol on 12.12.2000.
[†] Status: June, 2010.

and the persons concerned—frequently by use of violence or deception—respectively, systematically exploit the dilemma of the victims and force them to work as prostitutes.

Moreover, the phenomenon is often linked to organized crime. As HT is typically a type of transnational crime, the cooperation of several offenders is assumed in many cases, above all regarding the recruitment and smuggling of the victims into a country. In 2009, 20 police investigations were linked to organized crime in nightlife—14 of which concerned trafficking in human beings (the victims identified in the course of these were mainly Romanian, Hungarian, Nigerian, and Russian nationals). The offenders were typically organized in larger groups (approximately eight persons) and had been operating over a certain period of time (for 3.2 years on average) in hierarchical structures. Specifically, the Romanian organized crime groups dominated crime associated with nightlife, followed by Hungarian, German, Nigerian, and Turkish organized crime groups (i.e., the offenders typically operate from abroad and given the existing laws it is difficult to not only investigate but also prosecute such individuals). Consequently, it is quite difficult to identify the network structures that underlie such organized crime groups. The *modus operandi* of the offenders is partly very brutal. In some cases, multiple rapes, brutal physical violence and murder threats were reported as being used to force the persons concerned into prostitution. It was also reported that the offenders search out victims who managed to escape to their mother countries and threaten them or their families.

Similar to the trend prior to 2009, most of the 777 suspects and 710 victims registered by the German police in 2009 came from East European countries. Specifically, Bulgaria (suspects: 16%; victims: 19%), and Romania (suspects: 11%; victims: 20%) dominate the scene. Some 36% the suspects and 25% of the victims were German nationals. The age distribution of the victims is alarming: in 2009, 64% were under the age of 21; 20% were under age (younger than 18). Since 2005, the number of minor victims has continuously been increasing (2005: 8%); 41 victims (6%) were younger than 14 at the time of offence—so the number increased by more than 50% compared with that of the previous year. With respect to children, most victims come from Turkey and Bosnia; the German victims often have a migratory background.[*] The suspects came mainly to the attention of the police after being identified as pimps (380), followed by so-called intermediaries respectively recruiters (156 and/or 153), and brothel keepers (137). Forty-eight of the offenders were suspected of having raped the victims (Herz 2005).

For the successful implementation of the complex provisions against HT, sufficient resources and specially trained police officers are required. While proactive investigation is important for many offences, it is of particular importance when dealing with HT for gathering evidence and identifying victims of trafficking (i.e., police raids, monitoring of facilities suspected of providing sexual services, monitoring of media advertisements and so on). According to their own statements, only 20% of the specialized departments in charge of HT cases do not conduct checks in the Red-light districts. The other departments indicated conducting preventive checks or checks as a reaction to concrete grounds of suspicion. As it might be expected, the bigger the cities/places are, the higher the number of checks is (Herz 2005). At the level of the law enforcement authorities, specialized departments or even specially trained case officers are in many cases dealing with HT investigations. In a few individual cases, special investigation teams are set up (ibid).

---

[*] Between 31 and 40: 24%; between 41 and 50: 16%.

Example: Crime Suppression Focus West Africa/Nigeria

In recent years, there has been a steady increase in the number of leads that Nigerian HT groups have established in Germany and throughout other parts of Europe (e.g., the Netherlands, Italy, Belgium, Austria and Great Britain)—among them pimps, smuggled prostitutes, money launderers, passport lenders, document forgers and alien smugglers. In 2009 alone, 34 victims and 29 suspects from Nigeria came to notice in Germany. In early February 2010, controls were conducted—by recommendation and in coordination of the Bundeskriminalamt (BKA)—in the red-light districts all over Germany in order to identify HT victims from West Africa and to gather information about the offender structures in the background. Searches in approximately 600 brothels and brothel-like establishments were carried out in 13 Federal German states with more than 100 police offices having taken part.

In the course of these actions, 179 West African women were discovered, 44 of whom were provisionally arrested for violations of the aliens law. Initially, in 15 cases there was information that suggested suspected HT. It also became evident during that action that police often located possible prejudiced persons who are not willing to make any statement toward police—a phenomenon that considerably complicates investigations in the case of victims from West Africa (e.g., Nigeria). The victims are sometimes extensively prepared for the smuggling and indoctrinated by the offenders accordingly in their home countries: they are taught German by language teachers, practice role plays to be prepared for the border controls, and obtain forged identity documents.

In order to gain and maintain control over the women, complex Voodoo ceremonies are carried out in Nigeria. The women must swear before a priest to bear all incurring costs, not to run away, and to follow all instructions. Moreover, they must take an oath of silence. Because of their beliefs in voodoo-type practices, the "victims" are convinced that should they violate the oath that they will either die or become gravely ill. Although this may sound quite strange for readers who are not familiar with such cultural practices and beliefs—such ceremonies cause an extreme mental dependence of the victims; they feel themselves impelled to pay fictitious costs (often in the 5-digit range) for the smuggling and other expenses to the offenders (e.g., in one proceedings that sum amounted to 50,000–70,000 euro). It is very difficult for the investigators to gain access to the victims/ witnesses in these cases. It is quite common that police are also confronted with female offenders. After being smuggled, the persons concerned are handed over in Germany, or other European countries, to female Nigerian pimps, so-called "Madams." These "Madams" are frequently former victims who changed sides after they had worked off/paid back their "debts." For example in 2009, 22% of all HT suspects registered were women (BKA Annual Report 2010).

Decisive Role of Victim-Witnesses

Under German law, all acts that qualify as HT offences must involve an element or the intent of exploitation. In terms of HT, unless there is clear evidence of intent by the accused to exploit or law enforcement can in some way find other pieces of evidence, HT is almost impossible to prove without corroborating evidence from the victim.

In Germany, HT proceedings can only be successful if the victim is willing to cooperate with the police. Whereas victims from Africa usually stay illegally in Germany, prejudiced persons from Eastern Europe, meanwhile, often enter German legally and offer prostitution as an independent service. Preventive police measures are hardly possible in such cases. In particular, victims from Bulgaria and Romania are often suspected of fictitious self-employment (i.e., they are in fact dependent on pimps/backers; sometimes they have experienced the worst use of violence and many women are illiterate). If there is a suspicion of HT (i.e., coercion, exploitation of a destitute condition) the police officers concerned—just like in contact with Nigerian victims—must show empathy and cross-cultural competence.* In very few cases are the women willing to provide a statement and even when they do they frequently withdraw their statements or return to their home countries before the completion of the trial or case hearing.

Law enforcement officers also have to bear in mind that HT can be committed irrespectively of the victim's consent to work in prostitution. Also, German trafficking law does not require or include any provisions to detain the victim—even if for their own personal safety. There may be a number of other reasons that victims will not leave the exploitive situation including threats of violence to them or their families or because they had their documents taken away. For approximately 25% (170) of the HT victims registered in 2009, investigative leads had been developed that they were forced to work as prostitutes or were prevented from backing out of prostitution. The number of those who were recruited for prostitution (163 victims, 23%) by deception was almost as high as the above one. Nearly one-half of the victims (320 victims, 45%) stated that they had basically agreed to work as prostitutes—a phenomenon that is found with increasing frequency (BKA Annual Report 2010). In these cases, the women are often, however, misinformed about their future earnings and living conditions; moreover, they are forced to work off the costs caused due to their smuggling into the country and their lodging, thus making them still more dependent from the offenders (Herz 2005). Research shows that traffickers do not need to resort to physical control measures as victims are easily intimidated by threats and other forms of psychological coercion (Herz 2005). According to law enforcement officials judges are sometimes reluctant to apply trafficking law in the absence of physical means of control or if a victim consented to being trafficked (Herz 2005).

As a result, a high number of proceedings are discontinued because the victims are not available as witnesses. In addition, police and judicial authorities may avoid acknowledging the HT issue and conduct proceedings for other criminal offences, such as pimping, exploitation of prostitutes or violations of the aliens law because it is easier to gain evidence for these offences in practice and convictions are more likely as well (Herz 2005).

Given the above situation, it is very important for law enforcement authorities to involve specialized counseling services as early as possible as well as to involve them throughout the duration of the penal proceedings. In so doing, the victims' condition can be stabilized and their specific needs be met—which in turn enhances the likelihood of the police to obtain reliable testimony. Approximately 40 specialized counselling services in Germany have specialized on the care of HT victims (Schaab and Maragkos 2009). Nearly 25% of the HT victims identified by police underwent that care over the past years. Studies show that the involvement of specialized counseling services has a positive effect on the statistic figures in the field of prosecution: Victims who become subject of that care do more frequently obtain a residence permit and are more often willing to make a witness statement (Herz 2005). Persons who are presumed to be HT victims are granted a 4-week deadline

---

* Police officer receive cultural sensitivity training or awareness raising as part of police training courses on HT—mostly through presentations by NGOs.

in Germany to leave the country voluntarily, while they are supported by NGOs and may be persuaded to make a witness' statement in the penal proceedings. If the victims decide to do so, it is possible to issue a temporary residence title that suspends deportation for the duration of the penal proceedings. The cooperation between police and specialized counseling services in Germany is based on a cooperation model concept elaborated by a governmental working group in 1999* that includes also indicators for victim identification, an early involvement of the specialized counseling services in suspected HT cases and decision criteria for witness protection measures.

Police Training Efforts to Investigate HT Cases

The BKA offers advanced training courses in the field of HT for the entire German police—twice a year with the topic sexual exploitation and once a year with the topic exploitation of workers; approximately 30 police officers of the appropriate specialized departments usually take part in these courses. Among the instructors are police officers from specialized departments who deal with HT, social scientists, staff members of specialized counselling services, and lawyers. Focal points of the HT training involve learning the legal aspects of HT (e.g., the legal parameters of HT prosecution as well as the relevant provisions for alien legislation). In addition, officers are also informed about the nature and extent as well as structures of HT, problems with the indicators leading to suspicion as well as the collection and processing of information. Moreover, current operational priorities are presented on the basis of concrete cases, such as the extremely difficult prosecution of HT committed to the detriment of Nigerian women (keyword Voodoo), the currently largest group of victimized aliens (i.e., Romanian and Bulgarian women), and/or a closer involvement of the tax fraud investigation authorities. A third priority focuses on information in connection with the interviews of the victims and the measures necessary to recruit them as witnesses for the investigative proceedings. This includes the description of the role of the specialized counseling services and their optimum involvement in the investigations, the significance of intercultural communication during the interview of victims, as well as the occurrence of possible posttraumatic stress disorders.

Under a directive from the BKA, a catalog of guidelines on how to deal with traumatized HT victims was developed in 2009. The guidelines serve as a basis of action for police as well as judicial and municipal authorities (Schaab and Maragkos 2009). According to a study of 2010, also ordered by the BKA, in which 53 HT victims were interviewed, the prejudiced persons offered the following reasons for not contacting or addressing police investigators (Helfferich et al. 2010): (1) Violence and attempts to intimidate the victims used by the offenders; the desire to make a better living by migration to Germany and—along with that—the readiness to tolerate the "debt trap" as well as intimidations by the offenders; (2) barriers due to migration, such as lacking knowledge of language, writing and legal status and (3) fear of police or impression that police is cooperating with the offenders. The biggest inhibition thresholds were found in the case of those victims who had taken an oath of silence during Voodoo ceremonies or who were at the mercy of an organized crime system. The study also revealed that a comprehensive advisory service

---

* Besides representatives of seven Federal Ministries, the permanent working group consists of the Federal Government Commissioner for Matters Relating to Foreigners, representatives of the Bundeskriminalamt, the Federal German states and specialised counselling services.

has a positive influence on their willingness to make a statement. Most of the victims did, however, not know about the availability of advisory or support offers before they got into contact with such. Neither were they aware of their legal rights nor were they able to correctly estimate the role of police.

For a number of years, the BKA has also been conducting training courses in the typical countries of origin of victims and suspects of HT (e.g., Romania, Belarus, and Russia). Representatives of specialized counseling services also take part in these initiatives. One further focus is on victim-related investigative leads—taking into account the different cultural background of the victims and the influence of third persons—targeting at the collection of information on offender structures (e.g., the transfer routes of women in Germany with the intention to make the offenders feel unsafe). Moreover, much stronger involvement and sensitization of public prosecutors and judges working with such crimes are seen to be essential factors (see www.bka.de).

Summary

As noted throughout this book, trafficking in human beings is a very complex offence, HT cases are difficult to solve and consequently, intensive resources are required in this respect. Within the German police forces, there are notable differences and variations on how to prioritize HT cases. For example, some of the key challenges include: the establishment of counseling services and the professional qualification of the case officers (Herz 2005). The reason why the police's ability to detect, apprehend, and prosecute human traffickers in a timely manner is comparatively limited is mostly due to the difficult access to the victims and their reluctance to serve as witnesses. It is decisive that police and specialized counseling services support the victims who want to get out of their dilemma by their own efforts by offering them comprehensive means to lodge complaints—such as greater police presence in the milieu, multilingual flyers, and direct approaches. Regarding the interview of the victims/witnesses, great empathy and intercultural competence are required—besides origin and culture it must be taken into account that many women are very young. Therefore, it is absolutely necessary to provide comprehensive counseling to the persons concerned so that they can recognize police as a supporting entity and be informed exactly about their rights and possibilities (also see Chapter 8). Moreover, victims/witnesses must be provided necessary protection to avoid being further victimized. In order to guarantee the successful investigations of HT cases, institutionalized and international forms of cooperation, especially with the countries of origin, play a decisive role—a fact that is also at the center of most HT initiatives launched on an international or supranational level such as the UN, EU, OSCE, Europol, and Interpol.

We will now shift our focus to the situation in Russia.

Russia

Scope of the HT Problem in Russia

Since the fall of the Iron Curtain in the late 1980s, Russia—just as many other Central and East European countries—has become a country of origin, destination, and transit for HT, not only on a transnational but also increasingly on a domestic level. In the course of Russia's transformation process, the country has been trying to cope with the extreme economic and social imbalance among its own population, in particular between the poor rural population and the richer town inhabitants—as well as the rest of the world. The political upheaval did not only force many Russians, especially young women, to leave their country for new ways to earn their living but also offered a fertile breeding ground for organized crime and corruption (Stoecker 2005, Tiuriukanova 2005). In the aftermath of the socio-political changes, opportunity for trafficking grew dramatically with the recruitment and procurement of labor to such destinations as Western Europe, USA and China (Erokhina 2005). Meanwhile, the most common form of HT has become trafficking in persons for exploitation of labor. Moreover, an intense trafficking for sexual exploitation in and to Russia has become an increasing matter of concern. However, above all, Russia remains the country of origin for trafficking in women and children for sexual exploitation to more than 50 countries worldwide. The most common destination regions include Europe and North America and to a lesser extent various regions in Asia and the Near East. It has been estimated that approximately 175,000 women from Central and Eastern Europe as well as from the former Soviet Republics are recruited each year into HT. It is also estimated that 50,000 women from the CIS region (Community of Independent States) alone are illegally transported per year to foreign countries (Post 2008, UN/IOM 2006). Between 2000 and 2005, many of the foreign HT victims identified in Germany came from Russia. As expansive at HT is in Russia today, it was not until the late 1990s that the country began to address the problem of HT on an official basis—not least due to the pressure of NGOs and other countries, in particular, USA (Erokhina 2005).

Legal Situation

In 2000, Russia signed the UN Convention on Transnational Organised Crime inclusive with the Palermo-Protocol and ratified it in 2004.[*] Additional steps for the implementation on national level followed. Since 2003, the criminal offence of "human trafficking" has become part of the Russian Penal Code. In Russia, HT as well as the exploitation of slavery are now punishable offences; Section 127.1 (human trafficking) and 127.2 (use of slave labor) of the Russian *Penal Code* contain definitions based on the Palermo Protocol, stipulating a maximum sentence of up to 5 years—in serious cases up to 10 years.[†] Moreover, a *Witness Protection Act* entered into force on January 1, 2005.[‡] Since 2007, a national coordination agency at the governmental level exists in Russia, which controls and links all activities against HT.

Police Investigation in HT Cases

Every year since 2000, the U.S. State Department produces an annual report on the progress other countries have made in fighting trafficking, the Trafficking in Persons (TIP)

---

[*] The ratification was effected with the "Federal Law" of 26.04.2004 N 26-FZ. Although Russia is member of the Council of Europe, the Convention of the Council of Europe against Human Trafficking of 2005 has neither been signed nor ratified till now (state: June 2010).

[†] Section 127.1 (human trafficking) and section 127.2 (exploitation of slavery) entered into force with the "Federal Law", No. 162-FZ on 11.12.2003. A comprehensive "law against human trafficking" with 39 sections, initiated in 2002 has not been ratified so far despite international pressure and the intervention of NGOs, women's associations and the United States. For further details see Post, pp. 140 ff., 156 ff.

[‡] Federal Law No. 119-FZ of 20.08.2004.

report. Over the years, Russia has consistently performed poorly in this annual report, having been placed on the second-lowest level for insufficient efforts to combat trafficking in human beings particularly in providing assistance to victims. The Russian government is criticized for lacking political will to deal with the crime, continued refusal to fund victim protection services, and failure to establish a coordinating body to oversee antitrafficking activities. The main criterion for judging Russia's performance on HT has been the number of cases prosecuted under the new *Criminal Code* Articles 127.1 and 127.2.

In its 2004 annual watch list, the U.S. State Department upgraded Russia from the level Tier 3 to the level Tier 2. In the 2009 TIP, Russia's efforts to continue the fight against HT are confirmed but it is also stated that the action taken against the offenders is still not consistent enough. In particular, the efforts made by the law enforcement authorities are still unsatisfactory: Between 2004 and 2008, approximately 80 proceedings for HT with a view to sexual exploitation (Article 127.1) and 24 for exploitation of labor (Article 127.2) were registered each year (TIP 2009, see www.state.gov/g/tip).

After a first rise in the number of proceedings and convicted persons, only 111 penal proceedings for HT were conducted in 2008 (95 for sexual exploitation, 16 for exploitation of labor) (i.e., 28 fewer compared to the year before). Nine suspects were convicted for HT (this is also 80% less compared to the previous year). Many of these proceedings concern HT in Russia and from Russia abroad—whereas trafficking to Russia is hardly subject of prosecution.

As a comparatively new crime to Russian investigators, HT requires law enforcement to learn strategies for how to apply the new law effectively. The following factors are considered to constrain Russian investigators' capacity to enforce HT law (McCarthy 2008): (1) Corruption of state officials, border police and law enforcement personnel (viewed as both a cause and facilitating tool for HT); (2) complicated institutional structures and promotion criteria (as the system of promotion within Russian law enforcement is based on statistics on the number of cases and suspects convicted trafficking cases which are complicated to investigate do not have priority among law enforcement personnel); (3) difficulties inherent to applying HT law in practice (proof of intent of exploitation); (4) requirement of new investigative techniques regarding the crucial role of victim testimony (complicated role of victims who are also witnesses, techniques in dealing with traumatized victims, distrust of many victims in Russian law enforcement personnel); and (5) lack of supporting legislation (i.e., absence of a law granting victims temporary residence permits and shelter, insufficient measures regarding victim protection).

Trafficking takes significantly more resources, both time and manpower, since proactive measures are necessary and the evidence is so much more difficult to collect. However, the majority of the victims are not identified by the law enforcement authorities but the investigators mainly become active due to information obtained from victims or NGOs. Proactive police investigations only take place sporadically although information collected by police itself is indispensable and respectively verify suspicious facts or witnesses' statements. A differentiated approach in this respect is necessary because the persons concerned usually take the decision for an at least temporary labor migration knowingly and many of them are aware of the risks involved (Erokhina 2005). But the consent of persons with regard to migration does not automatically include the consent to prostitution; even in the case of an initial or basic consent to prostitution, it is possible that these persons become victims of exploitation and compulsory measures. A decisive aspect is not to criminalize the victims themselves (ibid).

In spite of the new legislation, Russian law enforcement officials have difficulty in applying the new laws and instead tend to defer to familiar articles of the *Criminal Code* which require less evidence (i.e., forgery of documents, recruitment for prostitution, etc.).*

Decisive Role of Victims as Witnesses

As is the case in Germany, HT requires Russian investigators to deal with victims whose testimony often is the crucial piece of evidence but who—for various reasons as stated above—are reluctant to cooperate with law enforcement officials. Moreover, it is still criticized that public authorities put in too little effort to provide the necessary support to the victim and leave such initiatives to the limited number of private institutions. Although persons who became victims of HT are officially recognized as such; in practice they are more likely to be deported especially if they have violated "Aliens" legislation at the same time. Due to the lack of protective legal provisions, it is at the discretion of the law enforcement authorities as to whether a right of residence is granted to HT victims or not. In practice, victim protection is mainly ensured by more than 100 NGOs (e.g., crime victim compensation, counseling, care, information campaigns) which, however, do not get a guaranteed financial aid by the government (Stoecker 2005, UN/IOM 2006).

Police Training Efforts to Investigate HT Cases

The Ministry of the Interior has intensified the training efforts for law enforcement and judicial staff over the past few years. Information on new laws and new techniques is disseminated through weekly meetings and briefings. For law enforcement professionals to be promoted they are also required to fulfill continuing education requirements. Specific training materials and instructional manuals on investigating HT have been developed and distributed to many regions throughout Russia. However, hands-on training courses, in which law enforcement professionals work with real case files, learn techniques for uncovering and investigating trafficking cases and learn how to work with victims to get reliable testimony, are mainly offered by NGOs. Many law enforcement professionals have participated in such local trainings run by NGOs, many of which have received grants for that purpose (McCarthy 2008).

Summary

Regarding the sheer size of the country as well as the fact that Russia is not only a country of destination for HT but also of origin and transit, Russia faces an even greater challenge to tackle HT effectively than Germany. With regard to the legal aspect, Russia has taken important measures for the suppression of HT but the real problems come to light above all when the legal provisions are to be implemented (also see Chapter 10). Here, Russian law enforcement professionals encounter many of the same problems as their German counterparts: the need for sufficient resources for proactive police measures, the need for highly specialized investigators trained in dealing with organized crime structures as much as with traumatized victim-witnesses, the dependence on reliable evidence from victim-witnesses who—for many reasons—are reluctant to cooperate with the police.

---

* In Russia, prostitution is not a punishable but an administrative offence. The recruitment for prostitution and the organisation of prostitution, for example, the running of a brothel, are liable to prosecution.

Nonetheless, the number of HT investigations annually registered in Germany is approximately three times higher than in Russia. All things considered, it is required the Russian investigative authorities must work toward a higher prioritization and sensitization in the phenomenal domain HT and to make available the respective investigative capacities. HT cases should be dealt with by specially trained law enforcement officers only but this requires a targeted state funding of basic and advanced training measures on a regular basis. Another important point is the problem of widespread corruption.

A better organization of the efforts in the field of victim protection and prevention in the future and a closer coordination between the parties involved would also be helpful. In addition to stronger efforts concerning prosecution it will be crucial for Russia to intensify its efforts—in view of the provisions on a legal residence status of foreign HT victims during prosecution, a closer cooperation between the authorities and NGOs, institutionalized state subsidies for the victims, specific information respectively recommended action for the job centers and other control agencies in charge of HT as well as prevention campaigns spreading information on HT among the population and—in particular—among persons willing to migrate.

Finally, of crucial importance, in Russia, is the need for an official action plan for the prevention of HT as well as awareness-raising programs launched at a national level concerning the risks of prostitution and the phenomenon HT, seen from the human rights' perspective.

Conclusion

Trafficking in human beings has become a worldwide profitable, low-risk business. Despite multiple efforts undertaken at national and international levels, it is due to inadequate laws, insufficient international cooperation in matters of criminal prosecution, lack of special authorities with professionally trained staff, corruption and the absence of effective victim and witness protection measures that offenders often go unpunished whereas the victims are criminalized in many cases. HT is a phenomenon with complex reasons and characteristics. The complexity of the problems requires a comprehensive, multidisciplinary approach as well as international coordination of actions by national governments and law enforcement officials as well as by multilateral organizations such as the UN, EU, OSCE, and Interpol, taking into account each of the so-called "3Ps," prevention, prosecution, and protection likewise and should involve all parties concerned (also, see Chapters 2 and 6). As organized and criminal organizations are operating at a transnational level, a close cross-border cooperation and coordination between the appropriate national institutions, the NGOs as well as regional and international organizations have become absolutely necessary. Investigative efforts have to be increased not only with regard to prosecution but also to victim and witness protection and preventive measures. The states concerned must establish coordination centers (National Rapporteurs) in the field of HT, serving as central points of contact which coordinate all ongoing initiatives.

The decisive problem of an effective prosecution remains, however, the application of the complex legal HT provisions and the victim identification in practice. National HT regulations based on UN and EU provisions focus on the various acts of influence and exploitation in connection with the recruitment and determination of persons for prostitution. Police and judicial authorities face three core problems in trying to clarify the acts of influence and exploitation (i.e., it is typical that offenders and victims cooperate for a certain period of time—although frequently on the basis of deception), and that the offenders primarily use psychological tactics. Moreover, the women concerned often make only limited statements of what they had to go through. This is due to the special situation of these persons in comparison to other groups of victims (i.e., their motivation for migration and employment in the country of destination, illegality and isolation, dependence on the offenders and their attempts of intimidation). And while this chapter has focused largely on the sex trade, HT has taken on other forms of exploitation such as exploitation of labor. Together they require police investigation to be sensitive to the diversity of HT and the fine line between HT and people smuggling. However, several of the problems described in connection with HT for sexual exploitation also apply to HT cases with a view to exploitation of labor—especially regarding the crucial but at the same time highly problematic role of the victim-witnesses.

The consequence is that—regardless of numerous initiatives and efforts on international and national level to successfully combat HT—the figures of police statistics on trafficking cases remain comparatively low and will likely be on that level in the future. It remains a crucial factor that the law enforcement authorities comprehensively handle the situation of the victims in cooperation with specialized counseling services and lawyers. The national penal provisions must be reviewed as to how the above-described difficulties in establishing and proving the acts of influence and exploitation can be overcome accordingly by means of amended provisions. It is also necessary to discuss the suppression of HT in close connection with the importance attached to migration and prostitution as well as all other forms of exploitation at the national level; this can for example, imply the protection of foreigners who want to work in another country, the statutory control of brothels, or similar establishments and the question as to whether clients of HT victims who work as prostitutes are to be punished.

Review and Discussion Questions

1. What are the central elements for successful investigation in human trafficking cases?
2. What obstacles do police investigations face when dealing with human trafficking cases?
3. What approaches are taken to overcome these obstacles?
4. On which broader issues do investigations in human trafficking cases touch?
5. What is understood by a broad, sustainable approach to fight human trafficking successfully?

References

AGIS. (2002–2007). http://ec.europa.eu/anti-trafficking/section;jsessionid=PpnyNn6Qf4T9mg82t mYN1ySTSVVCTJT9YLg9lKLxBpQhKsbs0x83!855818409?page=1&tag=AGIS&tagsList=& sectionId=ee0a97c9-c36f-4075-9c15-823c947f4aab&sectionType=TAG&breadCrumbReset= true (accessed August 18, 2010).

Bundeskriminalamt. 2010. Lagebild Menschenhandel 1994 bis 2009, Wiesbaden. Annual Report (available at www.bka.de).

Erokhina, L. 2005. Trafficking in women in the Russian described Far East: A real or imaginary phenomenon? In Stoecker, Sally/Shelley, Louise (Eds.), *Human Traffic and Transnational Crime—Eurasian and American Perspectives*, Lanham: Rowman & Littlefield, pp. 79–94.

Gallagher, A. 2001. Human rights and the new UN protocols on trafficking and migrant smuggling: A preliminary analysis, *Human Rights Quarterly* 23:975–1004.

Han, P. 2000. *Soziologie der migration*. Stuttgart: Lucius & Lucius.

Helfferich, C., Kavemann, B., and Rabe, H. (Eds.). 2010. *Determinanten der aussagebereitschaft von opfern des menschenhandels zum Zweck sexueller Ausbeutung—Eine qualitative Opferbefragung*. Bundeskriminalamt Köln: Wolters Kluwer Luchterhand.

Herz, A. 2006. The role of Europol and Eurojust in joint investigation teams. In Rijken, Conny/Vermeulen, Gert (Eds.), *Joint Investigation Teams in the European Union—from Theory to Practice*, The Hague: Asser Press, pp. 159–199.

Herz, A.L. 2005. *Menschenhandel*. Berlin: Duncker & Humblot.

Hofmann, J. 2002. *Menschenhandel—Beziehungen zur Organisierten Kriminalität und Versuche der strafrechtlichen Bekämpfung*, Peter Lang, Frankfurt a.M.

International Convention for the Suppression of the Traffic in Women of the Full Age. 1933. http://ec.europa.eu/anti-rafficking/entity.action;jsessionid=X2Y6NZ1DmykT2Zh73QZSLkGfm9G RYzYJncd6v1hmcKDDLnJtl9BG!1145937442?id=904ed57d-d500-4028-8392-c40575647b11 (accessed August 18, 2011).

IOM. 2000. *Migrant trafficking and human smuggling in Europe*. Geneva: IOM.

Kartusch, A. 2002. Menschenhandel—Eine menschenrechtliche Herausforderung für die OSZE. In Institut für Friedensforschung und Sicherheitspolitik an der Universität Hamburg (Ed.), *OSZE-Jahrbuch 2002*, Baden-Baden: Nomos, pp. 289–303.

Kreuzer, C. 2001. Initiativen zur Bekämpfung des Menschenhandels, *ZAR 5:* 220–226.

McCarthy, L.A. 2008. Beyond Corruption: An Assessment of Russian Law Enforcement's Fight against Human Trafficking (copy available at: http://ssrn.com/abstract = 1462842).

Milke, T. 2003. *Europol und Eurojust*. Göttingen: V & R unipress.

Oberloher, R.F. 2003. *Moderne Sklaverei im OK-Netz*. Wien: Facultas/WUV.

Post, C. 2008. *Kampf gegen den Menschenhandel im Kontext des europäischen Menschenrechtsschutzes—Eine rechtsvergleichende Untersuchung zwischen Deutschland und Russland*. Hamburg: Verlag Dr. Kovac.

Prostitution of others. 1950. http://treaties.un.org/doc/publication/mtdsg/volume%20i/chapter%20vii/vii-11-a.en.pdf (accessed August 18, 2011).

Rijken, C. 2003. *Trafficking in Persons: Prosecution from a European Perspective*. The Hague: Asser Press.

Schaab, E. and Maragkos, M. (Eds.) 2009. *Traumaleitfaden—Handbuch*. Wiesbaden: Bundeskriminalamt.

Sieber, U. and Boegel, M. 1993. *Logistik der Organisierten Kriminalität*. Wiesbaden: BKA-Forschungsreihe.

Stock, J. and Herz, A. 2008. Die internationale Kriminalpolizeiliche organisation (IKPO-Interpol), *Kriminalistik* 11/12, pp. 594–601, 651–655.

Stoecker, S. 2005. Human trafficking: A new challenge for Russia and the United States. In Stoecker, Sally/Shelley, Louise (Eds.), *Human Traffic and Transnational Crime—Eurasian and American Perspectives*, Lanham: Rowman & Littlefield, pp. 13–28.

The International Agreement on Fighting the Trafficking of Girls. 1910. http://www.dadalos.org/int/menschenrechte/Grundkurs_MR3/frauenrechte/warum/frauenhandel.htm (accessed August 18, 2011).

Tiuriukanova, E. 2005. Female labor migration trends and human trafficking: Policy recommendations. In Stoecker, Sally/Shelley, Louise (Eds.), *Human Traffic and Transnational Crime—Eurasian and American Perspectives*, Lanham: Rowman & Littlefield, pp. 95–113.

Trafficking in Women and Children. 1921. http://ec.europa.eu/anti-trafficking/entity?id=3e45bb04-38d9-4f66-b7f1-bde3ea47361e (accessed August 18, 2011).

Tolmein, O. 1999. *Europol*, StV 2, pp. 108–116.

UN/IOM. 2006. *Working group on trafficking in human beings: Human trafficking in the Russian federation*. Moscow: IOM.

UN/IOM. 2010. News and Events. www.unodc.org.en/human-trafficking/news-and-events.html (accessed August 18, 2011).

UNODC. 2009. *Global report on trafficking in persons*. Vienna: UNODC.

UNODC. 2010. *The globalization of crime*. Vienna: UNODC.

Vlassis, D. 1998. Drafting the United Nations convention against transnational organized crime, *Transnational Organized Crime*, 4:356–362.

Voß, T. 2003. *Europol: Polizei ohne Grenzen*? Freiburg: Max-Planck-Institut.

Helpful Web Links

http://www.humantrafficking.org/publications/451, a web resource for human trafficking that focuses on policing global human trafficking.

Prosecution of Trafficking in Human Beings Cases

8

MARIANNE WADE

Contents

Introduction

As has been articulated throughout this book, and in particular in Chapters 1 and 2, the plight of human trafficking is extensive globally. Trafficking in human beings and a suitable criminal justice response to it is a topic of highest interest in many supranational* contexts such as the United Nations and the European Union (EU). The decision of governments to raise efforts to combat this category of crimes to a governance level above the national is indicative of its nature; these are crimes to which one nation alone cannot respond comprehensively. They can legitimately be viewed as one of the catalysts and/or facilitators of the supranationalization of criminal justice. Despite all the initiatives undertaken, since 2000, of such activity, however, the rate of convictions for such crimes—perhaps the clearest indicator of criminal justice activity—remains low (see U.S. Department of State 2010).

---

* Of increasing importance to the criminal justice realm, supranational governance organizations such as the United Nations and the European Union are meant here. Fundamentally reference is to institutions resulting from the decision of sovereign states to work together at the international level to (better) tackle common problems.

For this reason among others, supranational activity in this area remains considerable. For example, significant efforts are currently underway at the EU level to prepare a proposal for the approximation* of law among the member states (see Gibb et al. 2004). The recently adopted 2010 Stockholm Programme, which sets the criminal justice policy agenda for the EU for the coming 5 years, dedicates a section to this offence as one deserving particular attention. Expressly mentioned in the Treaties, this is a crime clearly belonging to the category foreseen for EU action; one of sufficient seriousness and cross-border relevance to warrant and require action at the supranational level—also beyond the borders of the EU (European Council 2009). It is notable that EU efforts explicitly address prevention and investigations—dealt with in other chapters of this book (see Chapter 7)—remaining silent on the matter of prosecution of such crimes, however.

This silence stands in opposition to the United Nations and other efforts to combat trafficking in human beings centrally expressed in the United Nations "Protocol to Prevent, Suppress, and Punish Trafficking in Persons, Especially Women and Children" adopted in 2000 and also known as the Palermo Protocol which embraces the so-called 3P approach to combating these crimes "prevention, prosecution, and protection" (see Chapters 1 and 6 for further discussion). United Nations' efforts, specifically those of the Office on Drug and Crime (i.e., UNODC) in this field have been extensive to date leading to considerable improvement in terms of legislative provision for trafficking human beings offences, though in fact so far less successful in stimulating *prosecutions* (see UNODC 2009, p. 22 et seq. as well as the balance of efforts reflected in UNODC 2008). Efforts have necessarily focused first on ensuring criminalization (and with it, of course, the very first step to facilitate later prosecution) now increasingly turning to spurning prosecutions as will be explored in the following.

The EU's quieter stance on this point is doubtlessly linked to the 2009 Treaty of Lisbon's clear statement that national jurisdictions are to remain responsible for prosecution [Article 86 of the post-Lisbon Treaty of the Functioning of the EU (TFEU) concerning a potential European prosecutor explicitly states that he or she must bring cases to national courts], but is a significant omission and one which may well have a more reality-driven background than we might wish. As we shall see, even in contexts making strong political commitments to criminal prosecution of the perpetrators of human trafficking crimes, the resulting criminal justice action focuses elsewhere. This chapter by no means sets out to diminish the valuable efforts made at UN, EU or national level toward improving preventive action or investigations into trafficking human beings cases, rather it merely sets out to explore this one aspect; prosecution—in its own right. Naturally the coordination and concentration of such investigations (e.g., at the EU level) will assist in overcoming many of the challenges associated with transnational cases and (particularly in the Continental European context, where it is prosecutors who lead investigations of serious cases), *de facto* mean that prosecution-related efforts are likely to improve alongside and during these. Nevertheless, this chapter is dedicated to a prosecution-centric (see Box 8.1) view of efforts against human trafficking crimes and, unfortunately this means it is often an exploration of deficits which remains to be pursued in this chapter.

---

* This is the traditional procedure used within the EU to ensure the 27 member states' laws are harmonized to a certain extent by bringing them within predefined margins.

BOX 8.1   PROSECUTORS IN DIFFERENT CONTEXTS

Worldwide prosecutors are tasked with bringing cases to court aiming to trigger the imposition of a criminal sanction on criminal perpetrators. Their legal responsibility for the gathering of evidence to prove their cases, however, varies greatly with their respective legal system. While in *adversarial* systems the prosecutor is an intermediate figure receiving the results of police investigation to evaluate and prepare these for court, his/her equivalent in adversarial systems is often formally in charge of the investigation; the police are regarded as prosecution auxiliaries in this context. Relating to serious cases such as trafficking in human beings, this will mean that Continental European prosecutors are on the ground, leading an investigation tactically and potentially ensuring investigatory steps are taken to build their court cases from the very start—assuming of course, this is what the prosecutor is aiming for.

In reality, where complex investigations are launched aiming for criminal convictions in adversarial systems, investigators are perhaps likely to work closely with prosecutors asking their advice on how to proceed with the case. In other words, in such cases, reality may not see adversarial and inquisitorial systems working as differently as the law alone would indicate. However, continental European prosecutors (and those working in systems based on such models) per se have greater influence on the initiation and direction of investigations than their common law colleagues do.

Combating Trafficking in Human Beings: Some Priorities are More Equal than Others

As displayed above, United Nations' efforts to combat trafficking human beings are associated with three priorities (see, e.g., USA Department of State 2010, p. 5); nevertheless, a superficial look at the topic reveals a less balanced reality. To date, efforts to combat trafficking in human beings have focused, above all, on detecting and dismantling trafficking networks (see Potts 2003, p. 248) and prosecution has taken a secondary position.

This priority is arguably set even at the level of supranational treaties. As displayed earlier for the EU, this may be for quite unrelated reasons but it is also indicative of what priority measures truly enjoy. Thus, even the mother of the three Ps, the UN protocol states its purpose in Article 2 as

1. To prevent and combat trafficking in persons, paying particular attention to women and children,
2. To protect and assist the victims of such trafficking, with full respect for their human rights, and
3. To promote cooperation among States Parties to meet those objectives.

However, the Council of Europe Convention states in Article 1 that the purposes of the convention are

   a. To prevent and combat trafficking in human beings, while guaranteeing gender equality;

    b. To protect the human rights of the victims of trafficking, design a comprehensive framework for the protection and assistance of victims and witnesses, while guaranteeing gender equality, as well as to ensure effective investigation and prosecution; and

    c. To promote international cooperation on action against trafficking in human beings.

While prosecution is mentioned and certainly assisted by what is foreseen in these pieces of legislation, their main emphasis is on the broader idea of combating such offences and protecting victims. As displayed, their primary concern (and not without good reason) is first to ensure adequate criminalization of such offences and then arguably to turn to the prevention of such offences and victim protection. These are purposes that are also served by prosecution but not necessarily prosecution alone. Article 4 of the Palermo trafficking protocol expressly includes prosecution within the ambit of its provisions application but it proceeds then to regulate criminalization, to emphasize victim protection and prevention before turning to detailed provision to facilitate, above all, the discovery and prevention of such crimes. Naturally, discovery is also a vital precondition to prosecution. The very layout of the Protocol nevertheless clearly indicates those steps identified as most urgently necessary. Prosecution is set as a political priority but with detailed provision for immediate action made in the other priority areas. As we shall see, this is also the path primarily followed in the decade since the Protocol was adopted. The Council of Europe Convention features greater detail as to criminalization and prevention measures but only makes brief reference to prosecutions though the measures foreseen are clearly intended to facilitate and lay down conditions for these. The criminal justice response to trafficking human beings resulting from these and especially prosecution of such cases should possibly be regarded as "work (still) in progress."

In contrast, the European Council Framework Decision and particularly the related Directive are far more geared toward ensuring prosecution and facilitating judicial cooperation to allow for this. Indeed, one might argue that the Directive was introduced as a reaction to practices preventing prosecutions, but, as will be explored in the following, this is only one legislative stimuli and not that of central importance in the global efforts to combat the trafficking of human beings.

Although not the highest priority so far, prosecutorial efforts at various levels do accompany preventive and protective actions to combat the trafficking of human beings. These prosecutorial efforts are explored in the following. Although this chapter focuses largely on the EU because the most detailed data are available for those countries, as trafficking in persons is a global phenomenon, attention will be drawn to the situation and/or issues within a broader global context.

Domestic Efforts

The immediate problem facing any documentation of criminal justice activity in this field is that the statistical information available is limited (see UNODC 2009, p. 38 et seq., and Chapter 2 in this collection). Despite the concentration of efforts on disruption and prevention, domestic agencies naturally feature the desire to prosecute those who its criminal justice agencies discover to be running and participating in trafficking of human beings. Table 8.1 displays a statistical overview.

Table 8.1   Investigations, Prosecutions, and Convictions for Trafficking Human Beings

Country	Investigations (Cases)[a]	Number of Persons Prosecuted	Number of Persons Convicted
Asia and Europe			
1. Belgium	1204 (2007) N/A (2006)		223 (2007) 238 (2006)
2. Denmark	34 (2008) 34 (2007)	81 (2008) 52 (2007)	19 (2008) 31 (2007)
3. France	30 trafficking networks were dismantled in 2008)	N/A	19 (2007)
4. Ireland	96 (2008)	0 (2008)	0 (2008) 1 (2007)
5. Italy	2221 (2008–data not complete) N/A (2007)	480 (2008–data not complete) N/A (2007)	225 (2008–data not complete) 282 (2007)
6. Luxembourg	N/A (2008) N/A (2007)	7 (2008) 6 (2007)	7 (2008) 6 (2007)
7. Netherlands	N/A (2007) N/A (2006)	221 (2007) 216 (2006)	177 (2007) N/A (2006)
8. Norway	45 (2008) 19 (2007)	6 (2008) 6 (2007)	6 (2008) 6 (2007)
9. Sweden	23 (2008) 15 (2007)	13 (2008) 13 (2007)	12 (2008) 13 (2007)
10. United Kingdom	N/A	129 (March 2008–March 2009)	23 (of the prosecuted cases between March 2008 and March 2009 10 (same period in 2007)
11. Greece	40 (2008)	41 ongoing prosecutions (2008)	21 (2008)
12. Turkey	25 security officials (2008) (2007)	69 cases involving 273 suspected (2008) 160 suspected (2007)	58 trafficking offenders (2008) (2007)
13. Iceland	2 (2008) 0 (2007)	0 (2008) 0 (2007)	0 (2008) 0 (2007)
14. Germany	546 (2007) N/A (2006)	168 (2007) 193 (2006)	133 (2007) 150 (2006)
15. Austria	50 (2008) 89 (2007) N/A (2006)	N/A (2008) (N/A 2007) N/A (2006)	N/A (2008) 30 (2007) 18 (2006)
16. Cyprus	70 persons in 29 cases (2008) 45 persons in 27 cases (2007)	21 (2008) 17 (2007)	1 (2008) 8 (2007)
17. Switzerland	N/A (2007) N/A (2006)	20 (2007) 20 (2006)	25 (2007) 16 (2006)
18. Malta	N/A	N/A	N/A
19. Portugal	55 cases (2008)	57 cases with 190 charges (2008)	N/A
20. Spain	471 people arrested (2008) N/A (2007)	135 cases (2008) 102 cases (2007)	107 offenders (2008) 142 offenders (2007)
21. Liechtenstein	Not reported	Not reported	Not reported
22. San Marino	Not reported	Not reported	Not reported
23. Finland	9 (2008) 10 (2007)	9 (2008) 10 (2007)	9 (2008) 3 (2007)

continued

Table 8.1   (continued) Investigations, Prosecutions, and Convictions for Trafficking Human Beings

Country	Investigations (Cases)[a]	Number of Persons Prosecuted	Number of Persons Convicted
24. Hungary	21 (2008)	18 (2008)	18 (2008)
	48 (2007)	20 (2007)	17 (2007)
25. Poland	119 (2008)	78 (2008)	46 (2008)
	122 (2007)	62 (2007)	43 (2007)
26. Bulgaria	212 (2008)	87 (2008)	69 (2008)
	201 (2007)	78 (2007)	73 (2007)
27. Estonia	2 (2008)	N/A (2008)	2 (2008)
	2 (2007)	N/A (2007)	N/A (2007)
28. Lithuania	18 (2008)	20 (2008)	13 (2008)
	9 (2007)	8 (2007)	4 (2007)
29. Slovenia	7 (2008)	8 (2008)	6 (2008)
	6 (2007)	3 (2007)	5 (2007)
30. Czech Republic	81 (2008)	110 (2008)	64 (2008)
	11 (2007)	121 (2007)	78 (2007)
31. Slovakia	18 (2008)	3 (2008)	11 (2008)
	14 (2007)	16 (2007)	7 (2007)
32. Romania	494 (2008)	329 (2008)	125 (2008)
	232 (2007)	398 (2007)	188 (2007)
33. Andorra	N/A	N/A	N/A
34. Latvia	17 (2008)	15 (2008)	11 (2008)
	21 (2007)	N/A (2007)	28 (2007)
35. Albania	N/A (2008)	22 cases (2008)	26 offenders (2008)
	N/A (2007)	49 cases (2007)	7 offenders (2007)
36. Moldova	246 (2008)	127 (2008)	58 (2008)
	507 (2007)	250 (2007)	60 (2007)
37. Macedonia	N/A (2008)	14 cases (2008)	25 offenders (2008)
38. Ukraine	N/A (2008)	80 cases (2008)	99 offenders (2008)
	N/A (2007)	95 cases (2007)	128 offenders (2007)
39. Russia	111 (2008)	At least 9 (2008)	N/A (2008)
	139 (2007)	At least 46 (2007)	N/A (2007)
40. Croatia	15 people (2008)	12 (2008)	9 (2008)
	20 people (2007)	N/A (2007)	10 (2007)
41. Georgia	14 (2008)	10 (2008)	10 (2008)
	37 (2007)	18 (2007)	N/A (2007)
42. Armenia	13 (2008)	8 (2008)	4 (2008)
	14 (2007)	8 (2007)	11 (2007)
43. Azerbaijan	66 (2008)	61 cases (2008)	61 traffickers (2008)
	N/A (2007)	75 cases (2007)	85 traffickers (2007)
44. Bosnia and Herzegovina	94 (2008)	N/A (2008)	34 (2008)
	(at least) 26 (2007)	N/A (2007)	N/A (2007)
45. Serbia	94 persons (2008)	N/A (2008)	18 (2008)
46. Monaco	N/A	N/A	N/A
47. Montenegro	N/A (2008)	18 (2008–data not complete)	8 (2008–data not complete)

NonCoE Members in Asia and Europe

1. China	2566 (2008)	N/A (very few)	N/A (very few)
2. Indonesia	N/A (2008)	129 (2008)	55 (2008)

Table 8.1   (continued) Investigations, Prosecutions, and Convictions for Trafficking Human Beings

Country	Investigations (Cases)[a]	Number of Persons Prosecuted	Number of Persons Convicted
	N/A (2007)	109 (2007)	45 (2007)
3. Thailand	N/A	54 (whole reporting period)	4 (2006 and 2007)
4. Philippines	168 (2008)	97 (2008)	7 (2008) 12 (since 2003)
5. United Arab Emirates	N/A	20 cases (presumably 2008)	6 (presumably 2008)
North America			
Canada USA	183 (2008)	April 30, 2007–April 2009 82 individuals in 40 cases (2008)	5 (April 2007–April 2009[b]) 77 convictions in 40 cases (2008)
South America			
1. Brazil	57 (2008)	23 (2008)	28 sex and labor traffickers (since March 2009) 22 sex traffickers (since March 2008) 9 (2007)
2. Argentina	35 (10 additional cases were forwarded to courts (2008) N/A (2007)	N/A (2008) N/A (2007)	0 (2008) 10 (2007)
3. Peru	N/A (2008) N/A (2007)	54 (2008) 15 (2007)	5 (2008) 0 (2007)
4. Colombia	159 (2008) 182 (2007)	20 (2008) 44 (2007)	16 (2008) 6 (2007)
Africa			
1. Algeria	0	0	0
2. Tunisia	N/A (30,000 labor inspections in 2008)	1 (till April 2009) 0 (2008)	1 (till April 2009) 0 (2008)
3. Morocco	N/A (they dismantled 220 trafficking or smuggling rings in 2008)	242 (2008)	N/A
Australasia			
Australia	N/A (2009) N/A (2008)	5 prosecutions with 11 defendants (March 2009) N/A (2008)	N/A (2009) "significant convictions" (2008)

Source: Patt, M. 2009. *Human Trafficking and Modern-day Slavery. Country Reports.* Retrieved July 16, 2010, from http://gvnet.com/humantrafficking/; relevant country reports.

[a] The data in this table are based on data drawn from the U.S. State Department Trafficking in Persons Report, 2009. The data for each country are thus a compilation of all cases of "trafficking" compiled by embassies working with NGOs, researchers, and so on. See methodology USA Department of State (2010) p. 20 et seq. As such, this is a mixed figure including trafficking for sexual exploitation, labor, and so on.

[b] Perrin 2010, p. xix.

The data display, above all, a fairly low level of cases. This is normal for a serious crime but given the priority this crime has been lent during the past decade paired with international organizations' repeated assertions that criminalizing norms (let alone enforcement practice) are not wholly adequate, one might assume that these numbers are deficiently low. Research into the totality of the phenomenon and comparison with the rate of other serious crimes might as well bring further enlightenment. These are, however, not pursued here because this section is dedicated to the prosecution of discovered crimes. Relating to this, Table 8.1 is particularly interesting because it shows, for the main part (notable exceptions being: Denmark, Sweden, Finland, the Czech Republic, Azerbaijan, Brazil, and The USA) a steep fall between the number of cases and the number of persons prosecuted, let alone convicted.

The statistics are incomplete and incompatible (comparing numbers of cases to the number of persons prosecuted and convicted is far from ideal) confirming the UNODC's assertion that lacking data is a fundamental problem and drawing conclusions is challenging (also see Chapter 2). One should further note that a fall in number between cases, identified perpetrators, and convictions is entirely normal (Jehle 2009). However, one might also note that such a sharp fall is astonishing on the one hand because trafficking human beings (THB) cases have been lent such priority (in other words, one would not expect them to be filtered out of the criminal justice system at such a high rate) and on the other, because one might fairly expect this statistical relationship not to apply to such cases. THB cases automatically involve more than one perpetrator: Ones in the source and ones in the destination country as well as a potential for a number underway (transporters, corrupt border guards, and so on). Given this fact the statistical relationship displayed might as well be regarded as surprising.

Any attempt to present domestic efforts to combat any crime comparatively are faced with the considerable challenge of lacking common legal definitions, statistical compatibility, not to mention language barriers, reporting and recording practice and administrative variations (an overview of sorts of the situation in the EU can be gained in De Jonge [2005, p. 19]). For problems of statistical comparison, see Home Office et al. (2006), and Aebi et al. (2010, pp. 16–20). In interpreting the statistics in Table 8.1 a number of these caveats apply.* Nevertheless, the figures are sufficient to provide the clear impression that the usual diminishing relationship between investigations and prosecutions is of particular significance for these offence types. That is to say much investigative activity in most countries results in only very few corresponding court cases, let alone convictions.

This discouraging correlation is confirmed and added to by the latest U.S. trafficking in persons' report which estimates a mere 4166 "successful" prosecutions as having ensued worldwide in 2009 although 49,105 victims were identified. Moreover, these are presumed to represent only 0.4% of the estimated 12.3 million victims of such crimes (USA Department of State 2010, pp. 7, 13).

Naturally, an emphasis on *prevention* and *disruption* of trafficking activity as discussed earlier is a possible reason for this. These figures would be compatible with criminal

---

* As noted within the table, they apply to different offences, between the categories featured the unit counted changes and their reliability varies. There is also, naturally no correspondence between the number of cases discovered and convictions ensuing in any one year but given that that UNODC indicates there is a stable trend in the number of prosecutions brought for most of the countries featured, these should for the most part be broadly representative (see UNODC 2009, p. 37 et seq).

justice responses geared mainly at disrupting what activity they discover (thus hopefully preventing further offences). Overall, however, they demonstrate systems unable to deal with the extent of even crimes discovered. The data available thus certainly back up the idea that criminal justice activity currently focuses on disruption rather than prosecution of such networks (most clearly displayed by France providing investigation statistics relating to the number of networks disrupted). Investigative measures can act as disruptive action in themselves and thus not aim for the usual criminal justice "product" of convictions, perhaps explaining this. It is submitted, however, that prosecutors contemplating such cases are also faced with specific challenges that may also contribute to a lower level of cases in this field (see Segrave et al. 2009, p. 152). These are explored in the following sections.

The Challenges of Trafficking Human Beings' Prosecutions

Prosecutors wishing to bring cases against human traffickers to court are faced first with the decision as to how to charge. Trafficking-specific offences are new and often untested, thus placing prosecutors before a number of uncertainties in comparison with more traditional crimes committed as part of the trafficking and exploitation scenario (see Gallagher and Holmes 2008).

The crux of the matter is, prosecutors faced with the choice of ensuring a conviction for a more tried and tested component crime (such as bodily harm, rape and kidnapping—thus for evidential reason, charging can often scale down the offence or indeed relate to nonTHB-specific offences [see De Jonge 2005, pp. 21–2] or labeling a trafficker as a trafficker). In other words, the easier conviction may be gained by charging less or only a part of what has taken place—thereby nevertheless serving to disrupt and prevent trafficking activity. This will have to be weighed against the ultimately more appropriate but, in trial–tactical terms, riskier human trafficking-specific offence that would ensure more comprehensive prosecution and thus ultimately justice (see House of Commons 2009). This "Al Capone" approach is all too understandable but naturally imbues the danger that this phenomenon as a whole is underestimated and remains "under the carpet," as well as under the judicial radar. Given the immense caseload pressure under which even specialist prosecutors are (see in general Wade 2008), and the fact that nothing is more time intensive than days spent in court arguing one's case, it would not be surprising to find that prosecutors do all they can to avoid complications such as untried legal argument. Aside from the investigative difficulties present such as the clandestine nature of human trafficking, the challenges of apprehending perpetrators of human trafficking and so on, there may be purely legal–tactical reasons for prosecutions still being relatively rare (see Gallagher and Holmes 2008, p. 320).

In forging a case against human traffickers, prosecutors face enormous challenges building and bringing a case. Just as investigations are hampered by difficulties in identifying victims, and so prosecutors will suffer in seeking available and reliable witnesses from the way in which this issue is fused with actions against illegal migration (USA Department of State 2010, pp. 13–14). Once identified, victim witnesses will require a great deal of protection and may indeed be extremely traumatized meaning that the prosecutor faces—the human challenges laid to one side—considerable difficulties gaining suitable testimony (see Chapter 12 in this collection and Segrave et al. 2009, p. 68 note also the need for very extreme circumstances as facilitating courts in perceiving a victim as such p. 138).*

In 2007 in Germany, for instance, legislative effort was made to deal with a key challenge to prosecuting such crimes: the *lack of witnesses*. The statutory position of victims of human trafficking who were forced into prostitution or the pornography industry was changed to allow them to reside in Germany and indeed to work legally for as long as they are required to act as witnesses at least. The fate of this potential improvement is indicative of the multifaceted nature of problems (see also Konrad 2002, pp. 266–7) facing prosecutors: In 2009, the circa 700 registered cases of human trafficking for sexual exploitation led only to 45 victims being permitted to stay as witnesses (Confirming the general rarity of victim involvement—Gallagher and Holmes 2008, p. 338). According to NGOs active in the area, immigration officers are generally unwilling to allow victims to stay or even to inform them of their rights; presumably mistaking or viewing them primarily as illegal immigrants or even other types of criminal offenders rather than victims (this attitude is apparent on the metro-level of political agreements [see Chou 2008, pp. 80–81 and Segrave et al. 2009, p. 4]). On the massive efforts undertaken to counter such attitudes (and the need for them) in the USA see Zakhari (2005), pp. 132, 144). Prosecution is thus made impossible by deportation practice which prevents the majority of victims even considering this modest offer. As a result, prosecutions can relate only to structures uncovered by *razzias* and thus presumably only to a very limited aspect of the phenomenon (see Preuß 2010 and also Konrad 2002, p. 266). For consideration of what may be a more productive route see Gallagher and Holmes 2008, p. 334). By failing to pursue their prosecution possibilities, destination states are arguably neglecting their legal as well as moral duty (see Perrin 2010). As Gallagher and Holmes (2008, pp. 321, 332) point out, it is in these countries that the real profits are made and exploitation takes place. Evidence of the full picture of such offences is only available there in cooperation with victims. The failure to ensure that such evidential strands are brought together is the end of many a potential prosecution. The inextricable nexus of protection of victims with their cooperation in criminal proceedings has naturally been subject to strong criticism (Expert Group on Trafficking in Human Beings 2004).

This restrictive view in assessing victims is also reported as counterproductive. The Italian experience, for example, has apparently witnessed an increase in trials (though many investigations do not lead to prosecution) reportedly based on the comprehensive granting of residence permits because only once victims recover and realize that the authorities they are dealing with are not the same as those whose officials they saw bribed in the process of their trafficking, do they become cooperative (see Raffaelli 2009, p. 219). Similar experience is reflected in the advice provided by the 2010 U.S. Trafficking in Persons report (see USA Department of State 2010, p. 40) as well as by the UNODC whose Toolkit to combat trafficking in persons (which dedicates one of 10 sections to victim identification including a very detailed list of "indicators of trafficking" in Section 6.4) clearly indicating that criminal justice professionals are required to perceive those they deal with differently to recognize them as trafficking victims. The USA has made concerted efforts since 2007 to improve victim identification but still report "Victim identification, given the amount of resources put into

---

* The UNODC online toolkit to combat trafficking in persons which aims to aid criminal justice professionals in combatting trafficking human beings dedicates three of ten sections to victim-related issues and one section entirely to victim assistance. See http://www.unodc.org/unodc/en/human-trafficking/electronic-toolkit-to-combat-trafficking-in-persons—index.html

the effort, is considered to be low and law enforcement officials are sometimes untrained or unwilling to undertake victim protection measures" (USA Department of State 2010, p. 339). The latest government conclusions there thus rank highly in their work ahead on further training of criminal justice professionals in identifying and supporting victims in suitable ways (see USA Department of State 2010, p. 339 as well as U.S. Attorney-General 2009). In other words, the current scenario may leave most prosecutors, regardless of geopolitical location, faced with victims who are not given the necessary time to reveal their potential as witnesses upon which the former might base a prosecution.

In any case, the *complex nature of the structures* behind such crimes, their transnational nature on the one hand, and the incentive structures within which prosecutors work on the other will tend to lead them to restrict their cases to "manageable" elements (e.g., to events occurring within their jurisdiction—De Jonge 2005, pp. 28, 33–4; The European Commission has also felt it necessary to call upon member states to ensure charging reflects offence seriousness—indicative of unsuitable reductions being made—COM 2005 514 Final). Organizational structures of prosecution services may further mean that more local prosecutors, who would need to assume leadership of the case and certainly take it to court, may not be in a position to recognize the full scope of an offence (see De Jonge 2005, p. 36). Furthermore, evidential complications may be further compounded by the number of players and factors involved. For example, Eurojust* members report on the one hand that victims may have incentives to exaggerate their accounts to authorities hoping it may lead to their stay in the country being permitted, while on the other hand they may withdraw their testimony on being returned to their country of origin because they become subject to pressure from perpetrators (see De Jonge 2005, p. 40). The latter effect may of course also be achieved when perpetrators are able to threaten, apply pressure to, or harm the victims' families if these persons remain in the country of origin or are not sufficiently protected in the course of proceedings (see Potts 2003, pp. 239–40; Zakhari 2005, p. 143). Prosecutors attempting to truly get to the bottom of a case and to bring these as such to court face a difficult task (see Potts 2003, pp. 239–40; Zakhari 2005, p. 143) for Europe and North America, see also Segrave et al. (2009, p. 122) mentioning the same issues in relation to Australia, Thailand and Serbia illustrating that specific challenges are inherent to these prosecutions). The danger of retaliation attacks and related threats are, for example, specific to human trafficking cases in which an individual is held in servitude to any group with the ability to act in the country of origin. This automatically presents prosecutors with the necessity of protecting persons outside of their own jurisdiction, potentially on a massive scale and thus probably with a unique challenge.

Even if "logistically" enabled to testify, victims are confronted with their ordeal in the process. This fact alone presents prosecutors with a considerable challenge in considering which victims they ask to appear as witnesses and indeed how their testimony is to be facilitated (see Konrad 2002, p. 269). The cultural and social differences between the victim's background and the setting within which he or she is required to act as a witness may make this task complex in this context. On the other hand a number of human trafficking victims are also reported in part as unwilling to identify themselves as victims, having, for example, undertaken their trafficking voluntarily [which legally rarely

---

* Eurojust is the judicial cooperation unit of the European unit which incorporates a representative of each member state (and Norway) to facilitate judicial cooperation in specific cases—see www. Eurojust. europa.eu

makes a difference as far as the offence is concerned—see Conference of the Parties to the United Nations Convention against Transnational Organized Crime (2008) Section 11] as they see it or due to their relationship with their trafficker (see UNODC Section 6.2 and Segrave et al. 2009, pp. 75–6, 84). Where prosecution is intensified, witness protection measures and residence concessions are a precondition (see Konrad 2002, p. 271 and these may indeed need to extend to family in other countries as shown earlier [Potts 2003, pp. 239–40]). Furthermore, the need to provide psychological support and counseling may be overwhelming (see Chapter 12 in this book for further discussion). A decision to involve such witnesses, certainly vital to trafficking-specific charges, is likely to leave prosecutors facing enormous organizational as well as emotional challenges. Where such scenarios arise under time pressure because deportation decisions are pending, it is not difficult to imagine them becoming a disincentive to pursuing a prosecution.

Utilization of Victims?

Innate in the current approach to facilitating the inclusion of victim witnesses to facilitate precisely these broader prosecutions is the acceptance that victims will be protected and assisted only in so far as they are useful for prosecution. As described below the EU directive has set out boundaries for its member states to facilitate the accommodation of victims in so far as they participate in criminal proceedings while the U.S. government has opted to open the path to benefits and tracks to permanent residence status to victims of "serious forms of trafficking" who are "willing to assist in every reasonable way in the investigation and prosecution of severe forms of trafficking in persons" (107.b.1.E.i.I.) (see U.S. Attorney-General 2009, p. 34).* It is not difficult to imagine scenarios in which such an approach may appear highly questionable with prosecutors forced to demand that such potential witnesses make speedy decisions and indeed are likely to face witnesses desperate not to be returned to their country of origin having co-operated. As a whole, this scenario is not likely to make the prosecutor's work easy either in emotional or in evidence-securing and evaluating terms. Independent of whether this is regarded as an appropriate state reaction to such a situation, it is one which places criminal justice employees in highly demanding and difficult human scenarios, making life-changing decisions of the highest order.

Potential witnesses, especially those providing for the most solid prosecutions, are likely to be highly traumatized victims who have suffered extreme cruelty and deprivation (Segrave et al. 2009, pp. 138, 140 and 155). Broader prosecution strategies likely need to pay greater attention to these aspects. From a casuistic point of view alone, one would expect that these victims require a great deal of support and counseling to become reliable witnesses (as discussed earlier, see also Chapters 6 through 8 of UNODC toolkit). That it will

---

* See also Zakhari (2005, p. 131). U.S. legislation also "opens the door" for victims to be given temporary immigration status and accommodation in safe housing provided it is determined that such individual is a victim of a severe form of trafficking and a potential witness to such trafficking, in order to effectuate prosecution of those responsible"—107 (c) of the Trafficking Victims Protection Act of 2000. Section 107(b) does require the provision of medical care to all victims regardless of their immigration status. The U.S. approach can be seen as more generous to victims providing a possibility for victims to stay for up to three years and even to apply for permanent residence status; nevertheless, the key first hurdle is an assesment of usefulness to criminal justice proceedings perhaps explaining the relatively low number of such applications so far—see Zakhari (2005, p. 132).

also be a prosecutorial decision when to end such support may make prosecutors less keen to place themselves in this situation.

Aside from such utilitarian aspects, the legitimacy of such state behavior toward vulnerable victims abused on their territory can hardly be described as anything but questionable. Given the low rate of prosecutions brought, limiting more permanent protection and assistance to so-called useful witnesses greatly reduces the circle of persons likely to benefit from it. One might more radically argue it to represent a secondary form of exploitation. Victims are not assisted based on their needs (those most traumatized are imaginably least likely to make good [i.e., reliable witnesses without a great deal of help]) nor in an effort to make good their suffering by the society in which they suffered (and which as asserted earlier, therefore also bears the moral responsibility for the demand driving such crimes [see, e.g., Stoecker 2005, p. 24]), but are subjected to new "masters"; the coincidence as to whether they were trafficked by persons against whom a case can and will be made—as raw material for the criminal justice system.[*]

Legal Challenges

On an entirely other level: The substantive requirements of THB-specific offences are likely to place prosecutors before legal problems (see, e.g., the extensive guidance issued by the British Crown Prosecution Service—CPS 2009). Substantive alarm bells begin to ring at first sight of the supranational requirements (see infra) requiring the creation of such offences. Thus, for example, the UN Palermo Protocol uses terms such as "other forms of coercion" [Article 3(a)] and indeed "for the purpose of exploitation" proceeding to explain that "exploitation shall include, at a minimum, the exploitation of the prostitution of others or other forms of sexual exploitation, forced labor or services, slavery or practices similar to slavery, servitude or the removal of organs"; [Article 3(a)] the Council of Europe Convention adds the concept of "abuse of power" to these [Article 4(a); see also Articles 16–22] while the EU Council Framework Decision speaks also of a "position of vulnerability" [Article 1(c)] resulting in the victim having "no real and acceptable alternative but to submit to the abuse involved" [Article 1(c)]. These simply are not the easiest of legally determinable and certain concepts, let alone ones that can easily be proved (see Box 8.2). This fundamental, definitional problem would go some way in explaining Segrave et al.'s assertion that "this pattern of minimal numbers of convictions is consistent across nations regardless of the systems of justice in operation or the differences between legislative frameworks" (2009, p. 123—in reviewing legislation, the U.S. State Department is critical, above all, of failures to recognize trafficking as a problem in itself adequately—see also Apap et al. 2000). The difficulty of proving a victim as having been forced into a situation of exploitation or as having been in a vulnerable position has already proved a frequent, significant hurdle (see De Jonge 2005, p. 42). Charging for offences with a lesser evidential burden is a prosecutor's logical consequence.

[*] For examples of treatment causing revictimization and the utlilization and objectification of victims by criminal justice systems see Segrave, Milivojevic and Pickering (2009, p. 155 et seq). Such utilization is to be regarded even more critically given their study's indication (to quote their interpretation of one interviewee featured) "that the official response has no direct relevance to or benefits for victims"— p. 127 see also the accounts on pp. 128 and 139 which go so far as to suggest a certain degree of abuse inherent in victims treatment within the criminal justice process.

The following examples of legislation criminalizing trafficking for sexual exploitation in England and Wales and in Germany, as well as the definitional section of the U.S. American legislation serve as illustrations of the challenges lawyers may face in proving human trafficking-specific offences.

BOX 8.2   COMPLEXITY OF ANTITRAFFICKING LEGISLATION

Section 57 of the UK Sexual Offences Act 2003: Trafficking into the UK for sexual exploitation

1. A person commits an offence if he intentionally arranges or *facilitates* the arrival in the United Kingdom of another person (B) and either—
   a. he intends to do anything to or in respect of B, after B's arrival but in any part of the world, which if done will involve the commission of a relevant offence, or
   b. he believes that another person is likely to do something to or in respect of B, after B's arrival but in any part of the world, which if done will involve the commission of a relevant offence.
2. A person guilty of an offence under this section is liable—
   a. on summary conviction, to imprisonment for a term not exceeding 6 months or a fine not exceeding the statutory maximum or both;
   b. on conviction on indictment, to imprisonment for a term not exceeding 14 years.

Section 232 of the German Criminal Code: Human trafficking for the purpose of sexual exploitation

1. Whosoever exploits another persons *predicament* or *helplessness* arising from being in a foreign country in order to induce them to engage in or continue to engage in prostitution, to engage in exploitative sexual activity with or in the presence of the offender or a third person or to suffer sexual acts on his own person by the offender or a third person shall be liable to imprisonment from six months to ten years. Whosoever induces a person under twenty-one years of age to engage in or continue to engage in prostitution or any of the sexual activity mentioned in the 1st sentence above shall incur the same penalty.

Legally challenging concepts *emphasized* by author

Section 103 U.S. Victims of Trafficking and Violence Protection Act of 2000

2. COERCION—The term "coercion" means:
   (A) threats of serious harm to or physical restraint against any person;
   (B) any scheme, plan or pattern intended to cause a person to believe that failure to perform an act would result in serious harm to or physical restraint against any person; or

      (C) the abuse or threatened abuse of the legal process.
3. COMMERCIAL SEX ACT—The term "commercial sex act" means any sex act on account of which anything of value is given to or received by any person.
4. DEBT BONDAGE—The term "debt bondage" means the status or condition of a debtor arising from a pledge by the debtor of his or her personal services or of those of a person under his or her control as a security for debt, if the value of those services as reasonably assessed is not applied toward the liquidation of the debt or the length and nature of those services are not respectively limited and defined.
5. INVOLUNTARY SERVITUDE—The term "involuntary servitude" includes a condition of servitude induced by means of
      (A) any scheme, plan or pattern intended to cause a person to believe that, if the person did not enter into or continue in such condition, that person or another person would suffer serious harm or physical restraint; or
      (B) the abuse or threatened abuse of the legal process.

On a more practical note, reports of *overly lenient-sentencing* are not rare in this context; indeed relatively light sentences appear to be a regularity in such cases (see Gallagher and Holmes 2008, p. 322; Segrave et al. 2009, p. 152). This is apparently true also of the USA—a jurisdiction considered to be taking decisive action against trafficking offences—see Zakhari (2005, pp. 125, 130)—in spite of adjustments to the sentencing guidelines (p. 131, also pp. 139, 144). This may be due to the complexity of proving certain elements of the crime, the factual extent of the activity, or indeed because judges fail to appreciate the seriousness of the phenomenon (not entirely unlikely if prosecutors are more likely to bring partial, tactically simpler charges in most cases, meaning that courts have no chance to gain a full impression). UK efforts have, for example, focused particularly on trafficking for sexual exploitation (see, e.g., Home Office 2007 and 2008; between March 2008 and 2009 the UK government reported 129 ongoing prosecutions). Sentences ranged from 18 months to 14 years (an average of 5 years—Patt—UK; see also CPS Press Release 2005). A "cost/ benefit analysis" of this order is likely to act as a disincentive to prosecutors considering charging trafficking human-beings–specific offences. The unusual measure of a state appeal against a lenient sentence reported early on in UK efforts for such a case displays the importance attached to such convictions and, above all, the sentence level achieved (see CPS 2004). Sentences within the United States are reported as nominally higher (see U.S. Attorney General 2010, p. 49) though it is typical of the United States imposing higher sentences across the board in any case (see e.g., Zakhari 2005, p. 142) which notes sentence differences as in accordance with variation between U.S. states. Further study would be required to determine whether sentences are more punitive in the respective sentencing context.

    Successful prosecutions, especially for trafficking-specific offences will require strong prosecutorial guidance of investigative proceedings to ensure that the results of these can lead to comprehensive and ultimately just prosecutions;* prosecutors must not only

---

* Ensuring evidence of all aspects necessary is a challenge unto itself, see Gallagher and Holmes 2008, p. 332.

be familiar with the law and the broader contexts of the cases but should also be well equipped to deal with its complexities, witness protection, and the challenging interaction and protection of victim witnesses (see Gallagher and Holmes 2008, p. 327), as well as being prepared to face an "uphill battle" in court. A rational prosecutor, pushed for time, may well choose an alternative course of action as prosecutors worldwide can be seen to be doing in the face of case overload regardless of their formal duties (see Luna and Wade 2011).

The 2009–2010 EuroNEEDS Study

Prosecutors' experiences in dealing with transnational crimes including trafficking human beings' offences were explored as part of the EuroNEEDs study.[*] This study features interviews with 140 prosecutors from 18 EU member states. Seventeen of the prosecutors interviewed as specialist in transnational crime had expertise in cases of trafficking human beings. They, like all other interviewees, were questioned as to the problems they face in dealing with such cases, whether mechanisms introduced by the EU so far have or will help counter these problems and whether any further changes are necessary. The results of interest to the focus of this chapter are included here.[†]

Twelve of the seventeen (71%) specialist prosecutors interviewed estimated that all, or almost all, their cases have a transnational dimension. Two (12%) estimated a lower proportion while three did not answer this question. In other words, it would appear that prosecutors working in this area are certainly faced with the challenges of transnational evidence collection if not even deeper cooperation needs. Four (24%) interviewees explained that the international dimension of these cases make them far more complex while two attest to cases as failing because of this aspect. Four (24%) saw them hampered by legal problems, seven (41%) by procedural, and ten (59%) by practicalities. One interviewee criticized the lack of an internationally proactive approach saying that prosecutors must in fact initiate investigations to be able to successfully combat these crimes. Of the 15 who answered this specific question, 13 (87%) stated that the mechanisms by which they could seek assistance from abroad currently in place are sufficient and only two said that they were not. Ten (67%) said that the result would always depend on the effort made by the individual prosecutor, four (27%) said that these mechanisms ensured success, and one said that they would not. Nine (53% of the entire sample) interestingly stated no further mechanisms to be necessary while only three (18%) of those who chose to answer the question responded in the affirmative.

Confirming the international nature of their work in this field, of the 17 interviewees one (5.9%) stated using the European Arrest Warrant in all cases, one (5.9%) occasionally, eleven (65%) frequently and four (24%—stemming from a jurisdiction in which it is not available) never. In relation to Eurojust the numbers were as follows: one (5.9%) for all cases, eight (47%) frequently, two (12%) occasionally, one (5.9%) rarely, and five (29%)

---

[*] See http://www.iuscrim.mpg.de/ww/en/pub/forschung/forschungsarbeit/strafrecht/euroneeds.htm (retrieved July 28/10).

[*] A full analysis as well as raw interview data will be available within the EuroNEEDS publication and documentation activities see http://www.mpicc.de/ww/en/pub/forschung/forschungsarbeit/strafrecht/euroneeds.htm for details as of circa June 2011.

never. In relation to the European Judicial Network: one (5.9%) for all cases, six (35%) frequently, one (5.9%) occasionally, two (12%) rarely, and seven (41%) never.

Highlighting the difficulties prosecutors face in trying to ensure that they prosecute such cases fully, eight prosecutors said that they never limit their cases to matters of national relevance while nine admitted that they do so. Seven (41%) prosecutors claimed their system inherently contains disincentives to bringing such cases, five (29%) of these pointed to a lack of financial or personnel resources to deal with them.

It must be noted as background that nine (53%) of the prosecutors said that they carried out investigations themselves (a further 4%–24%—stating this role is played by the investigating judge—from two countries which feature these). Interestingly of those interviewed from one of these systems, only two (of four) said this was the case, a third mentioning that the investigating judges are also used but always with strong prosecutorial participation (i.e., leadership of such cases is shared). Of the 15 who answered the question, 11 (73% of those who answered) said that they would always prefer to be involved in investigative measures taking place abroad while only four said "no."

The EuroNEEDS study thus, above all, highlights a number of limitations as to what can be achieved in a domestic setting in combating trafficking human beings offences altogether. Clearly, decisions as to what to prosecute as well as how and where to do so require the same international cooperation to enable this. Investigations alone require prosecutors to engage the full range of special European cooperation mechanisms made available to them. Trafficking human beings prosecutions thus clearly require prosecutors to work outside their comfort zones: with dense links to other jurisdictions, laws, and cultural contexts. A supranational cooperation framework such as that found in the EU would appear necessary to facilitate prosecutions of this kind; yet interestingly here too, emphasis has been more on investigation and disruption so far. This is also reflected by the lack of formal rules (e.g., on jurisdiction as to who should prosecute what at the end of an investigation). Where prosecutors must operate using traditional mutual legal assistance channels, the challenges facing them in putting together a comprehensive prosecution case must be recognized as daunting.

Impact

Given that the prevention of such offences is ultimately also likely to be linked to prosecution and strategic decisions as to whom to prosecute as well as making sure there are no safe-havens from prosecution, prosecutors' decisions relating to trafficking human beings offences have importance well beyond their national jurisdictions. Trafficking offences often involve organized criminal networks (though naturally this is not always the case (see, e.g., Zakhari 2005 and Segrave et al. 2009, who report finding little indication of organized networks in their study) which are likely to respond to criminal justice pressure being applied on them (see Stoecker 2005). A lack of effective prosecution policies in one country will open the door to criminal activity affecting surrounding states to be based there (see Stoecker 2005, p. 21). The EuroNEEDS study clearly indicates the European context and thus also the Europe-wide ramifications of prosecutors work in this context. Currently, decisions when to initiate prosecuting proceedings are not in any way linked unless by a coordinated, cross-border investigation. As yet, there is no over-arching common strategy though initial efforts are being made, as we shall see.

It is interesting to note that it has so far been larger EU member states who are reported as bringing trafficking human beings cases to Eurojust for further facilitation and coordination (see De Jonge 2005), perhaps indicating that willingness and ability to recognize and act upon indications of a cases' international dimension is a matter of capacity (resource, financial, and political), specialization, and so on. Another interpretation is naturally that only these states experience such offences in a volume which make them willing to dedicate this degree of resources to them or perhaps only they are able to. Echoing other offences of concern to the EU, it would appear that the responsibility of nation states for prosecution of such cases must be regarded as a hindrance. Comprehensive prosecution, and with it plausibly effective prevention, hinges on having a perspective and indeed a criminal justice reach which goes beyond traditional borders. Trafficking human beings forms part of a group of offences for which a supranational perspective might as well be useful (see De Jonge 2005). The idea that these offences are—in this context, a European problem, requiring not only coordination but also recognition and drive at the European level to be comprehensive and thus effectively prosecuted is likely to mark future discussion on their prosecution there and with time perhaps that of a European public prosecutor's office. Naturally, discussions of such efforts are also unlikely to end at the periphery of the EU.

Supranational Efforts

As indicated in the previous section, trafficking of human beings is an offence area in which there is a clear need for criminal justice agencies to act beyond their national jurisdictional borders and indeed to make strategic decisions at an international level. By its very definition, it will involve the crossing of borders requiring international effort in any criminal justice response. Like drug smuggling, it is a classic transnational crime. Quite aside from its moral weightiness, its very nature demands an internationalized, tactical response. Since around 2000, this has been recognized and various actions have been undertaken at the supranational level. One should note, however, that this has not necessarily been related to the prosecution of these crimes.

As indicated earlier, supranational efforts have been central to measures combating trafficking human beings so far. The establishment of a requirement that trafficking be made a criminal offence at various supranational levels, including that of the *United Nations*, provides the broadest precursor for prosecution (Article 5 UN Protocol to Prevent, Suppress and Punish Trafficking in Persons, especially Women and Children supplementing the UN Convention against Transnational Organised Crime of the 15th of December 2000 [entry into force December 2003]). In a move later paralleled in relation to terrorism, the United Nations Office for Drug Control and Crime Prevention (UNODC) went so far as to offer assistance in aiding countries to draft anti-trafficking human beings legislation, also to avoid the creation of safe havens for traffickers (Potts 2003)—as well as to ensure their mobility cannot assist them in avoiding prosecution Gallagher and Holmes (2008, p. 334). Together with other supranational organizations (such as the, OSCE and the Council of Europe) the United Nations has provided an impulse to ensure trafficking human beings cases can be prosecuted in any relevant jurisdiction. Above all, supranational legislative efforts have been directed at ensuring the full nature of trafficking human beings offences is recognized, providing prosecutors with a new toolkit to comprehensively prosecute. Thus, Article 3 of the UN *Protocol to Prevent, Suppress and Punish Trafficking in Persons, especially Women and Children* (supplementing the UN Convention against Transnational Organised Crime) reads:

(a) "Trafficking in persons" shall mean the recruitment, transportation, transfer, harboring or receipt of persons, by means of the threat or use of force or other forms of coercion, of abduction, of fraud, of deception, of the abuse of power or of a position of vulnerability or of the giving or receiving of payments or benefits to achieve the consent of a person having control over another person, for the purpose of exploitation. Exploitation shall include, at a minimum, the exploitation of the prostitution of others or other forms of sexual exploitation, forced labor or services, slavery or practices similar to slavery, servitude or the removal of organs;

(b) The consent of a victim of trafficking in persons to the intended exploitation set forth in subparagraph (a) of this article shall be irrelevant where any of the means set forth in subparagraph (a) have been used;

(c) The recruitment, transportation, transfer, harboring or receipt of a child for the purpose of exploitation shall be considered "trafficking in persons" even if this does not involve any of the means set forth in subparagraph (a) of this article; and

(d) "Child" shall mean any person under 18 years of age.

The Protocol continues to require criminalisation in Article 5 according to the following terms:

1. Each State Party shall adopt such legislative and other measures as may be necessary to establish as criminal offences the conduct set forth in Article 3 of this Protocol, when committed intentionally.
2. Each State Party shall also adopt such legislative and other measures as may be necessary to establish as criminal offences:
   (a) Subject to the basic concepts of its legal system, attempting to commit an offence established in accordance with paragraph 1 of this article;
   (b) Participating as an accomplice in an offence established in accordance with paragraph 1 of this article; and
   (c) Organizing or directing other persons to commit an offence established in accordance with paragraph 1 of this article.

In other words, it is more than apparent that UN efforts are directed at ensuring broad and similar criminalization of anyone linked to, or assisting, such networks in any way (there is clear emphasis of the strong misbalance of power between victim and perpetrator taken advantage of in the criminal behavior thrown into focus). This effort is thus clearly directed at ensuring substantive harmonization providing prosecutors with a better basis on which to cooperate and to ensure that prosecution can ensue in any territory in which traffickers operate. Nevertheless, neither a sentence range [compare with Article 3(2) of the EU Framework Decision] nor procedural detail as to how the "assistance to enable [victims'] views and concerns to be presented and considered at appropriate stages of criminal proceedings" [as required by Article 6(2)] is provided. This perhaps serves to confirm that the drafters of this legislation were less mindful of the specificities of prosecution work. It is noted that this is a first step only, albeit an important one.

At a European level the efforts of the United Nations have been picked up in two supranational contexts. Firstly, at the broader level of the *Council of Europe*. This organization has a long tradition for taking initiative wherein cooperation is required at the international level and for propagating human rights (see in general http://www.coe.int/aboutCoe/index.asp?page=nosObjectifs&l=en). Paralleling the UN approach, in 2005, the Council of Europe Convention begins by defining the scope and nature of behavior that member states are required to criminalize. Accordingly Article 4 states:

(a) "Trafficking in human beings" shall mean the recruitment, transportation, transfer, harboring or receipt of persons, by means of the threat or use of force or other forms of coercion, of abduction, of fraud, of deception, of the abuse of power or of a position of vulnerability or of the giving or receiving of payments or benefits to achieve the consent of a person having control over another person, for the purpose of exploitation. Exploitation shall include, at a minimum, the exploitation of the prostitution of others or other forms of sexual exploitation, forced labor or services, slavery or practices similar to slavery, servitude or the removal of organs;

(b) The consent of a victim of "trafficking in human beings" to the intended exploitation set forth in subparagraph (a) of this article shall be irrelevant where any of the means set forth in subparagraph (a) have been used;

(c) The recruitment, transportation, transfer, harboring or receipt of a child for the purpose of exploitation shall be considered "trafficking in human beings" even if this does not involve any of the means set forth in subparagraph (a) of this article;

(d) "Child" shall mean any person under eighteen years of age; and

(e) "Victim" shall mean any natural person who is subject to trafficking in human beings as defined in this article.

The Convention then proceeds to require criminalization in Article 18:

Each Party shall adopt such legislative and other measures as may be necessary to establish as criminal offences the conduct contained in Article 4 of this Convention, when committed intentionally.

The Convention's requirements are thus less explicitly broad than those of the UN Protocol and indeed one might well argue that Article 19 sets out a clear difference in focus to the UN legislation. This focuses on the separate requirement to criminalize the use of services of a victim, in other words to allow criminal justice systems the potential to concentrate on protecting the victims within their jurisdiction. Article 19 states:

Each Party shall consider adopting such legislative and other measures as may be necessary to establish as criminal offences under its internal law, the use of services which are the object of exploitation as referred to in Article 4 paragraph a of this Convention, with the knowledge that the person is a victim of trafficking in human beings.

One cannot help but note that prosecution is only one element considered by the Convention and would certainly not appear to be its primary focus. As outlined above, Article 1 which states the purposes of the Convention apparently stresses the prevention and combating of this crime alongside the human rights of victims as the immediate concern of criminal justice systems. Ensuring comprehensive prosecution is facilitated but perhaps regarded as of secondary importance.

The second supranational activity level within Europe is that of the *European Union* (EU). Until recently, the EU provided for criminal justice-related legislation within a unanimous, intergovernmental context known as the "third pillar."[*] The production of a Council Framework Decision as early as 2002 indicates that this area was given high priority seeing all (at the time 15) Member States' governments agree to legislation at this level. This legislation adds greater detail to the bones of the previous United Nations work, specifying first which types of human trafficking are to be the focus of Member State action and in greater detail the requirements as to what should be criminalized. EU Council Framework Decision of July 19, 2002 on combating trafficking in human beings [2002/629/JHA (2002) OJ L 203/1] thus sets out:

Article 1: Offences concerning trafficking in human beings for the purposes of labor exploitation or sexual exploitation

1. Each Member State shall take the necessary measures to ensure that the following acts are punishable:
   - the recruitment, transportation, transfer, harboring, subsequent reception of a person, including exchange or transfer of control over that person, where:
     - (a) use is made of coercion, force or threat, including abduction, or
     - (b) use is made of deceit or fraud, or
     - (c) there is an abuse of authority or of a position of vulnerability, which is such that the person has no real and acceptable alternative but to submit to the abuse involved, or
     - (d) payments or benefits are given or received to achieve the consent of a person having control over another person for the purpose of exploitation of that person's labor or services, including at least forced or compulsory labor or services, slavery or practices similar to slavery or servitude, or for the purpose of the exploitation of the prostitution of others or other forms of sexual exploitation, including pornography.
2. The consent of a victim of trafficking in human beings to the exploitation, intended or actual, shall be irrelevant where any of the means set forth in paragraph 1 have been used.
3. When the conduct referred to in paragraph 1 involves a child, it shall be a punishable trafficking offence even if none of the means set forth in paragraph 1 have been used.
4. For the purpose of this Framework Decision, "child" shall mean any person below 18 years of age.

Article 2 proceeds to specify the breadth of criminal liability required, it reads:

Instigation, aiding, abetting and attempt

Each Member State shall take the necessary measures to ensure that the instigation of, aiding, abetting, or attempt to commit an offence referred to in Article 1 is punishable.

---

[*] The first two are the traditionally purely economic European community and the common foreign and defence policy.

Within the EU great effort was obviously put into ensuring the compatibility of legal definitions presumably to enable a greater degree of practical cooperation in combating these crimes. The offence definitions required naturally lay the ground for more detailed common action that can be witnessed within the EU. In its new legal framework for this area (see, e.g., Article 83 Treaty of the Functioning of the EU) the EU has emphasized THB offences as the ones for focus of relevant activity. Much effort has been invested in facilitating successful common investigations (see, e.g., Section 3.3.1. of the Stockholm Programme and the encouragement of the use of joint investigation teams by the Council, Section 4.3.1 [p. 40]. For more information on these, see http://www.eurojust.europa.eu/ jit.htm) and within these presumably disruptive actions. Nevertheless, such concerted action can be expected to have a "trickle-down" effect causing more prosecutions. Eurojust already plays a significant role in the investigative stage (see, e.g., the EuroNEEDs results mentioned earlier) meaning that strategic prosecutorial decisions will already be innate in these. The more cases arise, the more efforts will become visible at the European level in relation to prosecutors.

Recent EU policy was also developed precisely with the intent of facilitating prosecution of human trafficking offenders in mind (see Chou 2008, p. 82) via the Victim of Trafficking Directive* (adopted as a migration policy matter and thus in the—now defunct—first pillar as genuine supranational legislation). In other words, the EU level was used to address some of the challenges recognized as facing prosecutors in this area. Centrally, the Directive requires the Member States to encourage victims to come forward and assist authorities in prosecuting their traffickers by awarding them temporary residence permits and a number of further, related benefits. Where they are considered useful for investigation or prosecution proceedings, victims will be given a contemplation period (Article 6 of EU Directive) followed by a renewable residence permit valid for at least 6 months (Articles 7 and 8 of EU Directive). As shown above, this EU approach is the subject of considerable criticism (see above page 144).

This Directive stands next to the Framework Decision on Combating Trafficking in Human Beings which was created to alleviate the recognized lack of effective judicial (as well as law enforcement) cooperation. It is thus clear that the EU-level efforts were undertaken to ensure that highly practical changes were undertaken within the Member States. THB is an unusual policy area in that it witnesses the Member States formulating a very detailed common policy. This is naturally connected to the fact that THB offences are perceived as strongly related to illegal immigration which has been a genuine supranational policy area since 1999 (when the Treaty of Amsterdam saw this policy area brought into European Community responsibility [see Chalmers et al. 2006, p. 606]). Nevertheless, given the depth of criminal justice action emphasized in this area, it is an interesting development.

Alongside the legislative framework, the EU's organizational setup (including Eurojust as a facilitator, instruments based on mutual recognition such as the European Arrest Warrant alongside its inherent abolition of the double criminality requirement for, amongst others, these offences; see e.g., Keijzer and Sliedregt, 2009) is regarded as exemplary in this context (see Gallagher and Holmes 2008, p. 335), displaying clearly the

---

* Council Directive on the Residence Permit Issued to Third-Country Nationals who are Victims of Trafficking in Human Beings or who have been the subject of an action to Facilitate Illegal Immigration, who Co-operate with the Competent Authorities 2004/81/EC, [2004] OJ L 261/19.

kind of level at which such offences must be tackled. The supranational efforts within the EU go beyond formulating priorities and providing legal basis (see e.g., European Commission 2004). Trafficking human beings must be regarded as one of the drivers of EU criminal justice integration; the depth of police and judicial interaction (as well as the assignment of tasks and powers to supranational institutions such as Europol and Eurojust) is unusual displaying the Member States' evaluation of the need to cooperate as more important than their usual sovereignty concerns.* Practical consequences are ongoing for the investigation of such offences and we are only now beginning to see the impact on the prosecution stage.

UNODC efforts have, as described earlier, so far been concentrated on ensuring criminalization with efforts now beginning to turn to ensuring more comprehensive prosecution (see UNODC 2009, p. 37).

In comparison, the Council of Europe Convention approach can be recognized as having another function; providing a broader protective basis for victims and further steps to facilitate international cooperation as well as prosecution though its focus is regarded as being victim protection rather than the latter (see Raffaelli 2009, p. 212). These efforts are augmented within Europe by the Organization for Security and Co-operation in Europe (OSCE) and the Stability Pact for South Eastern Europe which also placed this issue high on the agenda creating the Stability Pact Task Force for Trafficking in Human Beings in June 2000 (see Konrad 2002, p. 260). Clearly, this is an area subject to a great deal of supranational attention in Europe. The results of this will become apparent and form an unprecedented example of supranational-based action in the criminal justice realm and prosecutorial policy within the next few years. These have just begun with the Commission's suggestion (e.g., approximate substantive criminal law and to revise legislation to ensure better victim protection [see European Commission 2009]). So far, however, the impact on prosecutions has been limited with even Eurojust tending to emphasize its role in disrupting networks and coordinating investigations.†

Finally, one should not neglect to mention the oldest supranational influence on European governments and criminal justice systems. More concretely than recent Council of European legislation, its *Convention on Human Rights* (Convention for the Protection of Human Rights and Fundamental Freedoms. It was signed on November 4, 1950 and entered into force on September 3, 1953) must also be regarded as relevant in such cases. The *Siliadin* judgement (*Case of Siliadin v. France*, 2005, VII. Application number 73316/01 [ECHR]) saw recognition of a positive state duty to ensure that private individuals are punished where they force a foreign minor to work without payment and rest arising from Article 4 of the Convention. Prosecutorial decisions in this context are thus placed at the forefront of human rights protection. What this will mean for prosecutors' work in the future remains to be seen.

---

* See, for example, the discussion surrounding the failed Framework Decision on Procedural Rights in Criminal Proceedings: In the case of *COMMISSION v. COUNCIL* (Application No. C-440/05), judgment of October 23, 2007, OJ C 315/9 of 22 December 2007, the official position of the Irish government was that "this is precisely the kind of action the EU has no competence to take." This was also stated, for example, at the Conference of the German Presidency and the Academy of European Law in February 2007 (for more information see Wade (2007).

† See, for example, Eurojust and Europol Joint Press 2010 and Release (2010 and 2008) and Eurojust Press Release (2008)—Note also that it is this function upon which the European Council lays emphasis for Eurojust's work for the next 5 years—see page 45 of the Stockholm Programme.

NGO Efforts

The role of NGOs in supporting victims is naturally of vital importance for the prosecution of human trafficking offences (also see Chapter 12 in this book). Among other
things, lobbying work and setting of standards are also of great importance in ensuring
adequate and just prosecution. Thus, for example, the Global Alliance against Traffic in
Women, The Foundation against Trafficking in Women, and Global Rights have issued
Human Rights Standards for the Treatment of Trafficked Persons (see Global Alliance
against Traffic in Women et al. 1999) including the following as one of eight central rights/
obligations:

> **Access to Justice**: The police, prosecutors and court shall ensure that their efforts to punish traf-
> fickers are implemented within a system that respects and safeguards the rights of the victims to
> privacy, dignity and safety. An adequate prosecution of traffickers includes prosecution, where
> applicable, for rape, sexual and other forms of assault (including, without limitation, murder,
> forced pregnancies and abortions), kidnapping, torture, cruel, inhuman or degrading treat-
> ment, slavery or slavery-like practices, forced or compulsory labour, debt bondage, or forced
> marriage. (p. 2)

The central role of NGOs in this area is doubtlessly to lobby for comprehensive prosecution
reflecting the severity of crimes, as well as for the consideration of victims' compensatory
claims when this occurs alongside their vital work supporting and assisting victims who
cooperate in prosecutions both by educating criminal justice agencies as to the sensibilities
of such cases on the one hand and in supporting individual victims concerned. Because of
the manifold challenges facing prosecutors in such cases, as well as the lack of adjustment
or familiarity of criminal justice systems with such cases, the burden on NGOs is and will
certainly remain considerable in these cases.*

Conclusion

This chapter set out to examine prosecution as an independent criminal justice response
to THB offences. It has shown that while international legislation spurring on criminal
justice reaction to these offences has certainly foreseen it as a desirable product, prosecution has so far been somewhat eclipsed by efforts to investigate these crimes, to prevent
them, or, in some cases, to primarily ensure that victims are protected. While this is in
many ways understandable, this chapter has pointed out that the lack of comprehensive
prosecution cannot be accepted in the mid- to long term because it is ultimately damaging,
also to these goals.

As has been shown, regardless of the jurisdiction, the prosecution of trafficking human
beings offences is a relatively rare event. This is probably due to the fact that challenges
raised for prosecutors as well as the fact that criminal justice responses to such offences
are still in a developmental stage. Action so far has correctly focused on ensuring criminalization and—in the EU context—the precondition for the necessary international

---

* Little information is available as to NGO work related directly to prosecution, again activities appear
to be strongly concentrated at initial, more fundamental support but see, for example, http://www.kok-
buero.de/index.php?idcatart = 94&lang = 1&client = 1 for NGOs working to support victims during trial
in Germany.

cooperation. As such aspects become more streamlined, attention is increasingly being drawn to prosecution. While prosecutions and convictions are not the only further action required, it appears uncontroversial that the number of prosecutions, convictions, and appropriate sentences must increase.

Nevertheless, practice so far draws our attention to a variety of issues—practical, legal, and philosophical, requiring further attention before more comprehensive prosecution of such offences can take place. Not the least of these is the way in which societies react to the victims of trafficking human beings offences and the mandate we therefore impose upon our prosecutors in dealing with them.

THB offences require all agents, even those far removed, of criminal justice systems to examine our perceptions and, above all, to perceive our work in its globalized context. Investigators and prosecutors must become connected with colleagues in immigration departments as well as in source countries to bring solid cases; victims must be better identified and supported in their recovery as well as their part of the criminal justice process. Where necessary, courts may also need their attention drawn to the necessity of understanding victims even if they fit less comfortably into the mould developed so far. The broader societies which these criminal justice systems serve, however, must facilitate and accompany such a development. Ultimately, prosecutor and court understanding of the THB phenomenon can only be changed by further knowledge of the true context of these crimes, of the modus operandi of perpetrators and the push and pull factors that lead to victimization as well as the various facets of this. Research illuminating the facts of THB offences as well as translating these into the new legal categories that are the justice systems' toolbox has a decisive role to play.

Review and Discussion Questions

1. Should the criminal justice response to trafficking cases be to attempt to achieve convictions?
2. When seeking to bring a prosecution, which duties does a prosecutor owe to which individuals with some nexus to the case?
3. How is a prosecutor to fulfill these obligations?
4. Are victims adequately served by the criminal justice process?
5. Should victims be granted longer-term immigration rights in exchange of their testimony?

References

Aebi, M. et al. 2010. *European Sourcebook of Crime and Criminal Justice Statistics.* Available online at http://www.europeansourcebook.org/ob285_full.pdf (last download January 14, 2011).

Apap, J., Cullen, P., and Medved, F. 2000. *Counteracting Human Trafficking: Protecting the Victims of Trafficking.* CFPS. Available online at http://www.belgium.iom.int/STOPConference/Conference%20Papers/01.%20Apap,%20J.-%20IOM%20final%20paper.pdf (last download January 14, 2011).

Chalmers, D., Hadjiemmaanuil, C., Monti, G., and Tomkins, A. 2006. *European Union Law.* Cambridge: Cambridge University Press.

Chou, M.-H. 2008. The European union and the fight against human trafficking: Comprehensive or contradicting? *St Antony's International Review*, 4(1), 76–95.

Conference of the Parties to the United Nations Convention against Transnational Organized Crime. 2008 *Implementation of the Protocol to Prevent, Suppress and Punish Trafficking in Persons, Especially Women and Children, supplementing the United Nations Convention against Transnational Organized Crime: consolidated information received from States for the first reporting cycle. Report of the Secretariat.* CTOC/COP/2005/3/Rev.2. Available online at http://www.unodc.org/documents/treaties/COP2008/CTOC%20COP%202005%203%20Rev2%20Final%20E.pdf (last download January 14, 2011).

Crown Prosecution Service. 2004. *Groundbreaking Sentence Increase for Human Trafficker.* Press Release 29/04/2004. Retrieved July 16, 2010, from http://www.cps.gov.uk/news/press_releases/118_04/.

Crown Prosecutions Service. 2005. *UK Hosts Conference to Fight Human Trafficking Across Europe.* Press Release 24/10/2005. Retrieved July 16, 2010, from http://cps.gov.uk/news/press_releases/154_05/.

Crown Prosecution Service. 2009. *Human Trafficking and Smuggling.* Legal Guidance of 5 November 2009. Retrieved July 16, 2010, from http://www.cps.gov.uk/legal/h_to_k/human_trafficking_and_smuggling/.

De Jonge, B. 2005. *Eurojust and Human Trafficking—The State of Affairs.* Retrieved July 16, 2010, from http://polis.osce.org/library/f/3273/2219/EU-NLD-RPT-3273-EN-Eurojust%20and%20Human%20Trafficking%20-%20The%20State%20of%20Affairs.pdf

Eurojust. 2008. *Successful Cooperation in Human Trafficking Case.* Eurojust Press Release 04/11/2008. Retrieved July 16, 2010, from http://www.eurojust.europa.eu/press_releases/2008/04-11-2008.htm.

Eurojust. 2010. *27 Prosecuted for Trafficking Children.* Eurojust Press Release 16/04/2010. Retrieved July 16, 2010, from http://www.eurojust.europa.eu/press_releases/2008/04-11-2008.htm.

Eurojust and Europol. 2008. *Eurojust and Europol Assisted in Dismantling a Trafficking in Human Beings Network.* Eurojust-Europol Joint Press Release 31/01/2008. Retrieved July 16, 2010, from http://www.eurojust.europa.eu/press_releases/2008/31-01-2008.htm.

Eurojust and Europol. 2010. *People Smuggling Network Disrupted.* Eurojust-Europol Joint press Release 22/06/2010. Retrieved July 16, 2010, from http://www.eurojust.europa.eu/press_releases/2010/22-06-2010.htm.

European Commission. 2004. *Report of the Experts Group on Trafficking in Human Beings.* Retrieved July 16, 2010, from http://ec.europa.eu/justice_home/doc_centre/crime/trafficking/doc/report_expert_group_1204_en.pdf.

European Commission. 2009. Impact Assessment. Accompanying document to the Proposal for a COUNCIL FRAMEWORK DECISION on preventing and combating trafficking in human beings, and protecting victims, repealing Framework Decision 2002/629/JHA. COM (2009) 136 Final. Available at: http://eur-lex.europa.eu/LexUriServ/LexUriServ.do?uri=SEC:2009:0358:FIN:EN:PDF (last download: 7.11.2010)

European Council. 2009. *The Stockholm Programme—An Open and Secure Europe Serving and Protecting the Citizens.* Retrieved July 16, 2010, from http://register.consilium.europa.eu/pdf/en/09/st17/st17024.en09.pdf.

Expert Group on Trafficking in Human Beings. 2004. *Report 100.* Can be found online at: http://ec.europa.eu/justice_home/doc_centre/crime/trafficking/doc/report_expert_group_1204_en.pdf (last download 17.7.2010) or http://www.coatnet.org/en/23957.asp (last download January 14, 2011)

Gallagher, A. and Holmes, P. 2008. Developing an effective criminal justice response to human trafficking—Lessons from the front line. *International Criminal Justice Review,* 18(3), 318–343.

Gibb, F., Tendler, S., and Ford, R. 2004, February 10. Rougher justice for drug barons and gangsters: Reasonable doubt should be set aside for worst crimes, says Blair. *The Times.*

Global Alliance Against Traffic in Women 1999. *Human Rights Standards for the Treatment of Trafficked Persons.* Retrieved July 16, 2010, from http://www.globalrights.org/site/DocServer/IHRLGTraffickin_tsStandards.pdf?docID=204.

Home Affairs Committee of the House of Commons, 2009. *The Trade in Human Beings: Human Trafficking in the UK*. Sixth Report of Session 2008–09, Vol. 1. London: The Stationery Office Limited.

Home Office. 2007. *UK Action Plan on Tackling Human Trafficking*. Retrieved July 16, 2010, from http://www.scottishrefugeecouncil.org.uk/arts/Trafficking_ActPlan.

Home Office. 2008. *Update to the UK Action Plan on tackling Human Trafficking*. Retrieved July 16, 2010, from http://www.irm.gov.hu/i/irm.gov.hu/files//downloads/Fooldal/Szakmai_munka/egyesult_kiralysag_emberkereskedelem_elleni_akcioter.pdf.

Home Office. 2006. *European Sourcebook of Crime and Criminal Justice Statistics*. Third Edition. The Hague: WODC.

Jehle, J.-M. 2009. *Criminal Justice in Germany—Facts and Figures*. Fifth Edition. Berlin: Federal Ministry of Justice.

Keijzer, N. and Sliedregt, E.v. 2009. *The European Arrest Warrant in Practice*. The Hague: T.M.C. Asser.

Konrad, H. 2002. Trafficking in human beings—The ugly face of Europe. *Helsinki Monitor*, 13(3), 260–271.

Luna, E. and Wade, M. (Eds.). 2011. *Prosecutors in Trans-National Perspective* (in print). UK: Oxford Press.

Patt, M. 2009. *Human Trafficking and Modern-day Slavery. Country Reports*. Retrieved July 16, 2010, from http://gvnet.com/humantrafficking/.

Perrin, B. 2010. *Invisible Chains*. Toronto: Viking Press.

Potts Jr., L. G. 2003. Global trafficking in human beings: Assessing the success of the United Nations protocol to prevent trafficking in persons. *The George Washington International Law Review*, 35, 227–249.

Preuß, R. 2010, March 8. Einsame Zeugen. *Süddeutsche Zeitung*.

Raffaelli, R. 2009. The European approach to the protection of trafficking victims: The council of Europe convention, the EU directive, and the Italian experience. *German Law Journal*, 10(3), 205–221.

Segrave, M., Milivojevic, S., and Pickering, S. 2009. *Sex Trafficking—International Context and Response*. Cullompton: Willan.

Stoecker, S. 2005. Human Trafficking: A New Challenge for Russia and the United States. In S. Stoecker and L. Shelley (Eds). *Human Traffic and Transnational Crime: Eurasian and American Perspectives*. Lanham: Rowman and Littlefield.

Telegraph. 2009. EU President Takes Office as Lisbon Treaty enters into Force. The Daily Telegraph, December 9, 2009, available under: http://www.telegraph.co.uk/news/worldnews/europe/eu/6696363/EU-President-takes-office-as-Lisbon-Treaty-enters-into-force.html (last download January 14, 2011).

UNODC Toolkit to combat trafficking in persons available at http://www.unodc.org/unodc/en/human-trafficking/electronic-toolkit-to-combat-trafficking-in-persons—index.html#6

UNODC 2008. An Introduction to Human Trafficking.

UNODC 2009. Global report on Trafficking in Persons.

USA Department of State. 2010. Trafficking in Persons Report, 10th ed. June 2010.

U.S. Attorney-General. 2009. Attorney General's Annual Report to Congress and Assessment of U.S. Government Activities to Combat Trafficking in Persons, Fiscal Year 2009, July 2010 available at http://www.justice.gov/ag/annualreports/tr2009/agreporthumantrafficking2009.pdf

Wade, M. 2007. Deep rifts on procedural guarantees mirrored at conference in Berlin. *Eucrim—The European Criminal Law Associations' Forum*, 1–2, p. 31. Retrieved July 17, 2010, from http://www.mpicc.de/eucrim/archiv/eucrim_07-01.pdf.

Wade, M. 2008. The Januses of justice—How prosecutors define the kind of justice done across Europe. *European Journal of Crime, Criminal Law and Criminal Justice*, 16(4), 433–455.

Zakhari, B. 2005. Legal cases prosecuted under the Victims of Trafficking and Violence Protection Act of 2000. In S. Stoecker and L. Shelley (Eds.), *Human Traffic and Transnational Crime: Eurasian and American Perspectives*. Lanham: Rowman and Littlefield.

Legal Documents

Council of Europe. 1950. *Convention for the Protection of Human Rights and Fundamental Freedoms.* European treaty Series—No. 5, Rome, November 4, 1950.

Council of Europe. 2005. *Convention on Action against Trafficking in Human Beings and its Explanatory Report.* Council of Europe Treaty Series—No. 197, Warsaw, May 16, 2005.

Council of the European Union. 2002a. Council Framework Decision of 19 July 2002 on Combating Trafficking in Human Beings. 2002/629/JHA, *Official Journal L* 203/1 of August 1, 2002.

Council of the European Union. 2002b. Council Framework Decision of 13 June 2002 on the European arrest warrant and the surrender procedures between Member States. 2002/584/JHA, *Official Journal L* 190/1 of July 18, 2002.

Council of the European Union. 2004. Council Directive of April 29, 2004 on the Residence Permit Issued to Third-Country Nationals who are Victims of Trafficking in Human Beings or who have been the Subject of an Action to Facilitate Illegal Immigration, who Cooperate with the Competent Authorities. 2004/81/EC, *Official Journal L* 261/19 of August 6, 2004.

European Council. 2009 The Stockholm Programme—An Open and Secure Europe Serving and Protecting the Citizens. 2010/C 115/01, *Official Journal C* 115/01 of May 4, 2010.

United Nations. 2000a. Convention against Transnational Organized Crime. Adopted by General Assembly resolution 55/25 of November 15, 2000.

United Nations. 2000b. *Protocol to Prevent, Suppress and Punish Trafficking in Persons, especially Women and Children.* Supplementing the United Nations Convention against Transnational Organized Crime. Adopted on December 15, 2000.

Cases Cited

Commission v. Council, Application No. C-440/05, judgment of the European Court of Justice on October 23, 2007, OJ C 315/9 of December 22, 2007.

Siliadin v. France, Application No. 73316/01, final judgment of the European Court of Human Rights on October 26, 2004.

Useful Links

http://ec.europa.eu/home-affairs/doc_centre/crime/crime_human_trafficking_en.htm

http://www.unodc.org/unodc/en/human-trafficking/electronic-toolkit-to-combat-trafficking-in-persons—index.html

http://gvnet.com/humantrafficking/

http://www.state.gov/g/tip/

http://www.humantrafficking.org/

http://www.justice.gov/olp/human_trafficking.htm

http://www.unodc.org/unodc/en/human-trafficking/index.html

Improving Law Enforcement Identification and Response to Human Trafficking

9

AMY FARRELL

Contents

Introduction

Since the passage of the Palermo Protocol in 2000,* 98 counties have adopted laws criminalizing trafficking and providing a framework to support antitrafficking efforts (United
Nations 2009). Critical to these responses is the ability of local law enforcement authorities
to enforce laws against trafficking, necessitating the proper identification of potential victims and the prosecution of offenders. Law enforcement agencies worldwide, however, have
generally been slow to respond to this new mission, often failing to train officers to properly identify indicators of human trafficking or adequately respond to traumatized and historically marginalized victims. In some cases, there is evidence that the police are in fact
facilitating and benefitting from trafficking activities (Hughes and Denisova 2001; Schauer
and Wheaton 2006). This chapter uses data from a national survey of local law enforcement agencies in the United States as a case study to describe the cultural, structural, and
organizational challenges facing police agencies in responding to the problem of human
trafficking. A series of recommendations are provided based on the U.S. data and drawing
on comparisons between the U.S. experience and challenges facing law enforcement in
other countries. While some of obstacles to an effective police response identified here are
unique to the United States, there are similarities between the struggles facing agencies in
the United States and those identified in other cultural contexts. Together these multiple
sources of data inform our understanding of the challenges that face local law enforcement agents tasked with identifying and responding to human trafficking and inform our
attempts to improve how the police respond to human trafficking.

The U.S. Antitrafficking Response

In the mid-1990s, U.S. officials became concerned about growing evidence of exploitation
of individuals, particularly women and girls, who were increasingly moving across borders
to find work. Evidence of growing illicit networks facilitating the smuggling of humans
coupled with concern that these networks had connections to transnational criminal syndicates heightened concern about the phenomenon termed as human trafficking (O'Neill
1999). While a complete review of how interest groups mobilized these concerns is beyond
the scope of this chapter (see Stolz 2005 for an in-depth discussion of interest groups politics and the passage of U.S. antitrafficking legation), activities framing the U.S. efforts are
described briefly.

Politicians and nongovernmental organizations engaged in international women's
rights work began sounding an alarm about the growing problem of sex trafficking following the United Nations World Conference on Women in Beijing in 1995, where the problem of sex trafficking was highlighted as a priority among women's rights issue. Following
a trip to Thailand focused on the rights of women and girls, First Lady Hillary Clinton and
Secretary of State Madeline Albright became particularly engaged in formulating policies
to stop the sale of women and girls into prostitution. In 1998, then President Clinton issued

---

* In addition to adopting the United Nations Protocol to Prevent, Suppress and Punish Trafficking in
  Persons, Especially Women and Children in 2000, the United Nations has established a set of stan-
  dard to guide nation state responses to human trafficking included in the Recommended Principles and
  Guidelines on Human Rights and Human Trafficking (2002).

a presidential directive to develop domestic and international policies aimed at reducing trafficking in women and children.

The groups charged with implementing the President's directive found support for their antitrafficking work from an already strong coalition of women's rights and religious advocates seeking to abolish prostitution. While these groups disagreed about the nature of women's agency in prostitution, the two groups formed an allegiance based on their common agenda to prevent exploitation of women (Weitzer 2007). At the same time, labor rights organizations and immigrant advocacy groups in the United States were pushing to strengthen existing involuntary servitude laws to protect workers exploited through nonviolent forms of psychological coercion and fraud that fell outside the protection of existing laws. Two high-profile cases of labor exploitation received significant media attention during this time alerting government officials to the problem of labor trafficking in the United States (see Box 9.1 and Figure 9.1).

Despite significant differences in their paradigms and approaches to the problem of human trafficking, groups looking to abolish prostitution and those seeking to protect laborers found common ground in an effort to stop "modern day slavery." Together they exerted significant pressure on the federal government to pass legislation criminalizing human trafficking and provide resources to combat the problem. In 2000, the federal government passed the *Victims of Trafficking and Violence Protection Act (TVPA)*. This law

BOX 9.1   EARLY U.S. LABOR TRAFFICKING CASES

In 1995, law enforcement officials discovered a sweatshop operating in an apartment complex in El Monte California where seventy-two Thai immigrants were kept in involuntary servitude (Maya 1997). Kept behind razor wire in a boarded-up apartment complex, the El Monte sweatshop workers were forced to work over 80 hours per week and paid just over $1.00 per hour for their labor. Workers were threatened with violence and deportation if they did not acquiesce to the demands of their exploiters. Federal and local law enforcement agencies in the region in partnership with nongovernmental organizations coordinated an emergency response to rescue the workers and prosecute the perpetrators. The seven perpetrators identified by the police in the El Monte sweatshop case were prosecuted federally for violation of civil rights.

Two years later, federal law enforcement officials discovered a ring of perpetrators who forced over 50 hearing impaired Mexican immigrants to beg and peddle trinkets mainly in subways in three major U.S. cities (Trafficking in Persons 2000). The twenty perpetrators involved in this scheme repeatedly assaulted victims to keep them in servitude and ensure the victims turned over all the money they earned peddling. One victim was tortured with electric shocks while another was chained to a bed for a week (Fisher 1997). The perpetrators were part of a ring of extended family members who recruited victims from Mexico with promises of prosperous jobs for deaf individuals who faced limited economic opportunities in their home county. Perpetrators were charged with conspiracy to violate federal civil rights laws against involuntary servitude, extortion, alien smuggling, and illegal transportation of aliens. Ultimately, the ring leader operation was sentenced to 14 years in prison and ordered to pay $1 million in restitution the victims.

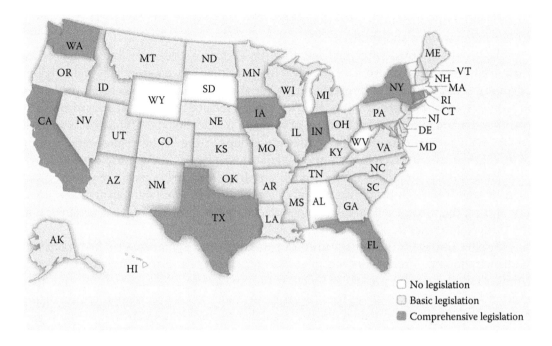

Figure 9.1 U.S. State Legislation. (Adapted from Center for Women Policy 2010.)

defined a new crime of human trafficking and enhanced penalties for existing offenses such as slavery, peonage, and involuntary servitude. Under the TVPA, a severe form of trafficking in persons was defined as:

> a commercial sex act induced by force, fraud, or coercion, or in which the person induced to perform such act has not attained 18 years of age; or the recruitment, harboring, transportation, provision, or obtaining of a person for labor or services, through the use of force, fraud, or coercion for the purpose of subjection to involuntary servitude, peonage, debt bondage, or slavery (TVPA, Section 103, 8a and b).

The TVPA definition does not require transportation of victims across borders or state lines, but instead rests upon the 13th amendment principles of preventing slavery, or involuntary servitude, in any form. The TVPA and its reauthorizations in 2003, 2005, and 2008 include provisions to protect victims, prosecute offenders, and prevent future trafficking. The TVPA establishes that noncitizen victims of human trafficking who participate in the investigation and prosecution of trafficking cases, or who are under 18 years of age, can qualify for nonimmigrant status through a special visa created for trafficking victims (i.e., T-visa). In the 10 years following the passage of the TVPA, 43 states have passed state legislation criminalizing human trafficking and some states have mandated more comprehensive mechanism such as police training, victim services, and data collection to improve local identification of victims and response to the crime (Center for Women Policy 2010).

Following passage of the TVPA, federal government officials tasked local agencies to be the "eyes and ears for recognizing, uncovering and responding to circumstances that may appear to be a routine street crime, but may ultimately turn out to be a human trafficking case" (U.S. Department of Justice 2004, p. 5). In the United States, over 17,000 municipal, county and state law enforcement agencies carry out the routine policing functions of local communities. To support the antitrafficking efforts of this large and diverse pool of local law enforcement agencies, the U.S. Department of Justice devoted over $64 million to support local law enforcement responses to human trafficking through the funding of *multiagency* task forces and police training.[*]

Despite the prioritization of human trafficking through new laws and devotion of resources to antitrafficking efforts, fewer human trafficking cases have been identified than estimates of the problem would predict. To date, the U.S. government has certified only 2009 victims of human trafficking and brought 531 trafficking suspects forward to federal prosecution (U.S. Department of Justice 2009; U.S. Department of State 2010). In response to concerns about the low numbers of identified victims, the U.S. Congress directed the Department of Justice to provide information on the extent and costs of human trafficking to justify continued expenditures in an annual report to Congress on antitrafficking activities. For the first time in 2010, the U.S. Department of State evaluated and ranked the response of U.S. agencies to human trafficking (U.S. Department of State 2010).

There are a number of potential explanations for the lower-than-expected numbers of identified human trafficking victims. The major challenges can be classified into five main areas that are discussed in more detail in the following section. They are

1. Failure of local officials to prioritize the problem of human trafficking and inadequate training to prepare law enforcement and other first responders to identify cases;
2. Difficulties identifying human trafficking;
3. Victim fear of the police and reluctance to participate in investigations;
4. Poor relationships between potential human trafficking victims and the police, particularly noncitizen victims and individuals involved in prostitution; and
5. Challenges securing arrest and taking cases forward to prosecution.

It is also possible that there are actually fewer victims of human trafficking than original estimates predicted (see, e.g., Chapter 2 in this volume), though it is difficult to address this question when local identification and response systems are inadequate. Missing from debate about the effectiveness of the U.S. government's antitrafficking program, however, is concrete information about the capacity of local law enforcement agencies to answer to this new mandate.

Using data from a nationally representative survey of local law enforcement agencies in the United States about human trafficking, the following discussion advances our understanding of the perceptions, preparation, and capacity of local law enforcement agencies in the United States to respond to human trafficking. In addition to providing the first national measures of local law enforcement response to human trafficking, there are a number of important recommendations based on these data to help improve the

---

[*] This figure was calculated based on data reported in the 2002 to 2007 U.S. Attorney General's Report to Congress and Assessment of U.S. Activities to Combat Trafficking in Persons, released annually by the U.S. Attorney General's Office.

identification, investigation, and prosecution of human trafficking cases and which may be generalized to other jurisdictions.

Challenges of Law Enforcement Response to Human Trafficking

Research on local law enforcement responses to human trafficking in the United States has focused mainly on the experiences of a small number of municipal police departments from large cities (Clawson et al. 2006; Wilson et al. 2006). These agencies differ from traditional agencies because they are perceived to be the most likely to come into contact with victims of human trafficking and often have received significant federal funding to support interagency task forces aimed at identifying human trafficking victims and prosecuting these cases. In the United States, policing is carried out primarily by thousands of different local agencies with a variety of different organizational structures and local environments. As a result, fully understanding how law enforcement perceives and responds to the problem of human trafficking necessitates inquiries into the experiences of a much wider set of agencies. While our knowledge about local law enforcement responses to human trafficking is limited, there are a number of potential barriers identified by previous research that may be expected to reduce the effectiveness of police responses to human trafficking.

Failure of Local Officials to Prioritize the Problem of Human Trafficking and Inadequate Training to Prepare Law Enforcement and Other First Responders to Identify Cases

At the outset, the prioritization of criminal justice system responses to this problem is relatively recent and local leaders may not even be aware of the problem. Even when leaders recognize the existence of a potential problem, they must manage a variety of local demands for police responses that affect the resources and time that can be devoted to new crime problems. The perceptions of local sovereigns (e.g., mayors and city council member) of community problems drive the type and degree of responses local police agencies can devote to a potential problem (Crank 1994; Katz 2001). Local agencies face increased pressure to implement other federal initiatives such as Homeland Security measures, and must cope with significant reductions in budgetary resources (IACP 2008). Collectively, this makes it difficult for police leaders to justify the devotion of resources to human trafficking investigations (Marsh 2007).

Since human trafficking is largely a clandestine phenomenon, its effects on the local community and victims residing in these communities may remain hidden, the crime receives a lower priority due to perceived nonexistence of the problem. Recent efforts by the federal government to improve local responses to human trafficking have prioritized investigations of domestic minor trafficking victims who may be more visible in local communities and represent more traditional victim groups.[*] Despite these efforts, local

---

[*] In 2009, the Office of Victims of Crime released the first solicitation aimed at improving local identification of and provisions of services to domestic minor trafficking victims. For more information about these awards see: http://www.salvationarmyusa.org/usn/www_usn_2.nsf/0/88A27DECA1EA357C85257 6B800656581/$file/AnnouncingOVCAwardees.pdf. Accessed August 13, 2010.

agencies still largely view antitrafficking efforts as a federal mandate as opposed to a locally driven police response.

Victim Fear of the Police and Reluctance to Participate in Investigations

Even when agency leaders identify human trafficking as a problem in their community, frontline and investigative officers face a number of challenges identifying and responding to potential victimization. Human trafficking victims rarely seek out the assistance of law enforcement (also see Chapter 12 in this book). The crime itself depends on the hidden nature of victimization and oftentimes victims cannot escape from their victimization to alert authorities of their abuse. Even when victims are able to flee from their situation of exploitation, they commonly have experienced trauma that makes it difficult for them to seek out assistance and provide information to law enforcement (Aron et al. 2004; Zimmerman et al. 2008). Victims often fear that contacting the police will result in retaliation by traffickers and in the case of foreign national victims, contacting the police puts victims at increased risk for deportation (Clawson et al. 2006). This necessitates both the proactive investigation of human trafficking crimes and networks within local communities and an awareness of frontline officers about how to identify the signs of potential trafficking situations while on routine patrol.

Local police face a number of additional complications when dealing with foreign victims. Human trafficking is easily confused with other forms of illicit people movement, such as migrant smuggling (see the Introduction in this volume). The citizenship status issues facing many human trafficking victims further complicates local law enforcement responses as many local agencies have made a decision not to inquire about citizen status during routine policing activities as a means of building trust and confidence in the local community (Ridgley 2008). In these situations, the organizational structure of an agency may inhibit officers from asking foreign victims questions about their immigration status that would be relevant to the identification of human trafficking.

Poor Relationships between Potential Human Trafficking Victims and the Police, Particularly Noncitizen Victims and Individuals Involved in Prostitution

Even with proper training, law enforcement officers may be reluctant to intervene in situations of human trafficking victimization (see Chapters 6 and 7 in this volume) due to a belief that victims were somehow complicit with their own victimization. In human trafficking cases, the police must provide services to groups of victims who in many cases have been under-served, by or had poor relationships with, law enforcement (e.g., migrants, immigrant community member, and poor women and girls). These historically poor relationships can be exacerbated further in the investigative process as highly traumatized victims, even when appropriately supported, may not be able to provide credible testimony about their experiences because victims of trauma are often not able to recall facts accurately (Women's Commission for Refugee Women and Children 2007). Without proper training in interviewing techniques for traumatized victims, police can become frustrated when victims change their testimony and demand additional interviews to clarify inconsistencies. Unfortunately, retelling one's story to the police in successive interviews can cause additional trauma, successively damaging one's ability to think analytically (Sadruddin et al. 2005). Human trafficking victims often have other problems that make the information they provide less credible, such compounding issues can include a history of substance abuse, long-term engagement in prostitution or illegal immigration. Because of these challenges, law enforcement may be unwilling to prioritize such investigations.

Challenges Securing Arrest and Taking Cases Forward to Prosecution

Challenges to successfully securing arrests and prosecuting human trafficking cases represent a final barrier to local law enforcement responses (see Segrave et al. 2009; Zhang 2007). The U.S. Department of State (2004) ranks human trafficking cases as "the most labor and time-intensive matters undertaken by the Department of Justice" (p. 24), due to the complexity of these cases and the challenges police face working with highly traumatized victims. When prosecutors are unwilling to take cases forward to state or federal prosecution, local law enforcement officials often become frustrated and are less willing to devote the time and resources toward identifying and investigating such crimes.

Results from the National Law Enforcement Human Trafficking Survey

To better understand the experiences and challenges agencies face identifying and investigating human trafficking, approximately 2000 municipal, county and state law enforcement agencies in the United States were surveyed in 2007 about their perceptions of human trafficking and experiences investigating such cases between 2000 and 2006 (see Farrell et al. 2010 for a detailed description of the survey methodology). The surveyed agencies were selected through a two-stage sampling process that included a national random sample of agencies supplemented with an oversampling of agencies serving medium-to-large communities (over 75,000 in population). Major results discussed in more detail below are first presented for all agencies and then differences between findings across types of agencies are presented.

Law Enforcement Leaders' Perceptions of Trafficking

Antitrafficking responses, particularly those that employ criminal legal structures to identify trafficking victims and prosecute offenders, depend on police in local communities identifying and investigating instances of human trafficking. As a result, recognition of the problem of human trafficking within the leadership of police organizations is a critical first step to a state's antitrafficking response. The national survey asked law enforcement leaders to indicate their perceptions of the prevalence of four different types of trafficking (i.e., labor trafficking involving foreign victims, labor trafficking involving domestic victims, sex trafficking involving foreign victims, and sex trafficking involving domestic victims) on a scale from "non-existent" (1) to "widespread" (4). Two-thirds of all local law enforcement officials reported that, to the best of their knowledge, all types of human trafficking were rare or nonexistent in their local community. There was little difference in agency leader perceptions about the prevalence across the different types of trafficking—law enforcement leaders perceived that all types of human trafficking were rare or nonexistent in their communities. Of the 1904 agency leaders surveyed, only 74 (3.8%) indicated that any type of human trafficking was "widespread" in their community. Agency leader perception that human trafficking was not a pressing problem in their community was also reflected in interviews with police leaders. Agency leaders characterized human trafficking as a "federal issue," a "problem for border communities" or simply something that "we just haven't seen much of it here" (Farrell et al. 2008). Some law enforcement leaders indicated that they have had suspicion of human trafficking in their community, but that obvious evidence of force, fraud, or coercion was not present, and agencies did not have the resources necessary to continue such investigations. Leaders generally were aware of the problem of human trafficking (though there was inconsistency in their definition of the phenomenon) and in some cases had devoted resources to training, but investigating human trafficking was not described as a priority for local agencies.

Perceptions about the prevalence of human trafficking did vary by size and type of agency. As illustrated in Table 9.1, agency leaders serving medium-to-large communities (populations over 75,000), county agencies in metropolitan statistical areas and state police agencies on average thought human trafficking was more prevalent in their local community. This finding suggests, either human trafficking is more concentrated in large urban centers or at a minimum that there is more awareness of the problem in larger urban areas.

For example, 20% of medium-to-large agencies indicated that sex trafficking involving international victims was "occasional" or "widespread" in their community compared to only 5% of agencies serving smaller communities (under 75,000 in population) who indicated sex trafficking involving international victims was "occasional" or "widespread." Agency leaders in the West and Southern parts of the United States were more likely to think that the problem of human trafficking was "occasional" or "widespread" (20% and 17% respectively) compared to agency leaders in the Midwest (10%), Southeast (13%), or Northeast (13%).

Table 9.1 Law Enforcement Leader Perceptions of Human Trafficking Problem by Agency Type and Size ($n = 1850$) (Scale: 1 = Nonexistent to 4 = Widespread)

Agency Type	Population Size	Foreign Labor Trafficking	Domestic Labor Trafficking	Foreign Sex Trafficking	Domestic Sex Trafficking
Municipal	Under 10,000	1.44	1.34	1.25	1.28
	10,000–24,999	1.49	1.36	1.32	1.35
	25,000–49,999	1.66	1.51	1.55	1.54
	50,000–74,999	1.52	1.43	1.56	1.55
	75,000–99,999	1.83	1.61	1.85	1.69
	100,000–249,999	1.89	1.71	1.90	1.92
	250,000 +	2.25	2.00	2.55	2.60
County	Non-MSA	1.60	1.40	1.34	1.35
	MSA	1.77	1.51	1.56	1.68
State police		2.46	1.96	2.16	2.13
Total		1.59	1.44	1.45	1.27

Agency Preparation and Capacity to Identify and Investigate Human Trafficking Cases

Nationally, local law enforcement agencies are not prepared to identify, or respond to, cases of human trafficking. Only 21% of local, country or state law enforcement agencies had any type of human trafficking training, just under 10% had a protocol or policy to guide law enforcement response to human trafficking cases and only 6% had designated personnel, or specialized, units to investigate these cases. Agency preparation also varies by agency size and type (see Table 9.2). Municipal agencies serving smaller communities and county agencies were generally less likely to have had training, a departmental policy on human trafficking, or any specialized personnel. Conversely, a third of large-sized agencies (serving populations between 75,000 and 250,000) and 66% of the agencies serving the largest population (over 250,000) have conducted training and 47% of state police agencies have conducted some type of training. While protocols and specialized personnel were rare for virtually all types of agencies, those agencies serving the largest populations (cities over 250,000) were much more likely to have specialized personnel (51%) or a written protocol (33%) to guide officer responses to trafficking than any other agencies.

From the national survey, we know some detailed information about the scope and type of training that agencies received on human trafficking. Even when agencies had human trafficking training, the reach of these training programs were relatively narrow. Two-thirds of the agencies who responded to the survey that they had some type of training program only trained between one and five officers and only 4% of agencies indicated having department wide roll-call training or training on human trafficking as part of the academy curriculum for new recruits.

Identification and Investigation of Human Trafficking Cases

Just under 10% of the municipal, county, and state law enforcement agencies surveyed investigated a case of human trafficking between 2000 and 2006 (see Table 9.3). While local law enforcement of all sizes and in all regions of the county reported some identification of human trafficking, agencies serving larger populations were most likely to

Table 9.2 Agency Preparation to Identify Human Trafficking Cases by Agency Type and Size (n = 1863)

Agency Type	Population Size	Percentage of Training	Percentage of Policy or Protocol	Percentage of Specialized Personnel
Municipal	Under 10,000	14.7	8.5	3.5
	10,000–24,999	20.9	9.3	2.8
	25,000–49,999	21.1	5.7	5.4
	50,000–74,999	17.5	7.5	5.3
	75,000–99,999	38.0	7.4	8.6
	100,000–249,999	29.0	8.1	7.1
	250,000+	65.6	32.8	50.8
County	Non-MSA	16.5	9.6	1.6
	MSA	16.5	12.5	10.1
State police		47.1	18.8	17.6
Total		21.0	9.8	6.4

Table 9.3   Identification of Human Trafficking Cases by Agency Type and Size

Agency Type	Population Size	All Agencies (*n* = 1834)	Agencies that Identified Cases (*n* = 180)			
		Percentage of identified at Least One Case	Average # Cases Identified	SD	Average # of Suspects Arrested	SD
Municipal	Under 10,000	3.7	1.80	(1.31)	4.50	(7.52)
	10,000–24,999	5.3	4.35	(6.35)	4.07	(6.36)
	25,000–49,999	10.1	15.2	(23.98)	8.6	(13.14)
	50,000 –74,999	14.6	4.0	(6.00)	6.5	(9.19)
	75,000–99,999	18.6	4.16	(5.47)	4.50	(7.64)
	100,000–249,999	25.2	13.36	(48.27)	3.95	(8.12)
	250,000 +	52.4	45.68	(102.44)	20.41	(42.13)
County	Non-MSA	7.0	4.00	(4.34)	5.14	(5.24)
	MSA	8.9	15.00	(16.05)	8.40	(5.45)
State police		34.3	55.25	(120.13)	2.33	(3.88)
Total		9.8	20.45	(65.11)	8.82	(23.43)

report identifying cases of human trafficking, identified the most cases on average and made the most arrests. Over half of the municipal law enforcement agencies serving very large populations (250,000 and above) indicated investigating a case of human trafficking, despite the fact that large city agency leaders were only marginally more likely to perceive human trafficking as a problem in their community compared to agencies that serve smaller jurisdictions.

Only 4% of municipal agencies serving populations under 10,000 indicate investigating a case of human trafficking. That figure more than doubles for agencies serving populations between 25,000 and 100,000 and increases sixfold for those agencies serving populations between 100,000 and 250,000. Agencies serving the largest cities (250,000 plus population) are nearly 15 times more likely to identify a case of human trafficking than those agencies in the smallest cities (under 10,000 population). Approximately 8% of all county law enforcement agencies and approximately one-third of State Police agencies have investigated a case of human trafficking since 2000. The numbers of identified cases and suspects arrested increased correspondingly to population size, though the variance in identified cases and arrests was quite wide across agencies where a handful of agencies may have a disproportionately large number of cases and arrests. State police agencies indicate investigating a large number of cases (average of 55 cases), only a small number of suspects (average of 2.3) had been apprehended and arrested by state police agencies.

Detailed information was collected from 118 agencies (6.2% of the original sample) that indicated investigating at least one case of human trafficking between 2000 and 2006.[*] Sex trafficking was the most common type of case identified. Sixty-four percent of the

---

[*] While 180 agencies indicated investigating human trafficking cases on the main survey, follow-up interviews with investigators to collect detailed information about the nature of these investigations could only be conducted with 118 of the 180 agencies.

118 agencies ($n = 75$) completing detailed interviews indicated investigating at least one sex trafficking case and over a third ($n = 37$) of these agencies investigated three or more sex trafficking cases during the study period. Half of the agencies also indicated that they investigated at least one labor trafficking case ($n = 60$), but with only 21% ($n = 25$) of agencies indicating they investigated more than three labor trafficking cases. The most common types of labor trafficking identified were domestic servitude cases, followed by labor trafficking in commercial agriculture and restaurants.

Predictors of Successful Law Enforcement Responses

Outcome Measures

There are a number of factors about police organizations and communities that make it more likely that the police will take steps to prepare officers to identify cases of human trafficking and that such cases will be successfully investigated and prosecuted. A set of logistic regression models[*] were estimated to test the effect of organizational characteristics, particularly leadership perceptions of human trafficking, on proactive responses (measured here as dummy variables indicating whether or not the agency adopted human trafficking training, developed written protocols or designated specialized personnel). A separate logistic regression model was estimated to test the effect of organizational preparedness and community factors on the identification of human trafficking cases (measured as a dummy variable where zero indicates no cases identified and one indicates at least one case identified in the study period). Table 9.4 presents descriptive statistics for all measures.

Table 9.4   Descriptive Statistics ($n = 1863$)

	Percent	Mean	SD	Min	Max
Population (logged)		9.37	1.82	4.25	15.89
Border state	36.4				
Owner occupied		68.32	13.40	0.30	97.70
Poverty		10.17	6.98	0.00	41.70
Foreign born		6.34	8.74	0.00	72.10
Legislation	33.4				
Perception		1.44	0.64	1.00	4.00
Municipal	79.7				
County	18.2				
Training	20.5				
Protocols	6.2				
Specialization	9.6				
Task force	8.9				
Proactive strategies		2.27	0.81	1.00	4.00

[*] Logistic regression is a statistical technique that analyzes the relationship between one dependent variable (here measured as proactive responses or identification of trafficking cases) and several independent variables. Logistic regression makes use of several predictor variables that may be either numerical or categorical

Test and Control Measures

Police organizations can take a number of different instrumental steps to increase the likelihood that officers within their agency will successfully identify and investigate crimes. Scholars and law enforcement practitioners suggest that because human trafficking is a particularly complex crime to investigate and has a number of associated victim–witness challenges, agencies need to develop specialized antitrafficking capacities within their agencies, through training or the dedication of specialized personnel to respond to these crimes (Interpol 2007; Gallagher and Holmes 2008). The national survey data suggests that such preparations are critical to human trafficking identification. Twenty-nine percent of agencies who had some type of human trafficking training identified cases compared to only 5% without training; 36%of agencies with written protocols identified cases compared to only 8% of agencies without protocols; and 56% of agencies with specialized personnel or units identified case compared to only 7% without such specialization. To measure the effect of agency preparation on human trafficking identification we created a series of dummy variables coded zero if agencies did not take a preparatory measure and coded one if they had taken such steps (i.e., measured separately for training, protocols and specialized personnel).

Additionally, the use of multiagency task forces that bring together local and federal law enforcement partners with victim service agencies and other stakeholders in the local community to comprehensively identify and serve victims of human trafficking has been suggested as a promising strategy for identifying and investigating cases of human trafficking (Braun 2007; de Baca and Tisi 2002). The data from the national survey support this conclusion. Agencies participating in regional or federal task forces were more likely to have training, policies and specialized personnel than other agencies and were much more likely to investigate cases of human trafficking than nontask force agencies (76% of agencies participating in human trafficking task forces investigated at least one case of human trafficking compared to 25% of medium-to-large-sized agencies overall). Agencies participating in task forces also reported investigating many more cases on average than nontask force agencies (36 on average for task force agencies compared to 15 on average for nontask forces agencies). Task force agencies made more arrests than nontask force agencies (average of 12 arrests compared to 8 for nontask force agencies) and their arrests resulted in more formal charges than nontask force agencies. For example, 55% of arrests in task force agencies resulted in federal charges compared to only 25% in nontask force agencies. A measure indicating whether or not the agency participated in a state, regional or federal task force (measured as zero for "no task force" and "1" for "task force participation") is included in the following analyses to control for the effect of task force participation.

Underlying the presumption of why agencies who develop specialization in human trafficking and those who develop partnerships with other law enforcement agencies and victim service providers were more successful is a belief that these agencies develop different kinds of skills that may facilitate the identification and successful response to human trafficking. Among those skills is the proactive investigation of potential human trafficking networks and operations in local communities. Proactive investigations involve police actively seeking out information on potential human trafficking operations in their local community through intelligence gathered by confidential sources, information from victims, and other proactive strategies such as surveillance and undercover operations. Agencies that had taken purely reactive stances to the problem of human trafficking (e.g., waiting for calls for service or referrals from victim service agencies) were anticipated to be less likely to identify such cases (Interpol 2007; IACP 2006). To measure whether proactive stances to human trafficking investigations predict the identification of such cases, we included a measure of the degree to which police leaders believe information gathered from proactive sources (i.e., tips from co-conspirators, tips from community partners or other ongoing investigations) leads the identification of human trafficking. This variable was an averaged scale ($\alpha = 0.93$) of the proactive strategies measured on a scale from one ("not likely" or "unsure") to five ("very likely").

There were, a number of local community-level factors that were also believed to contribute to the likelihood of trafficking in persons across communities, including the size of the population, high levels of undocumented immigrant residents and proximity to foreign borders (Andrees and van der Linden 2005), residential instability and poverty (Ebbe and Das 2007). To control for these community factors, we gathered data from the 2000 U.S. Census to measure the size of the population served (measured as the logged population), the percent of the population foreign born, the percentage of the population residing in owner occupied dwellings and the percent of the population living in poverty. A dummy variable was developed measuring whether or not the agency was in a state directly bordering Canada or Mexico.

Although any local law enforcement agency working in partnership with federal investigators could identify cases of human trafficking and charge those cases under the federal trafficking laws (TVPA 2000), agencies in States with state human trafficking legislation criminalizing trafficking may have additional incentives to identify such crimes. At the time of the study, eleven States passed antitrafficking legislation,[*] criminalizing human trafficking and providing support for training, public awareness, and research about the problem. To control for the impact of state legislation, a dummy variable was created to measure whether or not the agency was in a state with human trafficking legislation.

Multivariate Analyses

Table 9.5 presents the results from the multivariate logistic regression analyses examining whether agency leader perceptions of the problem of trafficking predict agency preparedness. As predicted by the bivariate analyses, the odds of an agency adopting training, developing protocols, and designating specialized personnel increased significantly as law enforcement leaders perceive that the problem of human trafficking is more severe in their local community. It is impossible to determine the direction of this relationship. It is, possible that agencies perceive trafficking to be a problem and in response invest in training and other efforts to increase the readiness of their officers to respond. It is also possible that agencies that adopt training come to perceive trafficking to be more prevalent in their community because they get better at identifying it and begin to understand the complexities of the crime. In either case, it is clear from the survey evidence that perceptions of the problem and readiness go hand-in-hand.

Agencies that adopt training, develop protocols, and designate specialized personnel were significantly more likely to identify cases of human trafficking than agencies that do not take such proactive steps (see Table 9.6). Agency leader perceptions about the

---

[*] States with early legislation include Arkansas, Arizona, California, Connecticut, Illinois, Kansas, Louisiana, Missouri, New Jersey, Texas, and Washington.

Table 9.5   Prediction of Agency Responses (n = 1863)

	Model 1: Training		Model 2: Protocols		Model 3: Personnel	
	B (SE)	Odds	B (SE)	Odds	B (SE)	Odds
Population (logged)	.140 (.056)*	1.15	−.027 (.071)	.97	.237 (.096)**	1.26
Border state	−.290 (.182)	.75	.030 (.228)	1.03	.352 (.316)	1.42
Owner occupied	−.002 (.007)	.99	.003 (.009)	1.00	−.002 (.012)	1.00
Poverty	.005 (.012)	1.01	.015 (.015)	1.02	.027 (.022)	1.03
Foreign born	.014 (.010)	1.02	.010 (.013)	1.01	.022 (.014)	1.02
Legislation	.243 (.174)	1.27	.047 (.226)	1.05	−.184 (.320)	.83
Municipal agency	.397 (.237)	1.48	−.387 (.279)	.70	.510 (.437)	1.66
Task force	.280 (.265)	1.32	−.622 (.407)	.53	.999 (.355)**	2.72
Leader perception	.892 (.121)**	2.44	.933 (.142)**	2.54	.893 (193)**	2.44
Constant	−4.464 (.915)**		−3.509 (1.019)**		−7.781 (1.686)**	
Pseudo R^2	.187		.108		.240	

* $p < .05$
** $p < .01$

value of various proactive policing strategies to identify human trafficking cases does not significantly predict investigation of such cases in this model. More work may need to be done to understand how different investigative strategies employed by investigators with specialized knowledge and training affect the type and quality of evidence gathered in support of prosecution. Conversely, most of the community level predictors were not significantly related to human trafficking identification, but larger agencies and agencies in border states were also more likely to identify such cases during the study period.

Table 9.6   Logistic Regression Models Predicting Law Enforcement Identification of Human Trafficking Cases (n = 1863)

				95% CI	
	B	(SE)	ExpB	Lower	Upper
Population size	.410	(.072)**	1.51	1.31	1.73
Border	.682	(.229)*	1.97	1.26	3.10
Owner occupied	−.005	(.009)	.99	.98	1.01
Foreign born	.010	(.012)	1.01	.98	1.03
Poverty	.008	(.016)	1.00	.97	1.03
Legislation	.276	(.213)	1.31	.84	2.07
Municipal agency	.229	(.305)	1.25	.69	2.28
Training	1.053	(.238)**	2.86	1.79	4.56
Protocols	1.648	(.271)**	5.19	3.05	8.83
Specialized units	1.277	(.317)**	3.58	1.92	6.67
Task force	−.180	(.403)	.84	.83	1.83
Proactive strategies	.176	(.127)	1.19	.38	1.53
Constant	−8.052**	(1.304)			
Pseudo R^2	.471				

Note: State police agencies excluded from present model, reference category for agency types is county agency.
* $p < .05$ level;
** $p < .01$ level

Recommendations for Improving Law Enforcement Response to Human Trafficking in the United States and Beyond

A number of recommendations to help improve police responses to human trafficking more can be drawn from the findings of the U.S. survey of law enforcement agencies and comparisons of these findings to the experiences of law enforcement in other countries. The following section discusses four main recommendations aimed at improving police leaders:

1. Increasing local law enforcement leadership buy-in about the problem of human trafficking and its potentially detrimental effects on community safety,
2. Enhance the ability of *frontline officers* to recognizing human trafficking,
3. Develop specialized and proactive investigation of human trafficking cases, and
4. Utilize *multiagency* approaches to ensure more prosecuted offenders and restored victims.

Recommendation 1: Increase Local Law Enforcement Leadership Buy-in about the Problem of Human Trafficking

Like many of its international partners (see Commission of European Communities 2005; African Union 2002), the U.S. federal government has provided resources and leadership to support local law enforcement agencies as they begin addressing human trafficking in their local communities. As a result, the issue of human trafficking is beginning to make its way into the broader community of police professionals. In 2006, the *International Association of Chiefs of Police* released a short guide on human trafficking identification and investigation providing law enforcement officials with basic information about the problem of human trafficking and suggesting a number of national resources for assistance (see www.theiacp.org). Additionally, the IACP has provided training to law enforcement executives through their police leadership program. They estimate that to date ~250 police enforcement leaders (only 1.5% out of ~17,000) have undergone leadership training including human trafficking material. In the United States a number of Regional Community Policing Institutes (RCPI's) have provided training to raise awareness about human trafficking in the law enforcement community and some states have passed legislation mandating statewide training. To date, however, the major police leadership organizations in the United States (e.g., Police Executive Research Forum, Police Foundation) have not addressed the issue of human trafficking with their membership.

Findings from the U.S. data suggest that local police leaders are reluctant to devote resources toward investigation of a problem that is not immediately visible and about which there are no local constituencies demanding action. While law enforcement officials in the United States openly oppose slavery and recognize the potentially devastating consequences of human trafficking to individual victims, they generally do not think such crimes occur in their communities. While social marketing campaigns implore law enforcement to "look beneath the surface" (U.S. Department of Health and Human Services 2009) to identify trafficking victims, they provide little concrete information about the types of resources necessary to expose hidden victimization or the benefits to local communities of exposing and preventing this crime. Looking "below the surface" requires police leaders to approve the time and resources necessary for investigators to pursue leads and begin proactive investigations even when the evidence of human trafficking is not clear.

Misrepresentations of the nature and costs of human trafficking in local communities also can impede political support for antitrafficking efforts. Given that media reports have commonly drawn direct links between violent organized crime groups and human trafficking, many law enforcement leaders expect that antitrafficking efforts will net arrests involving major crime syndicates. In reality, the links between organized crime and trafficking are less clear. While some organized network is presumed to be needed to facilitate illicit cross-national movement (Turner and Kelly 2009), human trafficking cases identified by the police more often involve networks of loosely organized entrepreneurs or local actors exploiting victims for their own personal gain (Bruckert and Parent 2002; Jahic and Finckenauer 2005). Disconnects between expectation and reality may lead some police leaders to lose support for antitrafficking investigations, perceived to be costly and time consuming.

Examples from outside the United States suggest that even with national-level prioritization and coordination, there are numerous barriers to effective local law enforcement responses. For example, in 2007, the United Kingdom developed an action plan to guide the government's antitrafficking response and prioritize the problem of human trafficking (Home Office 2007). Central to the UK strategy was the development of UK Human Trafficking Centre (UKHTC), which coordinated training and the development of operational expertise in human trafficking response among local agencies throughout the UK. Despite well-coordinated operational responses to human trafficking under Operation Pentameter in 2006 and Pentameter II in 2007, only a handful of offenders were ultimately prosecuted for human trafficking offenses, leaving some government officials to question the resources devoted to antitrafficking activities. A Home Office assessment of the Pentameter projects identifies "police officer's lack of knowledge and experience with trafficking for sexual exploitation" and lack of "internal support for the operation and insufficient staff" as main impediments to the operation (Avenell 2008, p. 1). Funding cuts in response to the national budget crises have led to reductions in the number of police personnel dedicated to human trafficking investigations in the United Kingdom, jeopardizing an already tenuous program of coordinated law enforcement responses to trafficking in persons (Dugan 2008).

Finally, gaining genuine police leadership support for antitrafficking activities is most difficult in contexts where corruption facilitates human trafficking. Research by Studnicka in 2010 confirms that a high level of corruption is a strong predictor for increased trafficking in persons. Unfortunately, police corruption remains a problem despite decades of police reform. Hughes and Denisova (2001) document a number of instances where high-ranking police officials in Europe have been complicit in sex trafficking networks accepting bribes, facilitating illicit border crossing and returning rescued trafficking victims to their pimps or traffickers. Additionally, local Bosnian police officers have been investigated for their participation in the sex trade (Potts 2003). Qualitative research in other contexts suggest that when police officials benefit financially from trafficking networks (Agbu 2003; Richards 2004), it is impossible to expect that government pressure to combat trafficking will ensure local police leadership support. Police officials may also face pressure from government officials to ignore human trafficking. For example, in Southeast Asia where the local economies depend heavily on a tourism industry presumed to cater to the commercial sex trade, police officials have been criticized for taking a more reactive stance to the problem of human trafficking (Samarasinghe 2003).

Recommendation 2: Enhance the Ability of Frontline Officers to Recognize Human Trafficking

Frontline officers are critical to the successful identification of human trafficking in a community. They often have the most regular access to places in the community where human trafficking victimization may occur and are likely to encounter incidents of human trafficking while on routine patrol (Clawson et al. 2006). Even when agencies develop human trafficking specialization among investigative officers, investigations are often dependent upon frontline officers identifying indictors of human trafficking victimization and bringing these incidents to the attention of investigators. Despite their critical role, most frontline officers do not know how to recognize the signs of human trafficking and when they do, they have few tools to help guide their response. Data from the United States confirm that most agencies lack basic training on human trafficking, but when agencies prepare their officers to investigate human trafficking cases, including having training or policies that direct how officers should respond if they encounter cases they are more likely to successfully identify and investigate human trafficking.

In their in-depth review of 12 U.S. human trafficking cases from originating from 1996 to 2002, Bales and Lize (2007) found that actions by frontline officers in the first few moments a human trafficking victim has contact with the police were critical to the successful prosecution of human trafficking cases. The frontline officers did not need to have specialized investigative skills, these investigations are often too complex and issues facing victims are too challenging for frontline officers to tackle on their own. Instead, frontline officers needed to know some basic information about the indicators of human trafficking and how to secure the scene, gather basic information, provide immediate assistance to potential victims where appropriate, and quickly forward information about the incident to specialists within their agency. Similar findings were reported by Winterdyk and Sundberg (2009) in their study of Canadian Border Security Agency frontline officers.

In many jurisdictions in the United States, frontline officers need additional support and training to increase their readiness to question potential noncitizen victims or suspects. Language barriers and concern about violating agency policies against inquiries into a person's immigration status known as sanctuary city policies make confronting potential noncitizen victims or suspects more difficult (Ridgley 2008). Appropriate training would provide officers with tools to identify potential indicators of human trafficking without violating policies against inappropriate involvement of local officials with immigration enforcement or offending noncitizen individuals in the community.

The challenges of training frontline law enforcement agents to recognize human trafficking is not new. Law enforcement often adapts to changing legal and social environments. For example, in the United States, until quite recently local law enforcement officials perceived domestic violence to be a personal or family problem rather than a criminal justice issue. The police were hesitant to become involved in people's intimate relationships even when they involved violence. Part of this resistance, we now know was based on the facts that officers did not feel that they had the proper tool and training to address such complex problems (Ferraro 1989). While police responses to domestic violence in the United States are arguably far from perfect, there is little confusion among the professional law enforcement community about the fact that domestic violence is a crime and there are policies in place in virtually all police agencies to guide frontline officers in responding to such incidents (Buzawa and Buzawa 2002). Similar types of protocols and training are needed to overcome the lack of awareness and confusion that many local officers may have about human trafficking and the role local police play in identifying incidents, interdicting officers and restoring victims.

There are a growing number of instructive examples for improving front line officer knowledge of trafficking indicators. For example, during Pentameter 2, the UK Human Trafficking Center worked with a local NGO to produce a list of indicators for all forms of human trafficking, including domestic servitude, which was issued to over 9000 local police agents in advance of the operation (Tackling Human Trafficking 2010; also see Chapter 5 in this volume). Additionally, model curriculum for roll-call trainings or in-service modules for current officers and academy training for new recruits should be designed to help frontline officers identify the signs of trafficking. In some cases curriculums specific to the local, or regional, risk factors may be more effective than a national model. In Southeast Asia, the ASEAN Training Program on Trafficked Persons for Front-line Law Enforcement Officials was launched in 2008. The training program has now been customized for use in Cambodia, Lao, PDR, Myanmar, Thailand, and Vietnam. Preliminary evaluations of the program indicate that it strengthened frontline officers' abilities to recognize signs of trafficking, provide immediate assistance to trafficking victims, and increase coordination between patrol officers and specialized investigators (Smith 2010). Most critical to any human trafficking training aimed at the generalist officer is messaging that affirms that human trafficking is a crime necessitating local police attention and response.

Recommendation 3: Support Specialized Investigators to Engage in Proactive Investigations

The complexity of human trafficking investigations necessitates the dedication of specially trained investigators (Gallagher and Holmes 2008; UNODC 2008). These specialists must receive information from frontline officers, communicate with other investigative agencies and prosecutors, and work closely with victim service providers who will be assisting identified victims. Given the complex and transnational nature of human trafficking specialization in a number of different areas is required. Specialists need training to conduct interviews with both adult and child victims, often who suffer from the effects of trauma and require specialized medical attention (Zimmerman et al. 2008). They need to develop expertise working with noncitizen victims who face language barriers and complex immigration issues often necessitating procurement of specialized visas or other forms of immigration relief (Srikantiah 2007). Human trafficking specialists also learn to negotiate relationships and work collaboratively with a host of local and federal law enforcement partners, victim service agencies, embassies, and other international officials. Ideally, specialists must develop international connections to investigate transnational aspects of trafficking crimes and have experience navigating international protocols that guide transnational investigations and extraditions (Williams and Vlassis 2001). Specialists should also serve as the hub of information about ongoing investigations in a community and be responsible for developing proactive investigative strategies to identify human trafficking networks, or patterns within a community.

At present, only 6% of local law enforcement agencies in the United States have personnel specially trained to investigate incidents of human trafficking in local communities.

Even in the largest cities, less than half of the agencies have investigators with any type of specialization in human trafficking investigations. Even when a police agency designates specialists, there are few tools to help them learn how to navigate the complexities identified above. Until recently, human trafficking training for local agencies targeted toward generalists as opposed to specialists (also see Winterdyk and Sundberg 2009 for similar results observed in Canada). While programs have been in-place since the mid-2000s to provide specialized training for federal agents, training for investigators in local agencies has been mainly "on the job" training where specialists learn best practices for investigating these complex cases while in the midst of ongoing investigations. In 2010, the Regional Community Policing Institutes in the United States offered the first advanced training courses of its kind in the United States. The course is aimed specifically at developing the capabilities of local investigators. While training for both generalists and specialists is also lacking outside of the United States, there are some promising examples of programs that bring together specialists from multiple countries in a region to develop transnational specialization. For example, the Organization for Security and Cooperation offers advanced online courses on human trafficking targeted at investigations in Eastern Europe, Serbia, and Kosovo through the Police Online Information System. Additionally, in 2010, Interpol sponsored multiday advanced investigator training on human trafficking investigations in West Africa. In doing so, they brought together investigators from the region to improve transnational investigative capacities.

Without specialization, human trafficking responses tend to be largely *reactive* in nature. Under such circumstances, law enforcement is alerted to a situation where victimization is occurring and intervenes through raids or other mechanisms to rescue victims from exploitation and arrest whoever is found at the scene. In the United States, human trafficking investigations tend to fall into the reactive category, relying heavily on victim cooperation and testimony (Bales and Lize 2007). The UNODC Toolkit for Combating Trafficking in Persons (2008) suggests that reactive investigations are inferior to proactive investigations because they depend too heavily on the cooperation of victims who may later resend their cooperation. Additionally, reactive investigations require immediate action, such as raids or arrests, meaning that the police may not be able to collect evidence and individuals in higher levels of the criminal organizations may be tipped off and evade arrest.

In *proactive investigations*, police obtain information about ongoing criminal activity through intelligence gathering mechanisms such as the use of confidential sources and surveillance and they have time to plan their interventions. While reactive investigations may be necessary in cases where victim harm is imminent and severe, dismantling human trafficking operations will require sustained efforts based on intelligence and analysis. After reviewing numerous cases of human trafficking in South-Eastern Europe, Surtees (2008) suggests, trafficking "is a complex and evolving industry and much has changed in recent years in how trafficking takes place. Not only have traffickers' profiles changed but so too have their strategies, behaviors and tactics. Traffickers are regularly responding and adapting to the social, economic and political arenas in which recruitment and trafficking take place, which makes it imperative that anti-trafficking actors are equipped with detailed and up-to-date information about traffickers and their activities" (p. 61). To do so requires local investment in proactive investigative strategies carried out by specially trained and dedicated investigative personnel working collaboratively across agency and regional boundaries.

Recommendation 4: Support Multiagency Partnership Approaches

Multiagency partnerships between local, state and federal law enforcement officials along with victim service providers and local advocates in a community increase the capacity of agents in those communities to identify and respond effectively to human trafficking. As the U.S. data clarify, law enforcement agencies participating in multiagency human trafficking partnerships with other investigative agencies, prosecutors, and victim service providers are more likely to have training, protocols, and specialized units or personnel devoted to human trafficking investigations and are more likely identify and prosecute human trafficking in their community.

The U.S. government has supported a multiagency task force approach to bring together local and federal law enforcement partners with victim service providers and community stakeholders. Between 2004 and 2009, the U.S. Department of Justice funded over forty multiagency task forces to improve the capacities of local communities to identify and investigate human trafficking crimes and provide services to identified victims. Recognizing the transient nature of human trafficking operations, fourteen states have also mandated the formation of statewide *antitrafficking task forces* through state (e.g., California, Colorado, Connecticut, Florida, Hawaii, Idaho, Kentucky, Maine, Minnesota, New Mexico, New York, Rhode Island, Utah, and Washington) legislation (Polaris 2010). Multiagency and multijurisdiction task forces are potentially powerful antitrafficking strategies but they depend on proper support and coordination among partner agencies (GAO 2007). Additionally, task forces need resources to help them overcome the challenges that are inherent to this approach. Multiagency partners come from different organizational and cultural background, often with conflicting organizational missions. To overcome these challenges, multiagency partners need to meet regularly and establish clear protocols to guide their individual and joint responsibilities and actions.

Since the crime of human trafficking often crosses borders, transnational partnerships are critical to effective antitrafficking responses. As law enforcement agencies in the United States struggle to establish multiagency partnerships within local regions or states, there are important lessons to be learned from the experiences of agencies attempting to form even more complex cross-border partnerships outside of the United States In some cases, cooperation is facilitated through formal agreements, such as mutual aid and extradition agreements. In other cases, informal collaboration occurs when investigative leaders share intelligence and develop strategic goals in a region. For example, in Southeast Asia, the heads of specialized trafficking investigative units from nine different countries met to share intelligence and review progress toward shared operational goals (Smith 2010). In addition, Europol has assisted in the coordination of investigations when illicit activities cross at least two European nations (Europol 2007).

Some of the challenges of a multiagency approaches that have been identified in U.S. communities (Farrell et al. 2008) such as differing definitions of the problem of human trafficking, differing approaches to how to best address the problem and measure success and interagency competition have also been identified in evaluations of cross-national collaborations (Reichel 2008). Additional challenges seemingly more relevant to cross-national collaborations include differing legal systems, differences in the types of officials responsible for antitrafficking interventions, language and cultural barriers, and problems related to government corruption (Reichel 2008). Studies in the United States and cross-nationally suggest that establishing common ground and developing trusting relationship among collaborative partners through networking is essential to overcoming the challenges of cross-agency and cross-cultural antitrafficking work. Experiences from agencies attempting transnational collaborations in Europe suggest that cross-national training is also critical to establishing expectations between officials about what types of responses are permissible and likely to occur across different countries.

Conclusion

The passage of laws criminalizing human trafficking and providing resources for its eradication provide the foundation upon which successful antitrafficking efforts can be built. Local law enforcement agents play a critical role in this effort, but they face a number of significant challenges. To this end, since 2000, government officials in the United States have laid a greater emphasis on equipping federal law enforcement agents to investigate and prosecute human trafficking cases, but local law enforcement, remains less prepared. The lack of readiness by local law enforcement agencies is particularly troubling considering the fact that these agencies are often the segment of the criminal justice systems that may be in the best position to provide protection and safety to largest number of human trafficking victims. Primary among the challenges facing local law enforcement is the failure of local leaders to prioritize the problem of human trafficking, inadequate training for both generalist and specialist officers, and ineffective mechanisms to coordinate law enforcement responses across local, state, and national boundaries. There is much to be learned from the experiences of law enforcement practitioners internationally who have taken preliminary steps toward addressing these challenges (see, e.g., REF). The recommendations and promising practices described above are intended to help inform local officials as they work to improve antitrafficking enforcement and fulfill the mandates of international, federal, and state antitrafficking laws.

Acknowledgment

This project was supported by Award No. 2005-IJ-CX-0045 awarded by the National Institute of Justice, Office of Justice Programs, United States Department of Justice. The opinions, findings, and conclusions or recommendations expressed in this presentation are those of the authors and do not necessarily reflect the views of the Department of Justice. Data for this project were collected in collaboration with Jack McDevitt, Stephanie Fahy and Nikos Passas from Northeastern University with assistance from Scott Decker and Nancy Rodriguez of Arizona State University and Vincent Webb of Sam Houston State University.

Discussion and Review Questions

1. Law enforcement agents struggle to identify cases of human trafficking proactively. One tool that has been proven to be effective is training officers to look for the signs of human trafficking during police responses for other routine crimes. What other types of crimes do you think most warrant a closer look for potential victims of trafficking? What are the most important indicators or "red flags" that would signal the possibility of human trafficking victimization?

2. Due to regional variation in factors that put victims at risk for human trafficking and the types of criminal organizations that facilitate trafficking, law enforcement responses to trafficking naturally must vary. Describe four factors that change the way the police respond to human trafficking in your local community.

3. Human trafficking investigations often necessitate sharing information and collaborating with partners outside of their agency. What are the main challenges that law enforcement agents in your community face when attempting to conduct cross-agency or cross-border investigations? How could those challenges be overcome?

4. Corruption of police officials may directly support or indirectly help facilitate local human trafficking operations. How should nation states most effectively address the problem of police corruption?

References

African Union, 2002. Draft Action Plan to Combat Trafficking in Human Beings Especially Women and Children. 2nd Ministerial Conference of the African Union, November 28.

Agbu, O. 2003. Corruption and human trafficking: The Nigerian case. *West Africa Review*, 4: 1094–2254.

Andrees, B. and van der Linden. 2005. Designing trafficking research from a labour market perspective: The ILO experience, in Laczko, Frank and Gozdziak, Elzbieta (eds) *Data and Research on Human Trafficking: A Global Survey*. Geneva, Switzerland: International Organization for Migration.

Aron, L., Zweig, J., and Newmark, L. 2006. *Comprehensive Services for Survivors of Human Trafficking: Findings from Clients in Three Communities*. Washington, DC: Urban Institute.

Avenell, J. 2008. *Trafficking for sexual exploitation: A process review of operation pentameter*. Research Report 7. UK: Home Office.

Bales, K. and Lize, S. 2007. Investigating human trafficking challenges, lessons learned and best practices. *Federal Bureau of Investigation Law Enforcement Bulletin*, April. 76: 24–31.

Braun, J. 2007. Collaborations: The key to combating human trafficking. *Police Chief*, 70(12): 68–74.

Bruckert, C. and Parent, C. 2002. *Organized Crime and Human Trafficking in Canada: Tracking Perceptions and Discourses*, Ottawa, Ontario: Research and Evaluation Branch, Royal Canadian Mounted Police.

Buzawa, E. and Buzawa, C. 2002. *Domestic Violence: The Criminal Justice System Response*. Sage Publications.

Crank, J.P. 1994. Watchman and Community: Myth and Institutionalization. *Policing, Law and Soc'y Rev.*, 28: 325.

Center for Women Policy Studies. 2010. U.S. Policy to Combat Trafficking, State Laws. http://www.centerwomenpolicy.org/programs/trafficking/map/default_flash.asp. Accessed August 15, 2010.

Clawson, H., Dutch, N. and Cummings, M. 2006. *Law Enforcement Response to Human Trafficking and the Implications for Victims: Current Practices and Lessons Learned*. Washington, DC: ICF International.

Commission of the European Communities. 2005. *Fighting Trafficking in Human Beings—An Integrated Approach and Proposal for an Action Plan*. Communication from the Commission to the European Parliament and the Council, Brussels, October 18.

de Baca, L. and Andrea T. 2002. Working together to stop modern-day slavery. *The Police Chief*, (August) 69: 78–80.

Dugan, E. 2008. Police team that investigated tide of human traffic is closed Investigators who saved victims of prostitution and child labour have funds withdrawn by Home Office. *The Independent*, (November 10).

Ebbe, O. and Dilip D. 2007. *Global trafficking of Women and Children.* Boca Raton, FL: CRC Press.

Europol. 2007. Trafficking in human beings in the European Union: A Europol Perspective. http://s3.amazonaws.com/rcpp/assets/attachments/644_665_EN_original.pdf. Accessed on April 15, 2010.

Farrell, A., McDevitt, J. and Fahy, S. 2008. *Understanding and Improving Law Enforcement Responses to Human Trafficking (Grant No. 2005-IJ-CX-0045).* Washington DC: National Institute of Justice, U.S. Department of Justice.

Farrell, A., McDevitt, J. and Fahy, S. 2010. Where are all the victims? Understanding the determinants of official identification of human trafficking incidents. *Criminology and Public Policy,* 9(2): 201–233.

Ferraro, K. 1989. Policing women battering. *Social Problems,* 36(1): 61–74.

Fisher, I. 1997. U.S. indictment describes abuses of deaf Mexican trinket sellers. *New York Times,* August 21.

Government Accountability Office. 2007. Human Trafficking: A Strategic Framework could Help to Enhance the Interagency Collaboration Needed to Effectively Combat Trafficking Crimes (GAO-07-915). Washington, DC.

Gallagher, A. and Holmes, P. 2008. Developing an effective criminal justice response to human trafficking lessons from the front line. *International Criminal Justice Review,* 18:318–343.

Home Office. 2007. UK Action Plan on Tackling Human Trafficking. Joint Scottish Executive/Home Office Action Plan, March 23 http://www.homeoffice.gov.uk/documents/human-traffick-action-plan. Accessed on July 15, 2010.

Hughes, D. and Tatyana D. 2001. Trafficking in women from Ukraine. *Trends in Organized Crime,* 6: 43–67.

International Association of Chiefs of Police. 2006. *The Crime of Human Trafficking: A Law Enforcement Guide to Identification and Investigation.* Alexandria, VA: International Association of Chiefs of Police, March.

International Association of Chiefs of Police. 2008. *The impact of the Proposed FY 2009 budget on state, tribal, and local law enforcement.* Alexandria, VA: International Association of Chiefs of Police, March.

International Criminal Police Organization. 2007. *Trafficking in human beings—Best practice guidance manual for investigators* (2nd ed.). Lyon, France: General Secretariat of the International Criminal Police Organization.

Jahic, G. and Finckenauer, J. 2005. Representations and misrepresentations of human trafficking. *Trends in Organized Crime,* 8: 24–40.

Katz, C. 2001. Establishment of a police gang unit: An examination of organizational and environmental factors. *Criminology,* 39: 37–74.

Marsh, D. 2007. Issues impacting human trafficking collaborations: A local law enforcement perspective, statement at *Crossing the Border: Immigrants in Detention and Victims of Trafficking, Part II,* March 20. Maya, R. 1997. Sex trafficking of Thai women and the United States: Asylum law Response. *Georgetown Immigration Law Journal* 12: 145.

O'Neill, A.R. 1999. *International trafficking in women to the U.S.: A contemporary manifestation of slavery and organized crime.* Washington, DC: Center for the Study of Intelligence.

Potts, Jr., L. 2003. Global trafficking in human beings: Assessing the success of the United Nations Protocol to Prevent Trafficking in persons. *George Washington Law Review,* 35: 227–250.

Richards, K. 2004. The Trafficking of Migrant Workers: What are the Links Between Labour Trafficking and Corruption? *International Migration,* 42: 147–168.

Reichel, P. 2008. *Cross-national collaboration to combat human trafficking learning from the experience of others.* Washington DC: National Institute of Justice, National Criminal Justice Reference Service, Document number 223286.

Ridgley, J. 2008. Immigration enforcement, police and the insurgent genealogies of citizenship in U.S. sanctuary cities. *Urban Geography,* 29: 53–77.

Sadruddin, H., Walter, N., and Hidalgo, J. 2005. Human trafficking in the United States: Expanding victim protection beyond prosecution witnesses. *Stanford Law and Policy Review*, 16: 379–415.

Samarasinghe, V. 2003–2004. Confronting Globalization in Anti-trafficking Strategies in Asia. *Brown Journal World Affairs*, 10: 91.

Schauer, E. and Wheaton, E. 2006. Sex trafficking into the United States: A Literature Review. *Criminal Justice Review*, 31: 146–169.

Segrave, M., Milivojevic, S., and Pickering, S. 2009. *Sex Trafficking: International Context and Response*. Oxford, UK: Willan Publishing.

Smith, G. 2010. The Criminal Justice Response to Human Trafficking Recent *Developments in the Greater Mekong Sub-region*, Strategic Response Information Network. http://www.artippro-ject.org/artip-tip cjs/resources/specialised_publications/SIREN%20GMS-08.pdf. Accessed on August 13, 2010.

Srikantiah, J. 2007. Perfect victims and real survivors: Victims in domestic human trafficking law. *Boston University Law Review*, 87: 157–211.

Stolz, B. 2005. Educating policymakers and setting the criminal justice policymaking agenda: Interest groups and the "Victims of Trafficking and Violence Act of 2000." *Criminology and Criminal Justice*, 5: 407–430.

Surtees, R. 2008. Traffickers and trafficking in Southern and Eastern Europe: Considering the other side of human trafficking. *European Journal of Criminology*. 5:39–68.

Tackling Human Trafficking – The Ongoing Development. Serious Organized Crime Agency. http://www.soca.gov.uk/about-soca/about-the-ukhtc/ukhtc-news/199-tackling-human-trafficking-the-ongoing-development, Accessed on August 15, 2010.

Trafficking in Persons, Before the Senate Subcommittee on Near Eastern and South Asian Affairs, Foreign Relations Committee, 106 Congress. 2000. Statement of William Yeomans, Chief of Staff, Civil Rights Division, U.S. Department of Justice.

Trafficking Victims Violence Protection Act of 2000, PL 106–386, Statutes at Large 114 (2000): 1464.

Turner, J. and Kelly, L. 2009. Trade secrets: Intersections between diasporas and crime groups in the constitution of the human trafficking chain. *British Journal of Criminology*, 49: 184–201.

United Nations. 2009. *Global Report on Trafficking in Persons*. United Nations Office on Drugs and Crime.

United Nations Office on Drugs and Crime. 2008. *Toolkit to combat trafficking in persons*. New York: United Nations Office on Drugs and Crime. http://www.unodc.org/documents/human-trafficking/HT_Toolkit08_English.pdf

United States Department of Health and Human Services. 2009. *The Campaign to Rescue and Restore Victims of Human Trafficking, Resources for Law Enforcement*. Washington, DC: United States Department of Health and Human Services.

United States Department of Justice. 2004. U.S. Department of Justice, Civil Rights Division. *Anti-Trafficking News Bulletin*, 1(11): 1–8.

United States Department of Justice. 2009. Attorney General's Annual Report to Congress and Assessment of U.S. Government Activities to Combat Trafficking in Persons Fiscal Year 2008.

U.S. Department of State. 2004. *Trafficking in Persons Report*. Washington DC: U.S. Department of State.

U.S. Department of State. 2010. *Trafficking in Persons Report*. Washington DC: U.S. Department of State.

Victims of Trafficking and Violence Prevention Act of 2000. PL 106–386, Statutes at Large 114.

Weitzer, R. 2007. The social construction of sex trafficking: Ideology and institutionalization of a moral crusade. *Politics and Society*, 35: 447–475.

Williams, P. and Vlassis, D. 2001. *Combating Transnational Crime: Concepts, Activities and Responses*. London, UK: Frank Cass Publishers.

Winterdyk, J. and Sundberg, K. 2009. Human trafficking: Need for reform in Canada. *Crime and Justice International*. (online).

Wilson, D., William, W., and Sherilyn, K. 2006. Trafficking in human beings: Training and services among U.S. law enforcement agencies. *Police Practices and Research*, 7(2): 149–160.

Women's Commission for Refugee Women and Children. 2007. *The U.S. Response to Human Trafficking: An Unbalanced Approach*. New York: Women's Commission for Refugee Women and Children.

Zhang, S. 2007. *Smuggling and Trafficking in Human Beings: All Roads Lead to America*. New York: Praeger.

Zimmerman, C., Mazeda, H., Yun, K., Gajdadziev, V. et al. 2008. The health of trafficked women: A survey of women entering posttrafficking services in Europe. *American Journal of Public Health*, 98: 55–59.

Helpful Web Links

United Nations Office of Drugs and Crime publications on law enforcement responses to human trafficking: http://www.unodc.org/unodc/en/human-trafficking/publications.html

International Association of Human Trafficking Investigators: http://iahti.org/

International Association of Chiefs of Police: http://www.theiacp.org/PublicationsGuides/ResearchCenter/Projects/ViolenceAgainstWomen/PoliceResponsetoViolenceAgainstWomen/tabid/372/Default.aspx

International Cooperation

YVON DANDURAND

10

Contents

Introduction

Human trafficking often occurs across borders and the criminals involved in this terrible trade too often manage to avoid detection, arrest, or conviction. They can operate with relative impunity because they are able to take advantage of the difficulty that national law enforcement and criminal justice agencies have in working together to prevent and control most forms of transnational crime. In practice, human trafficking is often difficult to distinguish from the smuggling of illegal immigrants (see Chapters 1 and 2). However, both of them are serious forms of transnational organized crime and countries of the world must learn to cooperate not just in preventing illegal immigration, but also in preventing these more serious crimes. As in other forms of transnational crime, such as drug trafficking or trafficking in firearms, international cooperation is essential to the success of efforts to prevent and control these crimes. In the case of human trafficking, more specifically, cooperation is also essential to the rescue, protection and, when necessary, the repatriation of victims.

While previous international cooperation has focused on border control and the management of immigration (see Winterdyk and Sundberg 2010a), there is now a need for a different kind of international cooperation. Measures to protect state security, to prevent infiltration by foreign spies, enemies, terrorists, or unwanted refugees always seem to take precedence over human security concerns. Even when governments are claiming to be taking certain measures to prevent human trafficking or to protect refugees and poor immigrants against criminal exploitation, one sometimes suspects that they are indeed moved by far less humanitarian motives.

In this chapter, we will suggest that what is required is a genuine victim-focused approach to the prevention of human trafficking at all levels, including at the level of international prevention and cooperation efforts. By this, at the least, we mean that a concern for the protection of victims and potential victims must be placed at the center of our strategies and practices and, whenever necessary, must supersede concerns for protecting our borders and preventing illegal immigration.

This chapter pursues the following four objectives:

1. Critically examining the motivation and impetus behind the apparent renewed international commitment to fight human trafficking and stop the smuggling of migrants
2. Understanding the crucial importance of international cooperation in preventing and controlling human trafficking and understanding the international legal framework developed within the context of the United Nations and other organizations to support such cooperation
3. Identifying the main obstacles to international cooperation in preventing human trafficking and the main reasons for its frequent failure
4. Reflecting on ways to improve international cooperation and effectively counter the human trafficking activities of criminal groups

The Need for International Cooperation

Background

In most western countries, governments are dealing with negative public attitudes toward illegal immigrants and they are pressured into taking action, including repressive measures such as the detention and deportation of illegal migrants irrespective of their personal circumstances. In Canada, a 2007 public opinion poll conducted for Citizenship and Immigration Canada showed that a majority of Canadians wanted all illegal immigrants arrested and deported, including those who came to the country legally and whose visa had expired, whether or not they have family in the country (*Ottawa Citizen* 2007).

In Europe, in response to a public perception that illegal immigration is getting out of control, in 2005 the European Commission (i.e., Council Regulation [EC] 2007/2004) created Frontex (from French "frontières extérieures" for external borders) as a pan-European model of integrated border security and operational cooperation aimed at curbing irregular migrant influx into the European Union. In 2009, French President Nicolas Sarkozy and Italian Prime Minister Silvio Berlusconi urged European Union leaders to step up their fight against illegal immigration. They urged Frontex to proceed expeditiously with the expulsion and deportation of illegal migrants (de Beaupuy 2009).

With the passing of the "Secure Fence Act of 2006," in September of 2006, the United States government began to build an enormous wall (a 21 ft tall and 6 ft deep under the ground fence) along the Mexican border. At the time of preparing this chapter, the wall runs for hundreds of miles from San Diego, California, all the way to Texas. It has been paid for by the American tax payers, the majority of whom—some polls suggest—support such measures as an appropriate way to prevent illegal immigration from the South. There is no equivalent fortification on the Mexican side. This is not a joint initiative to prevent human trafficking or the criminal exploitation of migrants by the "coyotes" (smugglers involved in smuggling Mexican immigrants into the United States) and criminal organizations. In fact both the past and current Presidents of Mexico, Vincente Fox, and Felipe Calderon have denounced the American initiatives as shameful and disgraceful and have likened the wall to the Berlin Wall that separated communist East Germany from West Germany for decades (*CanWest News Service* 2006).

In April 2010, the Governor of Arizona signed into law the toughest bill on illegal immigration in the United States, a law meant to facilitate the identification, prosecution, and deportation of illegal immigrants. According to the *New York Times*, the law "unleashed immediate protests and reignited the divisive battle over immigration reform nationally" (Archibold 2010). President Obama was politically compelled to intervene and dissociate his administration from that State initiative and the matter ended up before the federal court.

It should be obvious that much of the existing border control and immigration control apparatus was put in place to prevent illegal migration or unwanted immigrants from entering a country; in other words, to protect borders rather than the people. It can sometimes be confusing when we hear our governments and politicians advocate for and justify stronger border control measures under the pretence that they are required to prevent human trafficking. Their real motives are thinly veiled and often different from those they state. Worse still, it is both confusing and discouraging to observe how one very powerful country, the United States, uses the threat of withholding its development assistance to other countries to force it to "protect victims of human trafficking" or, as everyone should understand, to limit illegal immigration and help them protect their own borders.

So far, countries have demonstrated that they are far more interested in protecting their borders and territory against foreigners than protecting victims of human trafficking or human smuggling. Illegal migration and the unregulated movement of refugees are their primary concerns. In fact, it has been argued that by constructing human trafficking as a crime control issue and by presenting government interventions as attempts to protect victims, governments can present more restrictive immigration controls as if they were designed to protect victims and human rights (O'Connell Davidson 2005, p. 69). The criminalization of human trafficking serves to "divide the deserving 'victims' from the undeserving '**illegal immigrants**'" (O'Connell Davidson 2005, p. 65).

Critically examining how and why countries cooperate with each other—or fail to do so—to prevent human trafficking and protect its victims can be instructive. It helps us understand how and why, over the last century or so, the issue of human trafficking was taken up periodically by the international community and supported by local activists. We can also look at international cooperation in criminal matters, as it has been evolving over the last two or three decades, based on an uneven and still-growing international regime designed to address various forms of transnational crime. This chapter concentrates on both these issues and also looks at some concrete ways in which this regime can be strengthened. We must bear in mind that countries and their law enforcement agencies are not always transparent about how, and if, they cooperate to fight transnational crime (see Chapter 9). Predictably, there is a paucity of publically available information and so we must do our best with what is available.

International Attention to the Problem

The problem of abduction, enslavement, and exploitation of people, including women and children, goes back to times that cannot be remembered. Many ancient tribes held these forcible abductions as a kind of rite of passage for young males. International attention to human trafficking or its condemnation is more recent. The formal denunciation of this behavior and the accompanying moral panic goes back more than a century and are revived periodically. Since the late-nineteenth century, various groups denounced "la traite des blanches" (trafficking in white women and eventually "white trafficking") as a growing and dangerous problem. Newspapers were filled with sensational reports of poor innocent girls who were drugged, or kidnapped, and taken to work in foreign brothels; the theme and other similar ones were taken up by various antivice crusades in Europe and in North America (Barry 1982).

In Paris, in 1904, 12 countries signed an international agreement for the repression of trafficking in women (the *International Agreement of May 18, 1904 for the Suppression of the White Slave Traffic*). In 1910, the agreement was followed by the *International Convention of 4 May 1910 for the Suppression of the White Slave Traffic*. This was followed by the *International Convention of September 30, 1921 for the Suppression of the Traffic in Women and Children* (amended later by the Protocol approved by the General Assembly of the United Nations on October 20, 1947) (Toupin 2002). The 1921 Convention included a number of international cooperation measures, including the provision for *extradition* for the crimes defined by the Convention. Under the auspices of the League of Nations, another international agreement was adopted: *The International Convention of October 11, 1933 for the Suppression of the Traffic in Women of Full Age*.

In 1949, the United Nations adopted the *Convention for the Suppression of the Traffic in Persons and of the Exploitation of the Prostitution of Others*. The purpose of the convention is to repress prostitution. Its preamble includes the following statement: "(...) prostitution and the accompanying evil of the traffic in persons for the purpose of prostitution are incompatible with the dignity and worth of the human person and endanger the welfare of the individual, the family and the community" (Preamble). The parties to the Convention must agree to "punish any person who, to gratify the passions of another: (1) procures, entices or leads away, for purposes of prostitution, another person, even with the consent of that person; (2) exploits the prostitution of another person, even with the consent of that person" (Article 1). The efforts of moral entrepreneurs determined to abolish prostitution was at the heart of these early attempts to criminalize human trafficking (Piette 2002) and, as one would expect, that motivation is still very much present in the current movement to control human trafficking (Segrave et al. 2009).

Legal Framework for International Cooperation

There is now a considerable body of international law (regional and global) dealing with immigration and providing for a complex international cooperation regime. It governs such things as asylum, immigration of children, detention, expulsion, and deportation of illegal immigrants, border management, documentation, or carrier sanctions. Founded in 1951 with Headquarters in Geneva, the International Organization for Migration (IOM) provides an institutional basis to support that collaboration. In addition, there is the *Hague Convention on Protection of Children and Co-operation in Respect of Intercountry Adoption* (1993) which establishes a basis for international cooperation in protecting children and enforcing certain standards in the cases of international adoption.

There is also a rich body of international law concerning the protection of refugees, the principle of nonrefoulement, and many other key elements of human rights law. The basis of this law is the 1951 *United Nations Convention Relating to the Status of Refugees*. The Convention provides that countries who become parties to the Convention cannot "impose penalties, on account of their illegal entry or presence, on refugees who coming directly from a territory where their life or freedom was threatened: "(...) enter or are present in their territory without authorization, provided they present themselves without delay to the authorities and show good cause for their illegal entry or presence" (Article 31). Within the United Nations, the Office of the United Nations High Commissioner for Refugees is the institutional agency at the heart of an international regime for the protection of refugees. Since 1950, the Office coordinates international action to protect refugees and resolve refugee problems worldwide. It helps ensure that everyone can exercise the right to seek asylum and find safe refuge in another State.

Since 1989, the *Convention on the Rights of the Child* entails some clear obligations for States parties with respect to the protection of children against human trafficking and fraudulent adoptions. Article 35 of the Convention demands that States parties to the Convention "take all appropriate national, bilateral, and multilateral measures to prevent the abduction of, the sale of, or traffic in children for any purpose or in any form." Other articles of the Convention create additional obligations for the governments: the obligation to take measures to combat the illicit transfer and nonreturn of children abroad (Article 11); obligations to monitor and supervise intercountry adoptions (Article 21); obligations regarding children seeking refugee status (Article 22), or the obligation to take several measures to prevent the commercial sexual exploitation of children (Article 34). In 2000, the United Nations also adopted the *Optional Protocol to the Convention on the Rights of the Child on the sale of children, child prostitution and child pornography*. The Protocol addresses a "significant and increasing international traffic in children for the purpose of the sale of children, child prostitution and child pornography" (Preamble). The concern extends to the practice of sex-tourism to which children are seen to be especially vulnerable. Under the Protocol, States parties must prohibit the sale of children, child prostitution, and child pornography (Article 1).

Not all countries expressly recognize or define these and other behaviors as criminal. The Protocol requires States parties to define a number of specific offences, to establish its jurisdiction over these offences, to investigate and prosecute them and to extend wide cooperation to other countries in the investigation and prosecution of these crimes. The criminalization of a specific conduct is what triggers a criminal justice intervention and unless a conduct is criminalized in relatively similar terms in two countries, it is difficult for the criminal justice agencies of these countries to cooperate efficiently with each other.

In the 1990s, the increasing involvement of criminal organizations in these and other forms of transnational organized crime resulted in development of a comprehensive international treaty to facilitate cooperation in preventing and fighting international organized crime. Specific crimes such as migrant smuggling, trafficking in firearms, and corruption were identified as worthy of special attention.

During the negotiations that followed, it was agreed that a new Convention should be adopted to promote international cooperation in the fight against all serious international crimes involving criminal organizations. Since it was clear from the outset that not all countries involved in the negotiations would agree to specifically criminalize the smuggling of migrants, human trafficking, or trafficking in firearms, it was decided that these matters were better left to supplemental and optional protocols that State parties could elect to ratify or not. That way, objections or concerns about specific dispositions in the protocols would not constitute obstacles to the ratification of the main Convention by as many countries as possible.

Negotiations concerning the new international dispositions relating to the smuggling of migrants and human trafficking were complex and delicate. In fact, the most testing part of that process was reaching an agreement on the definitions of these two types of crime and on how they should be distinguished. Right up to the end of the negotiations, assorted versions of these definitions were included within brackets—a standard notation in drafting international treaties and resolutions to indicate that the text has not yet been agreed upon—in the various drafts of the proposed protocols. It was not until the "eleventh hour," that a compromise was found to resolve the disagreements over definitions. This little known fact is more than a piece of historical trivia: it was already a clear sign of the difficulty that countries had, and would continue to have, in distinguishing these two types of criminal activities. It also revealed the fact that countries had, and would continue to have, different motives and interests with respect to the prevention and control of these crimes. The definitions that were eventually agreed to were most important for the future workings of the treaties and for promoting criminal justice cooperation in fighting these crimes. However, surveys of States parties conducted over the last decade indicate that these definitions continue to create operational difficulties for the law enforcement and criminal justice agencies involved (United Nations CTOC 2008).

By December 2000, countries were prepared to adopt and sign the *United Nations Convention against Transnational Organized Crime* and its three supplementary protocols: the *Protocol to Prevent, Suppress and Punish Trafficking in Persons, Especially Women and Children*; the *Protocol against Smuggling of Migrants by Land, Sea and Air*, the *Protocol against the Illicit Manufacturing of and Trafficking in Firearms*. The main Convention and the Protocol against trafficking in persons, because they were signed in Palermo, Sicily, are often referred to as the "Palermo Convention" and the "Palermo Protocol." As of August 2010, the main convention against transnational organized crime had been ratified by 155 countries and the protocol against trafficking in persons by 137 countries.*

The TOC Convention

The United Nations *Convention against Transnational Organized Crime* is meant to promote and facilitate more effective international cooperation in fighting transnational organized crime, including human trafficking and the smuggling of migrants. Its stated purpose is to promote cooperation in the control and prevention of these crimes. It covers the following seven crucial aspects: (1) how parties must establish jurisdiction over offences; (2) the need to provide for the legal liability of legal persons (e.g., a corporation); (3) the identification, tracing, freezing or seizure of assets, and confiscation of proceeds of crime; (4) the protection of victims and witnesses; (5) special investigation techniques; (6) extradition; and (7) *mutual legal assistance*. The Convention sets a basic minimum standard for extradition for the offences it covers and encourages the adoption of various mechanisms to streamline the extradition process. The Convention also calls for the widest measure of mutual legal assistance in investigations, prosecutions, and judicial proceedings. It builds upon a number of previous multilateral and regional treaties.

The Trafficking in Persons Protocol

To become a party to the Protocol on trafficking in persons, a State must first ratify the main *Convention against Transnational Organized Crime*. This is because the general means through which countries can cooperate in fighting human trafficking are established in the main Convention. The trafficking in persons protocol deals with the definition of the offence of trafficking and some of the specific measures required to address this problem at the international level, notably its prevention, the provision of assistance to victims and issues of border control. Article 8 of the protocol requires the cooperation of States parties in arranging for the prompt and safe repatriation of victims. The obligations of States parties to facilitate and accept the return, or repatriation, of victims parallel the dispositions of the *Protocol of the Smuggling of Migrants*.

Especially Women and Children

The full title of the Trafficking in Persons Protocol is the *Protocol to Prevent, Suppress, and Punish Trafficking in Persons, Especially Women and Children, Supplementing the United Nations Convention against Transnational Crime*. The Protocol does not contain dispositions which distinguish between women, children, or men. Furthermore, the definition of the crime does not limit the offence to a special group of victims. Why then was it deemed necessary to emphasize women and children as potential victims?

Vermeulen (2001, p. 838) notes that from a criminal law perspective the fight against trafficking in and smuggling of persons is largely independent from gender differences.

---

*For a complete listing of current countries see: http://treaties.un.org/Pages/ViewDetails.aspx?src=TREATY&mtdsg_no=XVIII-12-a&chapter=18&lang=en, retrieved on August 7, 2010.

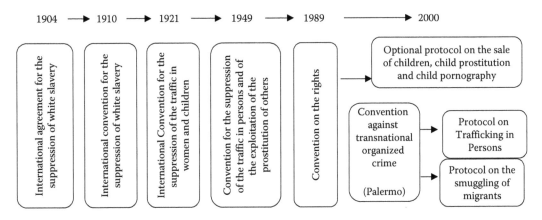

Figure 10.1 Evolving international legal framework to address trafficking in persons.

Why then did drafters of the Palermo Protocol feel a need to specify "particularly women and children?" If it is because women and children are most often the victims of human trafficking, it is necessary to ask how one knows that. Where is the evidence that such is really the case? In fact various attempts to measure the prevalence of various forms of human trafficking have shown how complicated it is (UNODC 2006b, 2009a, 2010a, pp. 39–52; also see Chapter 2 of this book). In particular, one must bear in mind that all of the official data available are affected if not biased by differences in national legal definitions of human trafficking and by varying law enforcement practices (UNODC 2010b, p. 39).

Regional Instruments

The above review of the legal framework for international cooperation does not cover the many bilateral arrangements and treaties which countries have concluded among themselves or the regional treaties and international legal instruments that also aim to promote international cooperation in the fight against human trafficking and the smuggling of migrants. There are many such regional arrangements. For example, the *Inter-American Convention on the Prevention, Punishment, and Eradication of Violence against Women* (also known as the Belém do Pará Convention) defines trafficking in persons as a form of violence against women (Article 2b) calls for international cooperation. In Europe, the *Commission of the European Communities* has adopted Framework Decisions on combating trafficking in human beings and on combating the sexual exploitation of children and child pornography. These decisions strengthen regional cooperation by impose binding minimum rules upon the EU Member States concerning the constituent elements of and sanctions for the crimes in question (see Figure 10.1).

Why International Cooperation Is Essential to Combat All Forms of Transnational Crime, Including Human Trafficking

Even those who have been involved in the field for many years continue to be surprised at how easily criminal groups operating across borders can avoid detection, arrest, and conviction by exploiting the weaknesses of various criminal justice systems and their inability to cooperate. For criminal justice agencies, national borders are what define and delimit their jurisdiction. If they exceed their jurisdiction, they risk encroaching on the jurisdiction and sovereignty of another country. For criminals, however, national borders often function more as a protective shield than an obstacle. Some of them, the smugglers and traffickers, even find ways to turn the borders into an opportunity for vast profits by illegally moving people, drugs, arms, and various other commodities across borders (United Nations 2010).

Without laws that criminalize similar conducts, in similar terms and with comparable severity, criminal justice agencies find it hard to cooperate internationally. Without agreements facilitating investigations across borders, the exchange of evidence, the extradition of criminals, the protection of witnesses, or the enforcement of court judgements, their efforts can easily get bogged down in procedural and sometimes political intricacies. In the absence of bilateral treaties, countries are often unable to cooperate with each other. There are more than 200 countries around the world and none of them has bilateral cooperation treaties with all the others. The shortcomings of national systems working alone and of existing bilateral arrangements have become obvious (Dandurand et al. 2007).

Experience shows that the best results in controlling and preventing human trafficking are obtained when law enforcement and prosecution agencies are able to work together effectively, both locally and across borders (Dandurand 2007). This is why multilateral treaties, or conventions, are critical in strengthening an international cooperation regime. This is why the *United Nations Convention against Transnational Crime* is so important in articulating a coherent regime of international cooperation in criminal matters. Countries that do not have specific arrangements to govern their relations with respect to mutual legal assistance, extradition, or the seizure and forfeiture of criminal assets or proceeds of crime can directly invoke the dispositions of that Convention. The Convention provides a framework for international cooperation in combating organized crime in general and human trafficking specifically.

The dynamic nature of transnational crime requires countries to constantly refine their cooperation strategies (Harfield 2008). They need to take into account how criminal elements are acting to defeat detection and prosecution. Generally speaking, not enough is known about the criminal patterns involved and the behavior of human traffickers (Surtees 2008). Countries must favor strategic approaches to the investigation and prosecution of transnational crime (see Chapters 6 through 8 in this textbook). International cooperation, particularly law enforcement collaboration, requires national efforts to comply with new international standards, encourage convergence, and compatibility of national legislation, introduce complex procedural reforms, develop a much greater investigative and prosecutorial capacity at the national level and strengthen the capacity to cooperate at the international level (Dandurand 2007).

Dealing with organized crime presents difficult challenges for all countries, but particularly for countries with a weak, or corrupt, criminal justice system.[*] They simply do not have the capacity to confront some of the powerful criminal organizations that take advantage of countries which are poorly equipped to stop them independently or to cooperate internationally. In some instances, they manage to corrupt public officials to ensure that international cooperation will be defeated, that they will continue to function with relative impunity and that the proceeds of their crimes are safely tucked away. Some countries are particularly vulnerable because they are the weakest links in the "chain" of international cooperation. As

---

[*] Transparency International provides a corruption perception index for countries. It can be viewed at: http://www.transparency.org/policy_research/surveys_indices/cpi/2009/cpi_2009_table

such, they attract the unwanted activities of criminal organizations. Countries in transition, or postconflict, countries are particularly vulnerable and they are often targeted as a source country for human trafficking. In recent years, this has been the case of Liberia, Haiti, the Democratic Republic of Congo, and the former Yugoslavia. For these and other vulnerable countries, building the basic capacity of their criminal justice system to function efficiently, let alone a capacity to cooperate internationally, is often a painfully slow and difficult process, one they cannot hope to achieve without international assistance.

The Importance of Internationally Agreed upon Legal Definitions as a Basis for International Cooperation

The international definitions found in the UN Protocol on Trafficking in Persons, the Protocol of the Smuggling of Migrants and the additional protocol to the *Convention on the Rights of the Child* were meant to provide consensus-based definitions that would facilitate international cooperation. With these definitions, the international community finally has a common basis for the criminalization of these conducts in national laws in a manner that may lead to greater international cooperation. The ability to reduce discrepancies in national laws could help ensure that offenders have no place to hide and can no longer exploit gaps and inconsistencies in the law (Dandurand 2005).

Article 3 of the Trafficking in Persons Protocol identifies the following three constituting ad necessary elements of the crime of the crime of "trafficking in persons" as follows: (1) the action (e.g., recruitment, transportation, transfer, or receipt of persons); (2) the means (e.g., threat or use of force, coercion, fraud, etc.); and (3) the purpose of exploitation (e.g., sexual, force labor, removal of organs, etc.) (UNODC 2006a).

The definition does not limit the offence to the criminal exploitation of individuals through various forms of sexual exploitation. Instead, it enumerates different and often more frequent forms of criminal exploitation in an attempt to distinguish human trafficking from forced prostitution. Note also that, according to the International Labour Organization, the majority of human trafficking in the world takes the form of forced labor—involuntary servitude (U.S. State Department 2009).

The emphasis on transportation and transfer of persons relate to what makes the crime a transnational crime and that is what is being targeted by the protocols and the convention. However, international transportation does not need to be emphasized within the national legislation (UNODC 2004a, pp. 275–276). The crime can be committed within a country. Whereas the offence of smuggling of migrants always involves an element of "*transnationality*," the offence of human trafficking does not.

The definition's emphasis on the means used to commit the offence was required to emphasize that lack of an individual's consent, at least in the case of adults, was relevant and important in defining the offence. This is because people who are smuggled across borders normally consent to it; indeed they are often prepared to pay large sums for that service (INTERPOL 2009; also see Chapter 2). They become victims of human trafficking only if there was no consent as in the case of abduction, or if the consent was obtained by threats, violence, fraud, or deception.

In the two protocols, smuggling of migrants and human trafficking both involve moving human beings for profit. However, in the case of human trafficking, two additional elements must be present beyond the act of smuggling: there must be some improper form of recruitment, without real consent, and there must be an exploitative purpose, although the purpose need not necessarily have been fulfilled. When children are involved, the method of recruitment and the child's consent is irrelevant. Trafficking in persons and smuggling of migrants are distinct crimes, but they represent overlapping crime problems. Actual cases may involve elements of both offences or they may shift from one to the other. In reality, victims of human trafficking are often smuggled into another country without being aware they are being trafficked or that they are being duped into a situation where they will be criminally exploited. This complicates international law enforcement cooperation because victims of human trafficking often come to the attention of the authorities not as victims, but as illegal immigrants, as migrant being smuggled into a country or as offenders because they are being forced to participate in various crimes as part of their criminal exploitation (e.g., drug production, prostitution, illegal work, etc.). Some forms of trafficking, such as trafficking for forced marriage or for adoptions, can be more difficult to detect than others (Bokhari 2009).

International Legal Definitions and Their Impact on National Laws

As we have seen, various international instruments create for the States that ratify them an obligation to establish in their laws some specific criminal offences relating to human trafficking. This is referred to as "the obligation to criminalize." This obligation, needless to say, is not always fulfilled.

One study, for example, described the difficulties encountered in Nigeria in prosecuting cases of trafficking Nigerian girls to Italy in spite of the heightened law enforcement cooperation between the two countries. These difficulties were due in part to the fact that Nigeria did not have specific legislation criminalizing human trafficking so prosecutors had to rely on other more general dispositions of the criminal law to build their case (UNICRI 2004).

It is difficult to know how much impact international legal definitions have had on national laws. Incorporation of the Palermo Protocols' definitions into national law has been more difficult than anticipated. Ten years after the adoption of the protocols and often many years after ratifying them, countries are still finding it difficult to bring their own criminal definitions into compliance with the international instruments. The United Nations *Convention against Transnational Organized Crime* provided for the establishment of a Conference of Parties to the Convention and its protocols whose main purpose is to review progress and assist in the implementation of these international instruments. Yet, a decade after the adoption of the Convention and its protocols, the slow implementation of these protocols continues to be a concern (United Nations CTOC 2009). As it strives to improve the capacity of States to combat trafficking in persons, the Conference of Parties has repeatedly called upon States parties to continue to strengthen their national legislations and policies for the implementation of the Trafficking in Persons Protocol.

The United Nations Office on Drugs and Crime, the UNICEF and other UN agencies provide technical assistance to requesting countries who are trying to achieve compliance of their laws with the new international definitions. A *Model Law against Trafficking in Persons* has been made available to them (UNODC 2009b) as well as a legislative guide (UNODC 2004a).

Difficulties Encountered at the National Level in Implementing International Definitions

When attempting to fully implement the legal definitions of the two or three relevant protocols, countries must often undertake a detailed review of their existing criminal law and criminal procedure codes (e.g., Ministry of Justice of Vietnam 2004). In some countries, like Vietnam, where children involved in prostitution are criminalized as a "social evil," the implementation of Protocol provisions, particularly those relating to the noncriminalization of victims, has been a challenge. The Cambodian *Law on Human Trafficking and Sexual Exploitation* refers generally to victim assistance and prevention but implies that the police may remove "suspected sex workers" and place them in facilities where they may be held against their will. People who assist them in avoiding arrest can be charged with "procuring" (Overs 2009). Box 10.1 presents examples of the confusion that prevails among the countries along the Mekong River.

Canada, for example, did not immediately bring its criminal law into compliance with the Convention and its protocols. Parliament first adopted some specific provisions in its new *Immigration and Refugee Protection Act* (2001). Sections 117 and 118 of that legislation created the offences of human smuggling and trafficking in persons, and attached a maximum penalty of life imprisonment and/or a fine up to one million dollars. At the time, the federal

---

BOX 10.1   LEGAL OBSTACLES TO COOPERATION*

Most countries of Southeast Asia need to cooperate in their efforts to curb human trafficking, but that cooperation is hindered by persisting confusion regarding the definition of human trafficking. A recent assessment of child trafficking by UNICEF/EAPRO reveals the general confusion among government officials about how to define the status of child victims of trafficking (UNICEF/EAPRO 2009). In the absence of clear legal definitions of trafficking, whether the situations of child trafficking are identified or not by various officials becomes a complicated matter of interpretation. This explains why many officials in Thailand treat the problem of human trafficking in terms of labor or immigration issues despite the region's well-documented human trafficking patterns. Since more people are voluntarily migrating from Cambodia or Myanmar to Thailand, it is difficult for Thai officials to determine whether the people coming to their attention are irregular migrants or trafficking victims. Furthermore, many of the irregular migrants also become victims even if they initially migrated voluntarily.

The cross-border confusion may also explain how Vietnamese border officials have apparently refused entry into Vietnam to Vietnamese victims of trafficking who presented themselves at the Vietnam–China border without adequate documentation. This is also how, in China, officials are deporting trafficking victims to Vietnam as they were no more than illegal migrants or even traffickers themselves. This, according to UNICEF, makes it difficult for Vietnam to provide appropriate services and protection to victims or even to distinguish them from human traffickers (UNICEF EAPRO 2009, p. 63).

---

* UNICEF/EAPRO. (2009). *Reversing the Trend—Child Trafficking in East and Southeast Asia*. Bangkok: UNICEF East Asia and Pacific Regional Office.

government claimed that these new offences were sufficient to bring Canada into compliance with international obligations under the Protocol on trafficking in persons and smuggling of migrants. Both offences were defined in terms of acts relating to "organizing entry into Canada" and "organizing the coming into Canada" (*Immigration and Refugee Protection Act* 2001, Sections 117 and 118). The illegal crossing of Canadian borders was an essential part of these offences. It was not until 2005, that the offence of human trafficking was introduced in the Canadian *Criminal Code* (Article 219.01) without reference to illegal immigration.

The Conference of Parties to the UN *Convention against Organized Crime* and its Protocols has established a working group to review the difficulties encountered by States parties in implementing the Protocol on trafficking in persons (United Nations CTOC 2010). The low rate of convictions for trafficking in persons globally (UNODC 2009a) continues to be a major source of concern. The working group is encouraging States parties to increase their efforts to investigate and prosecute cases involving trafficking in persons, including by making timely use of financial investigation techniques, special investigative techniques, and other tools designed to combat other forms of organized crime (United Nations CTOC 2010). To increase cooperation and coordination of efforts, it also suggests that countries enhance cross-border criminal justice action, including, where appropriate, by making increased use of joint investigations, special investigative techniques, and information sharing. In July 2010, the United Nations General Assembly adopted the *United Nations Global Plan of Action against Trafficking in Persons*. As expected, the plan includes a clear emphasis on enhancing international criminal justice cooperation (United Nations 2010).

Forms and Methods of International Criminal Justice Cooperation

The main forms of international criminal justice cooperation have evolved slowly over the years (Dandurand et al. 2007). At first, they resulted from bilateral treaties and arrangements among countries with similar interests in fighting crime, often immediate neighbors. In most instances, they are still quite cumbersome and relatively inefficient. There is, therefore, room for improvement.

We will briefly review here some of these mechanisms. All of them are directly applicable to human trafficking offences provided that these offences exist in national laws and that the countries have established their jurisdiction over them (UNODC 2010b).

Extradition

Extradition is a formal, and often treaty-based, process leading to the return or delivery of fugitives or alleged offenders to the jurisdiction in which they are prosecuted. When criminals are attempting to avoid prosecution in another country, extradition proceedings are required to bring them to justice in the prosecuting country.

The existing regime of international cooperation in criminal matters still needs major improvements to avoid legislative loopholes and eliminate safe havens.* For example, Canada has around 50 bilateral international agreements for extradition. Multilateral conventions and bilateral treaties on extradition are almost too numerous to track. Despite

---

* See http://www.treaty-accord.gc.ca/Treaties_CLF/TreatyList.asp?Type=All&Page=TL.

this, there are numerous situations where existing legal instruments are insufficient or do not cover the offence or the country concerned.

There remain many obstacles to expeditious and predictable extradition. States need to continue to perfect their treaty network and modernize their own extradition laws. Considerable work is being done internationally to implement best practices in these matters (UNODC 2004b). The United Nations has developed a Model Treaty on Extradition and a Model Law on Extradition.

Notwithstanding the previous comments, since 2000, some countries have seen progress through the principle of "mutual recognition." They improved judicial collaboration by replacing complex and cumbersome procedures with swift procedures which recognize the integrity of other legal systems. The best example is probably the European Arrest Warrant which, since 2004, effectively replaces extradition procedures by a system of surrender between judicial authorities in Member States of the European Union (Blekxtoon 2004; Council of the European Union 2002; Plachta 2003).

Mutual Legal Assistance

Mutual legal assistance is a formal process that countries use to provide and obtain government-to-government assistance in criminal investigations and prosecutions. As in the case of extradition, mutual legal assistance is based on bilateral and multilateral treaties, and relies on national legislation which either gives full effect to the relevant treaties or enables mutual assistance in absence of a treaty.

What is covered by these international arrangements varies but generally includes: taking of evidence and statements; locating and identifying witnesses and suspects; executing searches; executing seizure of property; executing legal documents; identifying and tracing proceeds of crime, providing information, evidentiary items and expert evaluations; or the transferring of prisoners to provide evidence (Dandurand et al. 2007; also UNODC 2004a). In recent years, countries have taken steps to improve their capacity to cooperate more fully in these regards. Countries are allowing the direct transmission of request for assistance, authorizing the cross-border use of technical equipment and the interception of communications, encouraging the establishment of joint investigation teams, and allowing controlled deliveries and covert investigations to take place across borders (Vermeulen 2001). Here also, a considerable amount of work has been done to identify and implement best practices. For example, a United Nations Informal Expert Working Group on mutual Legal Assistance Casework Best Practices noted that cooperation can be expedited through the use of alternatives to formal mutual assistance requests, such as informal police channels and communications mechanisms or joint investigation teams with a capacity to directly transmit and satisfy informal request for assistance.

Measures against Money Laundering

International cooperation has focused, in part, on controlling the laundering of proceeds of crime (Dandurand 2007). The international regime against money laundering is the result of a framework and international standards adopted in the context of various regional and international organizations. The United Nations conventions against transnational organized crime and against corruption both include provisions against money laundering. Measures against money laundering are often part of a law enforcement strategy that

consists of "following the money" and confiscating it as often as possible to deprive criminals of the proceeds of their crime (Commonwealth Secretariat 2005). However, there is
little convincing evidence that this approach is producing any significant results in terms
of controlling human trafficking.

International cooperation in the confiscation of criminal assets continues to pose
particular difficulties. The 2000 UN Convention against Transnational Organized Crime
offers some standards along which national laws and practices can be aligned.* The objective is to develop national legislative frameworks and practices that provide flexibility in
international cooperation while protecting the legitimate interests of third parties. The
successful investigation and prosecution of money laundering offences require the quick
identification and communication of information from banks and other financial institutions. Efforts are made to enlist the cooperation of the banking and financial sectors and
to ensure that relevant law enforcement authorities are familiar with the cooperation currently available from other countries and with the means to seek and obtain that cooperation (see Commonwealth Secretariat 2005).

In many instances, changes to bilateral treaties, or national laws, are required to allow
for the lawful and expeditious cross-border exchange of that information. Treaties and
international arrangements include provisions for prompt responses to requests for information on banking transactions of natural or legal persons, as well as for the monitoring of
financial transactions at the request of another State and for the spontaneous transmission
of information on instrumentalities or proceeds of crime to another State.

The existence of offshore centers also presents some practical problems from the point
of view of law enforcement cooperation. Corporate law, banking laws, and financial regulatory schemes vary from country to country. There are also issues with cyber-payments,
"virtual banks" operating in under-regulated offshore jurisdictions, and shell companies
operating outside of the territory of the offshore centre. Finally, control agencies are experiencing great difficulties in curbing money laundering in countries relying mostly on cash
economy or where participation in the "formal" financial system is low. Informal financial networks are used to transfer criminal proceedings and understanding these informal
financial networks and how criminal groups can abuse them becomes a law enforcement
priority (Passas 2003).

Cooperation in Assets Tracing, Freezing, and Forfeiture

The gathering of financial information to detect financial networks linked to organized
crime and human trafficking is an essential element of a strategic approach to fighting
human trafficking. The gathering and exchange of information by various countries
to detect financial networks linked to organized crime groups, including exchange of
information between law enforcement and regulatory bodies, are necessary to a strategic approach to combating organized crime. An extensive international regime exists to
prevent money laundering and to facilitate the tracing, interception, and confiscation of
criminal assets and the proceeds of crime. As part of that regime, countries are required to
establish "financial intelligence" units, an essential component of financial investigations
and international cooperation (Financial Action Task Force 2003).

---

* For further details on the Convention visit: http://www.unodc.org/unodc/en/treaties/CTOC/index.html

A number of strategies can be used to strengthen the law enforcement capacity to intercept criminal assets. These include the development of arrangements for timely exchanges of financial intelligence information between agencies, initiating assets confiscation or forfeiture proceedings independently of other proceedings, or entering into international agreements for sharing confiscated assets among countries involved in a case (see UNODC 2004a; Commonwealth Secretariat 2005).

Cooperation in Victim and Witness Protection

The threat that cross-border criminal groups represent to witnesses and victims is not confined to national borders. Physical and psychological intimidation of witnesses and their relatives can take place in many contexts (Dandurand 2010). Furthermore, witnesses may need to move from one country to another during lengthy investigations and criminal proceedings. Finally, there are cases where a country may not be able on its own to provide the required protection to the witnesses and ensure their safety. This is the case, for example, of several small island states such as those found in the Caribbean, or the South Pacific (Dandurand 2006).

For all these reasons, cooperation in the protection of witnesses and their relatives, including repatriated victims/witnesses of trafficking, and collaborators of justice becomes a necessary component of law enforcement cooperation. Furthermore, international cooperation may also be required at times to protect interpreters, the police or the prosecutors themselves and other judicial and correctional personnel. Victim intimidation is sometimes achieved indirectly by threat of violence against their family or relatives in their home country (Dandurand 2010). When intimidation becomes transnational, effective victim protection requires close cooperation among national authorities.

Effective protection of witnesses, victims, and collaborators of justice includes legislative and practical measures to ensure that witnesses testify freely and without intimidation. Such legislative and practical measures can include the criminalization of acts of intimidation, the use of alternative methods of providing evidence, physical protection, relocation programmes, permitting limitations on the disclosure of information concerning their identity or whereabouts, and in exceptional circumstances, protecting the anonymity of the person giving evidence.

The UN *Convention against Transnational Organized Crime* requires States parties to take appropriate measures within their means to effectively protect witnesses in criminal proceedings who give testimony concerning offences covered by the Conventions. To ensure greater international cooperation in effective witness protection, bilateral and multilateral instruments can be adopted for the safe examination of witnesses at risk of intimidation or retaliation and to implement temporary or permanent relocation of witnesses (Dandurand 2010). The absence of effective protection for victims and witnesses is one of the reasons why human trafficking victims often hesitate to come to the authorities or agree to testify.

Cooperation in Victim Repatriation and Victim Assistance

Victim repatriation is a unique aspect of international cooperation with respect to human trafficking (UNODC 2006a). Cooperation in this area is vital to the effective protection of victims and to their safe return to their country. Unfortunately, effective international cooperation in that area is oftentimes lacking, as exemplified by a recent study in Serbia

(Simeunović-Patić and Ćopić 2010). An IOM program works to facilitate the voluntary return of victims of human trafficking, but much more is needed. In some cases, countries simply expel, or deport, human trafficking victims, or treat them generally as illegal immigrants. On the other hand, more and more countries offer victims some practical assistance including a temporary residence permit to allow victims to recover, possibly testify against those who exploited them, and prepare for their safe return home.

The Frequent Failure of International Cooperation

Numerous practical, legal, and political factors hamper international cooperation in criminal investigations and prosecutions. The most common ones include differences in cultures, languages, legal cultures and traditions, or political orientations. To these we can add sovereignty protection issues, the absence of enabling legislation, the absence of channels of communication for the exchange of information and intelligence, divergences in approaches and priorities, and corruption of public officials.

Laws, bilateral treaties, conventions, and formal coordination mechanisms may pave the way to increased international cooperation, but success eventually depends on the relationships of trust, reciprocity, and mutual respect. When these relationships are solid and well supported institutionally they can accomplish a lot through the formal mechanisms mentioned above and through effective informal cooperation between criminal justice agencies.

There are, however, some major issues that cannot be ignored. For instance, it is important to note the fundamental asymmetry existing between the attitudes and motives of countries of origin as compared to those of destination countries with respect to the control of human trafficking. Countries of origin are limited in what they can do to prevent human trafficking. At their end of things, the phenomenon mostly consists of smuggling of migrants and illegal emigration; it is typically only after the victims have reached their destination that it is identified as a trafficking case. In countries, where a large portion of the population aspires to migrate to another country (mostly to improve their own economic situation), government measures to repress the illegal immigration and the smuggling of migrants are rarely popular. That asymmetry is quite obvious in the case of the United States–Mexico situation, where repressive measures to prevent illegal immigration are understandably quite difficult to justify to the population in Mexico. Such measures are always difficult to defend and sustain politically. Yet, these same countries are under considerable international pressure to prevent migrant smuggling and illegal immigration. Sometimes, they are essentially blackmailed into action by more powerful countries that threaten to suspend developmental assistance or other forms of assistance and cooperation.

The example referred to in Box 10.2 shows how one national initiative from a destination country attempts to compel some countries of origin to take unpopular and difficult measures to curtail illegal immigration, all under the guise of protecting potential victims of human trafficking.

The Importance of Relationships and the Frequent Lack of Reciprocity

Time and again, international cooperation is affected by the one participating agency's perception that the relationship is not a fair one. Reciprocity is what sustains these cooperative

BOX 10.2   COMPELLING OTHER COUNTRIES TO ACT*

Developing countries find it difficult to take measures to prevent illegal immigration and the smuggling of migrants. Countries that financially depend on foreign remittances from their citizens abroad and where large segments of the population aspire to immigrate into a new country, politicians are hard-pressed to take measures to prevent their own citizens from looking for a better future abroad. These countries are under a lot of international pressure, particularly from rich destination countries, to take active measures to curb illegal immigration and the smuggling of migrants. The fight against human trafficking can provide a cover for these pressures to be exercised under the guise of benevolent concerns for the plight of the victims.

The trafficking in persons (TIP) reports which the United States Department of State is required by law to submit each year to the U.S. Congress is ostensibly a measure to help eliminate severe forms of trafficking in persons. The report assesses other countries (the U.S. itself is not yet included in the assessments) on the success of their efforts to prevent human trafficking. They are then ranked and placed on one of the three tier lists mandated by law (United States' *Trafficking Victims Protection Act* of 2000). Countries are primarily rated on the basis of "minimum standards" defined by the American government and relating in large part to the government responses to trafficking. Countries which fail to satisfactorily meet these standards can be placed on a "watch list" or be denied nontrade-related foreign assistance.

The TIP reports are presented as a "diplomatic tool" for the U.S. Government to use to encourage continued dialogue and to help focus prosecution, protection, and prevention programs and policies (U.S. State Department 2009). Countries of origins are nevertheless compelled to take unpopular and difficult measures to curtail illegal immigration, all under the guise of protecting potential victims of human trafficking.

Please have a careful look at the criteria being used by the U.S. State Department and perhaps one of the most recent human trafficking reports published. In your opinion, how useful and justifiable is this form of diplomatic pressure in preventing human trafficking?

institutional relationships, even if they are rarely driven by the same priorities or motivation on both sides. One country may be giving priority to human smuggling or trafficking, when the other is more interested in recovering proceeds of crime or prosecuting drug traffickers or arms dealers. The expected reciprocity is never defined narrowly in terms of one type of crime. Cooperation treaties typically cover a range of offences and law enforcement priorities.

The Asymmetry of Means, Capacity, and Priorities

Understandably, countries do not necessarily have the same crime prevention and control priorities and will not have developed the same capacity to cooperate internationally. Some

* See previous TIP reports: http://www.state.gov/g/tip/rls/tiprpt/

countries have fledgling criminal justice institutions with limited financial and technical means. The collaboration that is expected of them by other countries is often beyond their means, yet powerful neighbors may pressurize them to be of assistance. Technical assistance programs exist—some of them are even mandated by international conventions—to help countries develop their basic criminal justice institutions, as well as their capacity to cooperate internationally. The delivery and effectiveness of that assistance sometimes appears to be problematic (Griffiths et al. 2005).

The Politicization of Criminal Justice Cooperation

Another issue is that of the politicization of criminal justice cooperation. Some countries, such as China, have become notorious for their frequent attempts to politicize international criminal justice cooperation. They may withhold, or extend, their cooperation depending on whether they can, in return, extract some political favors, concessions, or advantages. In most countries, law enforcement agencies are not typically in a position to grant these advantages and may in fact get themselves in to compromising situations by trying to interfere in political decisions. That politicization runs contrary to the broader and more stable bases of reciprocal criminal justice assistance that countries should be able to rely on.

Corruption and Its Impact on International Cooperation

One challenge that may not always receive sufficient attention is that of corruption. This has changed since the adoption of the *United Nations Convention Against Corruption* in 2003 because of which measures against corruption are explicitly included in the United Nations *Global Plan of Action against Trafficking in Persons* (United Nations, General Assembly 2010). The success of strategic approaches and cooperation initiatives is always dependent on the willingness of strategic partners to cooperate effectively. International coordination of law enforcement activities and the sharing of confidential information depend on trust and reliability, both of which are negatively affected by corruption or the perceived risk that another agency will compromise some crucial aspect of an investigation or prosecution.

Many criminal organizations are quite capable of acting strategically. There are numerous cases where they managed to use corrupt officials to obtain an advantage over other groups, create a monopoly, eliminate opponents, or obstruct justice (see, e.g., Punch 2000; Reuter 2009, p. 280). Corruption affects the general credibility and effectiveness of a justice system and compromises international cooperation in criminal matters, defeats coordination efforts, and condemns international initiatives to failure (Dandurand 2007). Perhaps more importantly, corruption can place victims, witnesses and justice officials at risk of intimidation and retaliation.

Criminal organizations may take advantage of security systems that are weakened by corruption by infiltrating and gaining control over them (Morris 1999). In extreme cases, dysfunctional state agencies can even be "captured" and held hostage by organized crime (Buscaglia and van Djick 2003). The State itself or some of its key institutions may fall under the control of professional criminals. In Columbia, for example, paramilitary groups involved in various forms of trafficking have exercised significant political power in large areas of the country (Fuentes and Kelly 1999).

Organized crime tends to flourish where public officials are corrupt. Corruption can help a group monopolize a market (i.e., legal or illegal) by enlisting the authorities in driving out or weakening the competition (Sukharenko 2004). Collusive ties between government officials and criminals are varied, the most common one being briberies to influence the functions of government (Fuentes and Kelly 1999).

There is abundant evidence of the frequent collusion in many countries amongst criminals and corrupt officials at all government levels. Case studies in Southern African countries have documented the patterns of activities of organized criminal groups in Africa and how they use corruption to facilitate their criminal activities, avoid punishment and infiltrate public institutions (Gastrow 2003). In Mexico, the federal government, under the leadership of President Felipe Calderon, has had to launch a vast initiative against drug syndicates and try to counter the infiltration of the drug cartels into the ranks of local police, politicians, and the armed forces (Tuckman 2010). Thousands of people have died since the beginning of the initiative in 2007. In June of 2010, Rodolfo Torre Cantú, a leading politician expected to win the forthcoming gubernatorial elections in the State of Tamaulipas, in the North of Mexico, was assassinated along with four members of his entourage (Tuckman 2010). A most obvious African example of political involvement in organized crime is that of the late Maurice Ibekwe, a former member of Nigeria's Federal House of Representatives and former Chairman of the House Sub-Committee on Police Affairs, arrested for fraud and conspiracy (UNODC 2005, p. 7).

More proactive investigations, the creation of special anticorruption agencies or units and other corruption prevention measures can help protect the integrity of the justice system against the pervasive effects of corruption. It can also strengthen the capacity and willingness of various agencies to engage in greater and more effective cooperation, information exchange, and joint operations (Dandurand 2007). Obviously, effective cooperation in the investigation and prosecution of corruption itself is also required.

More Effective Cooperation in Combating Human Trafficking

There are several ways to enhance international cooperation in preventing and controlling human trafficking. In fact, there is a growing consensus around some of the best means of improving international cooperation in the investigation and prosecution of serious crimes such as human trafficking (Dandurand 2007, UNODC 2010b). A key component of such efforts involves removing legal obstacles and establishing, at the national level, an effective and comprehensive legal basis for mutual legal assistance. At the international level, treaties to create binding obligations to cooperate with respect to a range of modalities must be initiated. Existing treaties and laws should be reviewed periodically and amended as necessary to keep pace with evolving practices and challenges in international cooperation. In addition, countries must depoliticize as much as possible the criminal justice cooperation process.

For years, countries have been encouraged to designate a strong and effective central authority for international cooperation in criminal matters. Such a central focal point provides the means for each country to coordinate its own request for assistance and stand ready to respond expeditiously to requests of cooperation it receives from other countries. At an advanced stage, these central authorities can engage in more strategic approaches to law enforcement and collaboration. Countries must also develop more effective approaches for the deployment of international law enforcement efforts, the exchange of information (including through new information management and communication technologies), and the strategic use of intelligence.

When human trafficking networks operate across borders, the countries concerned find it important to coordinate their investigations and prosecutions to more effectively target these groups and their transnational activities (Aden 2001; Dandurand 2007; UNODC 2010b). Coordination of cross-border investigation and prosecutions is still rare and requires considerable preparation through official channels. Frequently, multidisciplinary international teams or task forces are created, which can give their undivided attention to investigating human trafficking and related offences.

Addressing the Lack of Capacity of Weak States and Developing Countries

The success of strategic approaches to countering the activities of human trafficking networks is largely predicated on the capacity of strategic partners to cooperate effectively.

This should draw greater attention to the need to provide technical assistance, information exchange systems and training to requesting countries, and, in some cases, to financially support the development of a criminal justice capacity in developing countries or in countries in transition (Dandurand et al. 2007; Shaw and Dandurand 2006). In doing so, one must keep in mind the particular predicament of postconflict countries and failed States which not only provide a large pool of potential human trafficking victims, but must also rely on a weak criminal justice and law enforcement capacity (see Studnicka 2010). The public safety vacuum created by war or natural disasters benefits criminal organizations that are quick to exploit the situation and take advantage of people's desire for relocation. Waves of human trafficking activities can be traced to these situations. The recent earthquakes in Haiti and the devastation they left behind have brought international attention to various aspects of that problem, including fraudulent adoptions (Addley 2010) and the domestic servitude of the "restavecs"* both in and outside the country.

Adopting a Victim-Focused, Harm Reduction Approach

As was mentioned earlier, criminal justice agencies operate in the middle of a persistent tension between a state security (protection of borders and prevention of illegal immigration) and human security (placing people first) approach to human trafficking. Even if it is far from being the case, reducing the harm done by human trafficking activities and protecting victims and potential victims should really form the core of all international efforts to prevent human trafficking. The deployment of law enforcement efforts, which is currently focused on border control, need to be reconsidered. The identification, rescue, protection, and repatriation of victims of human trafficking needs to be placed at the core of law enforcement strategies and that needs to be reflected in how law enforcement resources are trained, developed, and deployed.

States party to the *Convention Against Transnational Organized Crime* and its protocols have already recognized that they must develop a comprehensive, multidimensional

---

* To learn more about the situation of children used as domestic servants, or the "restavecs" as they are known in Haiti—from the French "rester avec" for "one who stays with," see the personal experience account by Jean-Robert Cadet (Cadet 1998).

response to trafficking in persons as well as apply a victim-centered approach, with full respect for the human rights of victims of such trafficking (United Nations CTOC 2010). A Working Group of the Conference of Parties is recommending the development of guidelines for law enforcement officials on culture-, gender-, and age-sensitive responses to victims of trafficking in persons, including "standards and procedures for identifying and interviewing victims of trafficking in persons and methods for advising such victims of their rights" (United Nations CTOC 2010).

Cooperating More Effectively in Preventive Actions

There are other areas of international cooperation which deserve more attention. In particular, the area of human trafficking prevention is not receiving the attention it deserves (see Winterdyk and Sundberg 2010b). The *Protocol on Trafficking in Persons* includes some general provisions, calling upon State parties to endeavour to undertake measures such as research, information and mass media campaigns, and social and economic initiatives to prevent and combat trafficking in persons [Article 10 (2)]. Considerable resources are being spent on information campaigns whose effectiveness in preventing human trafficking is never evaluated, but little else seems to be done in a systematic way. Support for social and economic development is offered through official development assistant programs and, although it may achieve some success in alleviating poverty, it has not been shown to significantly reduce human trafficking. Immigration laws are part of what enables criminal organizations to take advantage of vulnerable victims and potential victims, yet countries are not yet showing a willingness to reconsider their immigration laws from that perspective.

Conclusion

International cooperation in preventing and controlling human trafficking is probably as essential as it is problematic. We can expect most countries to continue, all least for the foreseeable future, to jealously affirm their sovereignty and protect their borders, no matter what the real consequences of these attitudes may be for victims of human trafficking. More effective criminal justice cooperation is possible as is being demonstrated everyday by European Union countries. International cooperation efforts to date, including the adoption of various conventions and protocols whose main objective is precisely to enhance international cooperation in fight various forms of transnational crime, are far from being negligible. Gradually, countries are building a capacity to work more closely in preventing and controlling human trafficking. Unfortunately, there remains a profound asymmetry among countries and their respective capacity and willingness to effectively intervene to suppress human trafficking.

When it comes to preventing human smuggling and illegal immigration, countries of origins and countries of transition tend to have different motivations and attitudes toward these issues. While some countries are seemingly far more eager to close their borders to illegal immigration than to protect victims of human smuggling and trafficking, other countries simply do not have the capacity to prevent these forms of human exploitation. The tactical gap created in international law enforcement cooperation is something that sophisticated criminal networks exploit to their own advantage.

Addressing this gap requires that we all lay more emphasis on the protection of victims and potential victims as the first priority of international cooperation against trafficking in persons.

Much research remains to be done on the actual obstacles to more effective international cooperation in fighting human trafficking. In fact, there is nearly a total absence of systematic research on the current application and the relative effectiveness of existing international cooperation mechanisms. Most of the available evidence comes from attempts to collect and systematize the knowledge painstakingly acquired by various practitioners. The Conference of States parties to the *Convention Against Transnational Organized Crime* and its protocols has planned a fairly ambitious reporting mechanism to document the outcomes of the implementation of these international instruments. This will eventually provide a knowledge base for future policy consideration and for improving the capacity of all countries to address this complex problem.

Discussion and Review Questions

1. What are some of the recent examples of the importance of international criminal justice cooperation in combating human trafficking?
2. Why is reciprocity so crucial in the application of formal mechanism of international criminal justice cooperation?
3. How can we limit the detrimental effect of corruption of public officials on international cooperation in the fight against human trafficking?
4. What are the proven ways to improve international cooperation in fighting human trafficking and other forms of organized crime?
5. What would a victim-based approach entail in terms of future international cooperation in preventing and control human trafficking?
6. That innovative measures could countries adopt to cooperate more effectively in preventing human trafficking?
7. What measures has your country taken to combat human trafficking and how would you rate to another country of similar social, economic, and political characteristics?

References

Addley, E. 2010. Haiti earthquake: Aid agencies fear child trafficking. *The Guardian*, Friday, January 22, 2010. http://www.guardian.co.uk/world/2010/jan/22/haiti-warning-child-trafficking/print, retrieved August 7, 2010.

Aden, H. 2001. Convergence of policing policies and transnational policing in Europe. *European Journal of Crime, Criminal Law and Criminal Justice*, 9(2): 99–112.

Archibold, R. 2010. *Arizona Enacts Stringent Law on Immigration. New York Times*, April 24, 2010, p. A1.

Barry, K. 1982. *L'esclavage Sexuel de la Femme*. Paris: Stock.

de Beaupuy, F. 2009. *France, Italy Urge Tougher EU Fight Against Illegal Immigration*. Paris: Bloomberg, October 23, 2009.

Blekxtoon, R. 2004. *Handbook of the European Arrest Warrant*. Cambridge: Cambridge University Press.

Bokhari, F. 2009. *Stolen Futures: Trafficking for Forced Child Marriage in the UK*. London: ECPAT UK and Wilberforce Institute for the Study of Slavery and Emancipation.

Buscaglia, E. and I. van Djick. 2003. Controlling organized crime and corruption in the public sector. *Forum on Crime and Society*, 3(1–2): 3–34.

Cadet, J.-R. 1998. *Restavec—From Haitian Slave Child to Middle-Class American*. Austin: University of Texas Press.

CanWest News Service. 2006. Calderon compares U.S.–Mexico fence to Berlin Wall October 27, 2006. http://www.canada.com/topics/news/world/story.html?id=5c1d19c6-dd0a-47dc-9896-a2068b1393ea, retrieved August 7, 2010.

Commonwealth Secretariat. 2005. *Combating Money Laundering and Terrorist Financing*. London: Commonwealth Secretariat.

Council of the European Union. 2002. Council Framework Decision of June 13, 2002 on the European arrest warrant and the surrender procedures between Member States, (2002/584/JHA) http://eur-lex.europa.eu/LexUriServ/LexUriServ.do?uri=OJ:L:2002:190:0001:0018:EN:PDF, retrieved August 7, 2010.

Dandurand, Y. 2005. *Human Trafficking—Reference Guide for Canadian Law Enforcement*. Abbotsford: UCFV Press.

Dandurand, Y. 2006. Capacity building and technical assistance in small states, In Shaw, M. and Y. Dandurand (Eds.), *Maximizing the Effectiveness of the Technical Assistance Provided in the Fields of Crime Prevention and Criminal Justice*. Helsinki: HEUNI, pp. 42–56.

Dandurand, Y. 2007. Strategies and practical measures to strengthen the capacity of prosecution services in dealing with transnational crime, terrorism and corruption. *Crime, Law and Social Change*, 47: 225–246.

Dandurand, Y. 2010. *A review of selected witness protection programs*, a report prepared for the Research and National Coordination Unit, Organized Crime Division, Law Enforcement and Policy Branch, Public Safety Canada, Ottawa, March 2010.

Dandurand, Y., Colombo, G., and N. Passas. 2007. Measures and mechanisms to strengthen international cooperation among prosecution services. *Crime, Law and Social Change*, 47: 261–289.

Financial Action Task Force. 2003. *40 Recommendations*. http://www.fatf-gafi.org/dataoecd/7/40/34849567.PDF, retrieved August 7, 2010.

Fuentes, J. R. and R. J. Kelly. 1999. Drug supply and demand: The dynamics of the American drug market and some aspects of Colombian and Mexican drug trafficking. *Journal of Contemporary Criminal Justice*, 15(4): 328–351.

Gastrow, P. 2003. *Penetrating State and Business. Organised Crime in Southern Africa* (Vols. 1 and 2). Cape Town: Institute for Security Studies.

Griffiths, C. T., Dandurand, Y., and V. Chin. 2005. Development assistance and police reform: Programming opportunities and lessons learned. *The Canadian Review of Policing Research*, 2: 101–113.

Harfield, C. 2008. The organization of 'organized crime policing' and its international context. *Criminology and Criminal Justice*, 8(4): 483–507.

INTERPOL. 2009. *People Smuggling*. http://www.interpol.int/public/thb/peoplesmuggling/default.asp, retrieved September 12, 2010.

Ministry of Justice of Vietnam. 2004. *Assessment of the Legal System in Vietnam in Comparison with the United Nations Protocols on Trafficking in Persons and Smuggling of Migrants, Supplementing the United Nations Convention Against Transnational Organized Crime*. Hanoi: Department of Criminal and Administrative Law, Ministry of Justice; UNICEF; UNODC.

Morris, S. D. 1999. Corruption and the Mexican political system: Continuity and change. *Third World Quarterly*, 20(3): 623–643.

O'Connell Davidson, J. 2005. *Children in the Global Sex Trade*. Malden, MA: Polity.

Ottawa Citizen. 2007. *Canadians Want Illegal Immigrants Deported: Poll*. Ottawa: Canwest News Service, October 20, 2007, http://www.canada.com/topics/news/national/story.html?id=22dc364c-0bc8-44fa-ad5c-cbb68368f903, retrieved August 7, 2010.

Overs, C. 2009. *Caught between the Tiger and the Crocodile: The Campaign to Suppress Human Trafficking and Sexual Exploitation.* Phnom Penh: Asia-Pacific Network of Sex Workers—APNSW.

Passas N. 2003. *Informal value transfer systems, money laundering and terrorism,* Report to the National Institute of Justice (NIJ) and Financial Crimes Enforcement Network (FINCEN), Washington D.C.: http://www.ncjrs.org/pdffiles1/nij/grants/208301.pdf, retrieved August 7, 2010.

Piette, C. 2002. La scission politique du féminisme international sur la question du 'traffic des femmes'. *Migrations,* 15(2): 9–39.

Plachta, M. 2003. European arrest warrant: Revolution in extradition. *European Journal of Crime, Criminal Law and Criminal Justice,* 11(2): 178–187.

Punch, M. 2000. Police corruption and its prevention. *European Journal of Criminal Policy and Research,* 8: 301–324.

Reuter, P. 2009. Systematic violence in drug markets. *Crime, Law and Social Change,* 52: 275–284.

Segrave, M., Milivojevic, S., and S. Pickering. 2009. *Sex Trafficking: International Context and Response.* Cullompton, Devon; Portland, Oregon: Willan Publishing.

Shaw, M. and Y. Dandurand. (Eds.). 2006. *Maximizing the Effectiveness of the Technical Assistance Provided in the Fields of Crime Prevention and Criminal Justice.* Helsinki: HEUNI.

Semeunović-Patić, B. and S. Ćopić. 2010. Protection and assistance to victims of human trafficking in Serbia: Recent developments. *European Journal of Criminology,* 7(1): 45–53.

Studnicka, A. C. 2010. Corruption and human trafficking in Brazil: Findings from a multi-modal approach. *European Journal of Criminology,* 7(1): 29–43.

Sukharenko, A. 2004. The use of corruption by "Russian" organized crime in the United States. *Trends in Organized Crime,* 8(2): 118–129.

Surtees, R. 2008. Traffickers and trafficking in Southern and Eastern Europe—Considering the other side of human trafficking. *European Journal of Criminology,* 5(1): 39–68.

Toupin, L. 2002. *La question du 'trafic des femmes'—Points de repère dans la documentation des coalitions féministes internationales anti-trafic.* Montréal: Alliance de recherche IREF.

Tuckman, J. 2010. Leading politician Rodolfo Torre Cantú murdered in Mexico. *The Guardian,* June 29:22.

UNICEF/EAPRO. 2009. *Reversing the Trend—Child Trafficking in East and Southeast Asia.* Bangkok: UNICEF East Asia and Pacific Regional Office.

UNICRI. 2004. *Trafficking of Nigerian Girls to Italy.* Turin: United Nations Interregional Crime and Justice Research Institute.

United Nations CTOC. 2009. *Report on the Meeting of the Working Group on Trafficking in Persons held in Vienna on 14 and 15 April 2009,* Convention against Transnational Organized Crime. (United Nations CTOC/COP/WG.4/2009/2). http://www.unodc.org/documents/treaties/organized_crime/Final_report_English_TIP.pdf, retrieved August 7, 2010.

United Nations CTOC. 2010. *Report on the Meeting of the Working Group on Trafficking in Persons held in Vienna from January 27 and 29 2010* (United Nations, CTOC/COP/WG.4/2010/6). http://www.unodc.org/documents/treaties/organized_crime/2010_CTOC_COP_WG4/CTOC_COP_WG4_2010_final_report_E.pdf, retrieved August 7, 2010.

United Nations CTOC—Conference of the Parties to the United Nations Convention against Transnational Organized Crime. 2008. *Implementation of the Protocol to Prevent, Suppress and Punish Trafficking in Persons, Especially Women and Children, supplementing the United Nations Convention against Transnational Organized Crime: consolidated information received from States for the first reporting cycle.* Vienna, 25 August, 2008. http://www.unodc.org/documents/treaties/COP2008/CTOC%20COP%202005%203%20Rev2%20Final%20E.pdf, retrieved August 7, 2010.

United Nations, General Assembly. 2010. *United Nations Global Plan of Action against Trafficking in Persons.* http://documents-dds-ny.un.org/doc/UNDOC/LTD/N10/463/13/pdf/N1046313.pdf?OpenElement, retrieved August 7, 2010.

UNODC. 2004a. *Legislative Guides for the Implementation of the United Nations Convention against Transnational Organized Crime and the Protocols Thereto.* New York, NY: United Nations.

UNODC. 2004b. *Report of the Informal Expert Group on Effective Extradition Casework Practice.* Vienna: United Nations Office on Drugs and Crime.

UNODC. 2005. *Transnational Crime in the West African Region*. New York, NY: United Nations.

UNODC. 2006a. *Toolkit to Combat Trafficking in Persons*. New York, NY: United Nations.

UNODC. 2006b. *Trafficking in Persons—Global Patterns*. Vienna: United Nations Office on Drugs and Crime.

UNODC. 2009a. *Global Report on Trafficking in Persons*. Vienna: United Nations Office on Drugs and Crime.

UNODC. 2009b. *Model Law Against Trafficking in Persons*. Vienna: United Office on Drugs and Crime.

UNODC. 2010a. *The Globalization of Crime—A Transnational Organized Crime Threat Assessment*. Vienna: United Nations Office on Drugs and Crime.

UNODC. 2010b. *Trafficking in Persons and Smuggling of Migrants—Guidelines on International Cooperation*. Vienna: United Nations Office on Drugs and Crime.

U.S. State Department. 2009. *Trafficking in Persons Report, June 2009*. Washington, DC: Department of States, USA.

Vermeulen, G. 2001. International trafficking in women and children. *International Review of Penal Law*, 3(72): 837–883.

Winterdyk, J. A. and K. W. Sundberg. (Eds.). 2010a. *Border Security in the Al-Qaeda Era*. Boca Raton, FL, United States: Taylor & Francis Group.

Winterdyk, J. A. and K. W. Sundberg. 2010b. Accessing Public Confidence in Canada's New Approach to Border Security. *Journal of Borderland Security*, 25(3 and 4), 1–18.

Useful Web Links

http://www.ungift.org/ungift/en/stories/re_brazil_story_2.html: UN based organization offering commentary and links to the role and need for international cooperation to combat human trafficking

http://www.unrol.org/article.aspx?article_id=90: A UN link to the United Nations Rule of Law and overview of guidelines for international cooperation in antitrafficking and smuggling

Evaluating Responses to Human Trafficking

A Review of International, Regional, and National Counter-Trafficking Mechanisms

11

SANJA MILIVOJEVIC
MARIE SEGRAVE

Contents

Introduction

Human trafficking has maintained a priority status on the international agenda since the turn of this century. As a consequence, significant efforts have been made toward the development of counter-trafficking measures across the globe. These efforts have included international agreements that seek to define the issue and demarcate the appropriate international, national, and local response required to move toward the eradication of this exploitative practice. Yet while counter-trafficking policy commitments and the reporting of counter-trafficking data, particularly criminal justice data (such as number of victims, arrests, and convictions) proliferates, less attention has been paid to producing rigorous, empirical evaluation of either the counter-trafficking frameworks *or* the monitoring and reporting approach adopted by various agencies around the world. Indeed evaluation has largely been absent from the international debate regarding the definition of best practice. This chapter maps the role of evaluation in counter-trafficking policies at the international and national level to identify the benefits and limitations of current reporting practices in addition to key areas of consideration for the future development of more robust evaluation processes within the counter-trafficking field.

Underpinning this analysis is a research background in the area of human trafficking (most recently, Segrave et al. 2009) that brings a feminist critical criminological framework to bear upon contemporary counter-trafficking practices, which has challenged the early emphasis on sex trafficking and dominant assumptions about women as victims and which has contextualized human trafficking within broader patterns of gendered migration flows, globalization, and the exploitative practices that have accompanied border crossing, and labor processes (Agustin 2003, 2005; Andrijasevic 2004; Berman 2003; Bumiller 2008; Ditmore 2005, 2006; Doezema 2000; Goodey 2003, 2008; Kapur 2005; Kempadoo 2005; Miller 2004; Weitzer 2007; Wong 2005). We also draw on a criminological analysis that engages critically with the contemporary expansion of the state apparatus particularly at the border and in relation to migration status (see Pickering and Weber 2006). This literature is the foundation of the following analysis which endeavors not only to examine the practice of evaluation in relation to counter-trafficking frameworks but to recognize the importance of critically engaging with the framework itself.

Specifically, this chapter examines the issue of trafficking program evaluation at two levels—national and international—based on the distinction between evaluation and monitoring, whereby monitoring is a "management tool" focused on implementation indicators and evaluation involves "systematic and objective assessment" on "impact" and the value of the program (or, as we argue the whole framework) (IOM 2008:11). There are four key chapter objectives:

1. To identify how the dominant framework for understanding and responding to human trafficking informs the design of both counter-trafficking policies and evaluations of the impact/success of these policies
2. To highlight the operation and findings of international mechanisms of evaluation
3. To identify and examine national mechanisms to evaluate counter-trafficking programs within the nation
4. To outline potential areas for the development of counter-trafficking policy and evaluation at the national and international level

This chapter is divided into three parts. The first two parts examine the existing mechanisms (including monitoring tools and evaluation processes) to oversee the design and implementation of responses to human trafficking at the international and national level. The final part of this chapter draws on these findings to identify new ways forward for evaluation in counter-trafficking responses.

Evaluating Counter-Trafficking Initiatives and Policies

Two international mechanisms have driven contemporary counter-trafficking efforts: the United Nations Protocol to Prevent, Suppress and Punish Trafficking in Persons, Especially Women and Children ("the Trafficking Protocol" or "the Protocol") and the U.S. Trafficking in Persons (TIP) Report. Given the influence these two very similar models have had on the counter-trafficking policy response globally, this chapter argues for a more careful consideration of the foundations that underpin these two frameworks and the proliferation of specific types of human trafficking-related data that dominate the reporting they promote.

The primary concern central to this chapter is to identify the need for *evaluation* that can engage in more complex questions regarding the impact of counter-trafficking responses. In particular, this chapter recognizes the importance of developing frameworks for determining how we define effective criminal justice responses to human trafficking (see Gallagher and Holmes 2008; Shinkle 2007).* Currently, monitoring implementation largely dominates the global discussion over and above evaluation. The International Organisation for Migration has adopted a lead role as an international agency in partnering with nations in the development of counter-trafficking measures and in doing so have developed a considerable wealth of material and approaches, including releasing a *Handbook on Performance Indicators for Counter-Trafficking Projects* (IOM 2008). An important contribution of this Handbook is its encouragement for readers to recognize

---

* Specifically, the framework detailed by Gallagher and Holmes (2008) comprises eight specific components: 1. a comprehensive legal framework, in compliance with international standard, 2. a specialist law enforcement capacity to investigate human trafficking, 3. a general law enforcement capacity to respond effectively to trafficking cases, 4. strong and well-informed prosecutorial and judicial support, 5. quick and accurate identification of victims along with immediate protection and support, 6. special support to victims as witnesses, 7. systems and processes that enable effective international investigative and judicial cooperation in trafficking cases, and 8. effective coordination among international donors.

the difference between evaluation and monitoring and to recognize the limits of performance indicators in understanding the impact of policies and projects (IOM 2008, pp. 7–8). Yet, the Handbook is premised on the "Three Ps" framework as the best practice counter-trafficking model and there is little encouragement for analysis that would enable research and evaluation to examine the dominant international model as a whole. This chapter seeks to move beyond a simple identification of the monitoring systems in place at the international and national level, and develops a broader critique of existing efforts to evaluate program impacts and outcomes. We do this by first examining the international mechanisms (the Protocol, TIP Report, and regional mechanisms), followed by an examination of national efforts to review and assess contemporary counter-trafficking responses in relation to current mechanisms for reporting, evaluating, and analyzing the implementation and impact of these responses. We note at the outset that this chapter is neither comprehensive nor representational in its analysis; rather the chapter is designed to identify key issues for consideration in relation to contemporary trends in counter-trafficking mechanisms and evaluation.

International and Regional Mechanisms

Background

In the following section we outlined the design and operation of the key international counter-trafficking mechanisms dominating the counter-trafficking. While not detailing the historical intricacies of the international trafficking debate (see Doezema 2000; Saunders and Soderlund 2003; Sullivan 2003) this section outlines important elements of these frameworks that have been utilized by policy makers across the world in developing counter-trafficking policy responses that conform to the international consensus model.

The Trafficking Protocol

Counter-trafficking initiatives across the globe have largely been led by the United Nations Protocol to Prevent, Suppress and Punish Trafficking in Persons, Especially Women and Children ("the Trafficking Protocol" or "the Protocol"), one of three protocols linked to the UN Convention on Transnational Organised Crime. The Protocol was widely heralded as a significant achievement in the fight against human trafficking, signaling a contemporary international commitment to addressing all forms of human trafficking (Abramson 2003; Outshoorn 2005; Raymond 2002). Creating the Trafficking Protocol as a subset of the broader context of UN Convention against Transitional Organized Crime explicitly linked human trafficking to the transnational organized criminal practices associated more readily with trafficking in commodities such as drugs and weapons (Segrave et al. 2009). The Protocol established a framework for defining human trafficking and outlined the appropriate national and international response.

The structure of the Trafficking Protocol has come to be known as the "Three P's" model comprising prevention, protection, and prosecution. While this model suggests a broad approach, the backbone of the Trafficking Protocol is crime management through border security, criminal law, prosecution, and punishment of traffickers, where the emphasis is on combating transnational organized crime (Oberholer 2003; Segrave et al.

2009). Overall, the language and design of the Protocol enshrines the criminal justice focus; Article 1 of the Protocol explicitly links human trafficking and Transnational Organized Crime and the first chapter of the Protocol is focused on the prescriptive requirement of state signatories to build and implement a criminal justice counter-trafficking infrastructure. For example, Article 5 details the requirement for state parties to take a range of measures to criminalize trafficking and bring to justice those who perform, participate in, or organize trafficking offences.

This does not mean that broader issues including assistance and support for victims and recognition of the role of migration are absent from the Protocol. The language of these provisions, however, is less proscriptive and the provisions related to addressing push factors (Article 9–13) and to providing support to victims (including legal assistance, housing, counseling, medical and psychological assistance, employment and educational opportunities) are less proscriptive. Rather than being obligations, these provisions are "encouraged" for "appropriate cases" and "to the extent possible under … domestic law" (Article 6.1). Both receiving countries and countries of destination are urged to "consider" adopting mechanisms that will allow victims to remain either temporarily or permanently in "appropriate cases" (Article 7). What is evident is that the language the Protocol uses in relation to victims and noncriminal justice matters is "hedged with minimalism and ambiguity" (Sullivan 2003, p. 84). This emphasis is critical to understanding the current status of efforts to evaluate antitrafficking efforts and the prioritization on different "outcomes."

Reviewing Implementation: National Obligations and International Mechanisms

The Trafficking Protocol does not explicitly commit to evaluating the effectiveness of this framework nor the impact of policies introduced under the auspices of meeting obligations of the Protocol. Yet there is increasing research that challenges the logic of contemporary counter-trafficking responses that meet the standards set out within the Protocol. For example, one area of emerging research disputes the link between human trafficking and transnational organized crime which served as the foundation for the Trafficking Protocol (Finckenauer 2001; Sanghera 2005; Segrave et al. 2009; Turner and Kelly 2008). While the counter-trafficking momentum continues to strengthen, this research suggests that the framework is based on presumptions about the processes and key players that do not reflect the reality of the situation, creating additional challenges for police, policy makers, and victims alike (see Finckenauer 2001; Sanghera 2005; Segrave et al. 2009). Connected to this research are concerns raised regarding the impact of misplaced assumptions regarding victimization that are embedded within the protection, prosecution, and prevention model; concerns that highlight that the mechanisms put in place in the name of victim support appear to be driven by state assumptions about what victims may need and/or are limited according to the migration status of the victim (Berman 2003; Bjerkan 2005; Coomaraswamy 2002; Goodey 2003; Kapur 2005; Kempadoo 2005; Sassen 2000; Segrave et al. 2009). The Protocol, however, remains instrumental in defining State Parties' responses to human trafficking-delimiting the definition and the appropriate course of action, without a provision for ongoing research and evaluation by signatories to interrogate the assumptions that inform this approach and/or to ensure ongoing analysis on the impacts of counter-trafficking responses.

There is also no systematic evaluation of the Protocol at the international level. In contrast to other international mechanisms,* the Protocol and the broader Transnational Organised Crime Convention do not integrate nor define any explicit mechanisms to evaluate State Parties' efforts to address trafficking according to its standards.† While the Conference of the Parties to the UN Convention against Transnational Organized Crime and its Protocols (the Conference) (Article 42) has been established as the body responsible for periodic examination of the implementation of the Convention it is quite limited in its powers and scope. In relation to trafficking it has developed an assessment tool that prioritizes ensuring that states party to the Protocol have implemented "the basic criminalization and international cooperation standards and requirements" (UN Conference of the Parties 2006, p. 7). While more recent efforts to review implementation of Article 6 (Assistance and Protection of victims of TIPs) to Article 9 (Prevention of TIPs) have been in place since 2008, it has been argued that concerns regarding victims needs reflect the growing consensus that "victim-centered" approaches are central to successful criminal justice outcomes, such that the priorities of the response remain unchanged (Mattar 2008, p. 1400).

Also in 2008 the Conference established the Working Group on Trafficking to identify weaknesses, gaps, and challenges in implementation of the Protocol (UNODC 2010a). Despite the absence of any rigorous mechanism to ensure State Parties' meet obligations agreed to through ratifying the Protocol, the Working Group still concluded that the implementation of the Protocol is largely a success. This assessment is based on the *Global Report on Trafficking in Persons*, published by UNODC (February 2009), which states that of the 155 countries and territories covered by the Report 98 have criminalized trafficking. The Report also noted, however, that "in 40% of the States covered, not a single conviction for the specific offence of TIPs had been recorded" (Working Group on Trafficking in Persons 2009, p. 10). Again, the emphasis is on criminal justice practices rather than measures of effectiveness.

Finally, in 2009, several UN agencies, including UN Office on Drugs and Crime, UN High Commissioner for Refugees, UN Children's Fund, UN Development Fund for Women, and UN Interregional Crime and Justice Research Institute, published the *International Framework for Action to Implement the Trafficking in Persons Protocol* (UNODC 2010c). Designed as a technical assistance tool to assist member states in implementing the Protocol, this mechanism outlines key challenges in implementation of the Protocol and proposes measures to address them (UNODC 2010c, p. 3). While strictly following the "Three P's" framework, this document outlines knowledge and research, capacity-building, and monitoring and evaluation (numbers, information, and data sharing) as key challenges in implementing the Protocol. The framework for action as defined in this document has five key pillars: prosecution, protection, prevention, national coordination and cooperation, and international coordination and cooperation (UNDOC

---

* Such as the group of experts in Council of Europe Convention on Action to Combat Trafficking in Human Beings, or National Rapporteur in the OSCE Action Plan to Combat Trafficking in Human Beings (Mattar 2008).

† There was no lesson learned, for example, from the decision made after the establishment of the Convention on the Elimination of All Forms of Discrimination against Women that a permanent body is required to oversee the monitoring of implementation. The Committee on the Elimination of Discrimination against Women (CEDAW) is a body of independent experts that was established via an optional protocol.

2010c, p. 9). Thus, while it signaled awareness of the need for research it did not inject the importance of evaluation mechanisms into the ongoing discussion of best practice.

The lack of formal mechanisms to evaluate implementation of the Protocol mechanisms limit the ability for the international community to capture what is happening as a result of and beyond criminal justice activity. We return to these consequences in Part Three of this chapter. We now turn to the second major international framework and its process of review and evaluation: the U.S. Trafficking in Persons Report.

Trafficking in Persons Report

The second international mechanism that has wielded considerable influence in counter-trafficking efforts internationally is the U.S. TIP report, established by the United States independently of the Trafficking Protocol (see more detail below). The Trafficking in Persons report was introduced in 2001 as an assessment of counter-trafficking responses in selected nations around the world. Based on information collected by U.S. embassies and consulates as well as other sources (such as UN agencies and local non-governmental organizations [NGOs]* the report is submitted by the Secretary of State to the U.S. Congress annually [USDOS 2001] and is promoted by as the "most comprehensive worldwide report on the efforts of governments to combat severe forms of trafficking" [USDOS 2003, p. 13]). It is also heralded as a proactive and objective mechanism for ensuring the development and implementation of counter-trafficking measures and as such the TIP report plays a key role in the "overall strategy to combat trafficking worldwide" (USDOS 2003a, p. 56).

Unlike UN mechanisms for reviewing counter trafficking efforts the *modus operandi* underpinning the TIP Report is diplomatic pressure and the threat of coercion in the form of economic sanctions for nations that do not comply with U.S.-defined standards. We briefly explain the assessment framework and its limits below.

The Assessment Framework

Essentially the TIP report assesses in two ways. The first is to determine which nations come within its purview, based on data that determine which countries are "of interest" as countries of origin, transit, destination, or a combination (USDOS 2001). The major assessment, however, is the scrutiny of counter-trafficking policies in relation to U.S.-defined standards regarding the "Three P's" (prosecution, protection, and prevention) and "Three R's" (rescue, rehabilitation, and reintegration). These standards are enshrined in legislation, the *Victims of Trafficking and Violence Protection Act* (TVPA) (for details, see USDOS 2001, p. 5). While the assessment standards and focus has remained consistent, there have been some developments to the emphasis within the TIP Report over the past decade.

From 2002 to 2010, the TIP Report focus has shifted, as detailed in Table from a narrow emphasis on sex trafficking and criminal justice outcomes to an expanded recognition of all forms of human trafficking and a broader recognition of the context which enables human trafficking and the ways in which short-term criminal justice measures may have consequences that fuel further exploitative practices (Table 11.1).

---

* From 2002 shadow reports by NGOs are also included in the TIP report (USDOS 2002: 7).

Table 11.1 TIP Report and Addressing Trafficking

	2002 TIP Report	2010 TIP Report
Language	"Combating" trafficking	"Partnership" in addressing trafficking
Framework	"Three Ps" (prevention, protection, and prosecution)	"Three Ps" and "Three Ds": detention, deportation, and disempowerment are identified as common practices harmful for victims that have to be dismantled (USDOS 2010, p. 16).
Focus	Sex trafficking: "[i]n this modern form of slavery … [w]omen, children and men are trafficked into the international sex trade for the purposes of prostitution, sex tourism and other commercial sexual services and into forced labor situations" (USDOS 2002, p. 1)	Recognized the broader context of the feminization of migration and the breadth of labor trafficking
Success measured by	Almost exclusively criminal justice outcomes—legislative mechanisms, punishment that reflects "heinous nature of crime," and the number of prosecutions and convictions (USDOS 2002, p. 8)	Criminal justice outcomes but stressed the need to challenge current counter-trafficking measures that "rescue" women only to lock them "in "shelters" that look more like prisons than safe haven" and country of destination responses that consist of "repatriate[ing women] … as a matter of first instance" (USDOS 2010, p. 2)

While indicating that "numbers of trafficking prosecutions and convictions are important indicators of progress, the quality and impact of counter-trafficking law enforcement efforts are more significant" (USDOS 2010, p. 6), the focus is still on criminal justice outcomes. Country assessments reports do include efforts related to the protection of victims but emphasize the development and implementation of domestic criminal justice efforts as the primary indicators of a commitment to "fighting" human trafficking. An important development is that the 2010 TIP Report insisting on the separation of criminal justice and victim support mechanisms, shifting the focus away from witness protection to requiring nations to uphold the "needs and fulfil obligations that extend beyond the confines of a criminal case" (USDOS 2010, p. 13).

Overall then, the TIP report has broadened its focus in the last decade without abandoning the criminal justice emphasis. In and of itself this is not necessarily problematic; it demonstrates that there is room for the development of more informed responses to human trafficking. However, for researchers, a consistent concern with the TIP report remains the vagueness of both the methodological approach (which is broadly defined for the whole report without any specificity of the process in each nation and absent of references) and the assessment measures, the tier placements. Indeed, the tier placement remains a controversial measure of counter-trafficking efforts.

The TIP Report Implementation and Impact
Assessments are undertaken to rank each nation, whereby Tier One is the highest ranking and Tier Three the lowest, with a Tier Two and Tier Two Watch differentiating countries that do not comply but are "making significant efforts" (Tier Two) to

do so and countries that appear to not have implemented efforts to overcome areas of noncompliance as identified in previous TIP Reports (Tier Two Watch list, for full details, see USDOS 2004, p. 27). Countries in Tier Three are subject to potential sanctions by the U.S. Government if they do not respond to U.S.-determined "failures" in responding to human trafficking. Potential sanctions include termination of nonhumanitarian, nontrade-related assistance, and loss of U.S. support for loans from international financial institutions (Miko 2003; USDOS 2002 p. 10; USDOS 2001). It is important to note that such a warning may be interpreted as carrying greater weight for developing nations reliant on the United States aid and assistance; however, the broader political costs of a negative U.S. assessment has been noted to have had a direct impact on developed nations' efforts to address human trafficking. For example, the Australian response in 2003 has been noted as coming about as a consequence of U.S. diplomatic pressure as opposed to a national concern regarding the issue of human trafficking (see Alcorn and Minchin 2003; Maltzahn 2004; O'Brien and Wynhausen 2003). Thus, the diplomatic and political power wielded by the United State has enabled the TIP Report to play a significant role in influencing the introduction and design of national responses to human trafficking across the globe. This is evident by the willingness of nations to cooperate with the United States and provide information for each annual TIP Report, despite the absence of any legal duty to report, compared to the unwillingness to provide timely, detailed information to the Conference of Parties, as noted earlier (see Mattar 2008). Functioning as the "global sheriff" (Chuang 2006) enforcing its own standards of counter-trafficking practice and publishing assessments based on U.S.-defined processes have enabled the emergence of a unilateral, unchecked ranking process that is not without limitations.

The TIP report has been criticized for its lack of evidence and analysis, and arbitrary and insufficient data collection processes (Kempadoo 2005; Miko 2003; Segrave et al. 2009). The lack of transparency has also fueled concerns that the ranking system is driven by political interests as much as (if not more than) independent review and analysis (Skinner 2008). These concerns have often arisen in response to the shifting rankings of some nations that appear inequitable with other national placements (see Skinner 2008). While there have been changes over time to the TIP data collection and reporting processes, the arbitrariness of the process remains a contemporary concern.

This does not mean that the TIP report is without redeeming features. It should be noted that this process holds nations to account in a more comprehensive and consistent way than the existing UN-based bodies. While the data collection process remains contested, it nonetheless has sought to triangulate data sources including official and unofficial data provided by nongovernment agencies and civil society. As an annual report that nations are unable to opt out of it places pressure on nations to be vigilant to implementing a counter-trafficking agenda. These factors have enabled the TIP report have an instrumental role in the counter-trafficking policies and actions in place around the world (Mattar 2008; Segrave et al. 2009; Skinner 2008).

Regional Frameworks

While the international instruments have had significant influence on global counter-trafficking developments, a number of regional mechanisms have also influenced the design and implementation of national initiatives (see Gallagher and Holmes 2008). Generally these have not differed substantially from the dominant international frameworks, yet they have adopted different positions as illustrated in the subsequent discussion on the Council of Europe's (CoE) *Convention on Action Against Trafficking in Human Beings*, adopted in 2005 and the Association of Southeast Asian Nations' (ASEAN) *Declaration Against Trafficking in Persons, Especially Women and Children* (ASEAN 2010).

The CoE's* Convention on Action Against Trafficking ("the Convention") came into force in February 2008. Ratified by 26 countries (out of 47 member states of CoE), the Convention establishes the minimum standards of protection for victims and a specific monitoring mechanism for state parties' compliance with the Convention. While adopting the criminal justice emphasis seen in the Trafficking Protocol and TIP Report, the Convention also urges nation states to "take appropriate measures, as may be necessary, to enable migration to take place legally" (Article 5.4), pay attention to identification of victims and other forms of trafficking (such as labor trafficking), and uphold the right to compensation, assistance, and protection of privacy of victims. It preceded the U.S. shift in identifying the importance disconnecting victim assistance and participation in criminal proceedings (Article 12.6).

The review of implementation also differs to the international mechanisms. Implementation of the Convention was established within the Convention to be undertaken and monitored by GRETA (group of experts on action against trafficking in human beings) (Article 36.1) and the Committee of the Parties. While the Committee of the Parties is a political body, GRETA was designed as an independent, multidisciplinary expert group in the area of human rights, assistance, and protection for victims (Article 36). The evaluation process of State Parties' efforts is divided into rounds and involves multiple methodologies; however, the rigor of this mechanism of evaluation is yet to be determined as the first evaluation round began in 2010 and will not conclude until 2013. However, the focus and the methodology suggest a very different emphasis to the TIP Report. While still focused on law enforcement outcomes, the Convention adopts a more tangible human rights framework than the Protocol and TIP Report, in which responsibilities set to nation states in relation to upholding victims' rights play an equally important role in counter-trafficking strategies.

In comparison, ASEAN† still operates under the 2004 *Declaration Against Trafficking in Persons, Especially Women and Children*, a declaration that sought to reinforce the spirit and framework of the Palermo Protocol (Pollock 2007). The Declaration outlined key measures to combat trafficking that emphasized law-and-order measures targeted specifically at the issue of trafficking in women and children or the purposes of sexual servitude. The Declaration sought to enhance criminal justice cooperation between nations in the region and it has enabled this, as evidenced through developments such as the Thail-Cambodian 2003 *Cooperation for Eliminating Trafficking in Children and Women and Assisting Victims of Trafficking* Memorandum of Understanding. These formal commitments have been aimed at ensuring cross-border law enforcement cooperation and the protection and support of victims when returned to their country of origin (Pollock 2007).

---

* Council of Europe "covers virtually the entire European continent" (all European states except Belarus) and its mission is to "develop throughout Europe common and democratic principles based on the European Convention on Human Rights and other reference texts on the protection of individuals" (Council of Europe 2010: http://www.coe.int/aboutcoe/index.asp?page=quisommesnousandl=en).

† ASEAN member states are: Brunei, Cambodia, Indonesia, Lao PDR, Malaysia, Myanmar, Philippines, Singapore, Thailand, and Viet Nam.

Developments within the international sphere have also played an important role in shaping and legitimating the approach adopted by ASEAN, largely a reflection of the number of nations within ASEAN that are second and third world nations. The United Nations Inter-Agency Project on Human Trafficking in the Greater Mekong Subregion (UNIAP), established in 2000, was tasked with facilitating a coordinated response to trafficking within the region (UNIAP 2008), which became the Coordinated Mekong Ministerial Initiative against the Trafficking (COMMIT) initiative. This initiative focused on developing a cooperative regional system for responding to human trafficking, recognizing the cross-border nature of human trafficking. In 2004, the initiative produced the COMMIT Memorandum of Understanding based on the "Three P's" approach as the desired framework for counter-trafficking. It noted the importance of evaluation recognizing that "[m]onitoring and evaluation of trafficking interventions have generally been somewhat weak" (COMMIT SPA 2007, p. 54); however, to date evaluation has primarily involved reporting on progress relating to implementation and criminal justice indicators (COMMIT SPA 2007, p. 12).

Summary

Criminal justice mechanisms—ranging from policing and prosecution to border regulation—dominate as significant elements across the counter-trafficking international and regional mechanisms discussed. As a consequence, key performance indicators pertaining to implementing criminal justice processes (e.g., establishing legislation and reaching bilateral information sharing agreements) are often used in place of evaluation of these measures. Indeed, quantitative criminal justice data are the primary global "currency" in counter-trafficking assessments. Limited attention is paid to developing comprehensive reporting mechanisms that seek to *evaluate* existing responses rather than simply producing *monitoring* reports of processes in place. Within this setting there is limited recognition of the motivations that drive counter-trafficking responses, and the potential impact of counter-trafficking strategies that are developed for political expediency and to meet international expectations rather than been driven by close attention to the local contextual reality (Segrave et al. 2009). Recognizing that political priorities underpin national counter-trafficking efforts suggests that exploring more comprehensive evaluations and potentially developing *alternative* counter-trafficking measures will be anathema for some nations and a secondary concern to the broader aim of meeting international criminal justice priorities. This is an issue returned to in Part Three. Now we examine national counter-trafficking policies and evaluation approaches in place.

National Mechanisms

Shifting from the international to the national context, this section provides an overview of a selection of national counter-trafficking policies. Primarily we are interested in whether there is systematic evaluation of counter-trafficking measures and the design and conduct of any evaluation processes in place. We selected five case studies: Australia, Serbia, Thailand, South Africa, and the United Kingdom and provide a brief summary in Table 11.2. While a more detailed comparison of the background to and most recent developments in counter-trafficking in each nation cannot be provided here, we do elaborateon the Australian and

Table 11.2　Summary of Counter-Trafficking Frameworks in Each Country

Country	Status as Trafficking Nation	Trafficking Protocol Status[a]	TIP Ranking 2010[b]	Policy Framework[c,d] Title and Year Introduced	Policy Framework[c,d] Evaluation and Monitoring
Australia	Destination	*Signed:* December 2002 *Ratified:* September 2005	Tier One	*Australian Government's Action Plan to Eradicate Trafficking in Persons 2003*	Not legislated (details below)
Serbia	Source Transit Destination	*Signed:* December 2000 *Ratified:* September 2001	Tier Two	2006	Yes (details below)
Thailand	Source Transit Destination	*Signed:* December 2001 *Ratified:* Has not ratified	Tier Two Watch List (demoted from Tier Two 2010)	*National Policy to Combat Human Trafficking, Plan of Action to Prevent, Protect, Prosecute and Reintegrate.* Updated via *Anti-Trafficking in Persons Act B.E 2551* (2008) which expanded focus beyond sex trafficking	Data and evidence remain limited and firmly located within the reporting of criminal justice practice and outcomes (Pollock 2007). Critically, there is little to no reporting on the efforts related to the experience of Thai victims of trafficking *abroad* who return to Thailand, other than the production of statistics regarding the number of people assisted formally. The 2008 legislation established the Coordinating and Monitoring of Anti-Trafficking in Persons Performance Committee which was granted powers to monitor and evaluate the implementation of the act. However, the form and function of this evaluation remain to be seen, as does the frequency with which this is reported (which is not specified within the legislation). Independent research has raised concerns regarding implementation of counter-trafficking efforts in Thailand (Pollock 2007; USODS 2010)
South Africa	Source Transit Destination	*Signed:* December 2000 *Ratified:* February 2004	Tier Two	N/A Current legislative framework pertains specifically to sexual offences in relation to adults and children (*Criminal Law (Sexual Offences and Related Matters) Amendment Act,* No. 32 of 2007) and forced child labour [*Conditions of Labour Act* (1997)]. To date, victims	No. However, Sections 37 and 38 of the *Prevention and Combating of Trafficking in Persons Bill 2008* include the establishment of an Intersectoral Committee[e] responsible for monitoring implementation; however, progress of the proposed Bill remains to be seen (see Parliament of South Africa 2010; Watters 2010). See also Kempan 2008

			Signed: December 2000 Ratified: February 2006	assistance programs have been funded almost exclusively by the international community	Yes. *Official:* Two reports by UK Parliamentary Committee, Joint Committee on Human Rights (JCHR) (2006, 2007), both identified
England	Transit Destination	Tier One		*Action Plan on Tackling Human Trafficking* in 2007	several key areas that the Action Plan had failed to address and/or that urgently required attention. Home Affairs Committee inquiry 2008 identified and focused largely on how to improve and strengthen criminal justice efforts (HAC 2009, pp. 75–83). *Update to the UK Action Plan on Tackling Human Trafficking* report is more comprehensive than any equivalent in other nations assessed here—sets out targeted actions and progress in relation to prevention, criminal justice processes (investigation, law enforcement, and prosecution), protection and assistance to adult victims, and issues in relation to child victims. However, focus is on "Three P's" framework for responding to and reporting on counter-trafficking efforts and utilizes performance indicators to measure the implementation rather than the impact of the policy response. The absence of any formal *evaluation* of the response is reflected in the opening summary (UKHO 2009). *Independent Anti-Trafficking Monitoring Group*[f] (AntiSlavery.org 2010) formed in 2009/10 to undertake the first "robust and independent collection, analysis and reporting of evidence regarding the implementation of CoE's *Convention on Action Against Trafficking in Human Beings* in the United Kingdom" (Anti-Slavery 2010: np)

[a] UNODC 2010.

[b] USDOS 2010.

[c] This refers to the framework introduced as part of/to define the national counter-trafficking framework, if one is in place.

[d] Information taken from sources quoted in the country narratives.

[e] The Intersectoral Committee consists of—(a) the Director-General: Justice and Constitutional Development, who is the chairperson of the Committee; (b) the National Commissioner of the South African Police Service; (c) the Director-General: Home Affairs; (d) the Director-General: Foreign Affairs; (e) the Director-General: Social Development; (f) the Director-General: Health; (g) the Director-General: Labour; (h) the National Director of Public Prosecutions; and (i) the Chief Executive Officer: Government Communication and Information System.

[f] Specifically, Amnesty International UK; ECPAT [End Child Prostitution, Child Pornography and the Trafficking of Children for Sexual Purposes] UK; Helen Bamber Foundation; Immigration Law Practitioners' Association (ILPA); Kalayaan; POPPY Project (of Eaves Housing for Women); TARA (The Trafficking Awareness Raising Alliance, of Glasgow Community and Safety Services (GCSS)), and UNICEF, UK.

Serbian contexts to illustrate the diversity and similarity of responses and to bring to the fore key issues that we return to in Part Three of this chapter. These five countries are a limited selection and are demonstrative rather than representational—the social, political, and economic contexts differ substantially across all nations as does the counter-trafficking response.*

Table 11.2 indicates points of similarity and difference across all four nations. On examining Australia and Serbia more closely we gain further insight into the importance of attending to the context in which counter-trafficking responses are developed as well as ongoing issues regarding implementation when developing processes for evaluation.

Australia

Background

In 2003, the *Australian Government's Action Plan to Eradicate Trafficking in Persons [Action Plan]* was introduced. This was initially a 4-year, whole-of-government strategy designed to focus on "prevention, detection and investigation, criminal prosecution, and victim support and rehabilitation" (APTIC 2009, p. iii). In 2007, it was announced that the strategy would be funded for a further 4 years with minimal changes (Attorney-General's Department 2007). Australia's initial commitment to this issue arose in the political context where the criminalization of migration regulation processes both within the nation, at the border, and beyond Australia's border under the banner of "national security" dominated the public and policy agenda (Burke 2002; Carrington 2006; Gallagher 2005; Manne 2004; Marr and Wilkinson 2003; Pickering 2005). The right to remove illegal noncitizens from the nation was a condition of Australia's signature on the Trafficking Protocol, articulated within the caveat declaration that Australia upheld the sovereign right to refuse "to admit or retain within its borders persons in respect of whom Australia would not otherwise have an obligation to admit or retain within its borders" (UNODC 2010).

Despite this, the 2003 counter-trafficking policy reflected the dominant international frameworks, with an emphasis on criminal justice mechanisms including the establishment of a national police task force, legislative reform, and establishing a victim support model that was designed to assist witnesses through the legal process (for more details, see ANAO 2009; Segrave 2004; Segrave et al. 2009). While over time there has been some recognition of the rights of victims outside of the criminal justice process and a broadened definition of human trafficking, the logic of the "Three P's" model and the importance of criminal justice outcomes remains central as evident in the then Minister for Home Affairs declaration:

> [t]he strategy has three equally important needs: to do as much as we can to prevent people trafficking; to prosecute offenders; and to provide support to victims of trafficking, including by protecting their human rights. (O'Connor 2009, p. 2)

Since 2003, implementation of the whole-of-government policy response has been the responsibility of specific government departments including the Department of Immigration and Citizenship, the Australian Federal Police and the Office for Women (for

---

* We would note that these overviews are not intended to be comprehensive; for more detailed analysis of each nation considered in this chapter refer to the references in the text below.

details on roles and tasks, see ANAO 2009) with the Commonwealth Attorney-General's Department charged with oversight of the whole strategy.

Official Reporting Mechanisms

The Australian policy model, unlike models in other nations, was not established through legislation and no system of review or accountability was introduced. As a whole-of-government model, various Federal departments have consistently reported on their activities in relation to human trafficking according to their specific responsibilities since the introduction of the policy.* Largely, this has meant that the available data have been recorded criminal justice and visa information tracking implementation and trends, rather than a review and its impact as a whole. The reliance on these data as "evidence" was highlighted in 2007 when the then Attorney-General declared that Australia's newly established Rudd Government sought to continue the current policy in order to "build on the success of the existing initiatives" (Attorney-General's Department 2007). The success referred to was not based on any formal review or evaluation of the policy (see ANAO 2009).

Despite the lack of evaluation, Australia has retained a Tier One ranking in the TIP Report since 2004, reflecting the assessment of the Australian policy framework as the embodiment of the U.S.-preferred model (see USDOS 2010). Such international endorsement creates limited external pressure to analyze the appropriateness of the response as a whole. Indeed, at the national level, success remains unclear and undefined and this is embodied in two recently introduced reporting mechanisms.

In 2009, the inaugural annual report on the Australian government response was produced by the Counter-People Trafficking Interdepartmental Committee (APTIC) (APTIC 2009). It relies primarily on trend data with an accompanying discussion on the outcomes of the whole-of-government strategy, reporting on the framework itself, the legal parameters, and the outcomes of each aspect of the policy response. This document is purely driven to report *action* and *results*—rather than offering any interrogation of the framework of the response.

In addition, the Australian Institute of Criminology has been funded by the Attorney-General's Department to produce an annual Monitoring Report, the first of which was released on October 2009. This report is a "quantitative data monitoring project" that focuses on trend data in Australia and the Asia-Pacific (Joudo Larsen et al. 2009, p. 2) and does not offer per se an evaluation of the impact beyond considering and reporting on criminal justice, migration, and labor trend data in Australia and the Asia Pacific (Joudo Larsen et al. 2009).

Despite these two mechanisms, there remains limited comprehensive evaluation of the implementation of the policy response that has sought to assess or evaluate the impact of the efforts to date. There had been, however, some analyses offered by specific parliamentary inquiries that have provided some scope for recognition of the need for analysis of the policy response as a whole.

---

* See Annual Reports for DIMIA 2004–2005 and DIAC 2006–2009 at http://www.immi.gov.au/about/reports/annual; Annual Reports for AFP 2004–2009 http://www.afp.gov.au/media-centre/publications/annual-reports/afp.aspx.

Official Evaluation/Analysis

It has been specific Parliamentary Committees that have been closest to *evaluating* Australia's response to human trafficking. In 2004 and 2005, a partial analysis was conducted within Australia by the *Parliamentary Joint Committee on the Australian Crime Commission* (JCACC 2004, 2005). The establishment of the Committee was timely as it was able to include reports from the community, scholars, and government departments based on early findings from the implementation of the national policy response. The Committee's findings identified key areas for improvement of the response. One area included the clarification of the whole-of-government reporting process, noting that this model creates the opportunity for sections of the policy to be reported without any responsibility for the impact of the policy as a whole (JCACC 2004, 2005). Other critical areas were in relation to the protection visas created for victims of trafficking who were found in Australia without legal visas (JCACC 2004).

However, while these findings were tabled in Parliament and responded to by various Federal Departments, the recommendations remained unenforceable and those recommendation accepted and implemented primarily focused on ensuring that criminal justice mechanisms were in place (Attorney-General's Department 2004). One key recommendation was the need for the Auditor-General to carry out a performance audit of the management of the policy response. This happened 3 years later in 2008.

In 2009, the Australian National Audit Commission (ANAO) produced a report on the "Management of the Australian Government's Action Plan to Eradicate Trafficking in Persons" (ANAO 2009). The report was not designed to evaluate the policy but to assess the oversight of the Action Plan and whether the measures in place effectively manage, monitor, and assess performance (ANAO 2009). The ANAO examined the arrangements in place to monitor contributions to the achievement of outcomes focusing on four key agencies concluding that "greater discipline in seeking to measure the effectiveness ... would enable the agencies to refine their individual approaches, and better inform government and the Parliament as to the success of the overall anti-trafficking strategy" (ANAO 2009).

In June 2009, the Federal Minister for Home Affairs, the Hon Brendan O'Connor MP, made a statement regarding the Government's Response to Trafficking in Persons in response to the ANAO recommendations. He concluded that "there should be a more systematic annual reporting of outcomes under the anti-trafficking strategy" as this would benefit in the production of a single annual report (O'Connor 2009, p. 3).

The outcome of the ANAO report was the 2009 inaugural annual report on the Australian response as described above (APTIC 2009). Other key areas of concern raised by the Inquiry, such as the communication of information between authorities and other failures of the implementation of the response, were not pursued by the ANAO report due to its restricted mandate that did not allow for recommendations to be made regarding the appropriateness of the policy response per se. As such, the impact of the report was primarily to reaffirm the logic of the current response and to ensure an annual gathering and publishing of monitoring data, not evaluation.

Independent Reporting and Evaluation Mechanisms

Independent research into the *implementation* of the response in Australia has been limited. This can be partly attributed to the lack of transparency of implementation of all aspects of the official response. The analyses that have been published have focused on case studies and qualitative data drawn from migrant workers, victims of trafficking, and various agencies in addition to drawing on the available law enforcement data. This writing has emerged within the media (O'Brien and Wynhausen 2003), community sector (see Burn and Simmons 2005; Costello 2005; Roxon et al. 2004), and academia (Burn et al 2005; Gallagher 2005; Pearson 2007; Segrave 2004; Segrave and Milivojevic 2005). The key concerns raised have pertained to the criminal justice framework and problems associated with the visa system.

In addition, two key organizations have produced shadow reports on Australia's response to trafficking within the UN Committee reporting process: to UNESCO under Article 6, the freedom from forced work (National Association of Community Legal Centres 2008), and to CEDAW (YWCA 2009). The first focused primarily on the failure of the Australian government to protect the labor rights of temporary migrant workers and the limitations of the responses to victims of trafficking for whom compensation for unpaid work remains effectively unobtainable (NACLC 2008). The CEDAW Shadow Report focused more specifically on the treatment of women as witnesses for the prosecution and the failure to provide more comprehensive support to victims of trafficking.

These independent reviews, studies, and commentaries have highlighted the need to consider the response to human trafficking more broadly though identifying, for example, the many reasons why women may avoid engagement with authorities, the consequences of more restrictive immigration processes in countries of destination and origin, and the impact of being repatriated home with no financial compensation (Bjerkan 2005; Coomaraswamy 2002; Segrave et al. 2009; Soderlund 2005). In doing so, these reports have identified what GAATW (2007) refers to as the "collateral damage" of counter-trafficking initiatives that official reporting mechanisms fail to capture, as they sit outside the parameters of criminal justice trend data.

It is, however, worth noting that both internal reports and external pressures have created some positive changes, such as creating better conditions for the Witness Protection (Trafficking) visa system which in its original design was unworkable.* That said, despite critiques of the current response, the core focus of the policy has been consistent since it was introduced.

Summary

What is evident in the Australian context is that there has been some effort to produce accessible, clear data reporting on the outcomes of the policy response. However, there is no legislative oversight of this process, and the reporting model is a departmental report of processes and trends rather than *evaluation* and impact of these efforts.

Serbia

Background

Serbia is identified as a country of origin, destination, and transit for trafficked women (Bjerkan 2005; Nikolic-Ristanovic et al. 2004; Surtees 2005; USDOS 2010). Recognition of TIPs as an issue in Serbia (for both Serbian nationals and migrants trafficked to Serbia) by NGOs was largely ignored by the government until the fall of Slobodan Milosevic's regime

---

* See Burn and Simmons (2005) and Burn et al. (2006) for a discussion on this in detail.

in October 2000, after which followed the launching of counter-trafficking initiatives and campaigns largely funded and supported by international organizations (Lindstrom 2004; Simeunović-Patić 2005).

While the Protocol was ratified in 2001, it was not until April 2003 that trafficking in people was defined as a criminal offence (Article 111b of the Serbian Criminal Code, Official Gazette of Republic of Serbia, no. 67/2003).* Serbia has also signed the CoE's Convention in May 2005 (as Serbia and Montenegro), and ratified it in April 2009 (Council of Europe 2010).

In 2002, a National coordinator and the Republic Team for combating trafficking were established (Voice of Difference 2007). The role of a National Coordinator was reserved for high-ranked law enforcement officials, while the Republic Team enclosed representatives from both the government and the NGO sector. In 2006, *the Strategy for Combating Trafficking in People in Serbia* (the Strategy) was passed. This Strategy defines mechanisms for counter-trafficking, and process of evaluation of trafficking efforts in Serbia (Nikolic-Ristanovic and Copić 2010). According to the Strategy, Serbian national mechanism to combat trafficking has two levels: strategic (the Council for counter-trafficking, National Co-ordinator and Republic Team to combat trafficking) and operational (law enforcement agencies and the Service for coordination of protection of victims) (Nikolic-Ristanovic and Copić 2010).

The framework for action, however, is clearly set within "Three P's" framework, while numbers of identified victims and prosecuted offenders represent both required and undisputed mechanisms to evaluate trafficking efforts in Serbia. Although there have been considerable trafficking commitments in Serbia, these commitments primarily focus on criminal justice efforts, specifically targeting the trafficking of women into the sex-trade industry.

Official Reporting

In 2006, the National Coordinator for counter-trafficking in Serbia noted that "in the last couple of year Serbia significantly improved its response to trafficking" (*Vranje Press* June 15, 2006). However, Serbia's highest ranking (either as Serbia or Serbia and Montenegro) in TIP Report is Tier Two which it has maintained since 2005 (USDOS 2010), an improvement from 2004 when Serbia was placed on Tier Two Watch List (USDOS 2004) and 2001 in which Serbia (as Federal Republic of Yugoslavia) was placed in Tier Three (USDOS 2001). The key factors for Serbia's relatively low ranking is the lack of successful prosecutions, the corruption of complicit officials, incomplete law enforcement data, and limited victim support provisions (USDOS 2010).

Official Evaluation

Evaluation of trafficking initiatives as defined in the Strategy is based on a report by the Republic team for combating trafficking prepared for the Council for Counter-Trafficking. Nikolic-Ristanovic and Copić (2010, p. 16) argue that such mechanism cannot be effective, as it is based only on the report from the Republic Team, and more importantly—it is not prepared by an independent, expert body. Moreover, even though the *National Plan for Action 2009–2011*, passed in 2009 by the Serbian government, required evaluation of

---

* In 2006 trafficking was regulated by Article 388. New amendments of the Criminal Code in 2009 increased the sentence for trafficking: from 3 to 12 years of imprisonment (Official Gazette of Republic of Serbia, no. 72/09).

trafficking efforts in that year, results of this mechanism are still not available (Nikolic-Ristanovic and Copić 2010). Similar to Australia, Serbian trafficking efforts are becoming largely opaque,* while clear mechanisms for evaluation are still missing. Yet, the notion expressed by Serbian National Coordinator indicates that legislative changes, changed attitude among law enforcement officials, judiciary and media, are perceived as significant improvement in addressing the problem.

Independent Reporting

Serbian NGOs submitted several shadow reports to various international bodies, including CEDAW (Voice of Difference 2007) and UN Human Rights Committee in Geneva (ASTRA 2010). These reports also highlight good practice by Serbian government that focuses on criminal justice efforts, while reducing potential sanctions for trafficking offence and lack of police raids were key objections (Voice of Difference 2007, pp. 38–39)

Summary

While there has been a recent funding commitment and the development of a National Anti-Trafficking Coordinator in 2008, there remains limited oversight of this process, concerns regarding corruptions among officials (see USDOS 2009) and reporting that refers only to process outcomes rather than any attempt or commitment to *evaluating* the impact of effort to respond to human trafficking. In addition, as our previous research indicates, a key issue pertinent to Serbia, as a developing nation, is the role and influence of international NGOs whose agendas influence both the shape and the evaluation of responses (Segrave et al. 2009).

Overview of National Responses

Although Australia, Thailand, Serbia, South Africa, and the United Kingdom are nations vastly different from each other, they have adopted, or set in place measures to adopt, national responses to human trafficking that mirror the framework encouraged by the Trafficking Protocol and the U.S. TIP Report. None of these nations have a permanent independent body established to examine the national response to human trafficking and to evaluate the outcomes. Criminal justice mechanisms and data, including becoming a signatory to the UN and regional mechanisms, are reported as *progress* in the fight to address human trafficking. However, these are policy measures and "impact" remains undefined and largely absent from national efforts to report on these practices. Thus, we turn to consider key concerns and ways forward in evaluation.

Alternative Approaches to Evaluating Counter-Trafficking Efforts: Reviewing the International and National Analyses

There are many issues raised by the approaches to reporting and analysis adopted by the national approaches outlined above. We bring these together in this discussion to highlight key points for consideration.

---

* For more information, see Nikolic-Ristanovic and Copić (2010).

Conventions and Protocols: Reducing Responsibility

The first concern relates to the *limits* of international agreements. Signing and ratifying a broad international agreement in relation to any issue is often celebrated as a progressive step. Becoming a signatory indicates an acknowledgment of a phenomenon and a commitment to work toward national (and international) efforts to address the issue within the agreed framework for responding. Yet, the Trafficking Protocol also reveals that international agreements can enable states to relinquish responsibility to engage with the issue *beyond* the internationally defined obligations and priorities. The counter-trafficking model prioritizes criminal justice measures leaving less room for consideration of broader practices and experiences of exploitation. Similarly, there is little importance placed on ongoing analysis and evaluation to assess the impact of counter-trafficking including recognition of the myriad potential impacts counter-trafficking responses may have. As a consequence, nations can meet their obligations while avoiding responsibility for recognition of the complexity of the broader issues that are repeatedly brought to the fore by independent research.

As such, while the international stage is replete with counter-trafficking sentiment and assertions of the importance of the Protocol there is little critical engagement, through rigorous research, with the *status quo* on counter-trafficking best practice.

TIP Report: Operates Politically and Maintains *Status Quo*

The TIP Report does little to counter this. It lays emphasis on monitoring implementation—primarily criminal justice outcomes and victim support processes (USDOS 2010). While the TIP Report has shifted away from its narrow origins which focused on sex trafficking specifically, it remains a limited tool that is restricted in its contribution to enabling the international community to better understand the issue of human trafficking, and to better comprehend the impacts of current responses.

The TIP Report also effectively relinquishes responsibility for implementing counter-trafficking efforts beyond the requirements of the Trafficking Protocol. As the only comprehensive reporting of national efforts to address trafficking, the TIP report operates as the mechanism for assessing the extent to which nations have appropriate counter-trafficking policies in place. It does not undertake a rigorous evaluation of counter-trafficking measures and is unable (and does not seek) to establish any connection between the dominant counter-trafficking approach and the impact on the TIPs, nor does it seek to consider broader, unintended impacts of current policy approaches. Further, it does not require nations to ensure independent empirical evaluation is built into counter-trafficking responses. As a consequence, there is no imperative to commit to researching counter-trafficking responses; rather the commitment is to produce process data on activities and outcomes.

A further consequence of this is that given the weight of the TIP report findings—with U.S. sanctions and diplomatic consequences for nations that do not comply—we run the risk of counter-trafficking policies being implemented in inappropriate or limited ways by nations seeking to meet U.S. requirements first and foremost, rather than building responses that are appropriate to the specific patterns and practices related to trafficking underway within the nation. While it is not inherently problematic that nations' commitment to addressing issues such as human trafficking is influenced by multifarious factors (few of which may be directly related to concern for vulnerable and exploited populations), it is critical that we recognize these motivations. It has been identified in some nations, for example, that the pressure to meet international counter-trafficking requirements has led to questionable criminal justice practices that raise other human rights concerns (Nikolic-Ristanovic et al. 2004; Nikolic-Ristanovic and Copić 2010).

A final concern regarding the TIP Report relates to the methodology and ranking process that remains imprecise and the subject of some concern, given the political implications of ranking outcomes. There is considerable debate and contestation regarding the limits and politics of the TIP Report amongst nations, most often focused on the lack of clarity regarding how the determination of the Tier ranking is achieved and challenging the breadth of national policy responses that may all receive the same ranking. Although brief, the overviews of Serbia, Thailand, and South Africa as Tier Two and Tier Two Watch List ranked nations demonstrate that the attribution of the ranking level raises questions about the validity of this mechanism as a reviewing tool. All three nations are at very different stages in relation to establishing and implementing counter-trafficking efforts, with South Africa the least established, yet all were ranked Tier 2 in 2009 (USDOS 2009). A further concern is the ambiguity that surrounds the extent to which the broader context in the nation or region may be taken into account in a ranking. For example, in 2010, Thailand, a nation that has experienced significant political upheaval and instability over the past 12 months, was demoted to Tier Two Watch List with no recognition in the report of this political unrest and/or identification that these broader political uncertainties may have influenced the limited ground made on counter-trafficking efforts since the previous 2009 reporting period (USDOS 2010). These issues highlight the limited validity of the TIP Report as a reviewing mechanism. Yet, despite the consistent challenges and criticisms of the TIP Report, there is no international mobilization around the recognition for a more credible independent analysis of counter-trafficking efforts.

The Limits of the International Platform

Both the Trafficking Protocol and the TIP Report, combined with key regional mechanisms, view trafficking through the lens of transnational organized crime and through the criminal justice system where men, women, and children are simply and only victims or offenders. This results in a narrow interpretation of protection and assistance and, critically, means that the multiple and complex identities of victims of trafficking are ignored. This is at the peril of addressing exploitative migration and labor practices. There is a burgeoning critical research base (GAATW 2007; Segrave et al. 2009) that is calling for trafficking to be understood beyond the limits of a transnational organized crime and within broader migration and labor frameworks. As critical researchers have argued, migrant voices must be heard as must the experiences, frustrations, and concerns of those implementing policy on the ground (Agustin 2005; Kapur 2005). This requires an alternative template for review and analysis than that currently provided by the existing UN framework and/or the TIP report. This does not mean that existing counter-trafficking measures must be abandoned; rather, evaluations of current responses have to look beyond the implementation of the current framework to begin to document and identify the broader realities and impacts of counter-trafficking efforts. We will now outline four key considerations that need to be included in the development of a systematic *evaluation* process.

Multiple Voices

Reporting mechanisms tend to focus, naturally, on what has happened, on those who *have* been identified, on the outcomes of efforts. In part, as our detailed work in Thailand, Australia, and Serbia has demonstrated (Segrave et al. 2009), it is critical that we attend to those who are *absent* (also, see Chapter 12 in this volume). This is intuitive to the law-and-order logic and the victim-oriented rhetoric that dominates. What we know, however, is that the limits of existing data are frequently attributed to the challenges in identifying victims, in finding cases of human trafficking. Only reporting what we do find and the experiences of those who are recognized as trafficking victims means that we know little of what is happening beyond this. For example, we need to attend to the experiences and practices of those who experience exploitation who are not formally recognized as victims, who actively avoid recognition as victims of trafficking, who are engaged in complex, ongoing transnational migration journeys and those whose stories are rejected by criminal justice authorities due to lack of evidence or otherwise. This is possible through a commitment to rigorous research by social scientists and criminologists, who have well established the importance of recognizing the "dark figure" (i.e., stories that remain unreported or unrecorded) and we need to continue that commitment in the area of human trafficking (see, e.g., Kelly 2002; Lievore 2003). In part, this requires research that looks beyond human trafficking victims and data, to broader exploitative labor situations and migration trends, including policing practices in relation to illegal noncitizens.

Broader Contributing Factors

It is only when we look beyond the current frameworks that we see the influence of other practices and policies on human trafficking. To consider efforts to address human trafficking without also attending to the freedom to move as "the main stratifying factor of our late modern and post- modern times" (Bauman 1998, p. 2), and to what Sassen (1997) refers to as "growing inequality in earnings and profit-making capabilities" in relation to labor and migration trends, is to deny the bigger picture. This means we have to pay attention, for example, to the ways in which migration policies impact the ability of some populations to cross borders with ease. We cannot deny that increasing the difficulty of crossing borders creates opportunities for black market "entrepreneurs" to profit through assisting with alternative, illicit border crossings (see Andreas 2000). This brings to light the impact of contradictory policy proprieties and the impact this can have on the ground. This has been made evident by research into labor exploitation. For example, recent research into exploitation of temporary and illegal migrant workers in Australia has revealed that the same Australian authorities involved in identifying victims of trafficking (state police and immigration authorities) are also under pressure to identify and deport illegal laborers. This has given rise to exploited laborers who are potential victims of trafficking not been identified as such, despite the fact that their situations mirror those of women trafficked into the sex industry in every way, except that they are working in the agricultural or hospitality industry (Segrave 2008, 2009).

Recognition of Harm

Connected to the concern regarding silenced voices is the frustration that the international and national rhetoric gives the impression of "progress, of something being done, of a social-justice project being pursued in the name of the human rights" but that we can increasingly recognize that this progress "is emerging as a somewhat disingenuous and illusory project"

(Kapur 2005, p. 26). As Kapur notes, we must attend to the *harm* that can be caused by so-called humanitarian interventions. Our concern is that the Trafficking Protocol framework enables policy makers, NGOs, and human rights activists to, at times, frame their counter-trafficking efforts as benevolent gestures and interventions (e.g., through providing women with shelters and counseling, through raiding brothels and "rescuing" women from the sex industry) that are enabled and sustained by this framework. The logic appears to be irrefutable. Yet, as critical researchers, such as Kempadoo, (2005, p. xxi) argue, the "[h]yperbole, unsubstantiated claims, and sensationalism, while perhaps useful for rustling up indignation and moral condemnation about inhuman treatment and exploitation, can, and often do, lead to greater abuse and violations, even in the hands of well-meaning counter-trafficking policy makers and activists" Without research that attends to these experiences, victim-focused interventions remain unchallenged despite the fact that in some cases they may be further impinging on the human rights of already-vulnerable groups within the nation (see, e.g., Milivojevic and Pickering 2008). This was made evident in our own research, where, for example, women in shelters in Serbia were describing their experience as prison-like conditions (Segrave et al. 2009), or when women who wanted to travel to 2006 FIFA World Cup faced stricter visa regimes as a consequence of counter-trafficking initiatives (Milivojevic and Pickering 2008). Since the 2010 TIP report has identified some of these issues, it will be interesting to see what changes, if any, will follow such recognition.

Recognition of the Need for Review and Analysis

The key questions that the international community has broadly failed to address clearly relate specifically to the *recognition* of evaluation and the *purpose* of evaluation. It needs to be clear as to whether reporting mechanisms are about accountability, oversight, or some measure of effectiveness. If indeed it is to be effectiveness, then we need to consider whether it is enough to address human trafficking according to existing international frameworks when it is has connections with other exploitative practices including child adoption and labor exploitation with disconnections that are often blurred and create difficulties for those involved in implementation of policy responses.

We run the risk of remaining narrowly focused and not recognizing the broader trends and developments in relation to risk and vulnerability to exploitation if we continue to adopt the position that TIPs will *effectively* be addressed via the existing mechanisms developed almost a decade ago. The purpose of such an exercise is to move toward a response to forms of exploitation such as human trafficking that prioritizes recognition of the myriad of factors that give rise to the opportunity to exploit people, and adopt responses that begin from this basis.

Conclusion

We complete this chapter by identifying key elements for an alternative mechanism for evaluation that can work at *both* national and international levels, to ensure consistency in approach and emphasis at both the domestic and global level.

As we have noted elsewhere, while "the parameters of the understanding of and response to human trafficking have broadened, the details of the nature of the response have remained effectively unchanged" (Segrave 2009a, p. 205). The challenge arising from this chapter is to mobilize nations to make a commitment to engaging with the counter-trafficking framework, for which a starting point can be a commitment to empirical and evidence-based independent evaluation.

A human rights framework is not necessarily unproblematic (see GAATW 2007) as a beginning point. However, it is possible to develop an evidence base comprised of empirical triangulated data (i.e., utilizing multiple data collection methods that are transparently reported and conducted ethically and rigorously) that enables a more comprehensive picture to be built. One that respects and includes the "voice and agency of trafficked and migrant" persons because, as we've already noted, we need to attend broadly to the experiences of those crossing borders to understand better the nuances of why and where exploitation occurs (GAATW 2007). We echo Landau and Wa Kabwe-Segatti's (2009, p. 4) call for a model that moves "beyond the demographic and quantitative fixations [on criminal justice data]" toward "demographic and economic trends within broader socio-political formations ... [in order to] illustrate the intersections between human mobility and development" as well as, we would add, vulnerability and exploitation. Such a model requires careful development to enable these broad concepts to be usefully engaged.

We cannot begin to make sense of the complex interrelationship between migration and exploitation without developing more comprehensive research agendas and methodological approaches. Such work "must not and cannot be the responsibility of agencies involved in implementing counter-trafficking efforts" (Mattar 2009, p. 1415). We need a triangulated research agenda that draws upon NGOs, researchers from a range of areas of expertise (e.g., migration, criminology, law) and from a range of locations (i.e., countries of origin, destination, and transit), and which enables national authorities to cooperate and engage in the research process collaboratively rather than defensively. Such an approach also requires governmental commitment, including the appropriate apportioning of resources to evaluation (Shinkle 2007, pp. 12–13). Research and evaluation have to be undertaken with a constructive approach to critical engagement, whereby research can assist us to develop more targeted responses based on lessons learned, mistakes made, and a greater awareness of the complexity of the issues. In this process we must carefully attend to defining our scope and questioning what is success and what is effectiveness. These terms are loaded and used politically and, as such, engaging with the terminology must be central to the development of this process.

Indeed, determining impact is a significant consideration for the international community. Researchers at the micro- and macrolevels need to connect the multiple layers of impact that may be and are being measured. Through dynamic research that draws upon official crime data as well as reports from those working on the ground in official and nonofficial capacities we can begin to more robustly account for the impact of what is being implemented and to more quickly and thoroughly identify new and emerging issues to assist in tailoring and developing responses to news forms of exploitation as they occur.

We end by noting the challenge faced by the international community. As human trafficking, exploitative treatment of migrant laborers, and various forms of unregulated mobility continue without abatement, we must recognize the need to move beyond broad commitments to asking challenging questions about responsibility, accountability, effectiveness and impact, and success. This requires a commitment to constructive collaboration and a recognition that should remain committed to striving toward improvement and building on what is working and building anew what is not working. When the Universal Declaration of Human Rights was passed by the General Assembly in 1948, it was recognized by Jose Arce, then President of the General Assembly as "a remarkable achievement, a step forward in the great evolutionary process" (Smith 2007, p. 36). The international commitment to human trafficking is part of that process, and thus we must remain constantly committed to the improvement and development of international standards and approaches in order to achieve better outcomes for all.

Review and Discussion Questions

1. Is it possible or desirable to have a single international mechanism to evaluate counter-trafficking responses?
2. Can an international mechanism for evaluating counter-trafficking responses be effective in creating meaningful change?
3. Would it be more beneficial to evaluate specific areas of counter-trafficking (e.g., identifying potential victims, support mechanisms, criminal justice processes, etc.)?
4. What are the potential limits/possibilities of examining responses to human trafficking in relation to each industry/sector (i.e., agriculture, sex, domestic, and hospitality labor)?

References

Abramson, K. 2003. Beyond consent, toward safeguarding human rights: Implementing the United Nations Trafficking Protocol. *Harvard International Law Journal*. 44(2):473–502.

Agustin, L. 2003. Forget victimization: Granting agency to migrants. *Development*, 46(3):30–6.

Agustin, L. 2005. Migrants in the mistress's house: Other voices in the "trafficking" debate. *Social Politics*, 12(1):96–117.

Alcorn, G. and Minchin, L. 2003. A red light on trafficking. *The Age*, October 25: 5.

Andreas, P. 2000. *Border Games: Policing the U.S.-Mexico Divide*. Ithaca: Cornell University Press.

Andrijasevic, R. 2004. Gendered borders: (Il) legality, migration and trafficking in Italy among eastern European women in prostitution. *Studi Culturali* 1(1):59–82.

Anti-People Trafficking Interdepartmental Commission. 2009. *Trafficking in Persons: The Australian Government Response*. January 2004–April 2009. Canberra.

Anti-Slavery International. 2002. *Human Traffic, Human Rights: Redefining Victim Protection*. http://www.antislavery.org/homepage/resources/humantraffic/Hum%20Traff%20Hum%20 Rights,%20redef%20vic%20protec%20final%20full.pdf

Anti-Slavery. 2010. Anti Slavery.org. *Anti-trafficking Monitoring Group*. http://www.antislavery.org/ english/what_we_do/programme_and_advocacy_work/anti_trafficking_monitoring_group. aspx

ASEAN.org. 2010. *ASEAN Declaration against Trafficking in Persons Particularly Women and Children*. http://www.aseansec.org/16793.htm

ASTRA 2010. *About ASTRA*. http://www.astra.org.rs/eng/?page_id=7

Attorney-General's Department. 2004. *Australian Governments Action Plan to Eradicate Trafficking in Persons*. Canberra: Attorney-General's Department.

Attorney-General's Department. 2007. *More Resources to Combat People Trafficking*. Media Release May 8, 2007. http://www.ag.gov.au/www/agd/agd.nsf/Page/RWP7561D03F6952FB64CA2572 D4000BB873

Australian National Audit Office. 2009. *Management of the Australian Government's Action Plan to Eradicate Trafficking in Persons*. Canberra: Commonwealth of Australia. http://www.anao.gov. au/uploads/documents/2008-09_Audit_Report_30.pdf

Bauman, Z. 1998. *Globalization. The Human Consequences*. New York: Columbia University Press.

Berman, J. 2003. (Un)popular strangers and crises (un)bounded: Discourses of sex-trafficking, the European political community and the panicked states of the modern state. *European Journal of International Relations*, 9(1):37–86.

Bjerkan, L. 2005. *A Life on One's Own: Rehabilitation of Victims of Trafficking for Sexual Exploitation*, Oslo: Fafo.

Bumiller, K. 2008. *In an Abusive State: How Neoliberalism Appropriated the Feminist Movement against Sexual Violence*. Durham: Duke University Press.

Burke, A. 2002. The perverse perseverance of sovereignty. *Borderlands e-Journal*, 1(2).

Burn, J. and Simmons, F. 2005. Rewarding witnesses, ignoring victims: An evaluation of the new trafficking visa framework. *Immigration Review*. 24:6–13.

Burn, J., Blay, S., and Simmons, F. 2005. Combating human trafficking: Australia's response to modern day slavery. *Australian Law Journal* 79:543–52.

Burn, J., Simmons, F., and Costello, G. 2006. *Australian NGO Shadow Report on Trafficked Women in Australia: Report Submitted to the 34th Session of the Committee for the Convention on the Elimination of All Forms of Discrimination Against Women (CEDAW)*. http://www.antislavery. org.au/pdf/CEDAW_ShadowReport2006.pdf

Carrington, K. 2006. Law and order on the borders in the neo-colonial antipodes. In *Borders, Mobility and Technologies of Control*. Eds. S. Pickering and L. Weber. The Netherlands: Springer.

Chuang, J. 2006. The United States as global sheriff: Using unilateral sanctions to combat human trafficking, *Michigan Journal of International Law*. 27:437–94.

The COMMIT Sub-Regional Plan of Action 2007. *Achievements in Combating Human Trafficking in the Greater Mekong Sub-Region, 2005–2007*. http://webapps01.un.org/vawdatabase/uploads/ Cambodia%20-%20COMMIT%20report%202005–2007.pdf

Coomaraswamy, R. 2002. Fishing in the stream of migration: Modern forms of trafficking and women's freedom of movement. In *International Association of Refugee Law Judges (Conference Proceedings) 5th Conference 2002*. Wellington, New Zealand.

Costello, G. 2005. *2004 Donald Mackay Winston Churchill Fellowship to Study People Trafficking Law and Policy in Italy and the USA*. May 25, 2004. The Winston Churchill Memorial Trust of Australia. http://www.churchilltrust.com.au/res/File/Fellow_Reports/Costello%20Georgina %202004.pdf

Council of Europe 2010. *Action against Trafficking in Human Beings*. http://www.coe.int/t/dghl/ monitoring/trafficking/default_en.asp

Ditmore, M. 2005. New U.S. funding policies on trafficking affect sex work and HIV-prevention efforts world wide. *SIECUS Report* 33(2):26–29.

Ditmore, M. 2005a. Trafficking in lives: How ideology shapes policy. In *Trafficking and Prostitution Reconsidered: New Perspectives on Migration, Sex Work, and Human Rights*. Eds. K. Kempadoo, J. Sangera and B. Pattanaik. Boulder: Paradigm Publishers.

Ditmore, M. (Ed.). 2006. *Encyclopaedia of Prostitution and Sex Work*. Portsmouth, NH: Greenwood Press.

Doezema, J. 2000. Loose women or lost women: The re-emergence of the myth of white slavery in contemporary discourses of trafficking in women. *Gender Issues*. 18(1): 23–50.

Finckenauer, J. 2001. Russian transnational organized crime and human trafficking. In *Global Human Smuggling—Comparative Perspectives*. Eds. D. Kyle and R. Koslowski. Baltimore, MA: The Johns Hopkins University Press, pp. 166–86.

GAATW. 2007. *Collateral Damage: The Impact of Anti-Trafficking Measures on Human Rights around the World*. Bangkok: GAATW.

Gallagher, A. 2005. Human rights and human trafficking: A preliminary review of Australia's response. In *Human Rights Year in Review*. Ed. M. Smith. Melbourne: Capstan Centre for Human Rights Law, Monash University.

Gallagher, A. and Holmes, P. 2008. Developing an effective criminal justice response to human trafficking: lessons from the front line. *International Criminal Justice Review*, 18(3):318–343.

Group of Experts on Action against Trafficking in Human Beings (GRETA) 2010. *Questionnaire for the Evaluation of the Implementation of the Council of Europe Convention on Action against Trafficking in Human Beings by the Parties.* http://www.coe.int/t/dghl/monitoring/trafficking/Source/GRETA(2010)1_en.pdf

Goodey, J. 2003. Migration, crime and victimhood: Responses to sex trafficking in the EU. *Punishment and Society*, 5(4):415–431.

Goodey, J. 2008. Human trafficking: Sketchy data and policy responses. *Criminology and Criminal Justice*, 8(4):421–42.

Human Trafficking.org. 2007. *Country Report: Thailand.* http://www.humantrafficking.org/countries/thailand

IOM. 2008. *Handbook on Performance Indicators for Counter-Trafficking Projects.* http://www.iom.int/jahia/webdav/shared/shared/mainsite/published_docs/brochures_and_info_sheets/pi_handbook_180808.pdf

Joint Committee on the Australian Crime Commission. 2004. *Australian Crime Commission's Response to Trafficking in Women for Sexual Servitude.* Canberra. : http://www.aph.gov.au/senate/committee/acc_ctte/completed_inquiries/2002-04/sexual_servitude/report/report.pdf

Joint Committee on the Australian Crime Commission. 2005. *Supplementary Report to the Inquiry into the Trafficking of Women for Sexual Servitude.* Canberra: Secretariat of the Parliamentary Joint Committee on the Australian Crime Commission.

Joint Committee on Human Rights. 2006. *Human trafficking Twenty-sixth Report of Session 2005–06* Volume I. London: UK Parliament. http://www.publications.parliament.uk/pa/jt200506/jtselect/jtrights/245/245.pdf

Joint Committee on Human Rights. 2007. *Human Trafficking: Update Twenty-first Report of Session 2006–07.* London: UK Parliament. http://www.publications.parliament.uk/pa/jt200607/jtselect/jtrights/179/179.pdf

Joudo Larsen, J., Lindley, J., and Putt, J. 2009. *Trafficking in persons monitoring report July 2007–December 2008 AIC Monitoring Report No 6*, October 23, 2009, Australian Institute of Criminology Canberra. http://www.aic.gov.au/documents/E/9/A/%7BE9A61B2E-F333-41F2-B670-B11C39FCE2B1%7Dmr06.pdf

Kapur, R. 2005. Cross-border movements and the law: Renegotiating the boundaries of difference. In *Trafficking and Prostitution Reconsidered: New Perspectives on Migration, Sex Work, and Human Rights.* Eds. K. Kempadoo, J. Sangera, and B. Pattanaik. Boulder: Paradigm Publishers. pp. 25–41.

Kelly, L. 2002. The continuum of sexual violence. In *Sexualities: Critical Concepts in Sociology.* Ed. K. Plummer. London: Routledge.

Kempadoo, K. 2005. Introduction: From moral panic to global justice: Changing perspectives on trafficking. In *Trafficking and Prostitution Reconsidered: New Perspectives on Migration, Sex Work, and Human Rights.* Eds. K. Kempadoo, J. Sangera and B. Pattanaik. Boulder: Paradigm Publishers.

Kempan, A. 2008: *Victims of a Hidden Population—Human Trafficking Servamus Safety and Security Magazine.* March 4, 2008.

Landau, L. and Wa Kabwe Segatti, A. 2009. *Human Development Impacts of Migration: South Africa Case Study. United Nations Development Programme Human Development Reports Research Paper 2009/05* April 2009. http://hdr.undp.org/en/reports/global/hdr2009/papers/HDRP_2009_05.pdf

Larsen, J. J., Lindley, J., and Putt, J. 2009. *Trafficking in Persons Monitoring Report July 2007–December 2008.* Canberra: Australian Institute of Criminology.

Lievore, D. 2003. *Non-reporting and Hidden Recording of Sexual Assault: An International Literature Review.* Canberra: Australian Institute of Criminology and Commonwealth Office for the Status of Women. http://www.aic.gov.au/publications/reports/2003-06-review.html

Lindstrom, N. 2004. Regional sex trafficking in the Balkans: Transnational networks in an enlarged Europe. *Problems of Post-Communism*, 51(3):45–52.

Manne, R. 2004. Sending them home: Refugees and the new politics of indifference, 13th edn. *Quarterly Essay*, March 13.

Maltzahn, K. 2004. *Paying for Servitude: Trafficking in Women for Prostitution, Pamela Denoon Lecture 2004*. Viewed February 20, 2008. http://www.projectrespect.org.au/resources/payingservitude.pdf

Marr, D. and Wilkinson, M. 2003. *Dark Victory*. Crow's Nest, NSW: Allen and Unwin.

Mattar, M. 2008. Comparative models of reporting mechanisms on the status of trafficking in human beings. *Vanderbilt Journal of Transnational Law* 41:1355–1415.

Miko, F. 2003. Trafficking in women and children: The U.S. and International response. In *Trafficking in Women and Children: Current Issues and Developments*. Ed. A. Troubnikoff, New York: Nova Science Publishers. pp. 1–25.

Miller, A. 2004. Sexuality, violence against women, and human rights: Women make demands and ladies get protection. *Health and Human Rights*. 7(2):17–47.

Milivojevic, S. and Pickering, S. 2008. Football and sex: The 2006 FIFA World Cup and sex trafficking. *Temida* 11(2):21–47.

National Association of Community Legal Centres, the Human Rights Law Resource Centre and Kingsford Legal Centre. 2008. *Freedom, Respect, Equality, Dignity: Action*. Sydney: Australian National Association of Community Legal Centres. www.hrlrc.org.au/files/MP9JMGYX55/Final.pdf

Nikolic-Ristanovic, V. and Copić, S. 2010. *Pomoc i podrska zenama zrtvama trgovine ljudima u Srbiji*. Belgrade: Victimology Society of Serbia.

Nikolic-Ristanovic, V., Copić, S., Milivojevic, S., Simeunovic-Patić, B., and Mihic, B. 2004. *Trafficking in People in Serbia*. Belgrade: OSCE.

Oberholer, R. 2003. To counter effectively organized crime involvement in irregular migration, people smuggling and human trafficking from the East. Europe's challenges today. In *Organized Crime, Trafficking, Drugs: Selected Papers Presented at the Annual Conference of the European Society of Criminology*. Eds. S. Nevala and K. Aromaa. http://www.heuni.fi/uploads/v2t9skuki.pdf

O'Brien, N. and Wynhausen, E. 2003. Officials "hound" sex slave informers. *The Weekend Australian*. September 27, 7.

O'Connor, B. 2009. *The Government's Response to Trafficking in Persons*. Statement by the Minister for Home Affairs, the Hon Brendan O'Connor MP, June 17, 2009.

Outshoorn, J. 2005. The political debates on prostitution and trafficking of women. *Social Politics: International Studies in Gender, State and Society*. 12(1):141–155.

Parliament of South Africa (2010) *Portfolio Committee on Justice Welcomes Bill on Human Trafficking*. Media Statement. March 25, 2010. http://www.info.gov.za/speeches/2010/10032909451003.htm

Pearson, E. 2007. Australia. In *Collateral Damage: The Impact of Anti-Trafficking Measures on Human Rights around the World*. Bangkok: GAATW.

Pickering, S. 2005. Crimes of the state: The persecution and protection of refugees, *Critical Criminology*. 13:141–163.

Pickering, S. and Weber, L. 2006. Borders, mobility and technologies of control. In *Borders, Mobility and Technologies of Control*. Eds. S. Pickering and L. Weber. The Netherlands: Springer.

Pollock, J. 2007. Thailand. In *Collateral Damage: The Impact of Anti-Trafficking Measures on Human Rights around the World*. Ed. M. Dottridge. Bangkok: GAATW.

Raymond, J. 2002. The new UN trafficking protocol. *Women's Studies International Forum*. 25(5):491–502.

Roxon, N., Maltzahn, K., and Costello, G. 2004. *One Victim of Trafficking is One Too Many: Counting the Human Cost of Trafficking*. Collingwood: Project Respect.

Sanghera, J. 2005. Unpacking the trafficking discourse. In *Trafficking and Prostitution Reconsidered: New Perspectives on Migration, Sex Work, and Human Rights*. Eds. K. Kempadoo, J. Sangera and B. Pattanaik. Boulder: Paradigm Publishers. pp. 3–24.

Sassen, S. 1997. *Informalization in Advanced Market Economies. Issues in Development Discussion Paper*. International Labour Office. Geneva. http://natlex.ilo.ch/wcmsp5/groups/public/ed_emp/documents/publication/wcms_123590.pdf

Sassen, S. 2000. Women's burden: Counter geographies of globalisation and the feminisation of survival. *Journal of International Affairs*. 53, 2:503–524.

Saunders, P. and Soderlund, G. 2003. Threat or opportunity? Sexuality, gender and the Ebb and flow of trafficking as discourse. *Canadian Women's Studies*, 22(3–4):16–24.

Segrave, M. 2004. Surely something is better than nothing? The Australian response to the trafficking of women into sexual servitude in Australia. *Current Issues in Criminal Justice*, 16(1): 85–92.

Segrave M. 2008. Trafficking in persons as labour exploitation. In *Proceedings of the 2nd Australian and New Zealand Critical Criminology Conference*. Eds. Cunneen C and Salter M. The Crime and Justice Research Network, University of New South Wales. http://www.cjrn.unsw.edu.au/critcrimproceedings2008.pdf

Segrave, M. 2009. Order at the border: Examining national responses to trafficking in women. *Women's Studies International Forum*. 32(4):251–260.

Segrave, M. 2009a. Illegal labour and labour Exploitation in regional Australia. In *Australian and New Zealand Critical Criminology Conference Proceedings*, ed. M. Segrave. Melbourne: Monash University. pp. 205–214.

Segrave, M. and Milivojevic, S. 2005. Sex trafficking: A new agenda. *Social Alternatives*. 24(2): 11–16.

Segrave, M., Milivojevic, S. and Pickering, S. 2009. *Sex Trafficking: International Context and Response*. Devon: Willan Publishing.

Shinkle, W. 2007 Preventing human trafficking: An vvaluation of current efforts. *Transatlantic Perspectives on Migration Policy Brief* #3. August 2007. Institute for the Study of International Migration, Walsh School of Foreign Service, Georgetown University.

Simeunović-Patić, B. 2005. Protection, assistance and support of trafficked persons: Current responses. In *A Life on One's Own: Rehabilitation of Victims of Trafficking for Sexual Exploitation*. Ed. L. Bjerkan. Oslo: Fafo.

Skinner, B. 2008. *A Crime So Monstrous: A Shocking Expose of Modern-Day Sex Slavery, Human Trafficking and Urban Child Markets*. Edinburgh and London: Mainstream Publishing.

Smith, R. 2007. *Textbook on International Human Rights*. Oxford, New York: Oxford University Press.

Soderlund, G. 2005. Running from rescuers: New US Crusades against sex trafficking and the rhetorics of abolition, *NWSA Journal*. 17(3):64–87.

Sullivan, B. 2003. Feminism and new international law. *International Feminist Journal of Politics*. 5(2):67–91.

Surtees, R. 2005. *Second Annual Report on Victims of Trafficking in South-Eastern Europe*, Geneva: IOM.

Turner, J. and Kelly, L. 2008. Intersections between diasporas and crime groups in the constitution of the human trafficking chain, *The British Journal of Criminology*. 49(2):184–201.

UK Home Affairs Committee HAC. 2009. *The Trade in Human Beings: Human Trafficking in the UK*. London: UK. Parliament. http://www.publications.parliament.uk/pa/cm200809/cmselect/cmhaff/23/23i.pdf

UK Parliamentary Committee: Joint Committee on Human Rights (JCHR). 2006, 2007.

United Nations Conference of the Parties to the UN Convention against Transnational Organized Crime. 2006. *Review of the implementation of the Protocol to Prevent, Suppress and Punish Trafficking in Persons, Especially Women and Children, supplementing the United Nations Convention against Transnational Organized Crime*. http://www.unodc.org/pdf/ctoccop_2006/V0656230e.pdf

United Nations Inter-Agency Project. 2008. *United Nations Inter-Agency Project on Human Trafficking*. http://www.no-trafficking.org/uniap–frontend/default.aspx

UN Office on Drugs and Crime. 2009. *Global Report on Trafficking in Persons, UN.GIFT*. http://www.unodc.org/documents/human-trafficking/Global_Report_on_TIP.pdf

United Nations Office on Drugs and Crime. 2010. *Conference of the Parties to the United Nations Convention against Transnational Organized Crime and Its Protocols.* http://www.unodc.org/unodc/en/treaties/CTOC/CTOC-COP.html

United Nations Office on Drugs and Crime. 2010a. *First Meeting on the Working Group on Trafficking in Persons, Vienna Austria.* http://www.unodc.org/unodc/en/treaties/CTOC/working-group-on-trafficking-in-persons-protocol.html

United Nations Office on Drugs and Crime. 2010b. *Protocol to Prevent, Suppress and Punish Trafficking in Persons, Especially Women and Children, supplementing the United Nations Convention against Transnational Organized Crime Country List.* http://www.unodc.org/unodc/en/treaties/CTOC/countrylist-traffickingprotocol.html

United Nations Office on Drugs and Crime. 2010c. *International Framework for Action to Implement the Trafficking in Persons Protocol.* New York: United Nations. http://www.unodc.org/documents/human-trafficking/Framework_for_Action_TIP.pdf

U.S. Department of State. 2001. *Victims of Trafficking and Violence Protection Act 2000: Trafficking in Persons Report.* http://www.state.gov/g/tip/rls/tiprpt/2001/index.htm

U.S. Department of State. 2002. *Victims of Trafficking and Violence Protection Act 2000: Trafficking in Persons Report.* http://www.state.gov/g/tip/rls/tiprpt/2002/index.htm

U.S. Department of State. 2003. *Trafficking in Persons Report.* http://www.state.gov/g/tip/rls/tiprpt/2003/index.htm

U.S. Department of State. 2003a. Victims of Trafficking and Violence Protection Act 2000. In *Trafficking in Women and Children: Current Issues and Developments.* Ed. A. Troubnikoff, New York: Nova Science Publishers. pp. 51–67.

U.S. Department of State. 2004. *Trafficking in Persons Report.* http://www.state.gov/g/tip/rls/tiprpt/2004/index.htm

U.S. Department of State. 2009. *Trafficking in Persons Report.* http://www.state.gov/g/tip/rls/tiprpt/2009/index.htm

U.S. Department of State. 2010. *Trafficking in Persons Report.* http://www.state.gov/g/tip/rls/tiprpt/2010/index.htm

YWCA with Australia and Women's Legal Services Australia. 2009. *NGO Report on the Implementation of the Convention on the Elimination of All Forms of Discrimination Against Women (CEDAW) in Australia.* Submission to the Committee for the Elimination of All Forms of Discrimination Against Women. July 2009. Dickson: YWCA. http://www.ywca.org.au/sites/ywca.org.au/files/docs/FINAL-CEDAW-NGO-Report-Australia-July09.pdf

United Kingdom Home Office. 2009. Update to the UK Action Plan on Tackling Human Trafficking, October 2009. Available at: http://www.unhcr.org/refworld/docid/4ae574602.html [accessed July 26, 2011].

Voice of Difference. 2007. *Alternative Report to the CEDAW Committee.* Available at http://www.astra.org.rs/en/pdf/serbia_alter_rep.pdf

Watters, C. 2010. *The Anti-Trafficking Bill, the Immigration Act and the Refugee Appeal Board. Polity. org.za* April 7, 2010. http://www.polity.org.za/article/the-anti-trafficking-bill-the-immigration-act-and-the-refugee-appeal-board-2010-04-07

Weitzer, R. 2007. The social construction of sex trafficking: Ideology and institutionalization of a moral crusade. *Politics and Society*, 35(3):447–75.

Wong, D. 2005. The rumour of trafficking: Border controls, illegal migration and the sovereignty of the nation-state'. In *Illicit Flows and Criminal Things: States, Borders and the Other Side of Globalization.* Eds. W. van Schendel and I. Abraham Bloomington, IN: Indiana University Press.

Working Group on Trafficking in Persons, Conference of the Parties to the UN Convention against Transnational Organized Crime. 2009. *Report on the Meeting of the Working Group on Trafficking in Persons Held in Vienna on 14 and 15 April 2009.* Available at: http://www.unodc.org/documents/treaties/organized_crime/Final_report_English_TIP.pdf

Useful Web Links

Australian Government, Department of Families, Housing, Community Services and Indigenous Affairs: http://www.fahcsia.gov.au/sa/women/progserv/violence/Pages/AntiPeopleTraffickingStrategy.aspx/

Global Alliance against Trafficking in Women: http://www.gaatw.org/

NGO ASTRA, Serbia: http://www.astra.org.rs/ South African Government, Human Trafficking strategy: http://www.info.gov.za/issues/humantrafficking/strategy.htm/.

UK Human Trafficking Centre: http://www.soca.gov.uk/about-soca/about-the-ukhtc/ Australian Government, Department of Foreign Affairs and Trade: http://www.dfat.gov.au/illegal_immigration/index.html/

U.S. Trafficking in Persons Report: http://www.state.gov/g/tip/rls/tiprpt/

UN Office on Drugs and Crime, Human Trafficking page: http://www.unodc.org/unodc/en/human-trafficking/index.html/

Victims of Human Trafficking 12
Meeting Victims' Needs?

SANJA ĆOPIĆ
BILJANA SIMEUNOVIĆ-PATIĆ

Contents

This chapter focuses on the plight of human trafficking victims. The primary focus is on victims' needs and the question as to whether their needs are being met through the existing antitrafficking services and protocols. Drawing on some recent research and our own experience we concentrate mostly on jurisdiction and experiences of the Western Balkans' region to present and illustrate the points of discussion. Where possible, we make reference to other jurisdictions as well.

The chapter is divided into two main parts: In the first part we explore who the victims of trafficking in persons (TIPs) in the Western Balkans' region are, what is the impact of victimization, and what are the victims' needs, as identified in our grassroots work and research on trafficking. In the second part we outline some issues relating to victim assistance and support.

Four key objectives covered in this chapter include

1. To point out who are those who are identified as victims of trafficking.
2. To explore whether the image of the "ideal victim" in the field of human trafficking is still present.

3. To explore the impact of, and outline victim's needs after victimization
4. To explore what type(s) of assistance and support is/are available to the victims and to identify limitations of such services

In the section pertaining to concluding remarks we try to point out how universal victims' needs are in the aftermath of the trafficking situation, as well as how universal the problems with regard to assistance and support are.

Introduction

Trafficking in persons (TIPs) is a global phenomenon affecting almost every country in the world, and as such has become a priority for the governments worldwide (Dixon 2008; UNODC 2009a; USDS 2009; Laczko and Danailova-Trainor 2009). Since 2000 and the adoption of the UN Protocol to Prevent, Suppress and Punish Trafficking in Persons, Especially Women and Children (more commonly referred to as the "Palermo Protocol"), strong efforts were put in place to combat this form of crime on global, regional, and local levels. Although TIPs as "a complex multifaceted crime" (UNODC 2009b, p. 12) can be approached from different angles, such as slavery, prostitution, organized crime, migration, health policy, labor, or security issues (Lee 2007; Romcharan 2002), it should primarily be viewed as a human rights violation (Omelaniuk 2005). Consequently, the social response to human trafficking should be established on the human-rights-based approach, which is strongly advocated on both European and international levels (Rijken and de Volder 2010), as well as among most nongovernmental organization (NGOs) (Goodey 2008). This means that human trafficking should not be treated only "as a criminal activity but one that has profound human-rights implications both for victims and for the governments and NGOs that must deal with them" (Kröger et al. 2004, p. 10). Thus, there is a need of an integrated approach to TIPs (Rijken and de Volder 2010), which should include the "three P's" paradigm—prosecution, protection, and prevention, but also adding the fourth pillar—monitoring, which shall ensure that what has been undertaken actually works.

However, combating TIPs so far has been based on the narrow perception of human trafficking as a criminal justice problem (Rijken and de Volder 2010). It has been primarily focusing on traffickers and "to a lesser extent, protecting their victims" (Chuang 2006, p. 148), although victims' protection seems to be crucial for an effective response of the state agencies to the trafficking issue (UNODC 2008b, p. 12). In light of these observations, the focus of this chapter is on the protection side of the antitrafficking response. Protecting victims' rights both in the destination country and the country of origin, and preventing a victim from being returned to the unsafe and abusive context should be a central task of each antitrafficking policy (Simeunović-Patić 2005). Not accidentally, the 2009 US TIPs Report turns the attention from the "three P's" paradigm (see Chapters 2 and 6) to the "three R's" concept, which includes "rescue, rehabilitation, and reintegration" of victims, encouraging the states "to go beyond initial rescue of victims and restore to them dignity and the hope of productive lives" (USDS 2009, p. 6). What we try to examine through this chapter is whether the existing antitrafficking policies are based on such a concept or they rather fit into the newly developed concept of the "three Ds" (USDS 2010): detention, deportation, and disempowerment of victims. This new paradigm is "a competing, more unfortunate, paradigm," impeding "greater anti-trafficking progress" (USDS 2010, p. 16).

Drawing on the previous observation, this chapter has several aims. The first one is to point out who are the persons identified as trafficking victims and to what extent the image of the "ideal victim" still remains in this field. The second aim is to point out the victim's needs in the aftermath of the trafficking situation, and to examine if theses needs are met through the existing forms of assistance and support offered by different stakeholders. Third, we want to stress on some identified problems and shortages of the antitrafficking mechanisms with regard to assistance and support, which may be considered as obstacles for proper and efficient identification and treatment of trafficking victims.

We discuss the above-mentioned issues using Serbian data and examples from other Western Balkans' countries.[*] The first research deals with the rehabilitation of victims of trafficking for the purpose of sexual exploitation (Bjerkan 2005), the second one is on the scope, structure, and characteristics of male trafficking in Serbia (Nikolić-Ristanović 2009b), while the third explores the system of support and assistance to female victims of trafficking in Serbia (Nikolić-Ristanović and Ćopić 2010). In addition, the chapter is based on the analysis of the broader literature addressing different issues of assistance and support to trafficking victims in this region, giving a broader insight into the structure and nature of identified victims and framework of assistance and support (Surtees, 2005, 2006, 2007; Brunovskis and Surtees 2007). In addition, we look into the global reports on human trafficking (i.e., the 2009 and 2010 TIP reports) and the UN Office on Drugs and Crime's Global Report on TIPs (UNODC 2009a), which enabled us to notice some similarities and differences between the countries. Finally, the chapter draws on the literature around crime victim issues as this literature can help us to better understand the existing gaps and problems with regard to victims' status, needs, assistance, and support in a broader context, as well as some concerns in relation to these issues.

Victims of Trafficking in Human Beings in the Western Balkans

The Western Balkans serves as a source, transit, and destination region for trafficking in men, women, and children (RCP 2003; Nikolić-Ristanović et al. 2004; Bjerkan 2005; UNODC 2009a; USDS 2010).[†] This is due, in large part, to the fact that the region includes postsocialist countries experiencing deep socioeconomic downfall resulting in significant rise of unemployment, sharp social polarization, and feminization of poverty, as well as

---

[*] The Western Balkans is the term used by the European Union for the subregion comprising Albania, Bosnia and Herzegovina, Croatia, Montenegro, Serbia, and Kosovo under UNSCR 1244 and the Former Yugoslav Republic of Macedonia.

[†] According to the latest Trafficking in Persons Report of the US Department of State (USDS 2010), Albania is a source country for men, women, and children trafficking for the purpose of sexual exploitation and forced labor, including forced begging of children (p. 58); Bosnia and Herzegovina is primarily a source country for women and girls who are trafficked particularly for forced prostitution within the country, but it is also a destination and transit country for foreign female victims trafficked for forced prostitution in Bosnia and in Western Europe (p. 86); Croatia is country of destination, source and transit for men, women, and children trafficked primarily for forced prostitution and forced labor (p. 124); Macedonia is a source, transit and destination country for women and children trafficked specifically for forced prostitution and forced labor (p. 218); Montenegro is a transit, source and destination country for men, women, and girls trafficked primarily for forced prostitution and forced labor (p. 239), Serbia is a source, transit, and destination country for men, women, and children trafficked for the purpose of sexual and labor exploitation (p. 289), while Kosovo is a source, transit, and destination for women and children trafficked primarily for forced prostitution, and children for forced begging (p. 201).

postconflict countries and areas where peacekeeping military forces have been deployed for years. In this section, we point out who is identified as a trafficking victim, which, as we try to show later, may impact on the construction of the trafficked victim's profile and maintain the image of the "ideal" victim, impeding the recognition and identification procedures, leaving many others out of the system of assistance and support.

Available data indicate that for a long period of time, the vast majority of identified trafficked persons in the Western Balkans' have been women and girls (see Surtees 2005; Bjerkan 2005). They were mainly trafficked from the Ukraine, Romania, and Moldova to Italy and other Western European countries, while women and girls from the Balkan countries were exploited within the Balkan region, but also in Western Europe (Surtees 2005). The majority of identified female victims were quite young (mainly between 18 and 24 years of age), unemployed, and had been often previously exposed to different forms of violence and social marginalization (Nikolić-Ristanović et al. 2004; Pleša-Golubović 2006; Omelaniuk 2006). The number of minors (i.e., those under the age of 18) among identified female victims trafficked within or from the Western Balkans, particularly from Montenegro, Serbia, and Bosnia and Herzegovina, is notable, with an increasing trend in the last couple of years (see Nikolić-Ristanović and Ćopić 2010).[*] According to the Regional Clearing Point (RCP)'s data for 2004, almost 60% of victims from Bosnia and Herzegovina, 65% from Serbia, and even 80% from Montenegro were minors (Surtees 2005). Some data have also indicated that some adult women trafficked for the purpose of sexual exploitation experienced their first victimization as minors (see IOM Counter-Trafficking Service 2004: 23). Sexual exploitation was found to be the major form of exploitation of both adult and minor female victims. However, victims were also trafficked for labor, begging, while trafficking for multiple purposes has also been noticed—combinations of sexual exploitation and labor exploitation or begging/delinquency (Surtees 2005).

On the other hand, trafficking in male persons has been rather neglected (see Box 12.1), while the "dark figure" of this form of trafficking is identified as significant, limiting the possibility for reliable estimates on the scope of this form of victimization (Kovačević-Lepojević and Dimitrijević 2009). One recent survey on male victims of trafficking in Serbia revealed this problem in the region (Nikolić-Ristanović 2009b), pointing to the Western Balkans as being primarily a transit area and the cross of both trafficking and smuggling routes that run from the Middle East, Africa, Eastern, and South-Eastern Europe to the EU, but also a source region (see Ćopić 2008; Nikolić-Ristanović 2009b).

According to available data, the majority of male victims of human trafficking identified in the Western Balkans are adults. The majority of trafficked men are between 18 and 50 years of age, while in this category, most are between 30 and 40, being capable for work (Surtees 2005). Poor economic background and unemployment is, similarly to women, rather common among male trafficked victims. Poverty pushes the victims toward migrating to Western European countries: a number of identified male victims of trafficking in Serbia previously had tried, at least once, to leave the country illegally (Ćopić 2009).

In recent years, the majority of identified underage male victims (those under the age of 18) in the Western Balkans' countries were domestic nationals (Stamenkova Trajkova et al. 2007). They usually originate from economically poor environments, large families,

---

[*] This increase may be the result of various factors, but most probably it is contributed by the improvements in the victims' detection and identification (Stamenkova Trajkova et al. 2007: 47–48).

BOX 12.1   CASE IN POINT: RECRUITING MEN IN SERBIA FOR CONSTRUCTION WORK ABROAD

In 2007, a criminal group recruited men from several towns in Serbia and Bosnia and Herzegovina for the construction work in Dubai. Through the private employment agency, which had offices in several towns in Serbia and on the internet, the victims were promised jobs, working papers and solid wages ($1200 for the unqualified and $1600 for the skilled craftsmen). Prospective candidates had to pay 500 RSD [app. $6] for the membership, and subsequently $500 for the trip... Around 150–200 men aged from 20 to 50 went to Dubai ... Upon arrival, their passports were taken away (as alleged, in order to obtain work permits) ... The victims lived in poor conditions, in the barracks (with 20–40 people in one barrack) without basic health care and hygiene, and on poor diet ... They worked up to 10 or 12 hours a day, with no right for a break (they were threatened with a pay cut if they do, a pay which they never got in the first place). They were also threatened with "being sent to the war in Iraq". or hurting their family if they complain to someone or not act according to demands. The victims took the threats very seriously... They ended up being there from one to three months. Many victims were punished for violation of immigration laws and deported... Upon return, 39 of them reported the victimization to the police and several members of the criminal group from Serbia were arrested. Later on it had been revealed that the boss of the group had created similar "nets" in some neighboring countries...

(Interview with an official from the Ministry of Interior of the Republic of Serbia conducted in 2008 by the research team of the Victimology Society of Serbia as a part of the project *Male trafficking in Serbia*, Nikolić-Ristanović 2009b).

and are experiencing difficult family situations (Surtees 2005; Žegarac 2007). Minors are more often exposed to internal trafficking than adult men (Ćopić 2009). Boys of Roma nationality are in increased risk from trafficking for the purpose of begging and delinquency in Albania, Serbia, and Bosnia and Herzegovina (see Box 12.2). The recruitment of minor victims is usually initiated through family networks (ibid).

Adult male victims are mostly trafficked for labor exploitation while minors are usually trafficked for begging and committing crimes (e.g., stealing).[*] In addition, when speaking of male victims it should be noticed that a significant number of trafficking victims is hidden behind illegal migrants or smuggled persons. Namely, victims of smuggling may also be easily trapped in the trafficking chains (Ćopić 2009). Victims of smuggling, if they reach the country of destination, almost inevitably turn to other illegal markets and informal economy (Ely-Raphel 2002; Nikolić-Ristanović 2003), being forced to accept "dirty, dangerous and difficult jobs" (Kelly 2005, p. 54). On the basis of these

---

[*] Particularly vulnerable for trafficking for the purpose of begging and delinquency are minors of Roma minority. It should be noticed that Roma minority is considered one of the poorest and socially most deprived and marginalized minority groups in the majority of the countries of Southeast Europe (UNICEF 2004).

BOX 12.2   ROMA BOYS AT RISK

Excerpt from the interview with a representative of the NGO from Belgrade (Serbia) (Ćopić 2009, p. 104):

> Begging was traditionally a job of the Roma people—through the centuries it has been their traditional way of survival. Petty criminals, abusing poverty and bad financial situation of Roma families, put the parents in "debt bondage." If these people are not able to pay back to the criminals, they have to give their own children to petty criminals who are then forcing children to begging or prostitution. [...]Between 10% and 20% of children from the "traffic light" [refers to the children who beg on the crossroads] go to Italy, Spain.

facts we further elaborate on the problems in locating, identifying, and assisting trafficking victims and, as a result, meeting or not meeting their needs.

Impact of Human Trafficking

Understanding the complexities and impact of trafficking on victims is essential not only to understand their victimization, but also for designing adequate victim support and rehabilitation programs (Nikolić-Ristanović 2005). Trafficking victims often face a variety of health, legal, and social complexities as a consequence of trafficking. They may be subjected to physical, psychological, and sexual abuse and physical violence while trafficked. Some experience forced use of illegal substances and severe deprivations including limitation of freedom to movement, access to food and medical care, and poor hygienic and living conditions. All these experiences may have both physical and psychological consequences, since trafficking often includes repeated episodes of violence and prolonged traumatic experience (see Raymond et al. 2002; Clawson et al. 2008; UNODC 2008b; Zimmerman et al. 2003, 2006, 2008).

Research conducted in the Western Balkans' showed that women and children trafficked for sexual exploitation face serious health risks, including physical injuries as a result of beating, sexually transmitted infections, other reproductive tract infections, and unwanted pregnancies (RCP 2003). Victims may also suffer from posttraumatic stress disorder, anxiety, and substance abuse. The research on trafficking in women for the purpose of sexual exploitation conducted in Serbia (Nikolić-Ristanović 2005) identified also feelings of anger, eating disorders, intensive feelings of fear and insecurity, feeling of guilt, and the lack of trust in other people. Abused before, during, and sometimes after the trafficking; victims experience self-blame, lack of control over their life, exclusion, and helplessness (Herman 1992). The lack of trust in other people is also connected to the fear of revictimization by traffickers. Finally, trafficking has severe negative effects on victims' relationships with family and others (Nikolić-Ristanović 2005). Trafficked victims may also face legal consequences as far as they are often not identified exclusively as victims but as violators of immigration or other laws, and ultimately they may be detained, punished, or deported (Segrave et al. 2009).

Bearing this in mind, we may argue that proper identification of victims by authorities and addressing their needs is essential for further protection of victims and their human rights. It depends on the identification procedures, as well as on sensibilization and training of professionals who are likely to come into contact with victims. Such training should lead to more understanding of complexities of trafficking, and ultimately assist in abandoning the stereotypes on "ideal victim" (Christie 1986).

"Ideal Victims" and Real Victims' Needs

Phenomenological characteristics of human trafficking arising from the existing data about those already identified as victims of trafficking are usually linked to the issue of recognition and identification of victims. Many researchers have indicated a lack of recognition of trafficking victims outside of sex industry, both within general public and professionals engaged in antitrafficking activities (Simeunović-Patić 2009). This "hierarchy of victims" and a stereotype of an "ideal victim" of trafficking are notable. The official discourse reinforces the image of trafficking as something that happens to young, naïve, impoverished, helpless, and disadvantaged women with prior experience with victimization, who are coming from undeveloped or developing countries (Kapur 2002; Goodey 2004; Milivojević and Ćopić 2010). They are abducted, forced, or deceived by "evil" people and trafficked for sexual exploitation. This possibly impacts the "dark figure" of trafficking, in terms of an absence of "undeserving victims," which we are going to turn to later in this chapter.

Established stereotypes regarding "ideal victims" impact the recognition/legitimacy of those victims who do not share such defined demographic and personal characteristics. For example, it minimizes the recognition of adult male victims, which generally takes place in the broader context of illegal (i.e., economic) migrations (Simeunović-Patić 2009). On the other hand, using stereotypes of "ideal" versus "real" victims of sex trafficking might prompt women to compete for an (unambiguous) victim status (Simeunović-Patić 2009). While analyzing the link between the media, foreign donors, NGOs, professionals, and researchers, Bjerkan and Dyrlid (2005, p. 151) identified "a call for suffering" (i.e., physical violence/brutal force), which "has become the ideal, or normative, description of stories of trafficking for sexual exploitation."

Specific to this issue is the relationship of HT and migrant smuggling. While empirical data indicate similarities in relation to the socioeconomic status of trafficked persons and smuggled migrants, there is a tendency to "overlook the structural factors which prompted unauthorized cross-border movements and to stigmatize irregular migrants as either 'undeserving' victims or persons with criminal intent" (Lee 2005, p. 2). However, as it has been noted in the literature (see Salt 2000; Aronowitz 2001), it is not easy to distinguish human trafficking from migrant smuggling. The trafficking concept is frequently used to solve the problem of illegal migration or prostitution. As Srikantiah (2007, pp. 192, 194–195) pointed out while commenting the "migrant-victim spectrum" and the concept of "iconic victim":

> […] The iconic victim concept assumes situations where the necessary force, fraud, or coercion is so extreme as to overwhelm the typical situational push factors. […] In short, the iconic victim concept contemplates a victim totally under the trafficker's control and trafficked for sex. […] The iconic victim is the counterpoint to the iconic lawbreaker.

Keeping the above-mentioned issues in mind, there is a need of breaking the existing stereotypes, broadening the concept of the trafficking victim, and establishing the social response to trafficking on a much broader respect of human rights. Human-rights-based response should provide victims with opportunity and assistance to restore and strengthen their own personal resources. Victims need to be secure and protected from violence and exploitation by traffickers, to get compensation, information in relation to their rights as victims and witnesses, and to be provided with practical, administrative, legal, psychological, medical, and social assistance in the process of recovery. Some of these issues will be further discussed.

Assistance and Victim Support

TIPs should be understood as a process, a "continuum," which includes different levels of abuse, exploitation, and positions of vulnerability of victims (Kelly 2007, p. 86). Consequently, providing assistance and support to victims should be seen as a process which is not always linear and which may vary dramatically in terms of time and resources. Such variability is dependent on victims' condition, needs, and other circumstances in the aftermath of the trafficking situation (Albert and Santos 2004). As a result, support and assistance should encompass variety of activities, throughout this process: from identification, recovery, and rehabilitation, to the court procedure (if any), and return and reintegration. All these activities should be based on the following principles: respect for and protection of human rights, informed consent, nondiscrimination, confidentiality and right to privacy, self-determination and participation, individualized treatment and care, comprehensive continuum of care, and equitable distribution of resources (IOM 2007).

A framework of assistance and support to trafficking victims is set forth by the key anti-trafficking documents articulated at the international and European level—the "Palermo Protocol" and Council of Europe Convention on Action against Trafficking in Human Beings (hereinafter referred to as the Council of Europe Convention).* Although the Palermo Protocol was developed and framed "predominantly as a law enforcement instrument" (Segrave et al. 2009, p. 17), or "an international crime control cooperation treaty" (Chuang 2006, p. 148), whose "focus rests with crime against state parties rather than on individual victims of trafficking" (Goodey 2008, p. 424), it is the first document that regulates protection and assistance to victims of trafficking. Article 2 of the Protocol indicates that a purpose of this instrument is to protect and assist the victims of TIPs, with special emphasis on upholding their human rights. Furthermore, Article 6 calls for the protection of victim's privacy, identity, and safety. Specifically, this article indicates that State parties shall provide for such measures as physical, psychological, and social recovery, including appropriate housing, counseling and information, psychological and material assistance, and educational and training opportunities.

Another step forward was taken by the Council of Europe Convention, which "emphasizes the human rights of trafficked persons" (Anderson 2007, p. 5), imposing "measures to increase the protection of trafficking victim's human rights" (Rijken and de Volder 2010,

---

* Efforts on the EU level in regard to strengthening the combat against trafficking in persons are significant. On March 29, 2010 the European Commission presented a proposal for a Directive on preventing and combating trafficking in human beings and protecting victims, which should replace the existing legal framework on the EU level. It foresees higher standards of victim assistance and support. It particularly focuses on development of national mechanisms for early identification and assistance to victims, providing shelters, medical and psychological assistance, information, and interpretation services. Finally, it foresees special protective measures for child victims.

p. 59). As with the Palermo Protocol, it also focuses on physical and psychological assistance and support, particularly referring to secure accommodation, translation and interpretation services, and assistance in criminal proceedings against offenders. In addition, the Convention calls for Member States to provide access to the labor market, vocational training, and education, but limiting these services to victims who lawfully reside within the territory of a respective country.

Based on these documents, the general-level expertise in relation to victims' identification, care and protection has "successfully" and "significantly" increased since 2000 (Dixon 2008, p. 110), but it is still far from being satisfactory. Source, transit, and destination countries are still facing numerous problems, some of which we try to address and analyze in the following section. We first discuss the four different stages in the process of assistance and support for victims. In doing so, we try to critically refer to these issues, analyze shortages and gaps within the system of assistance, and support and identify whether victims' needs are met by the existing antitrafficking mechanisms.

Identification of Victims

Early identification of trafficking victims is a crucial precondition for a prompt and timely inclusion of a victim in the system of assistance and support. Only accurate identification enables trafficking victims to be protected, supported, and assisted; at the same time, it prevents them from being treated as law-breakers, criminals, or nonpersons (Simeunović-Patić 2005). In addition, early identification and assistance "promote recovery and may in turn have a positive future impact on the reduction of trafficking, by preventing re-trafficking" (Dixon 2008, p. 92). However, identification of trafficking victims still presents one of the biggest challenges in combating this form of crime and it will remain an even bigger challenge in the future due to the changes in trafficking patterns (Brunovskis and Tyldum 2004; Simeunović-Patić 2008).

Locating and identifying victims of trafficking is "more complex process that in the case of more traditional crime" (Segrave et al. 2009, p. 45), due to the hidden nature of trafficking and the problems in distinguishing it from other similar forms of victimization, particularly smuggling. Recognition and identification of trafficking victims can be done through the outreach programs of social services or NGOs, SOS hotlines, and activities of state agencies (Simeunović-Patić 2008). In other words, victims can be identified by law enforcement, staff of nongovernmental and international organizations, embassy personnel, social and health workers, labor inspectors, as well as by other persons who are not directly involved in antitrafficking activities such as transport agencies, religious organizations, citizens, families, or friends of the victim (Surtees 2007; IOM 2007; Newton et al. 2008). As some surveys suggest, victims may also be identified by clients and victims themselves (self-referrals or self-disclosure) (Surtees 2007; Newton et al. 2008). However, the most frequent form of identification is by the law enforcement, immigration and border services, or other state agencies, which could be considered as in cases of crime victims in general "'gate-keepers' who decide *who* will enter the system and *how* they will enter" (Cunneen 2001, p. 132, emphasis in the original).

Due to the complexity of the trafficking phenomenon, identification may require a certain period of time (Kröger et al. 2004). It is an ongoing process, which can be very "stressful" and "informed by a wide range of emotions and reaction" (Surtees 2007, p. 56). As "gate-keepers," professionals who are likely to come into contact with victims have to be trained to undertake more active efforts in identifying victims. It is also argued that for the efficient identification of trafficking victims there is a need for developing indicators that could guide professionals in this procedure (Ogrodnik 2010). Otherwise, identification of victims may rely on basic observations and arbitrariness, rather than a more comprehensive approach (Danziger 2006). As a result, UN Office for Drugs and Crime (UNODC 2008a) and US Department of State's Office to Monitor and Combat Trafficking in Persons (US Government Accountability Office 2007) developed lists of general and specific indicators for timely and efficient identification of victims.

Developed lists of indicators can provide some consistency and transparency in identification, but it is difficult to believe that any list can reflect complexities and fluency of the trafficking phenomenon. We may argue that these instruments actually deepen and strengthen the already-existing prejudices and stereotypes around trafficking. As a result, professionals may find themselves trapped with stereotypes on "how a victim should 'look' and 'behave'" (Segrave et al. 2009, p. 51), which in turn impacts on victim's (non)identification: only those who fit into the narrow notion of an "ideal victim" will be located and identified. This is why lists of indicators cannot be considered a "perfect tool" that will by itself improve the procedure of identification (Simeunović-Patić 2008, p. 82). As stated in the 2008 Council of Europe's Recommendations on Identification and Referral to Services of Victims of Trafficking in Human Beings, indicators should be understood as a "flexible instrument, to be used for case by case assessments," but at the same time avoiding "further stereotyping and victimization of presumed trafficked persons" (Simeunović-Patić 2008, p. 4). As a result, indicators can be considered only "basic tools" that require assessment and enhancement, which could only serve as guidelines for professionals. In this respect, there is a need of more professionals trained in identification and equipped with necessary information (Surtees 2007, p. 42), while education should be organized systematically, not ad hoc, as is the case in many countries today (Danziger 2006).

Apart from education, it is also important to develop more proactive approach of both officials and NGO activists to trafficking cases, and not rely only upon the so far dominant forms of identification: "independent raid and rescue missions and migration compliance raids" (Segrave et al. 2009, p. 45). Without changes in identifying patterns of trafficking victims, the risk of not identifying a pool of others will intensify, leading to the "missed identification opportunities" (Surtees 2007, p. 55). Consequently, a significant number of victims will remain out of the system of support and assistance, and ultimately will be removed from the country, criminalized or retrafficked (Ogrodnik 2010).

Reflection Period

Once having escaped from the trafficking situation, victims often need a certain period of time to recover from the trafficking experience (Simeunović-Patić 2005). They will need to reflect on their situation and make an informed decision about their lives and possible cooperation with state agencies. Therefore, the reflection period is recognized as "an effective best practice and humanitarian measure aimed at protecting the human rights of trafficked person" (UNODC 2008a, p. 120). It should limit immediate deportation, protect a victim from prosecution, and allow a person to get free from the traffickers' influence, as well as to start the recovery process and make informed decisions, including whether to testify against the perpetrators (Simeunović-Patić 2005; Dixon 2008). In addition, authorities may "profit" from the victim's recovery during this period, because the victim could be also encouraged to testify against a trafficker and thereby also support the prosecution (Dixon 2008: 92).

According to the Council of Europe Convention, each State should ensure the recovery and reflection period of at least 30 days "when there are reasonable grounds to believe that the person concerned is a victim" (Article 13). However, the practice shows that the reflection period varies from country to country (Dixon 2008; USDS 2009). For example, most European (mostly destination) countries accepted the suggested timeframe of 30 days (e.g., Austria, Germany, France, Sweden, Switzerland, and Hungary); some countries are more flexible in allowing for a reflection period between 30 and 60 days (e.g., Denmark and Portugal), while other countries provide for a recovery and reflection period of up to three months (e.g., The Netherlands, Romania, and Slovenia). Just occasionally, this period is longer—for example, reflection period extends to 6 months in Norway.*

Bearing in mind Norway's experience, as well as the report of the European Commission Experts Group on Trafficking in Human Beings from 2004, it could be argued that the time period of 30 days is an insufficient amount of time for victims to recover and make sound decisions about their future. As a result, the Group suggested the duration of at least 3 months, because reflection period must have "adequate duration bearing in mind its multiple goals" (European Commission Experts Group on Trafficking in Human Beings from 2004, p. 10). A short reflection period may pressurize a victim to make a decision about key issues for her/his future life shortly after the trafficking experience, while after this period, victims are usually returned to their homes, often suffering revictimization or reprisals from traffickers (UNODC 2008a). Therefore, we suggest that in most cases 30 days is too short for the victims to process and acquire the skills and knowledge necessary to move forward with their life and avoid future victimization. Victims should be provided for at least 3–6 months for recovery, with the possibility of the extension of this period but which should not be made conditional on their willingness to testify in the proceedings.

Referral Mechanisms

Once identified, victims should be referred to victim support services. Referrals should be made on victims' informed consent, and based on their needs. Addressing victims' needs requires cooperation of different antitrafficking actors, such as law enforcement, social welfare services, NGOs, and so on. The Palermo Protocol and the Council of Europe Convention emphasize that assistance, support, and protection should be provided for by the State, but in close cooperation with nongovernmental and other civil society organizations. In this context, we may argue that NGOs should also play an important role of a watchdog mechanism, monitoring the implementation of human rights commitments by the State.

Developing national *referral systems* enables victims equal access "to a wide range of services throughout the country, tailored to their needs and interests," and, at the same time maximizes the use of the existing resources (Surtees 2006, p. 7). Referral mechanisms can be understood as a means of efficient protection from revictimization, protection of victims' rights, and providing for the necessary support in the process of recovery and reintegration (Simeunović-Patić 2005). An example of such a framework

---

* Norway's experience instigated the process of reconsidering the duration of reflection period set forth in the Council of Europe Convention (Austad 2009, p. 3).

is the model of national referral mechanism developed by the Office for Democratic Institutions and Human Rights (ODIHR) in Warsaw, Poland (Kröger et al. 2004). Whenever possible, the partnership between the referral mechanisms should be formalized, with defined specific roles and duties of each respective party. Yet, this framework has to be as inclusive and flexible as possible in order to enable handling of every individual case (ICMPD 2006).

The central part of each referral mechanism is the process of victim's identification and her/his referral to different agencies that offer safe accommodation, protection, and other forms of assistance and support (Kröger et al. 2004). Yet, official national referral mechanisms do not exist in all countries (e.g., Italy, Mexico, and the Dominican Republic) (UNODC 2009a). Instead, some unofficial, ad hoc or operational systems of referrals are in place for either all trafficking victims (e.g., Italy) or for some victims, such as foreigners (e.g., Mexico) or adult victims of sex trafficking (e.g., Dominican Republic) (see Table 12.1). In other countries, such as Bulgaria, a national referral mechanism is still developing (UNODC 2009a, p. 241). Finally, in countries where referral mechanisms do exist, there is considerable variability between them, resulting in a variety of problems and inconsistencies (UNODC 2009a).

Table 12.1 Examples of Referral System Models

Form of the Referral Mechanism	Actors Included in the Referral Mechanism	Role of the Referral Mechanism	Example of Countries
Inter-ministerial or inter-state agency bodies	Representatives of state institutions or ministries (foreign affairs, interior, social policy equal opportunities, etc.)	Coordinating the work of State institutions and/or NGOs or referring victims to appropriate services	Albania, Macedonia, Afghanistan
Inclusive referral mechanisms	State and non-state institutions and civil society organizations	Referring victims to other appropriate services	Czech Republic, Turkey
One organization or institution appointed as a referral mechanism	State or non-state organization appointed in this charge	Coordinating referrals to shelters and other service delivery organizations	Serbia, The Netherlands[a]
Several referral systems	Social welfare centers on the provincial level Bureau of Anti-Trafficking in Women and children on the central, state level Thailand embassies in foreign countries	Referrals to relevant organizations and institutions	Thailand

Source: UN Office on Drugs and Crime (UNODC) 2009. *Global Report on Trafficking in Persons.* Global Initiative to Fight Human Trafficking. http://www.unodc.org/documents/Global_;Report_;on_;TIP.pdf. Accessed on March 31, 2010.

[a] For example, in The Netherlands this task is the responsibility of the NGO Foundation against Trafficking in Human Beings (UNODC, 2009: 267). In Serbia the Agency for Coordination of Protection of Victims of Trafficking in Human Beings, as an organizational unit of the social welfare system, is seen as the core part of the referral mechanism, being "the first point of contact for victims after they have encountered the police or other actors" (Simeunović-Patić, Ćopić, 2010: 50), but clear mandates of the Agency and cooperation with other actors "have not yet been formalized" (UNODC, 2009: 276; Nikolic-Ristanovic, Copić, 2010).

It could be argued that official national referral mechanisms are "essential for the standardized and systematic" (Surtees 2005, p. 45) approach to victims and providing them adequate services. As correctly stated in the UNODC Toolkit to Combat Trafficking in Persons, "a network of professionals and agencies" should be involved in both identification and assistance of trafficking victims, working together and ensuring referrals "without gaps" (UNODC 2008a, p. 265). Yet, in many countries, rather low number of professionals are involved in identifying and referring victims to a rather small number of victim support agencies, which unduly keep the exclusivity of providing support to this category of victims for a few organizations that gain the monopoly not only over the victim support, but also over the victims (see, e.g., Nikolić-Ristanović 2009b; Nikolić-Ristanović and Ćopić 2010). This certainly impacts on the negative rivalry among victim support services, which compete for the victims and, consequently, for additional funding of the services, but also limiting possibilities of many others to approach them and receive support and assistance.

Social recovery from trafficking experience and rehabilitation should be considered primary goals of programs of assistance and support to victims of trafficking (Segrave et al. 2009). In the aftermath of the trafficking situation most victims need to reestablish safety, to restore control over their lives and bodies, and to reconnect with the social environment and ordinary life (Herman 1992). In such a context, rehabilitation is seen as "a process that aims at improving person's ability to function in society on independent and equal terms" (Norman et al. 2003; quoted in Bjerkan and Dyrlid, 2005, p. 121), as well as the process of linking the past, present, and future life (Bjerkan and Dyrlid 2005). As a result, the first step in the process of recovery should be physical and psychological protection, and social support and assistance (Simeunović-Patić 2005).

According to international standards, all trafficked persons should have equal "access to comprehensive assistance and protection schemes" (Orfano 2010, p. 10), both in the countries of destination and the countries of origin upon their return. The programs for victims should be "diverse and appropriately sophisticated" (Surtees 2007, p. 41). Generally speaking, in order to meet a victim's needs and individualize the treatment it is necessary to take into account the type of crime, the psychological characteristics of the victim, and the factors in his/her social environment (Pemberton 2009). In addition, assistance and support should not to be made conditional on victim's willingness to testify in the criminal or other court procedure (Article 12 of the Council of Europe Convention), which seems rather disputable in practice.

Assistance and support to victims can be seen as an initial or short-term, and long-term assistance. Initial, immediate, short-term care and assistance are provided for in the place/country of destination. It usually includes safe accommodation, emergency medical and psychological assistance, food and clothing, issuing documents, and legal assistance. However, for victims' "efficient reintegration" (IOM 2007, p. 85) and social inclusion, a long-term assistance plan is required, enabling a victim to heal from the trauma, reduce her vulnerability, and the risk of being retrafficked (Tyldum et al. 2005). As suggested by the existing research, long-term assistance is only offered after a victim's return to the place or the country of origin, and refers to medical care, legal assistance, counseling, education, skills training, accommodation, financial assistance, and so on. (Surtees 2006; IOM 2007). With (temporary or permanent) residence permits in destination or transit countries, victims might be able to stay even longer in the respective country and receive a variety of long-term assistance. Unfortunately, these forms of assistance are still primarily eligible only for those victims who are ready and willing to cooperate with investigation agencies and to testify in the criminal proceedings against traffickers (Segrave et al. 2009), which is opposed to the human-rights-based approach advocated by the Council of Europe Convention.

On the other hand, assistance and protection to trafficking victims are still primarily shelter based. Shelters certainly play "a vital role in anti-trafficking assistance" (Surtees 2008, p. 36), being considered "as the most appropriate solution" for meeting victims' needs (Simeunović-Patić 2005, p. 31), which particularly refers to the immediate and short-term assistance, primarily in the cases of sex trafficking. Apart from safe accommodation, victims are offered medical care, psychological and legal assistance, and support. Shelter accommodation, as well as other forms of assistance and support are almost exclusively provided through initiatives of local NGOs worldwide (Nikolić-Ristanović and Ćopić 2010; USDS 2009, 2010). As stated in the 2008 Council of Europe Recommendations on Identification and Referral to Services of Victims of Trafficking in Human Beings, NGOs and other civil society organizations "can more easily ensure a victims' friendly approach" (p. 7). In this respect, NGOs should also play a sort of corrective role, which means to be more critical toward the state policy and "assist governments to implement international human rights obligations in the framework of national anti-trafficking policies" (p. 7).

Return and Reintegration

The third phase of victim's protection and the third "R" in the aftermath of trafficking situation refers to reintegration. Reintegration is a complex process of victims' inclusion in the social environment and return to normal life. What usually precedes the reintegration is victims' return to their home county or a place of residence (Brunovskis and Tyldum 2004), which should be followed by concrete forms of a long-term assistance and support.

The process of return, or repatriation, is rather complex for foreign citizens. The latest TIP report indicates that repatriation of trafficked victims should be voluntary and safe (USDS 2010). In other words, repatriation should involve "a number of steps designed to ensure the safe and dignified return of each individual victim" (Surtees 2007, p. 106). Otherwise, return can "pose a risk to victims" (Surtees 2007, p. 133). As some surveys indicated, apart from positive emotions (i.e., excitement, relief, and reassurance), victims may also express negative emotions, such as fear, disappointment, stress, frustration, and confusion (Surtees 2007). Therefore, providing victims clear and sufficient information, but also assistance during his/her return seems to be of a particular importance for victims' safe repatriation.

Yet, the latest TIP report questions how consensual "voluntary repatriation" actually is (USDS 2010, p. 18). The report concludes that "many governments, believing they are acting in the victims' best interests, make concerted efforts to return victims to their countries of origin as quickly as possible" (USDS 2010, p. 18). That is very often justified by victims' wishes to return home, but the real reasons are much more complex: the lack of information about alternatives, inability to work in the local economy, and having no access to government assistance programs (USDS 2010). In such context we can hardly speak of victims' informed consent as meaningful; consequently, it can be argued that this kind of voluntary return could be seen just as a sophisticated form of deportation.

In addition, it has been noticed that victims' return to home countries could be also unassisted (Surtees 2007). The term "unassisted return" refers to either deportation or self-returns that certainly increase the level of negative feelings, as well as the risks of being retrafficked. It can be argued that deportation is closely linked to the "inappropriate victim" (i.e., illegitimate or nontypical victim), quite often those punished for the trafficking-related offences, such as prostitution, illegal migrations, and undocumented labor (UNODC 2008a).

After repatriation, victims may face serious challenges such as extreme poverty, an absence of psychological support, threats from the traffickers (UNODC 2008a). Being forced to return may contribute to victims' attempts to reemigrate. Thus, some victims may also wish not to be returned, manifesting their need to avoid stigma, rejection, and the life in the unsafe environment. Consequently, each State should consider the possibility of granting victims not only temporary, but also permanent residence permits.

Granting a residence permit enables a victim to remain legally in the transit or destination country for a certain period of time. Practice shows that temporary residence permits are usually granted after the reflection period (UNODC 2008a), with the possibility of renewal. Following the guidelines of the Convention (see Article 14), in most countries temporary residence permit is usually granted for victims who are willing to cooperate with law enforcement and judiciary (UNODC 2008a).

Limiting the issuance of temporary residence permit to victims' willingness to cooperate with law enforcement is "indicative of the limited rights afforded to trafficking victims" (Goodey 2008, p. 440), which is inconsistent with the human-rights and victim-centered approach. As pointed out by Rijken and de Volder, "the residence permits will expire when the relevant legal proceedings end, regardless of the reasons for the proceeding's termination" (2010, p. 73). So, the lack of alternatives may actually push a victim into the "voluntary" return to the home country. Besides, grounding the issuance of the residence permit on victim's willingness to cooperate with law enforcement and judiciary puts aside consideration of the severity of violence and the threats victim could be exposed to (Rijken and de Volder 2010). These limitations reflect the still-prevailed approach to human trafficking, which is still focused on the state's interests and the necessity of the criminal justice response to TIPs. Nevertheless, there are examples of a good practice, such as Italy (UNODC 2008a). In addition to being able to grant temporary residence permit for 6 months, with the possibility of renewal of up to 1 year, but irrespective to their readiness to testify a broad range of services are also accessible to these victims, including education and employment.*

Another limitation for victims' stay in the country of transit or destination refers to the lack of appropriate reintegration programs (e.g., the Western Balkans' region). Countries of origin are often not well equipped with reintegration programs as well. As a result, returned victims are usually offered only some forms of short-term and limited assistance and support, which is not enough for their empowerment and return to independent life, rather to disempowerment. In addition, gender-based differences are also visible in terms that there are even less or no services and programs for reintegration and social inclusion for male victims. Furthermore, the cooperation between countries of origin and destination in the process of return and reintegration is still rather poor

---

* Nevertheless, as pointed out on October 18, 2010 (on the EU Antitrafficking day) by Cecilia Malmström, EU Commissioner for Home Affairs, "just a small number of residence permits are issued to victims of trafficking in a majority of EU Member States". http://europa.eu/rapid/pressReleasesAction.do?reference =IP/10/1346andformat=HTMLandaged=0andlanguage=ENandguiLanguage=en, Accessed on November 21, 2010.

(Surtees 2005). What is required is international capacity building and support (see Chapter 10 in this volume). It can be argued that the establishment and further development of transnational referral mechanisms could make a basis for better cooperation in this field and provide better protection of victims and prevention from further trafficking experience (Orfano 2010).

Identified Problems and Issues in Protection of Victims of Trafficking

In the following section some key challenges in relation to victim support will be outlined. Special attention will be paid to (1) "invisible" victims who are left out of the system of support, (2) victims who do not accept victim status, (3) lack of the informed consent for victim's inclusion into the assistance program, and (4) "eligible" and "noneligible" victims.

"Invisible" Victims

As observed by Surtees (2007, p. 41), the "identification mechanisms for victims of trafficking was initially developed to respond to what was perceived to be the prototypic trafficking victim—a young, adult woman trafficked for sexual exploitation" or the "ideal victim." Unfortunately, with some exceptions, identification and assistance still remain primarily focused on this "prototype" as they were at the beginning of the twenty-first century and "generally lack[s] broader, more inclusive criteria" (Surtees 2007, p. 41).

Trafficking for the purpose of labor exploitation and begging, and other forms of trafficking (e.g., debt bondage, arm conflicts, domestic servitude, etc.) are rarely recognized as trafficking (Simeunović-Patić 2009, p. 208). As Surtees (2005, p. 16) points out, in the South Eastern European (SEE) region, many service providers were actually trained to identify victims of sex trafficking; consequently, they are overlooking other victims. In addition, as correctly noted by Milivojević and Segrave (forthcoming), TIPs is often viewed "through the lens of the transnational organized crime" and the criminal justice response which strictly places men, women and children in the position of either offenders or victims. As a consequence, cases of trafficking that do not fit into the rhetoric of organized crime remain out of the system, without proper assistance and protection.

The image of "ideal victim" has an impact in terms of victims' gender and age; impoverished and uneducated women are more easily identified as victims of trafficking in comparison to men, while adult victims will be more visible than children. Thus, a large number of victims remain "invisible" and unidentified.

The image of "invisible" victims deepens the already existing victim stereotype which has a strong impact on the development of the system of assistance and support, contributing to the "persistent selective development of the provision of assistance and support to the victims" (Simeunović-Patić 2009, p. 217). This, in turn, produces the need for further capacity building of all those who are likely to come into contact with trafficking victims.

Rejecting "Victim Status"

When identified as victims by relevant stakeholders, it happens that trafficked women and men reject "victim label" (Spalek 2006, p. 9) (i.e., refuse to be identified and treated as victims (Tyldum et al. 2005; Newton et al. 2008). This is often motivated by such factors as fear of revenge, being revictimized, risk of being deported which actually pushed a victim into the trafficking situation, as well as fear of law enforcement (Tyldum et al. 2005). On the other hand, the term "victim" "may also help to stimulate the unpleasant feelings experienced in the process of being victimized" (Lamb, quoted by Spalek 2006, p. 9), which can also result in rejecting victim's status. In addition, trafficked persons may not see themselves as victims as they might not recognize their experience as victimization (Lamb, quoted by Spalek 2006; Strobl 2010). Refusing to be identified as a trafficking victim can also derive from the lack of confidence and trust in possibilities and readiness of different stakeholders to provide assistance and support and protect the victim(s) (Tyldum et al. 2005).

Gender identity contributes a great deal to (non)acceptance of victim status: it can be argued that men are more reluctant than are women to accept victim status (Nikolić-Ristanović 2009a). This is closely connected to the notion of a victim as a passive and help-lessness person, which are dissociated with hegemonic masculinity (Spalek 2006).

Refusing to be identified as a victim is also closely connected to the fact that some victims are rather confused and disoriented in the phase of identification, as they are "shocked, desperate and fearful" (Surtees 2007, pp. 61, 76). But, such feelings can be provoked by a lack of information about the procedure, their victim status, and rights.

Victims often do not know if they are rescued, arrested or trafficked again (Brunovskis and Surtees 2007). These observations suggest that during the identification phase it is important to provide victims with adequate and sufficient information on their position, rights, and available services. Informing victims and raising their awareness on victimization, their status and rights require considerable resources and knowledge. However, as far as most of the assistance and support is provided for by NGOs, we may argue that they may find themselves trapped, particularly because of the lack of resources, facing with serious challenges.

Lack of Informed Consent

Once identified, victim should be referred for assistance and support. A crucial precondition for victims' inclusion is their informed consent. Providing information about their status and other possibilities presents a "powerful tool" (Albert and Santos 2004, p. 63), which can enable victims to regain the control over their lives. Unfortunately, getting informed consent is frequently neglected both by the state and non-state service providers. Even if obtained, it is questionable how meaningful the consent is. This certainly has a negative impact on the victims' rehabilitation process: victim can feel "confined and denied of basic freedoms," which are the "hallmarks of trafficking experience" (USDS 2009, p. 35).

"Eligible" and "Noneligible" Victims

Closely connected to the notion of "ideal" and "invisible" victim is the notion of "eligible" and "noneligible" victim. To understand this division, we need to pose the following question: For whom are the existing programs of assistance and support reserved? This question can be answered from the following standpoints: (1) for *collaborators of the state in the process against the perpetrators*, and (2) for *prototypical or ideal victims*.

As stated by Segrave et al. (2009, p. 98), "provision of victim support in the aftermath of identification is driven by the ability and willingness of victims to support investigations." But, there is also another consideration which reflects the fact that victims' "willingness" to cooperate with the law enforcement is also driven by their endeavor "to establish that they did not contribute to victimization by engaging in illegal/immoral ventures such as illegal migration and sex work" (Milivojević and Ćopić 2010, p. 294). We suggest that victims find themselves in a position to have to prove their "innocence" and to convince law enforcement, judiciary, and victim support services that they actually fit into the category of "eligible" or "legitimate" victims. Making assistance and support conditional on cooperation with state agencies can be counterproductive for the overall antitrafficking policy (Rijken and de Volder 2010). As these authors pointed out, the results of such a policy will be short term because trafficked persons will likely become "suspicious of law enforcement agencies, unwilling to talk to them and, thereby, will hinder rather than help with the prosecution of traffickers" (Rijken and de Volder 2010, p. 79).

On the other hand, in most countries the systems of assistance and support are created to meet the needs of (foreign) female victims of sex trafficking—the "ideal victims." As expected, these systems appear to be inappropriate for other victims "who do not fit into this narrow category" and hence they are not likely to receive assistance or support (Milivojević and Ćopić 2010, p. 286). Another void that needs to be addressed relates to categories of "otherness" (i.e., to marginalized groups) who "do not correspond to the widespread image of the ideal victim" (Strobl 2010, p. 11) (e.g., victims with addiction and behavior problems, victims who have mental health problems, particular ethnic groups such as Roma populations in some countries) (Nikolić-Ristanović and Ćopić 2010).

Declining Assistance and Support

As reflected in the literature, victims of trafficking may decline offered assistance and support (Brunovskis and Surtees 2007). Some of the reasons include not trusting the authorities and assistance providers, not understanding the nature of the offered assistance due to a lack of information, fear from criminal sanctions and deportation, reluctance to return to their home country, not considering themselves as victims, or just wanting to leave the past behind and return to "normal" life. They often originate in lack of information about their status. In addition, refusing assistance may also be motivated by the desire to avoid the label of "victimhood" and/or simple denial of victimization (Spalek 2006, p. 9). It can be argued that men are more likely to decline assistance than are female victims (Nikolić-Ristanović 2009a). This is possibly driven by the rather narrow and often shelter-based scope of possible measures of support and assistance, which is not acceptable/suitable for men. The second explanation relates to gender roles and identities, which have particularly strong impact in the patriarchal societies. As noted earlier, gender identities prevent men to think about themselves as victims (Nikolić-Ristanović 2009a), resulting in their absence from assistance and support programs.

Shelter-Based Assistance

As mentioned above, most programs for victims of trafficking are shelter based. Without calling into question the importance of shelters for trafficking victims, we agree with the notion that shelter accommodation "is not a panacea" (Surtees 2008, p. 36). Thus, shelters and shelter-based assistance and support are not always an adequate solution for victims of trafficking. In most countries, shelters are designed only for women and sometimes for adolescent girls (Segrave et al. 2009). Insight into global reports on human trafficking (either the United States or the UNODC) suggest that many source, transit, and destination countries are facing a lack of housing for adult male victims. In the absence of adequate facilities and assistance programs for men, some *ad hoc* solutions are offered to victims.* In addition, in most countries there is no specialized accommodation for child victims (USDS 2009); they are often placed in shelters for adult women, orphanages, or other facilities for children without parental supervision, or in facilities for children with disorders in behavior. Not surprisingly, these facilities are usually not equipped with personnel educated and sensitized for dealing with trafficking victims, with no appropriate and systematic programs aimed at rehabilitation of trafficking victims.

Victims accommodated in the shelters are placed in a subordinate position and the situation similar to the trafficking one, which present an obstacle for real understanding of the concept of sheltering as victim-oriented service (Bjerkan and Dyrlid 2005; Nikolić-Ristanović and Ćopić 2010). During the stay in the shelter, victims are often treated as clients and objects that need protection, which according to Segrave et al. (2009) is opposed to the notion that shelters should work for the benefit of victims. Victims are even not allowed to talk to other persons (e.g., researchers) about their pre/posttrafficking experiences (Nikolić-Ristanović and Ćopić 2010). This is a direct consequence of the strong paternalistic and protective approach of service providers, which actually disables victims to regain the control over their lives. Thus, victims may find themselves being dependent on those providing assistance and support, even in the open-type facilities. Restricted mobility and strict rules of living in the shelter accommodation can transform "the practice of protection" into "the repression of victims' rights" (Anti-Slavery International, quoted in Segrave et al. 2009).

Conclusion

As Wemmers (2006, p. 6) has noted, meeting the needs of victims "enhances" their recovery from victimization, contributes to their rehabilitation, and serves as a conduit to their reintegration and social inclusion. In addition, there are "certain primary needs common to all," which include "information, medical and emotional support, practical support, reparation, protection, and inclusion in the criminal justice system's processes" (Wemmers 2006, p. 6). The needs of victims of TIPs do not differ much in comparison with the needs of victims of crime in general.

The analysis offered in this chapter lead us to two main conclusions. The first one relates to the predominant image of an "ideal" victim and the fact that only needs of "ideal" victims are met, even though not sufficiently. The second conclusion refers to the appropriateness of the existing antitrafficking systems to meet the needs of all the victims.

Unfortunately, the practice of support and assistance is not meeting the needs of trafficking victims, while the voices of those identified as victims are not heard by those who design and plan programs for trafficking victims. As was argued in this chapter, the lack of prompt, clear, and consistent information may result in refusing victim's status, declining

---

* For instance, in Saudi Arabia, which appears to be important destination country for adult men trafficked for labor exploitation, male victims are sent in deportation centers, hospitals or other available housing programs provided by charitable organizations (USDS 2010). Similar situation is noted in Afghanistan, where adult men are kept in detention centers (USDS 2010), which may lead to the conclusion that they are treated not as victims rather as criminals.

assistance and support or simply putting a victim in the situation similar to the trafficking experience. Without providing adequate information obtaining informed consent is questionable, in contrast to the international standards and the human-rights-based approach to trafficking. This may also deter victim's willingness to testify against perpetrators and participate in the court proceedings.

The existing systems of protection and assistance are meeting the needs of only "eligible" or "ideal" victims. This means that the system of protection and assistance is reserved for those who fit the image of the prototypical or desirable victim, while "others" or "undesirable" victims are left without appropriate treatment, treated as a serious threat to the security and safety of the society, detained, punished, and deported. As a result, "antitrafficking strategies require the disruption of the hegemonic victim subject and individualization of rehabilitation programs" (Segrave et al. 2009, p. 119). Otherwise, it is difficult to imagine how the antitrafficking mechanisms will be further developed and to whom they will serve. It can be argued that as long as the existing "trafficking victim paradigm" remains unchanged, fewer people will be recognized as victims and there will services and support will remain insufficient.

The second conclusion relates to the need for more inclusive, diverse, and responsive antitrafficking mechanisms, which will be permanently monitored, evaluated, and modified according to the needs of all victims. However, in order to build such a system, it is necessary to broaden the field of victim protection and to strengthen capacities of those who are likely to come into contact with victims.

Broadening victim protection refers to "decentralization" and relocation of assistance and support from the shelters. This requires a broader use of all the existing resources and distancing from insisting on specialized services for trafficking victims. If we consider victim's needs to be more or less the same as the needs of other crime victims, then we do not foresee obstacles in meeting these needs by victim support services that are offering support to a broad range of victims of crime. Even the need for safe housing is not the exclusive need of trafficking victims. Thus, sheltering may be provided by those organizations that have experience in running the shelters, but other forms of assistance and support should be provided for by a wide range of both NGOs and state services.

In order to develop a responsive system of assistance and support, based on the human rights approach, proactive approach to victims and better meet of victims' needs, it is necessary to develop permanent and efficient education programs for those who are likely to come into contact with (actual or potential) trafficking victims.

As observed by Goodey (2008, p. 434): "it is clear that a shift towards a victim-centered response to trafficking has developed over recent years, as increasing emphasis and resources are being placed on victim assistance." But, despite the noted progress, Goodey concludes that: "[t]he real test of how far these initiatives are 'for' victims is whether they exist separate to conditions that stipulate that the victim should co-operate with the authorities in order to receive certain services." As has been described throughout this chapter, most services are still rather dependant on victims' willingness to support prosecution of traffickers. It certainly casts a shadow on the recent development of a victim-centered response. Such a situation is generally supported by the rhetoric of a "soft law" that is used primarily in the Palermo Protocol, but also in the Council of Europe Convention in regard to victims' protection (Goodey 2008). This rhetoric confirms the notion that international legislation in the antitrafficking field is primarily offender oriented, while protection is predominantly seen as a mechanism to support the prosecution.

Discussion and Reflection Questions

1. In your opinion, what can be done in the course of demystification of human trafficking victimization? Why this demystification is important?
2. What puts people who have suffered trafficking victimization at greater risk of being "invisible" victims? How would you explain the phenomena of "invisibleness" of particular classes of victims?
3. Are the needs of victims of human trafficking different from those of other crime victims? How are trafficking victims' needs met in your country?
4. How is the system of assistance and support organized in your country in comparison with the issues raised in this chapter? What are the similarities and the differences?
5. In order to secure protection, assistance, and support to victims of human trafficking, would it be necessary to improve international legal framework in this domain? If yes, what it should be done in this respect?
6. What is your opinion to the shelter issues expressed in this chapter? Are the mentioned problems unique or are there differences in different countries?

References

Albert, I. and Santos, I. 2004. 5 day workshop at the shelter for survivors of human trafficking, in G. Schinina (ed.), *Psychosocial Support to Groups of Victims of Human Trafficking in Transit Situation* (Vol. 4, pp. 59–74). IOM: Psychosocial notebook

Anderson, B. 2007. *Motherhood, Apple Pie and Slavery: Reflections on Trafficking Debates*. Working paper No. 48, Center on Migration, Policy and Society, University of Oxford.

Aronowitz, A. 2001. Smuggling and trafficking in human beings: The phenomenon, the markets that drive it and the organisations that promote it, *European Journal on Criminal Policy and Research*, 9(2), 163–195.

Austad, J. 2009. Norway extends reflection period for victims of human trafficking, *Global Eye on Human Trafficking*, May (5), 3.

Bjerkan, L., (ed.) 2005. *A Life of One's Own: The Rehabilitation of Victims of Trafficking for Sexual Exploitation*. Oslo: Fafo-report 477.

Bjerkan, L. and Dyrlid, L. 2005. A sheltered life, in L. Bjerkan (ed.), *A Life of One's Own: The Rehabilitation of Victims of Trafficking for Sexual Exploitation* (pp. 121–156). Oslo: Fafo-report 477.

Brunovskis, A. and Surtees, R. 2007. *Leaving the Past Behind? When Victims of Trafficking Decline Assistance*. Oslo: Fafo-report 40.

Brunovskis, A. and Tyldum, G. 2004. *Crossing Borders—An Empirical Study of Transnational Prostitution and Trafficking in Human Beings*. Oslo: Fafo-report 426.

Christie, N. 1986. The ideal victim, in E. Fattah (ed.), *From Crime Policy to Victim Policy* (pp. 125–134). New York: St Martin's.

Chuang, J. 2006. Beyond a snapshot: Preventing human trafficking in the global economy, *Indiana Journal of Global Legal Studies*, 13(1), 137–163.

Clawson, H.J., Salomon, A., and Goldblatt, L. 2008. *Treating the Hidden Wounds: Trauma Treatment and Mental Health Recovery for Victims of Human Trafficking*. Issue Brief, U.S. Department of Health and Human Services, Office of the Assistant Secretary for Planning and Evaluation. http://aspe.hhs.gov/hsp/07/humantrafficking/Treating/ib.pdf. Accessed on August 18, 2010.

Ćopić, S. 2008. Putevi trgovine ljudima u Evropi i pozicija Srbije na njima ("Routes of human trafficking in Europe and the position of Serbia on it"), *Temida*, 4, 49–68.

Ćopić, S. 2009. The characteristics of male trafficking in Serbia, in V. Nikolić-Ristanović (ed.), *Male Trafficking in Serbia* (pp. 81–133). Belgrade: Victimology Society of Serbia.

Cunneen, C. 2001. *Conflict, Politics and Crime: Aboriginal Communities and the Police*. Crows Nest: Allen and Unwin.

Danziger, R. 2006. Where are the victims of trafficking?, *Forced Migration Review*, 25, 10–12.

Dixon, J. 2008. The impact of trafficking in persons, in UN Office on Drugs and Crime (UNODC) 2008b. *An Introduction to Human Trafficking: Vulnerability, Impact and Action* (pp. 81–100). Vienna: UNODC.

Ely-Raphel, N. 2002. Trafficking in human beings, in D. Vlassis (ed.), *Trafficking Networks and Logistics of Transnational Crime and International Terrorism*, International Scientific and Professional Advisory Council of the United Nations Crime Prevention and Criminal Justice Programme, pp. 173–175.

Goodey, J. 2004. Sex trafficking in women from Central and East European countries: Promoting a "victim-centred" and "woman-centred" approach to criminal justice intervention, *Feminist Review*, 76, 26–45.

Goodey, J. 2008. Human trafficking: Sketchy data and policy responses, *Criminology and Criminal Justice*, 8(4), 421–442.

Herman, J. 1992. *Trauma and Recovery*. New York, NY: Basic Books.

International Centre for Migration Policy Development (ICMPD) 2006. *Guidelines for the Development and Implementation of a Comprehensive National Anti-Trafficking Response*. Vienna: ICMPD.

International Organization for Migration (IOM) 2007. *The IOM Handbook on Direct Assistance to Victims of Trafficking*. Geneva: IOM.

IOM Counter-Trafficking Service 2004. *Changing Patterns and Trends of Trafficking in Persons in the Balkan Region: Assessment carried out in Albania, Bosnia and Herzegovina, the Province of Kosovo (Serbia and Montenegro), the Former Yugoslav Republic of Macedonia and the Republic of Moldova*. IOM. http://www.iom.hu/PDFs/Changing%20Patterns%20in%20Trafficking%20 in%20Balkan%20region.pdf. Accessed on March 31, 2010.

Kapur, R. 2002. The tragedy of victimization rhetoric: Resurrecting the "native" subject in international/post-colonial feminist legal politics, *Harvard Human Rights Journal*, 15, 1–37.

Kelly, L. 2005. *Fertile Fields: Trafficking in Persons in Central Asia*. Vienna: IOM, Technical Cooperation Centre for Europe and Central Asia, http://www.iom.int/jahia/Jahia/cache/offonce/pid/1674;jsessionid=1662869D20A3ECBD2F7CB0D85C1E8CB2.worker02?entryId=8002, Retrieved April 13, 2008.

Kelly, L. 2007. A conductive context: Trafficking of persons in Central Asia, in M. Lee (ed.), *Human Trafficking* (pp. 73–91). Devon: Willan Publishing.

Kovačević-Lepojević, M. and Dimitrijević, J. 2009. The review of the results of previous research and other available data on male trafficking worldwide and in Serbia, in V. Nikolić-Ristanović (ed.), *Male Trafficking in Serbia* (pp. 17–49). Belgrade: Victimology Society of Serbia.

Kröger, T., Malkoč, J., and Uhl, B. 2004. *National Referral Mechanisms: Joining Efforts to Protect the Rights of Trafficked Persons—A Practical Handbook*. Warsaw: OSCE/ODIHR.

Laczko, F. and Danailova-Trainor, G. 2009. *Trafficking in Persons and Human Development: Towards A More Integrated Policy Response*. United Nations Development Programme Human Development Reports Research Paper 2009/51 http://mpra.ub.uni-muenchen.de/19234/ Accessed on July 13, 2010.

Lee, M. 2005. Human trade and the criminalization of irregular migration, *International Journal of Sociology of Law*, 33, 1–15.

Lee, M. 2007 Introduction: Understanding human trafficking, in M. Lee (ed.), *Human Trafficking* (pp. 1–25). Devon: Willan Publishing.

Milivojević, S. and Ćopić, S. 2010. Victims of sex trafficking: Gender, myths, and consequences, in S.G. Shoham, P. Knepper, and K. Martin (eds.), *International Handbook of Victimology* (pp. 283–302). Boca Raton: Taylor & Francis Group.

Milivojević, S. and Sagrave, M. (forthcoming). Evaluating responses to human trafficking: An analysis of the applications of contemporary international, regional and national counter-trafficking mechanisms, in Winterdyk, J., Perrin, B., and Reichel, P. (eds) Human Trafficking: International issues and perspectives. Boca Raton, Fl: Taylor and Francis.

Milivojević, S. and Sagrave, 2011. Evaluating responses to human trafficking: A review of international, regional, and national counter-trafficking mechanisms.

Newton, P., Mulcahy, T., and Martin, S. 2008. *NORC Final Report Finding Victims of Human Trafficking.* Document no. 224393, presented to: National Institute of justice Office of Justice Programs U.S. Department of Justice, Washington, DC. National Opinion Research Center (NORC) at the University of Chicago. https://www.ncjrs.gov/pdffiles1/nij/grants/224393.pdf, accessed on November 21, 2010.

Nikolić-Ristanović, V. 2003. Ilegalna tržišta, trgovina ljudima i transnacionalni organizovani kriminalitet (Illegal markets, trafficking in human beings and transnational organized crime). *Temida*, 4, 3–13.

Nikolić-Ristanović, V. 2005. What victims went through and how they survived, in L. Bjerkan (ed.), *A Life of One's Own: The Rehabilitation of Victims of Trafficking for Sexual Exploitation* (pp. 89–119). Oslo: Fafo-report 477.

Nikolić-Ristanović, V. 2009a. Support, assistance and the protection of male victims of trafficking: Results of the research, in V. Nikolić-Ristanović (ed.), *Male Trafficking in Serbia* (pp. 219–234). Belgrade: Victimology Society of Serbia.

Nikolić-Ristanović, V. (ed.) 2009b. *Male Trafficking in Serbia.* Belgrade: Victimology Society of Serbia.

Nikolić-Ristanović, V. and Ćopić, S. 2010. *Pomoć i podrška ženama žrtvama trgovine ljudima u Srbiji (Assistance and Support to Women Victims of Trafficking in Persons in Serbia).* Beograd: Viktimološko društvo Srbije i Prometej-Beograd.

Nikolić-Ristanović, V., Ćopić, S., Simeunović-Patić, B., Milivojević, S., and Mihić, B. 2004. *Trafficking in People in Serbia.* Beograd: OSCE.

Office of Women in Development, US Agency for International Development 2007. *The Rehabilitation of Victims of Trafficking in Group Residential Facilities in Foreign Countries—A Study Conducted Pursuant to the Trafficking Victim Protection Reauthorization Act, 2005.* Available on http://pdf.usaid.gov/pdf_;docs/PNADK471.pdf. Accessed on November 21, 2010.

Ogrodnik, L. 2010. *Towards the Development of a National Data Collection Framework to Measure Trafficking in Persons.* Ottawa: Statistics Canada, Canadian Centre for Justice Statistics, Catalogue no. 85-561-M, no. 21.

Omelaniuk, I. 2005. *Trafficking in Human Beings.* New York: UN Expert Group Meeting on International Migration and Development, Population Division, Department of Economic and Social Affairs, United Nations Secretariat.

Omelaniuk, I. 2006. *Trafficking in Human Beings—CEE and SE Europe.* The paper submitted to the UN Commission on the Status of Women Fiftieth session, New York, February 27–March 10, 2006. http://www.un.org/womenwatch/daw/csw/csw50/statements/CSW%20HLP%20 Irena%20Omelaniuk.pdf. Accessed on March 31, 2010.

Orfano, I. 2010. *Guidelines for the Development of a Transnational Referral Mechanism for Trafficked Persons in Europe: TRM-EU.* Department for Equal Opportunities—Residency of the Council of Ministers Italy and International Centre for Migration Policy Development (ICMPD).

Pemberton, A. 2009. Victim movements: From diversified needs to varying criminal justice agenda's, in A. Pemberton (ed.), *The Cross-Over: An Interdisciplinary Approach to the Study of Victims of Crime* (pp. 175–201). Apeldoorn, Antwerpen, Portland: Maklu.

Pleša-Golubović, V. 2006. Croatia, in J. Škrnjug (ed.), *Mechanism for the Monitoring of Trafficking in Human Beings Phenomenon: Bosnia and Herzegovina, Croatia, Serbia* (pp. 37–60). Belgrade: IOM.

Raymond J.G., D'Cunha, J., Ruhaini Dzuhayatin, S., Hynes, P.H., Ramirez Rodrigues, Z., and Santos, A. 2002. *A Comparative Study of Women Trafficked in the Migration Process: Patterns, Profiles and Health Consequences of Sexual Exploitation in Five Countries (Indonesia, the Philippines, Thailand, Venezuela and the United States).* http://action.web.ca/home/catw/attach/CATW%20 Comparative%20Study%202002.pdf. Accessed on August 18, 2010.

Regional Clearing Point (RCP) 2003. *First Annual Report on Victims of Trafficking in South-Eastern Europe*. Belgrade: IOM, Stability Pact for South Eastern Europe—Task Force on Trafficking in Human Beings and ICMC.

Rijken, C.R.J.J. and de Volder, E.J.A. 2010. The European Union's struggle to realize a human rights-based approach to trafficking in human beings: A call on the EU to take THB-sensitive action in relevant areas of law, *Connecticut Journal of International Law*, 25(49), 49–80.

Romcharan, B. 2002. Human rights and human trafficking, in F. Laczko, I. Stacher, and A. Klekowski von Koppenfels (eds.), *New Challenges for Migration Policy in Central and Eastern Europe* (pp. 161–171). The Hague: IOM and ICMPD.

Salt, J. 2000. Trafficking and human smuggling: A European perspective, *International Migration*, 38(3), Special Issue 2000/1, 31–56.

Segrave, M., Milivojevic, S., and Pickering, S. 2009. *Sex Trafficking: International context and response*. Dvon: Willan Publishing.

Simeunović-Patić, B. 2005. Protection, assistance and support of trafficked persons: current responses, in L. Bjerkan (ed.), *A Life of One's Own—Rehabilitation of Victims of Trafficking for Sexual Exploitation* (pp. 23–70). Oslo: Fafo-report 477.

Simeunović-Patić, B. 2008. Prepoznavanje viktimizacije trgovinom muškarcima ("Recognizing the trafficking in human beings victimization"), *Temida*, 4, 69–86.

Simeunović-Patić, B. 2009. Sensibility of professionals and the recognition of male victims of trafficking, in V. Nikolić-Ristanović (ed.), *Male Trafficking in Serbia* (pp. 205–217). Belgrade: Victimology Society of Serbia.

Simeunović-Patić, B. and Ćopić, S. 2010. Protection and assistance to victims of human trafficking in Serbia: Recent developments, *European Journal of Criminology*, 7(1), 45–60.

Spalek, B. 2006. *Crime Victims—Theory, Policy and Practice*. Hampshire: Palgrave MacMillan.

Srikantiah, J. 2007. Perfect victims and real survivors: The iconic victim in domestic human trafficking law, *Boston University Law Review*, 81(1), pp. 157–211.

Stamenkova Trajkova, V., Bogoevska, N., and Trbojevic, S. 2007. *Study of Child Trafficking in the FYR of Macedonia*. http://www.unicef.org/tfyrmacedonia/STUDY_;ON_;CHILD_;TRAFFI CKING_;IN_;MACEDONIA_;Final_;Oct._;07_;-_;clean_;version.doc. Accessed on March 31, 2010.

Strobl, R. 2010. Becoming a victim, in S.G. Shoham, P. Knepper, and M. Kett (eds.), *International Handbook of Victimology* (pp. 3–25). Boca Raton, FL: Taylor & Francis Group.

Surtees, R. 2005. *Second Annual Report on Victims of Trafficking in South-Eastern Europe 2005*. Regional Clearing Point, IOM.

Surtees, R. 2006. *Evaluating Anti-Trafficking Victim Assistance in Southeastern Europe: A Strategic Planning Paper for the King Baudouin Foundation*. Prepared by the NEXUS Institute to Combat Human Trafficking in Vienna, Austria for the King Baudouin Foundation in Belgium.

Surtees, R. 2007. *Listening to Victims: Experiences of Identification, Return and Assistance in South-Eastern Europe*. Vienna: International Centre for Migration Policy Development.

Surtees, R. 2008. *Why Shelters? Considering Residential Approaches to Assistance*. Vienna: NEXUS Institute to Combat Human Trafficking.

Tyldum, G., Tveit, M., and Brunovskis, A. 2005. *Taking Stock—A Review of the Existing Research on Trafficking for Sexual Exploitation*. Oslo: Fafo-report 493.

UN Children's Fund (UNICEF) 2004. *Trafficking in Children in Kosovo, A Study on Protection and Assistance Provided to Children Victims of Trafficking*. Pristina: UNICEF. http://www.unicef. org/kosovo/kosovo_;media_;pub_;prot.009.04.pdf. Accessed on March 31, 2008.

UN Office on Drugs and Crime (UNODC) 2008a. *Toolkit to Combat Trafficking in Persons*. Global Programme against Trafficking in Human Beings. New York: UN. http://www.unodc.org/documents/human-trafficking/HT_;Toolkit08_;English.pdf. Accessed on March 31, 2010.

UN Office on Drugs and Crime (UNODC) 2008b. *An Introduction to Human Trafficking: Vulnerability, Impact and Action*. New York: UN. http://www.childtrafficking.com/Docs/ unodc_;08_;human_;action_;0109.pdf. Accessed on March 31, 2010.

UN Office on Drugs and Crime (UNODC) 2009a. *Global Report on Trafficking in Persons. Global Initiative to Fight Human Trafficking.* http://www.unodc.org/documents/Global_; Report_;on_;TIP.pdf. Accessed on March 31, 2010.

UN Office on Drugs and Crime (UNODC) 2009b. *International Framework for Action to Implement the Trafficking in Persons Protocol.* New York: UN. http://www.unodc.org/documents/human-trafficking/Framework_;for_;Action_;TIP.pdf. Accessed on July 13, 2010.

US Department of State (USDS) 2009. *Trafficking in Persons Report.* http://www.state.gov/documents/organization/123357.pdf. Accessed on April 1, 2010.

US Department of State (USDS) 2010. *Trafficking in Persons Report.* http://www.state.gov/g/tip/rls/tiprpt/2010. Accessed on July 13, 2010.

US Government Accountability Office 2007. *Human Trafficking: Monitoring and Evaluation of International Projects are Limited, But Experts Suggest Improvements.* GAO-07-1034 Report. Washington, DC.

Wemmers, J.A. 2006. *Reparation and the International Criminal Court: Meeting the Needs of Victims.* Report of the Workshop held on January 28, 2006 organized by the Research Group Victimology and Restorative Justice, International Centre for Comparative Criminology, University of Montreal. http://www.cicc.umontreal.ca/recherche/victimologie/reparation_;icc.pdf. Accessed on April 1, 2010.

Zegarac, N. 2007. *Deca govore: rizik od trgovine ljudima i rezilijentnost dece u Jugoistočnoj Evropi (Children Speak Out: The Risk from Trafficking and Resilience of Children in Southeast Europe).* Beograd: Centar za prava deteta and Save the children.

Zimmerman, C., Hossain, M., Yun, K., Gajdadziev, V., Guzun, N., Tchomarova, M., Ciarrocchi, R.A. et al. 2008. The health of trafficked women: A survey of women entering posttrafficking services in Europe, *American Journal of Public Health*, 98(1), 55–59.

Zimmerman, C., Hossain, M., Yun, K., Roche, B., Morison, L., and Watts, C. 2006. *Stolen Smiles: A Summary Report on the Physical and Psychological Health Consequences of Women and Adolescents Trafficked in Europe.* London: The London School of Hygiene and Tropical Medicine.

Zimmerman, C., Yun, K., Shvab, I., Watts, C., Trappolin, L., Treppete, M., Bimbi, F. et al. 2003. *The Health Risks and Consequences of Trafficking in Women and Adolescents. Findings from a European Study.* London: London School of Hygiene and Tropical Medicine (LSHTM).

Helpful Web Links

Victimology Society of Serbia, www.vds.org.rs
ASTRA—Anti-trafficking Action, www.astra.org.rs

Epilogue

PHILIP REICHEL
BENJAMIN PERRIN
JOHN WINTERDYK

Contents

As reflected throughout this thematic volume, human trafficking is a complex and often hidden crime. As has also been illustrated and described in the chapters of this volume, the issue of human trafficking can be defined and examined in a number of different ways and can be approached from an array of perspectives. Human trafficking can be categorized by geographical areas, gender and identity, or the method of exploitation, to name a few. Further, human trafficking can be accounted for through many existing legal models, including criminal justice, human rights, migration and globalization, feminist legal theory, and labor rights, amongst others.

The need for better data collection methods was a strong theme throughout this volume. While most chapters in this volume recognized the need for improved data collection and knowledge of human trafficking, several issues about how these data should be collected and analyzed, as well as "success factors," were also raised. Data collection must be "contextualized" as was discussed by Smith in Chapter 2, so that the data can serve as a sound foundation for future studies and implementation of policies. Decontextualizing data renders the results less scientifically rigorous (i.e., reliable and/or valid) and creates the possibility of misuse or misinterpretation; as was mentioned by Goodey in Chapter 3, "there is a real risk that policy responses are developed that do not reflect the realities on the ground." Current efforts of data collection to date have also been highly criticized by a number of the contributors in this volume as being too focused on criminal justice information, and on implementation of criminal justice measures, rather than focusing on the *impact* of such measures. In addition, the current state of data collection does not allow for sharing of information and ease of cooperation between sources as there is a lack of harmonization in data collection process. As mentioned, one reason for this is likely the lack of harmonization in legal definitions of human trafficking; however, various contributors in this volume also point to a lack of transparency, clarity and rigor in data collection methods.

While the past decade since the inception of the Palermo Protocol has created many dichotomous debates around the "best" approach to human trafficking, what all this indicates is in fact that there is no "one size fits all" solution, but a need to develop a comprehensive approach to combating human trafficking which can account for the complexities and overlapping issues inherent in this crime. To achieve a more comprehensive approach, throughout this volume and employing different perspectives, several of the contributors suggest that the first step requires an increased harmonization and consistency in legal definitions and interpretations within and amongst states. For example, several of the contributors highlighted both the need for this, as well as the substantive issues which arise out of a lack of harmonization and consistency, which include incomparable and incomplete data and statistics; ineffective police investigation and prosecution efforts; and, barriers to cooperation amongst various actors and between nations or regions. Consistent legal definitions and interpretations will enable data on human trafficking to be captured in a more accurate and precise manner. The suggestion is in fact calling for the application of more standardized policies and practices as they pertain to the issue of human trafficking. Further, harmonization and consistency will go a long way to understanding the breadth of the crime as including more than trafficking for sexual exploitation and the "ideal victim." In Chapter 4, Kaye and Winterdyk provide further area for thought on this issue, highlighting the consequences of a noncomprehensive approach to defining human trafficking, such as victims being deported alongside illegal migrants, victims going unidentified due to confusion with migrant smuggling, human trafficking becoming an increasingly sensationalized and moralized topic, and the agency of the victim being disrespected or unaccounted for in protection and assistance regimes. In Chapter 4, Kaye and Winterdyk call for a sociologically grounded "rights-based approach" to human trafficking which would account the human rights of victims in a broad sense which is able to encompass socioeconomic factors, gender issues, and the reality of globalization and migratory patterns, among others, through the use of an "interdisciplinary lens."

Building on the issue of data collection, in a number of the chapters (e.g., Chapters 7 and 10) of this volume, the contributors discussed the need for increased exchange of information and cooperation between the various actors involved in combating human trafficking. A focus on criminal justice actors was prevalent, although several chapters questioned the crime control approach as a whole. Examples of joint investigation teams in the European Union and the United States showed an increase in knowledge of human trafficking and successful investigations. However, several of these contributors also highlighted the need for social work actors (e.g., Chapter 6) to be involved in the investigation process where a victim has been identified and is in the custody of the authorities. As the authors for Chapter 12 reported, early involvement of counselling services resulted in a positive impact on victim protection and willingness to cooperate with authorities. Coupled with increased cooperation and exchange of information, several chapters pointed to the urgent need for increased training, particularly amongst law enforcement authorities. Research results highlighted in Chapter 9, Farrell established that a lack of training, at least in part, accounted for a lack of proactive investigation by local authorities because of the "dark figure," or "hidden nature" of the crime being misunderstood or unrecognized by these authorities. The lack of consistent and clarified legal definitions, coupled with the problems of data collection to date and ineffective investigatory capacity of many law enforcement authorities, has also hampered efforts to prosecute traffickers.

In several of the chapters (especially in Chapter 12), the contributors also highlighted the on-going issues in relation to the "victim" in human trafficking. First, victim identification continues to plague authorities and actors involved in human trafficking. While a lack of training and data collection inhibits victim identification because of the continued hidden nature or "dark figure" of the crime not being brought to light, the notion of the "ideal victim" also plagues victim identification, particularly by law enforcement and immigration authorities. The "ideal victim"—the "young, naive, impoverished, helpless, disadvantaged women from developing countries" who are "abducted, forced or deceived by 'evil' people" for sex trafficking is still the predominant "visual" of human trafficking victims. Authorities appear to have particular difficulty reconciling the idea of agency with the notion of a human trafficking victim. Victims not meeting the profile of the "ideal victim," or who, due to limited national legislation, are not defined as "victims" may simply be left out of the system. Further, some victims may be unwilling to self-identify as a "victim" and/or may be uncooperative with police. For these "ineligible" victims, as Ćopić and Patić (Chapter 12) discussed, assistance will not be adequate, if provided at all.

Building on the issue of victim identification is an on-going issue of linking protection measures to cooperation with authorities. Several States examined in the chapters of this book continue to link protection measures to cooperation with law enforcement (see Chapter 9) and prosecutorial authorities (see Chapter 8), which, when looked at from a human-rights or social-work approach, is arguably unacceptable. However, in addition to the highly questionable ethics of such mechanisms, some chapters also indicated that these mechanisms were likely to decrease victim cooperation because of the limited timeframe for decision and minimal access (if any) to counseling and other services which may bring the victim to a more stable state of mind. However, several chapters also acknowledged the importance and necessity of victim cooperation in successful prosecution, highlighting the on-going balancing act between criminal justice and human rights in human trafficking cases.

As the efforts, discourse and research around human trafficking continue to evolve, there is a need to reflect holistically on the past decade of progress. Throughout this volume, a number of the contributors commented on the notion that the Palermo Protocol has outgrown its roots as a criminal justice mechanism. In particular, several of the contributors discussed the need to shift evaluation mechanisms from monitoring implementation and progress, to determining the impact of policy measures. Most reporting around the globe continues to center on criminal justice data, which does not accurately reflect the expansive nature of the problem. Further, reports primarily center on implementation of criminal policy as successful outcome factors, rather than evaluating the *impact* of initiatives. As discussed within different perspectives but with a common focus, several of the contributors concluded that the issue of human trafficking must move beyond its initial creation as a criminal justice issue, and must be evaluated in the broader context of globalization, migration, socioeconomic factors and distribution of wealth, among many other overlapping issues. As the global effort to confront human trafficking moves into its second decade under the Palermo Protocol, a need for serious and substantive reflection is readily apparent to guide policy and research in a way which will provide meaningful insights and lasting solutions to this complex phenomenon.

Looking Forward: A Forecast for Human Trafficking

The 11 chapters in this thematic collection have served to underscore the human trafficking issues being focused on by contemporary scholars and researchers, practitioners, and policy makers. Several of the chapters have also touched on topics about which we need additional information or have suggested topics that are likely to draw attention in the coming years. Acknowledging areas where information is lagging and forecasting areas not yet fully on our radar are important activities for everyone interested in preventing and combating trafficking in persons. By engaging is such mental gymnastics we are able to propose research agendas, suggest educational and training programs, and prepare policy makers for coming trouble spots or opportunities. To that end, we take some time in this

Epilogue to expand a bit on one specific topic: recognizing the multidisciplinary nature of human trafficking.

Research endeavors that are multidisciplinary in nature are often touted as useful ways to broaden understanding of a particular topic. Unfortunately, due to some of the challenges, it is too often an after-thought when first considering a problem. Typically, when considering a research topic, we begin by looking at what has been done in our own field. Doing that is the obvious starting point, but the approach may exclude relevant literature and research questions from other disciplines.

Crime prevention and crime control seems an especially good example of an area that benefits by input from a variety of disciplines. In fact, the United Nations considers one of the basic principles underlying the guidelines for crime prevention to be

> Crime prevention strategies, policies, programmes and actions should be based on a broad, **multidisciplinary** foundation of knowledge about crime problems, their multiple causes and promising and proven practices (United Nations Office on Drugs and Crime, 2010, p. 22 [emphasis added])

The complex nature of human trafficking makes it an especially well-suited topic for multidisciplinary attention. Interestingly, however, the research endeavors remain primarily in law and criminal justice. Goździak and Bump (2008) conducted an extensive review of English language research-based literature on human trafficking through 2007. They compiled 741 trafficking EndNote citations and divided them into three main categories: books (represented 19% of the citations), reports (58%), and journal articles (29%). Of the 218 journal articles, 51% of the articles they identified as falling into the law/criminal justice category. Interestingly, most of the articles were nonempirical in nature. Of those that were based on empirical research, all but one used qualitative methodologies and 66% used convenience samples. From the perspective of research methods employed, such approaches are not considered overly robust and are primarily used in an exploratory context.

The finding that the pre-2008 journal-published research on human trafficking was focused on law and criminal justice topics and that it tended to be nonempirical in nature (or qualitative, when it was empirical) suggests a more discipline-specific than a multi-discipline approach to the topic. This is unfortunate, and has been consistently cited as a serious gap in the research. Adepoju (2005) notes that a battery of research methods is needed to capture the many sources, causes, and dynamics of human trafficking and to ensure that research findings can be generalized. Goździak and Collett (2005) point out the need for both qualitative and quantitative research (i.e., a mixed-methods approach) that can provide macro- and micro-level understanding of the trafficking phenomenon. The International Organization for Migration (2009) laments the lack of empirical research and interdisciplinary studies. There seem to be no claims that nonempirical research, or studies relying only on qualitative methodologies, is exactly what is needed to understand human trafficking. Further, it seems unlikely that there are many proponents for applying only a law or criminal justice perspective to the human trafficking phenomenon.

A greater involvement by disciplines other than law and criminal justice to the study of human trafficking is clearly needed. Some of the knowledge gaps identified in the human trafficking literature may be of particular interest to other disciplines. There have been calls for more and better studies presenting the victims' viewpoints (an area where disciplines such as psychology, sociology, and social work might be helpful). Others have suggested a need for greater consideration of how social norms and cultural values might facilitate both the pool of and demand for human trafficking victims (something anthropologists might find intriguing). Thinking about "demand," what new knowledge might be gained from an economic perspective of human trafficking as a market system?

The good news is that since Goździak and Bump's (2008) review of research-based literature on human trafficking, there appear to be a broader range of disciplines represented. Without undertaking anywhere near the extensive review completed by Goździak and Bump, an even cursory search has resulted in a forecast for a more multidisciplinary look at human trafficking. Examples upon which that optimism is based are provided in the brief comments below about activities in just a few disciplines beyond law and criminal justice.

Our intent in providing this review is not to suggest any specific disciplinary or methodological approach as primary—in fact, we hope this review does just the opposite. That is, scholars and researchers interested in the topic of human trafficking should actively seek out the theoretical musings and active research being done in disciplines outside one's own. The end result would not have to be a collaborative effort nor even be an example of multidisciplinary research, but it would serve to remind authors and readers that other disciplines have something to say about the topic. In other words, we simply want to show that one or two disciplines cannot provide a full spectrum understanding of a complex international problem such as trafficking in persons.

Communication Studies: Media portrayal of human trafficking has implications ranging from public education to policy making. Koerner et al. (2010) looked at how newspapers in 13 countries covered human trafficking. Using conceptual frameworks (community structure model) and methodologies (Media Vector scores) from their discipline, they looked at how national characteristics are linked to newspaper coverage of human trafficking.

Economics: Human trafficking is important to economists, in part, because it affects the global economy as source countries lose part of their labor supplies and transit and destination countries deal with the costs of illegal immigration. In a particularly interesting article that takes an economic perspective, Wheaton et al. (2010) present an economic model of human trafficking that encompasses all known economic factors affecting human trafficking both across and within national borders. Using a rational-choice framework of human trafficking, the researchers explain how the social situation of vulnerable populations can lead them to become human trafficking victims, the impetus for being a trafficker, and the decisions made by employers of trafficked individuals. Their research suggests that increased legal pressure on the demand side of human trafficking may be the most effective deterrent.

But economists see more to the problem than simple supply and demand issues. One example is a study by Akee et al. (2009), who argue that trafficking in persons must be understood through the "incentive" (in the economic sense of the term) of legislative forces and human rights policies that are in place in the destination countries. Their specific question concerns how incidences of trafficking might be due to perverse incentives created for traffickers by the provision and enforcement of policies that grant human rights (such as amnesty) to trafficked victims. They argue that the incentive for traffickers provided by legislation surrounding antitrafficking activities is an important but unexplored issue. We argue that while the policy of amnesty does protect the rights of trafficked victims in host countries, it cannot be viewed as a policy that deters traffickers, but as one that may in fact increase the incentive to select countries that offer amnesty as destination countries for victims.

Geography: Using mapping data to analyze the spatial patterns of slavery cases in Brazil, Thery et al. (2011) use social and economic factors to create a statistical and cartographical index that evaluates the probability of a given place to harbor undetected slave laborers and to estimate how vulnerable that place is to recruitment of trafficking victims. The researchers hope information of this type can facilitate the repression and prevention of modern slavery in Brazil's rural areas.

Marketing: There do not appear to be many marketing scholars or researchers who are tackling the topic of human trafficking, but those who have offer a unique perspective. Unique, that is, for law and criminal justice, but certainly not unique from their own discipline. Their beginning statement tells it all: "If you understand a marketing system, you can understand how to disrupt it" (Ball et al., 2010, p. 3). Using child slavery in the cocoa trade in West Africa as their case example, the authors describe the problem as a marketing system then suggest how that system can be disrupted. This is an excellent example of looking at the problem from a new disciplinary perspective.

Medicine: The importance of research in the health disciplines is quickly understood when we consider that "health care providers are often the only professionals to interact with trafficking victims who are still in captivity" (Dovydaitis, 2010, p. 462). Goździak and Bump (2008) found only a few research-based articles in health and medical journals—a point echoed by Silverman et al. (2007), who note the inadequate empirical data to characterize the related health consequences of human trafficking. Several current articles are educational rather than empirical and advise health care providers on recognizing health problems associated with human trafficking victimization (Siva, 2010) and with the relationship between trafficking and HIV (Vijeyarasa and Stein, 2010). But other articles are research-based and consider such issues as the relationship of trauma to mental disorders among trafficking victims (Hossain et al., 2010) and the importance of providing newly identified trafficked women with immediate attention to address posttrauma symptoms and adequate recovery time before making decisions about participating in prosecutorial or immigration proceedings or returning home (Zimmerman et al., 2008).

Political Science: Contrarian perspectives are found in all disciplines, and political science offers a particularly interesting one regarding good intentions with unintended bad results. Smith and Smith, for example, consider the impact of the United Nations intervention in crisis areas (specifically, Kosovo, Haiti, and Sierra Leone). They argue that UN involvement has the unfortunate and unintended effect of increasing the rates of human trafficking sex trafficking trade into the crisis areas. Our work concludes that the UN should proceed with caution into crisis areas and have plans in place to avoid the potentially devastating externalities of otherwise well-intentioned efforts. Specifically, a seemingly benevolent UN action, intended to bring peace, serves to promote a shadow economy with dramatic and negative consequences.

Social Work: David and Cynthia (2007) explain that international sexual trafficking of women and children has received little attention. In the social work literature, and their article attempts to provide information that can assist social workers in advocating on behalf of women and children and in providing services to victims of trafficking. Although sex trafficking remains a predominate topic in social work journals, there are some interesting takes on the topic of international adoption of children (e.g., McCreery et al., 2009; Roby and Ife, 2009)—which some identify as a form of human trafficking needing further attention. As an example of how other disciplines can provide a new perspective and raise new questions, consider the interesting study by Brunovskis and Surtees (2007), which reports on interviews with trafficking victims and others in an attempt to determine why some victims decline the assistance that is offered to them—a research question we haven't found asked in the law and criminal justice research.

Sociology: The victim's voice is not presented as often as many victim advocates would like. Some sociologists have tried to address this problem through qualitative studies that consider the complexity of the victim's situation and make appropriate links to theoretical considerations (Skilbrei and Tveit, 2008). Other sociologists are interested in how social stratification processes link to the issue of human trafficking for sex and labor purposes. Williams (2008) developed a social politics theory to connect concepts from social stratification to the study of human trafficking. Citing sources from Australia and Sweden, she shows how national laws and policies regarding prostitution can contribute to or discourage human trafficking for sex and labor purposes.

Obviously, researchers from a variety of disciplines are engaged in quite interesting research into many aspects of human trafficking. However, the end result brings to mind Abbott's observation:

> If we ask academics why poor people are poor or why cities grow as they do or why certain bills fail in legislatures, different disciplines will answer these questions in their own unique ways: each with certain kinds of data, certain methods, certain habits of thinking about the problem.... [A result] is what to outsiders seems like an amazing lack of reciprocal knowledge (Abbott, 2001, p. 142).

Abbott's comments on the varying responses we can expect from different disciplines regarding questions about poverty, urbanization, and legislation, would certainly hold for questions about trafficking in persons as well. But, as we suggested before providing the overview of research activity outside of the law and criminal justice areas, that is not necessarily a bad thing. The variation in data, methods, and ways of thinking about the problem results in a level of analysis and understanding that could not be achieved with a single-discipline approach. This, of course, is what planned multidisciplinary research seeks to achieve. The resulting benefits to theory, practice, and policy recommendations could be enormous where more multidisciplinary collaborations occur. But even if the project itself does not involve researchers from multiple disciplines, we encourage all researchers to familiarize themselves with perspectives and methodologies from at least some disciplines other than their own. Through such an effort, we hope that a new direction for human trafficking studies will eventually lead toward multidisciplinary endeavors that go beyond simply acknowledgment of other perspectives to full-fledged cooperative research projects representing multiple disciplines.

References

Abbott, A. D. 2001. *Chaos of Disciplines*. Chicago: University of Chicago Press.

Adepoju, A. 2005. Review of research and data on human trafficking in sub-Saharan Africa. [Article]. *International Migration, 43*(1/2), 75–98.

Akee, R. K. Q., Basu, A. K., Bedi, A. S., and Chau, N. H. 2009. Combating trafficking in women and children: A review of international and national legislation, coordination failures, and perverse economic incentives. *Journal of Human Rights and Civil Society*, (2), 1–24. Retrieved from http://www.protectionproject.org/wp-content/uploads/2010/09/JHU_Journal_vol2_final.pdf

Ball, D., Pennington, J., Hampton, R., and Nguyen, A. 2010. *A Market Analysis of Human Trafficking Systems*. Paper presented at the Second Annual Interdisciplinary Conference on Human Trafficking, University of Nebraska, Lincoln. http://digitalcommons.unl.edu/humtrafconf2/12/

Brunovskis, A., and Surtees, R. 2007. Leaving the past behind? When victims of trafficking decline assistance. (Fafo-report 2007:40). Retrieved from http://www.fafo.no/pub/rapp/20040/20040.pdf

David, R. H., and Cynthia, A. L. 2007. The international sexual trafficking of women and children: A review of the literature. *Affilia, 22*(2), 163.

Dovydaitis, T. 2010. Human trafficking: The role of the health care provider. *The Journal of Midwifery and Women's Health, 55*(5), 462–467.

Goździak, E. M., and Bump, M. N. 2008. Data and research on human trafficking: Bibliography of research-based literature. (NCJRS Document No. 224392). Retrieved from NCJRS Publications website: http://www.ncjrs.gov/App/Publications/abstract.aspx?ID = 246352

Goździak, E. M., and Collett, E. A. 2005. Research on human trafficking in North America: A review of literature. [Article]. *International Migration, 43*(1/2), 99–128.

Hossain, M., Zimmerman, C., Abas, M., Light, M., and Watts, C. 2010. The relationship of trauma to mental disorders among trafficked and sexually exploited girls and women. *American Journal of Public Health, 100*(12), 2442–2449.

International Organization for Migration. 2009. Human trafficking: New directions for research. Retrieved from http://www.iom.int/jahia/webdav/shared/shared/mainsite/microsites/IDM/workshops/ensuring_protection_070909/human_trafficking_new_directions_for_research.pdf

Koerner, M., Harrison, J., Omland, J., Rush, A., and Pollock, J. 2010. *Cross-national newpaper coverage of human trafficking*. Paper presented at the International Communication Association, Suntec City, Singapore. http://www.allacademic.com/meta/p403741_index.html

McCreery Bunkers, K., Groza, V., and Lauer, D. P. 2009. International adoption and child protection in Guatemala. *International Social Work, 52*(5), 649–660.

Roby, J. L., and Ife, J. 2009. Human rights, politics and intercountry adoption. *International Social Work, 52*(5), 661–671.

Silverman, J. G., Decker, M. R., Gupta, J., Maheshwari, A., Willis, B. M., and Raj, A. 2007. HIV prevalence and predictors of infection in sex-trafficked Nepalese girls and women. *JAMA: The Journal of the American Medical Association, 298*(5), 536–542.

Siva, N. 2010. Stopping traffic. *The Lancet, 37*(69758), 2057–2058.

Skilbrei, M.-L., and Tveit, M. 2008. Defining trafficking through empirical work. *Gender, Technology and Development, 12*(1), 9–30.

Smith, C. A., and Smith, H. M. 2011. Human trafficking: The unintended effects of United Nations intervention. *International Political Science Review, 32*(2), 125–145.

Thery, H. E., de Mello-Thery, N. A., Girardi, E. P., and Hato, J. 2011. *Slave Work's Geography in Brazil*. Paper presented at the Association of American Geographers Annual Meeting, Seattle, WA.

United Nations Office on Drugs and Crime. 2010. Handbook on the crime prevention guidelines: Making them work. *Criminal Justice Handbook Series*. Retrieved from https://www.unodc.org/documents/justice-and-prison-reform/crimeprevention/10-52410_Guidelines_eBook.pdf

Vijeyarasa, R., and Stein, R. A. 2010. HIV and human trafficking–related stigma. *JAMA: The Journal of the American Medical Association, 304*(3), 344–345.

Wheaton, E. M., Schauer, E. J., and Galli, T. V. 2010. Economics of human trafficking. *International Migration, 48*(4), 114–141.

Williams, L. M. 2008. Social politics: A theory. *International Journal of Sociology and Social Policy, 28*(7–8), 285–292.

Zimmerman, C., Hossain, M., Yun, K., Gajdadziev, V., Guzun, N., Tchomarova, M. et al. 2008. The health of trafficked women: A survey of women entering posttrafficking services in Europe. *American Journal of Public Health, 98*(1), 55–59.

Index

Note: n = footnote

For Product Safety Concerns and Information please contact our EU
representative GPSR@taylorandfrancis.com
Taylor & Francis Verlag GmbH, Kaufingerstraße 24, 80331 München, Germany

www.ingramcontent.com/pod-product-compliance
Ingram Content Group UK Ltd.
Pitfield, Milton Keynes, MK11 3LW, UK
UKHW051834180425
457613UK00022B/1246